The Cost of Inaction

Case Studies from Rwanda and Angola

Sudhir Anand

Chris Desmond, Nadejda Marques and Habtamu Fuje

Foreword by Amartya Sen

Published by the François-Xavier Bagnoud Center for
Health and Human Rights

Distributed by Harvard University Press
Cambridge, Massachusetts, and London, UK
2012

François-Xavier Bagnoud Center for Health and Human Rights
Harvard University
Harvard School of Public Health

Center for Health and Human Rights

ISBN 978-0-674-06558-1

Library of Congress Control Number: 2012935216

Printed by Webcom, Toronto, ON Canada
Design and production: Digital Design Group (www.ddgdesign.com)

Table of contents

Acknowledgements

I would like to acknowledge support from several institutions and individuals during the research for and writing of this book. Much of the research for this book was done at the FXB Center for Health and Human Rights at Harvard University, and much of the writing of it was done at the Department of Economics and St Catherine's College, University of Oxford. The FXB Center hosted me during the entire period and provided excellent logistical support and research facilities, including an office in Cambridge, MA. I am extremely grateful to its former Director, Jim Yong Kim, for taking on the Cost of Inaction (COI) project, and to its current Director, Jennifer Leaning, for helping me complete it in this published form.

While I was working on the COI project at Harvard, my main academic appointment was Visiting Professor of Global Health and Social Medicine at the Harvard Medical School. I was also Distinguished Visiting Scholar at the Harvard School of Public Health. I am very grateful to Jim Yong Kim, former Chair of the Department of Global Health and Social Medicine at Harvard Medical School, and to his successor Paul Farmer, for appointing me Visiting Professor at Harvard University for three years.

The idea behind the "cost of inaction" is due to Albina du Boisrouvray. Her insistence on actions on behalf of neglected children, and insights into the costs arising from inaction, have helped me develop the framework proposed in this book. She has also provided immeasurable support and understanding throughout the period of the COI project, which have been critical to its success.

My conversations with Amartya Sen on the concept and content of the "cost of inaction" have been invaluable. He has helped tremendously in both sharpening and extending the COI analysis presented here. I cannot thank him enough.

I would also like to acknowledge the great support and friendship of Lincoln Chen over the years, including the period of working on this book. He has allowed me an affiliation with the China Medical Board of which he is President, and provided me wise counsel on many different aspects of the COI project.

Several individuals have helped in the production of this book. I would like to acknowledge assistance on the references from Terra Ziporyn and Lauren Bateman, and on the Index from Aby Bidwell. A special word of thanks is due to the designer of this book, Marc Kaufman of Digital Design Group. He has produced page proofs quickly and efficiently, and has been indulgent in allowing me to dictate corrections and edits to the proofs over long transatlantic telephone calls. I am indeed grateful to him.

Sudhir Anand
Professor of Economics, University of Oxford
and Senior Fellow, St Catherine's College, Oxford
March 2012

I would like to acknowledge the support of the many people who made the Cost of Inaction project possible. Firstly, I would like to thank Prof. Amartya Sen for his guidance and insightful contributions, his comments played a major part in shaping the work presented in this book. I would also like to thank the following people who assisted greatly with background research: Mylena Aguilar, Vanessa Boulanger, Annie Chu, Bevan Dowd, Shalini Dutta, Brian Garvey and Anya Guyer. The project was supported by a number of interns to whom I am grateful, they include Lisa Lim, Mika Matsuzaki and Sonya Soni. I would also like to thank Kate Falb and Terra Ziporyn for their help with the references. Special thanks go to Agnes Binagwaho whom I collaborated with on our consultation process in Rwanda. I am also grateful to the staff of Faith Victory Action (FVA) in Rwanda who assisted with the research and provided logistical support during our consultation, and to Delma Monteiro and Acção Humana who did the same in Angola. I am thankful to the many individuals from NGOs, multilateral organizations, government departments and community groups who took the time to talk to us about areas of inaction in both Rwanda and Angola. We could not have identified our interventions without their input. Finally, I would like to thank colleagues at the FXB Center as well as others at the Harvard School of Public Health for their help and support over the three years of the project. In particular I would like to note the support of the following FXB colleagues: Lauren Bateman, Theresa Betancourt, Jacqueline Bhabha, Arlan Fuller, Robyn Libson Gray, Patricia Spellman and Bettina Stevens. The leadership of the FXB Center changed during the course of the project and I would like to thank both the current and former directors, Jennifer Leaning and Jim Yong Kim, respectively.

Chris Desmond
Research Associate, FXB Center for Health and Human Rights,
Harvard University

FXB Center for Health and Human Rights

The FXB Center for Health and Human Rights at Harvard University is an interdisciplinary center that works to protect and promote the rights and wellbeing of children in extreme circumstances worldwide.

Founded in 1992 through a gift from the Association François-Xavier Bagnoud, the FXB Center aims to build a conceptual and empirical basis for realizing rights inherent in protection of children and in empowerment of adolescents and youth trapped throughout the world in grave poverty and deprivation, harsh oppression, major disaster, and war.

Through the lens of health and human rights, the Center's faculty conduct research; teach and supervise students and engage faculty throughout the University; periodically convene leading academics, policymakers and practitioners to address pressing research or policy issues; and work generally to develop and promote evidence-based policy that has positive impact on the rights and wellbeing of children, adolescents, and their families globally.

The Cost of Inaction (COI) is an approach to the economic and social evaluation of interventions that draws attention to the consequences of a failure to take an action. The COI approach aims at highlighting the negative impacts that result when an appropriate action is not taken. In the context of actions that are known to improve the situation of vulnerable children and adolescents, the COI analysis highlights the direct and indirect consequences of not providing adequate support in time to make a substantial difference in the life prospects of this crucial population of young people. The COI approach provides a framework to support the evaluation of responses to inaction and offers a methodology for marshaling the evidence that can then support a transparent discussion of priority setting. Difficult decisions have to be made by policymakers in allocating resources. The COI approach seeks to promote such discussion and deepen understanding.

Jennifer Leaning
Director

Foreword

Amartya Sen

This is a far-reaching book with a deceptively modest title. The book does include case studies from Rwanda and Angola (as the title promises), and the lessons they offer are extremely important. But more generally, what the book really does is to present a new way of looking at policy analysis. The new insights and procedures can have fruitful application in a large number of public choice problems. Rwandan and Angolan case studies offer guidance on how the demands of rational policy making in those countries can be met, but they also powerfully illustrate the rationale and perspicacity of the general approach splendidly explored by Professor Sudhir Anand and his co-authors.

Indeed, the publication of this book is a good occasion to think about some foundational issues in the evaluation of public policy. This I will try to do in this Foreword, concentrating mainly on what I see as the central points that emerge from this significant contribution, which has been led with admirable skill by Professor Anand. The work was initiated by the insights of the visionary activist, Albina du Boisrouvray, whose clear-headed understanding of the consequences of inaction has inspired and driven this research effort, conducted at the FXB Center for Health and Human Rights.

Consider the use of cost-benefit analysis in project evaluation. The basic rationale of the analysis is simple enough: if the benefits that can be expected to flow from the project exceed the costs that have to be incurred in undertaking the project, then the project can be seen as making a net positive contribution, and well, that surely would seem like a case for going ahead with the project. There are, however, two rather fundamental issues in cost-benefit analysis that are often ignored, and sometimes dealt with in rather crude ways:

1. The complexity of including *benefits forgone* by *not* doing something (what economists call "opportunity costs"), and

2. The possibility of *assessing together* a number of diverse benefits and

costs to arrive at an overall judgment (in the odd terminology of cost-benefit analysis this is described — not entirely accurately — as the *measurability* of benefits and costs in a common scale).

On both of these rather heavy-weight problems, this book has a great deal to offer.

The opportunity of doing something else

In discussing the problem of benefits forgone, or opportunity costs, let me begin with a very different — and rather classic — issue. Suppose Projects A and B both yield positive net benefits, which would suggest that we should do both. But there may be interdependences between them, contrary to each other or mutually reinforcing, which would give us reason to consider the two projects together. Let us call the combined project A+B. If it has a positive net benefit, then that may look like a case for doing A+B together.

But what if the net benefit from A+B, though positive, is less than that from, say, doing project A alone? Somehow we must take into account the fact that by doing A+B we forgo the alternative of *doing project A alone*. And if the opportunity cost of doing A+B together is seen to include the sacrifice in the form of "benefit forgone" by not doing A alone, then the "opportunity-cost-netted" benefit from doing A+B together would, in this case, show up as negative. This reverses the initial judgment of doing A+B together, and more generally, the opportunity cost perspective has to be integrated into cost-benefit analysis in a fuller way than in standard practice.

This is not "cost of inaction," of course, but it is relevant to it. The foregoing analysis reflects a recognition of the fact that the opportunity cost of any action, in this case of doing A+B together, includes the loss of the opportunity of doing alternatives that are precluded by the chosen action, in this case of doing action A *alone*.[a] The point of this example is to illustrate the fact that cost-benefit analysis is integrally connected with checking what the alternatives are (in terms of doing this or that, or *not* doing them), and doing any particular thing which precludes other things that could have been done instead entails costs in the form of benefits forgone. This extends readily to the case in which nothing is done at all (sheer "inaction"), when all the things that could have been done instead become potential sources of cost.

Cost of inaction

Now, consider the costs and benefits from inaction. One understanding, which may even be blessed (undeservedly as it happens) as being seen as "basic common sense," is to say that if we do nothing then there is no cost to be incurred and no benefit to be reaped. Having done nothing, we need not go around with a heavy heart for having done some harm to the world, since in this allegedly common-sense view, we have done no such thing. This is where Albina du Boisrouvray's questioning mind revolts in agony, as well as in solid reasoning. "You say you are doing no harm, but what about the deprived kids you could have saved through doing something positive for them — aren't you simply neglecting the harm of ignoring that?" To return to formal terminology, this surely is the *opportunity cost of doing nothing*, for it involves the cost of the benefits forgone that could have been generated through doing something, instead of just sitting on your bum (the last bit was not, I suppose, particularly formal terminology).

As can be readily seen, cost of inaction is a heavy duty concept, with huge application and reach. Doing nothing seems far from innocent — indeed depending on our understanding of human obligation to others, it can be full of potential folly, and perhaps even the basis of a sense of actual guilt (much would turn on what view we take of Thomas Scanlon's far-reaching question "What We Owe to Each Other?").[b] But no matter how we extend all this into matters of personal morality and political duty, there can be no question at all that rational evaluation of public policy has to take on board the complications of opportunity costs in terms of benefits forgone, by not doing something that could have been done.

And the complications are quite formidable. It is to that extremely difficult challenge that Sudhir Anand and his colleagues have provided a response of magnificent reach and strength. Chapters 1 and 2 provide a powerfully lucid account of how the demands of this difficult exercise can be met. And then the book goes into application, armed with the theoretical clarity and the practical steps (or algorithms) that emerge in the earlier part of this well-integrated work. Policy issues in Rwanda and Angola related to health care and public policy get sorted out in this carefully analyzed framework, and they have, of course, importance of their own (and not just as good illustrations of Anand's general approach).

Variety of consequences

If an appropriately broader understanding of the idea of costs is one major engagement of this work, a fuller understanding of benefits is another. One clarification comes early, but with a huge set of implications. Some of the benefits of a project may be "constitutive" in the sense that they straightforwardly result from the project, and are part of the direct fruits of it. But there may be very important indirect consequences as well. If, for example, ill health of a child makes that child drop out from school, then we have to add to the direct benefit of better health resulting from a project of health-related intervention, the indirect benefits of education of the child who may now have the opportunity of continuing his or her studies, helped by better health. In the light of what has been discussed earlier here — and much more extensively in the book by Anand — these different constitutive and consequential effects can all be analyzed and investigated as part of "costs of inaction" when the intervention in question is not undertaken, yielding bad results that could have been avoided by appropriate action.

So the benefits end up being a bundle of good things — or averted bad things — that a project generates, in one form or another. The question that arises next is how to put them all together in some common metric. Or, at least, that is the question that standard cost-benefit analysis would ask as the next step. Here Anand et al. make another remarkable departure, disputing that we do need to do this at all. Why can't we judge, say, two diverse outcomes seen together as a multidimensional (in this case, two-dimensional) outcome, and then use our ability to do reasoned evaluation, which can of course take many different forms, to rank the multidimensional results respectively coming from different projects (or project combinations)? To give an analogy, if a person prefers to have bran flakes and a banana for breakfast rather than fried eggs and toast (and she can perhaps even tell us the reasons for her choice), the decision does not have to be made by reducing, first, all the different things — bran flakes and banana as well as eggs and toasts — into some common metric. Education, health, prevention of mortality may all be good things, and a decision of public choice must be based on reasoning, but the reasoning need not take the form of reducing them all into some common units, such as "their equivalent money value."

Of course, if we can rank two alternatives, then any mathematician can point out that there is a numbering system that can "represent" that ranking in the sense that the preferred alternative has a higher number than the one less preferred (this is a simple mathematical point, but I do not of course want to suggest that anyone who can see this obvious truth must be a mathematician — I think sanity may be involved somewhere). The question to discuss is this: must we *start with* getting some numbering system that puts the multidimensional bundles into a common metric and then count (as in the standard cost-benefit procedure), or whether we can, instead, think and scrutinize and decide on the relative merits of the different bundles (and then of course some — indeed many possible — numerical representations will *follow* from this)? The preferred alternative bundle would have a higher number in either case, but the association of a higher number with a preferred alternative is not based on any requirement that the numbering system must be arrived at *first* (even though two centuries of the utilitarian mode of thinking has made many people — even very sagacious people — inclined to get some numbering system, like that of utility, first, and then simply count, as a shepherd counts his flock).

Anand et al. follow the full disclosure route, and even go beyond "multidimensionality," that is each aspect being numerically measurable in the form of a "dimension" (yielding a "vector space" — to use a technical term here). Some important concerns may not be quantifiable in quite that way. Anand et al. make room for that, so that the results are seen as "a *multidimensional vector* whose components are recorded in different units" supplemented by "non-quantifiable benefits...listed separately" (Chapter 1). Some times the choice over such "bundles" — they are formally called "*n*-tuples" — would be easy, and sometimes quite difficult, but the assessors cannot grumble that they are not being told what the respective results of alternative courses of action really are. What Anand et al. show — in their empirical studies — is that often enough the choice would be quite easy to make given the standard value system that drives us, including saving lives, making people healthy and educated, and so on.

Even when the decisions are not entirely easy to reach, it is surely better to have public discussion on what is being chosen and why, rather than steam-rolling the different concerns and issues into some common homogeneous metric which serves as a kind of a veil on the distinct concerns. We need not insist that a policy maker and an intelligent critic cannot talk about diverse issues taken together, and are able only to *count* predigested numbers. To the extent that any policy analysis should disclose as much as possible for public discussion and scrutiny, subject to the picture not being unmanageably baroque, the methodology pursued by Anand et al. has much to offer as an input to public reasoning as well.

And in this respect too, the case studies help greatly as illustrations, since the choices look well sorted out by the methodology chosen. I shall not try to spell out the conclusions reached — or strongly suggested — for Rwanda and Angola by Anand et al. (they are discussed with great clarity by the authors), but I will emphasize here the sharpness with which the costs and benefits come through in the empirical part of this wonderful contribution to policy analysis. If the world is unduly complacent about not doing things that can be easily done, with huge benefits for disadvantaged people (often severely deprived children), the reason cannot be based on the intractability of the benefits of the neglected actions (or, in the language of the book, of "the costs of inaction").

I end by recommending the book strongly not only to those interested in Rwanda or Angola (important as the empirical and policy findings are in this book), but also to any policy analyst in general and analyst of development policy in particular. It would be hard to praise the book too much.

Endnotes

a.   The same line of analysis can be used to understand a basic problem in dynamic investment programming, which was the subject matter of Stephen Marglin's outstanding senior thesis at Harvard half a century ago (the work was later published as: *Approaches to Dynamic Investment Planning*, North Holland, 1963). Suppose project A yields a higher net benefit than project B alone, and also project A+B together. Then, if we include in the cost of each project the sacrifice — the opportunity cost — of not doing other things, then project A alone will have positive "opportunity-cost-netted" benefits, whereas the other options will not (they will be swamped by the loss of not doing project A). Easy enough so far (at least I hope so). But since the world is not going to end today, we have to consider the fact that by having project A *today* we forgo the opportunity of doing it *tomorrow*. And, in a telling example considered by Marglin, it may turn out that while project A today has a larger net benefit than project B today, the sequence "A today and B tomorrow" (AB for short) can have a smaller aggregate return than "B today and A tomorrow" (BA for short). In which case, we may be well advised to do project B today rather than project A (even though B gives a smaller net benefit than A done today), since B today can be followed up by the BA sequence, which would yield higher aggregate benefits than AB. The sequencing problem adds a huge complication to cost-benefit analysis, which Marglin's thesis identified and analyzed.

b.   Thomas Scanlon, *What We Owe to Each Other*. Cambridge, MA: Harvard University Press, 1998.

CHAPTER 1

Introduction

Primum non nocere—first, do no harm—is one of the pillars of medical ethics. Harm occurs not only as a result of doing, but also of *not* doing. A focus on the former may unduly draw attention away from the latter. Such lack of attention can be serious, as harms caused by omission can be large.

Inaction in relation to children can be particularly serious because it can impede their development and lead to negative outcomes in later life which may be large and irreversible. Investing in children's nutrition, health and education are actions that avoid such negative outcomes with long-lasting consequences. The area of child development thus provides an important illustration of the costs that arise from inaction. In this book we demonstrate the costs of inaction through case studies of actions relating to children.

Children and their families who subsist in difficult circumstances lack the basic capabilities to escape from poverty and other types of deprivation. Malnutrition, ill-health and lack of education are conditions that severely constrain individuals' basic capabilities and affect their life chances and contributions to society and the economy. In desperate circumstances, children and other individuals may also adopt behaviors that harm themselves and others in society, such as drug abuse and crime.

As the costs of inaction in relation to children are likely to be large, this book presents case studies of different types of investment in child development and capability expansion. The book begins by examining the meaning and definition of 'cost of inaction', and our approach to its measurement. The proposed framework for evaluating the cost of inaction is then applied to case studies focusing on children affected by poverty in two countries—Rwanda and Angola.

1.1. The concept of cost of inaction

The cost of inaction (COI) draws attention to the consequences of a failure to take an action. The cost of inaction is not the cost of doing nothing: it is the cost of not doing some *particular* thing. The COI approach aims to highlight the negative consequences that follow when an appropriate action is not taken; it does not imply that all negative events are costs of inaction.

For example, consider the lack of action in regard to infant health in Angola, where the infant mortality rate (IMR) is 98 per 1,000 live births.[1] Every death is a tragic loss, but not all deaths can be averted; some deaths would occur no matter what was done. Even in Sweden, which has one of the lowest IMRs in the world, there are 2 infant deaths per 1,000 live births.[1] Deaths that are inevitable cannot be considered costs of inaction.

Given that an IMR of 2 per 1,000 is achievable in Sweden, can we conclude that 96 deaths (98-2) per 1,000 is the cost of inaction in Angola? The answer is no, because it is not possible that the healthcare system and economic situation of Sweden can be replicated in Angola in the near future. The question is what actions are feasible in Angola to improve infant health. Once these are identified, the costs of inaction can be estimated relative to these actions.

It may be more appropriate to estimate the reduction of IMR in Angola if its government took the same actions as the government of neighboring Zambia, where IMR is 70 per 1,000 live births. This may, however, be setting the bar too low since Angola is almost four times richer than Zambia: in 2010 Angola's GDP per capita was US$4,423 and Zambia's US$1,253.[1] Perhaps the comparison should be with actions taken in Tunisia where GDP per capita in 2010 was US$4,199, and IMR was 14 per 1,000 live births.[1] Even if Tunisia is chosen as the comparator, it cannot simply be assumed that the COI in Angola is 84 deaths (98-14) per 1,000 live births. While Tunisia is not as different from Angola as Sweden is, it is still quite different. Not all actions implemented in Tunisia are replicable in Angola, and even if some could be replicated they might not have the same impact. The actions against which COI is assessed must be carefully selected. We should consider actions that are feasible in a specific country context and are likely to generate positive net benefits. It is against such actions that COI should be evaluated.

Economic evaluations typically focus on the cost of undertaking an action, and on what in this book we call the constitutive benefits of an action. Constitutive benefits are the direct benefits that characterize an action—the benefits of what the action is about (or "constitutes"). For a healthcare intervention the constitutive benefit is improved health; for an intervention to expand secondary schooling it is the educational gains that result. The cost and constitutive benefits of an action are important factors in deciding whether to implement it. The COI approach, however, goes beyond this and emphasizes the importance of also including the consequential benefits of an action. The consequential benefits of an action are the indirect benefits that arise as a consequence of the action—e.g. the negative consequences that the action avoids (or the positive externalities that it generates). For instance, if a healthcare intervention is not implemented the continued ill-health of children may lead them to drop out of school, and thus to a lower educational attainment. Dropping out of school may lead to increased risk behaviors (such as crime) and other negative outcomes. Taking account of the benefits of avoiding such negative consequences can substantially increase the magnitude of total benefits of an action, and hence its desirability.

The COI approach proposes that an action should be evaluated in terms of both its constitutive and consequential benefits—net of its implementation cost. Rather than requiring every benefit to be quantified in monetary terms when it is included in the analysis, the approach allows for the consideration of benefits in non-monetary and even non-quantitative terms. We recognize that in many instances a monetary value cannot be placed on benefits, at least not without making dubious value judgements. Rather than make such judgements, the quantifiable benefits can be presented in the form of a multidimensional vector whose components are recorded in different units; the non-quantifiable benefits can be listed separately. The question of whether the total benefits are worth the cost of the action can be examined following such a description in summary form. The presentation of this information allows policymakers to consider the many value judgements and trade-offs involved in assessing the costs of inaction.

An area of action that allows the concept and potential of the COI approach to be illustrated is that of early childhood development (ECD). ECD actions clearly have both constitutive and consequential benefits.[2] Such actions lead to health and developmental gains, which are constitutive benefits. In the future, they also lead to improved school performance, reduced risk-taking behavior and lower engagement in criminal activity.[2] These are consequential benefits. A full evaluation of an ECD action should consider how the costs stack up in relation to the total benefits—constitutive and consequential.

Many consequential benefits are determined by what other actions are, or are not, being undertaken. The COI approach considers this linkage explicitly. For example, one of the consequential benefits of ECD is improved school performance in the future. However, this takes for granted that there is a school for children to go to. If there is no school, it might be appropriate to consider a set of complementary actions that include ECD, building a school, and training and deploying school teachers. The idea is not simply to evaluate a single action in isolation, but to identify complementary actions that remove constraints or jointly lead to a greater benefit than the sum of the benefits of each action considered separately. If the net benefit is greater for a set of actions than for a single action, then that set of actions should be used as the appropriate intervention against which to assess the costs of inaction.

When used to evaluate an action or set of actions, the COI approach draws attention to the consequential benefits that might otherwise be ignored. It also highlights the importance of examining complementarities among different actions. By doing both of these things, the approach suggests that it may be seriously inadequate to examine the benefits and costs of actions within a single sector only, e.g. the health sector. Health interventions can have consequential benefits for education and economic productivity. The consequential benefits of health interventions will be greater if they are complemented by actions in other sectors such as education, where a school may need to be built and teachers trained. The application of the COI approach often forces the evaluator to consider the implications of an action in one sector for actions in other sectors.

The need to evaluate the cost of inaction relative to specific actions makes the selection of such (counterfactual) actions critically important. A COI analysis should endeavor to identify counterfactual actions which are expected to lead to constitutive and consequential benefits that are large relative to the cost of the action. To demonstrate the application of COI analysis and the importance of identifying specific actions, we undertake case studies in two countries. We examine the costs of inaction relating to children affected by poverty and HIV/AIDS in Rwanda and Angola. The next section describes how these case studies were conducted.

1.2. Case studies in Rwanda and Angola

To demonstrate the application of the COI approach we conducted case studies in two countries—Rwanda and Angola. The studies focus on children affected by poverty and HIV/AIDS because we believe this area provides a powerful illustration of the cost of inaction. The COI analysis can, of course, be usefully applied to a number of other areas—such as environmental protection and the prevention of maternal mortality. But applications to other areas are beyond the scope of this book.

Rwanda and Angola are similar in some relevant respects but are quite different in others. Both countries have low HIV prevalence, high rates of poverty, and have recently experienced major civil conflicts. A major difference between the two countries is that Angola has a much higher income per capita (US$4,423 in 2010) than Rwanda (US$530 in 2010).[1] Another difference is that whereas Rwanda has been active in responding to its social problems, Angola is seen by many to be doing far less than it could.

The two countries were selected because they permit interesting applications of the COI approach. As the countries face similar social problems, comparisons between them can be informative. In each country we identify areas of inaction in relation to children affected by poverty and HIV/AIDS—hereafter called priority areas—and actions in the area that we believe will have a large positive net benefit—hereafter called actions of special interest. In Rwanda it is more difficult to identify such actions than it is in Angola, beause Rwanda is already engaged in these priority areas—despite its resource limitations. With less being done in Angola, it is easier to identify areas of inaction there with which large costs are likely to be associated.

A COI study needs to take account of the country's economic and social situation, its existing policies and programs, and actions that are under consideration by policymakers there. This allows us to identify priority areas and actions of special interest. Specifically, we are interested in actions that will have a large net benefit. There is considerable evidence about interventions that are effective in reducing the burden of HIV/AIDS and poverty on children: we compiled a list for which the international evidence is substantial. The list was narrowed to take into account country constraints that might hinder effectiveness, and compared it with the set of current programs in each country. This process generated a short list of potentially desirable actions in Rwanda and Angola that have not yet been undertaken.

It was not feasible to consider all the potentially desirable actions for children affected by HIV/AIDS and poverty. To identify priority areas and generate a list of actions of special interest, we followed a process that involved three stages: a desk study, a country consultation, and a consolidation phase.

In the course of the desk study, we reviewed the available information and literature (published and grey) on the socio-economic background of each country. The topics reviewed include the country's recent history, political and administrative system, economic development, demographics, and future prospects. We also compiled information on existing government policies affecting children in the areas of poverty reduction, HIV/AIDS, child protection, health, and education. Part of the desk study involved assembling evidence from international sources on the effectiveness of interventions for children affected by poverty and HIV/AIDS. The desk review led to an initial identification of priority areas and list of potential actions.

Following the desk study, in-country consultations were undertaken in Rwanda and Angola with government, multilateral agencies, NGOs, faith-based organizations, and community groups. The COI team of researchers conducted semi-structured interviews intended to prompt responses on the appropriateness of different priority areas and actions identified in the desk review.

Following the country consultations, we considered the case for additional priority areas and potential actions that were suggested by respondents. In this third stage, the evidence on the effectiveness of the suggested actions was reviewed, and the priority areas and actions were revised.

In order to move from the list of all potential actions to a shorter list of actions of special interest, we examined each potential action and assessed its prospects of generating a positive net benefit, isolating those actions that we believed would have large net benefits. The actions of special interest include both single actions and sets of (complementary) actions.

We produced a list of actions of special interest for Rwanda and another list for Angola. From each list we selected three actions for COI analysis. We chose actions which demonstrate significant aspects of the COI approach and are likely to contribute to the policy debate in the country. In Rwanda we selected a scaled-up FXB (SFXB) intervention, expanded secondary schooling (ESS), and an expanded school-feeding program (ESFP). In Angola we selected a community healthcare system (CHS), an intervention to strengthen the education system (SES), and adult and infant male circumcision programs (AMCP and IMCP). For each intervention we conducted a detailed COI analysis, which involved specifying the design of the intervention and estimating its costs and its constitutive and consequential benefits.

1.3. Outline of the book

This book is divided into four parts which present, respectively, the conceptual framework of the COI approach, the case studies from Rwanda, the case studies from Angola, and a summary and comparison of the case studies with concluding remarks on the COI approach.

Part I, which consists of chapters 1 and 2, introduces and develops the concept of the cost of inaction. Following the introductory chapter 1, chapter 2 examines alternative ways in which the cost of inaction can be conceptualized, defines the key terms used, and presents our approach to evaluation and measurement.

Part II, which consists of chapters 3-7, deals with the case studies from Rwanda. Chapter 3 provides a socio-economic review of Rwanda. Chapter 4 presents the priority areas and actions of special interest which emerge from the country-consultation process. Chapter 5 presents our analysis of a scaled-up FXB intervention, which is an integrated poverty reduction program in Rwanda. It examines the benefits and costs of implementing a three-year intervention designed to help families meet their immediate needs while at the same time enhancing their income-generating capacity and other capabilities. Chapter 6 presents our analysis of a set of actions to expand secondary schooling in Rwanda. The country has had much success in improving primary-school enrollment, which has led to increasing demand for secondary-school places. If more schools are not built, and more teachers are not trained and deployed, there will be large costs of inaction because the current secondary-school system is too small to absorb the increasing numbers of primary-school graduates. Chapter 7 presents our analysis of an expanded school-feeding program in Rwanda. It examines the constitutive and consequential benefits, and the costs, of increasing the coverage of the existing program.

Part III, which consists of chapters 8–12, deals with the case studies from Angola. Chapter 8 provides a socio-economic review of Angola. Chapter 9 describes the priority areas and actions of special interest that were identified during the country consultation. Chapter 10 presents our analysis of a community healthcare system. Angola's health infrastructure was badly damaged during the 27-year civil war. A community healthcare system will provide primary care to an estimated 60% of the population without placing demands on the services of specialist medical personnel who are in very short supply. Chapter 11 presents our analysis of an intervention designed to expand access to education, including access to ECD services. Building schools and training teachers will allow more children to attend school, which will generate a wide range of benefits. Chapter 12 presents our analysis of an adult male-circumcision program and an infant male-circumcision program for Cunene province in Angola. Male circumcision reduces the risk of HIV transmission, and Cunene province has the highest rates of HIV/ AIDS in Angola with few men who are circumcised.

Part IV consists of the concluding chapter 13. It provides a summary and comparison of the case studies in the two countries. The chapter ends with a brief discussion of applications of COI analysis to other areas, and an assessment of the distinctive features of the COI approach.

References

1. World Bank. *World Development Indicators 2011*. Washington, DC: World Bank, 2011.
2. Shonkoff JP, Phillips DA. *From Neurons to Neighborhoods: The Science of Early Childhood Development*. Washington, DC: National Academy Press, 2000.

CHAPTER 2

The cost of inaction: Concept and content

2.1. Introduction

There are a variety of meanings of 'cost of inaction' and different conceptualizations are possible. Alternative formulations will have an impact on the nature and substance of a study on the cost of inaction, and it is important to be clear at the outset about what is meant. This chapter attempts to outline alternative ways of understanding and characterizing the 'cost of inaction'.

To begin with, it is important to distinguish what can and cannot be considered costs of inaction. If certain negative consequences are unavoidable whatever action were to be taken, then these consequences cannot be regarded as costs of inaction. Thus it will not be enough simply to count as costs of 'inaction' all adverse events that are observed. Only those events that could be avoided by *some* action can be considered a cost of inaction. In general, different actions will avoid different negative consequences. Hence, each action will typically imply a different cost of inaction.

By definition, it is possible to prevent avoidable negative consequences by undertaking some action or actions. However, these actions may not necessarily be warranted given the magnitude of their costs. It would appear to be of limited value to estimate the cost of inaction relative to an action that is clearly unwarranted. We need to identify a desirable action or actions with respect to which the cost of inaction is assessed. This inevitably requires us to consider the principles involved in identifying and choosing desirable actions.

In characterizing the cost of inaction, there are three dimensions to consider:
1. Choice of principle to determine desirable or optimal actions.
2. Identification of the specific action with respect to which the cost of inaction is measured.

3.   Selection of costs that are to be considered in the analysis.

The first dimension concerns the principles that guide the choice of a desirable or optimal set of actions, relative to which inaction can be compared and costed. Three approaches are discussed in this chapter: (i) identify the negative consequences avoided by undertaking an action, and compare these with the cost of the action; (ii) compare the costs of the negative consequences avoided by the action, *plus* the *constitutive benefits* of the action, with the cost of the action—i.e., effectively conduct a full benefit-cost analysis; and (iii) examine the cost of meeting goals that have already been agreed. Approach (iii) takes the goals as given and is similar to cost-effectiveness analysis.

We distinguish between the constitutive and the consequential benefits of an action as follows. The constitutive benefits of an action are the (direct) benefits of what the action is about, i.e., what the action "constitutes". The consequential benefits of an action are the (indirect) benefits that arise as a consequence of the action—e.g. the negative consequences that the action prevents, or the positive externalities that the action generates.

The second dimension in defining the cost of inaction relates to the appropriate counterfactual. To state that there are costs of inaction is to recognize the possibility of some action that could have avoided these costs. As inaction is assessed relative to an action that could be undertaken, the manner in which this action is identified and justified will be central to the determination of what are considered to be costs of inaction. If a desirable program of action over time which covers a range of policy interventions is considered as the counterfactual, the costs of inaction will be different from comparison to a one-off action limited to a single intervention. Much of the difficulty in identifying the counterfactual action relates to the policy areas and interventions that are considered to be feasible. The interaction of policy variables in determining outcomes must also be taken into account, together with the background conditions or context. An example is the interaction of interventions targeted to reduce HIV/AIDS and the background condition of poverty (and policies to reduce poverty). Where the counterfactual action has already been identified, a major part of the exercise will effectively have been accomplished. This will be the case, for example, when a plan of action exists but has not yet been implemented.

The third dimension in defining the cost of inaction concerns the costs that are deemed appropriate for inclusion. A variety of views can be taken on this matter, and the selected view will shape the analysis. The costs considered could be limited to those experienced by the individuals directly affected, e.g. children. More generally, the consequences on families, communities, society and the economy could also be taken into account and costed.

The different dimensions give rise to a range of alternative conceptualizations. At this stage, we are not proposing one or other of these alternatives. Rather, our purpose is to outline different possible ways in which the 'cost of inaction' can be understood and interpreted. To this end, we elaborate each of the three dimensions in the following sections. Our discussion of the cost of inaction is not restricted to a particular area of action or intervention. But we will illustrate it by considering actions in relation to children affected by HIV/AIDS.

2.2. The principles that guide the choice of an action

The selection of an action as the counterfactual against which to compare inaction will be governed by the principles that guide the choice of desirable actions. We consider three approaches to inform such a choice.

i.   Identify the negative consequences prevented by an action and compare the costs it avoids with the cost of the action.
ii. Add the constitutive benefits of the action to the costs of the negative consequences avoided by it, and compare this total with the cost of the action.
iii. Minimize the cost of meeting an agreed goal.

Each of these approaches has counterparts in standard frameworks used to evaluate actions or interventions. Approach (i) can be seen as similar to a limited benefit-cost analysis which identifies the benefit of an action simply in terms of the costs of the negative consequences it avoids, and compares this with the cost of the action. Approach (ii) is similar to a full benefit-cost analysis which compares the constitutive benefits of the action *plus* its consequential benefits (the costs of the negative consequences avoided by it), with the cost of the action. Approach (iii) is based on cost-effectiveness analysis, which takes the objective as given and identifies least-cost actions to achieve it.

The most desirable actions are not necessarily those that have the largest gross benefit. Benefit-cost analysis must take account of the cost of an action and calculate the *net benefit* that arises, i.e., gross benefit minus cost. The most desirable action is one which yields the largest net benefit, not the largest gross benefit. For example, consider the prevention of transmission of HIV from mother to child. The probability that HIV will be transmitted to a child as a result of the mother's infection can be reduced by 50% by means of simple and relatively inexpensive interventions. Further reductions in the probability can be achieved only by means of increasingly large expenditures. Some additional expenditure may well be desirable given the additional benefit that results. However, once marginal cost exceeds marginal benefit, further expenditure is not warranted in the benefit-cost calculus. A state-of-the-art intervention may consist of the mother being placed on a full course of highly-active antiretroviral treatment at an early stage of her pregnancy and the use of caesarean section. The expenditure on drugs may well be desirable. Caesarean sections, however, are very expensive and may not be warranted. While inclusion of a caesarean as part of the intervention leads to a further reduction in the probability of infection of the child, the additional cost may outweigh the additional benefit. In such a situation the action with the largest gross benefit includes caesarean section whereas the action with the largest net benefit does not.

Approach (i) to choosing a desirable action simply involves costing the negative consequences avoided by undertaking an action and comparing these costs with the cost of the action. Identifying the costs avoided by undertaking an action is a critical but incomplete part of analyzing its benefits. If the costs avoided by undertaking an action exceed the cost of implementing it, then there is already a case for undertaking the action independent of its constitutive benefits. However, this is an excessively conservative approach to selecting an action as it does not account for the *total* benefits that result from it, and judges the action solely in terms of the negative consequences it avoids. Because the avoidance of negative consequences is indeed a benefit of the action, approach (i) is akin to a limited exercise in benefit-cost analysis. If the costs it avoids are greater than the costs it incurs, then the action is clearly worthwhile even without counting its constitutive benefits.

As an example of approach (i), consider a secondary-schooling project whose constitutive benefits are the education received by the children enrolled. However, an organization charged with crime prevention might evaluate this intervention only in terms of its consequential benefits. By children attending school, the project helps to keep them off the streets and thus reduces crime The constitutive (educational) benefits of schooling are not relevant to the organization's evaluation of the project. Avoiding the costs of crime are its sole concern. In comparing only this consequential benefit with the cost of the action, it conducts a limited benefit-cost exercise.

In approach (ii), the constitutive benefit of an action is counted in addition to its consequential benefit of avoiding certain negative consequences. The constitutive benefit should obviously be incorporated into a full benefit-cost analysis of the desirability of an action. Not undertaking the action then involves two types of benefit foregone: the constitutive benefit of the action, and its consequential benefit in preventing certain negative consequences. A full benefit-cost analysis is then equivalent to comparing the sum of these two types of benefit with the cost of the action. Thus if approach (ii) were used to evaluate the secondary-schooling project above, both the constitutive benefit of school attendance as well as the consequential benefit of reduced crime by keeping children off the streets would be compared to the cost of the action.

Approach (ii) may also be illustrated with the example of old-age pensions against the background of poverty in South Africa. The constitutive benefits of old-age pensions are an improvement in the living standards of the recipients and their families. But there is also considerable evidence of consequential benefits. When pensioners living in poverty spend their pension income on children in the household, this can result in an improvement in the children's nutritional status and school attendance, among other benefits. The expenditure on children yields positive externalities to broader society in the form of reduction in anti-social behaviors, gains in productivity, future participation as citizens, better parenting by them of the next generation, etc. Hence, with approach (ii), the desirability of old-age pensions is evaluated by summing the constitutive benefits (improvement in living standards for the pensioners and their families) and the consequential benefits (positive externalities from investment by the pensioners in children), and comparing the *sum total* of these benefits with the cost of the action.

Another illustration of approach (ii) concerns interventions that prevent adults becoming infected with HIV. The avoidance of illness and death from HIV/AIDS are constitutive benefits to the adults. But there are also significant consequential benefits for children. If adults are not infected with HIV, they do not infect their children. In addition, many negative impacts on children that are associated with adult illness are avoided. Adult illness leads to both reduced earning capacity and diversion of expenditure to medical care. The reduction in the household's income and its diversion to healthcare can result in the withdrawal of children from school and reduced levels of household consumption. In approach (ii), the consequential benefits of avoiding such negative outcomes of adult illness are added to the constitutive benefits of the action in the benefit-cost calculation.

Approach (iii) is not based on an explicit benefit-cost calculation, limited or full. It takes for granted the desirability of meeting a goal by a certain date, e.g. one of the Millennium Development Goals. From the set of alternative (time paths of) actions that achieve the goal, an action is chosen to minimize (the present value of) costs. In this case, the cost of not undertaking the action can be measured directly in terms of the goal benefits foregone. The cost of a *delay* in meeting the goal can be measured in two parts: the cost to individuals of a delay (e.g. through illness, death, etc.), and the change in the present value of costs (e.g. through missed opportunities for prevention and hence higher costs of treatment). Approach (iii) is similar to cost-effectiveness analysis, as it takes the desirability of meeting the goal as given and examines the costs of alternative (time paths of) actions to achieve the goal.

As an example of approach (iii), assume that a state has accepted an obligation to ensure that the basic needs of children are met (e.g. in terms of food, shelter, healthcare, security, etc.). When families are unable to meet their children's basic needs owing to extreme poverty, the state must take responsibility to act on its obligation. Suppose that the least-cost action by the state in this situation is to enhance the income-generating capacity of families through an integrated poverty reduction program (as in chapter 5). If this action is not undertaken, the consequences will be twofold: the direct cost to children of their needs not being met, and the likely higher cost of fulfilling the state's obligation later—including the additional cost of addressing the negative consequences that arise from unmet children's needs.

Approach (i) can be seen as a building block for approach (ii) and, in part, for approach (iii). Approach (i) requires identifying and estimating the cost consequences of not undertaking an action. These cost consequences can form part of a limited or full benefit-cost analysis, or a cost-effectiveness analysis. Indeed, all three approaches require estimating the consequences of not implementing an action.

Conceptually, the full costs of not implementing an action can be disaggregated into (a) the actual (consequential) cost incurred by not undertaking the action, and (b) the (hypothetical) constitutive benefit foregone by not undertaking the action. Obversely, the full benefits of implementing an action can be disaggregated into (a) the (hypothetical) consequential cost avoided by undertaking the action, and (b) the actual (constitutive) benefit that accrues by undertaking the action. Approach (i) considers only the actual cost incurred in failing to take an action but not the constitutive benefit foregone. Approach (ii) considers the full benefits of an action, including both its constitutive benefit and its consequential benefit.

In general the three approaches will identify different counterfactual actions or alternatives against which to assess the cost of inaction. The perspective of the evaluator performing the analysis will determine which of the three approaches is adopted to identify desirable actions, and which benefits and costs are selected for inclusion. Indeed, our own perspective may be different from that of an evaluator who identifies a desirable action through, for example, a partial benefit-cost analysis which considers only the constitutive benefits. We may adopt this action as a counterfactual against which to measure the costs of inaction, but choose to include also the consequential benefits foregone from not undertaking the action.

In this section we have tried to outline alternative ways in which an action is identified relative to which the costs of inaction are assessed. The different possibilities will lead to different demands for data and analysis. The next section describes how the cost of inaction is determined by the counterfactual that is identified.

2.3. Which counterfactual action?

By 'intervention' or 'action' we do not necessarily mean a single action, or actions confined to a single sector. The counterfactual action might well involve a set of actions drawn from several sectors. For example, the appropriate action for children affected by HIV/AIDS may include, among other things, medical care for children and their care-givers, financial support to the family, and school-feeding programs. Such an action would be multisectoral across the health, welfare and education sectors.

Measuring the cost of inaction requires identifying a counterfactual action that can avoid, at least to some degree, the negative consequences of doing nothing. There must be at least one action which reduces the negative consequences of inaction. Typically, there will be many actions that mitigate or avoid these negative outcomes.

The cost of inaction will differ depending on the action that is selected as the counterfactual. The counterfactual actions themselves can be different in several respects: for example, the action can be a program of interventions over time or a one-off action. The action can also be distinguished in terms of generating greater or smaller gross benefits. These possibilities are illustrated in table 2.1 below.

Table 2.1. Intervention by type of action and magnitude of gross benefit

	Intervention with greater gross benefit (GB)	Intervention with smaller gross benefit (SB)
Program of action over time (PAT)	PATGB	PATSB
One-off action (OA)	OAGB	OASB

Measuring the cost of inaction relative to a program of action over time with greater gross benefit (PATGB) can lead to very different results from comparison to a program of action over time with smaller gross benefit (PATSB). For example, take a program of action designed to prevent mother-to-child transmission of HIV and assume that reduction in child infections is the only benefit of the action. With no action, approximately 30% of children will be infected with HIV if their mother is HIV positive at the time of her pregnancy. The benefit of the action is to reduce the rate of transmission of HIV from mother to child. Ceteris paribus, the greater the gross benefit of the counterfactual action, the greater will be the cost of inaction. In terms of benefits foregone, inaction relative to PATGB by definition incurs a greater (gross) cost than inaction relative to PATSB. But the cost of implementing

PATGB is likely to be higher than the cost of implementing PATSB, and it is the *net* benefit foregone that should signify the cost of inaction.

Consider further the gross benefits of the two actions, PATGB and PATSB. PATGB may be a full course of antiretroviral drugs for the mother and child taken over an appropriate period, with adequate postnatal support for infant feeding (and possibly caesarean section). Assume that such a program of action reduces transmission to (an unavoidable) 2%—from 30% with no action. Hence the benefit foregone from not doing PATGB is 28 fewer infections out of 30. Compare this to PATSB which in this example may be a single dose of antiretroviral drugs and irregular postnatal support for infant feeding (the norm in much of Africa). Assume that such an intervention reduces transmission to 15%—from 30% with no action. Here the benefit foregone is 15 fewer infections out of 30.

One-off actions might also be considered appropriate counterfactuals in some situations: they place fewer demands on the health system in terms of financial and human resources. However, one-off actions tend to generate smaller gross benefits as they usually involve a single interaction with the health worker—e.g. dispensing a single dose of a more or less effective drug with no postnatal support. As a result of the drug's lower effectiveness, the gross benefit foregone from not doing OAGB (a one-off action with greater gross benefit) or OASB (a one-off action with smaller gross benefit) will be lower than that from not doing either PATGB or PATSB.

The above example illustrates the importance of identifying the counterfactual action relative to which the cost of inaction is assessed. The gross benefits foregone from not doing an action and the cost incurred in doing it will both vary depending on the counterfactual action that is chosen. It also raises the question of the cost of *inadequate* action where actions with larger net benefit are available. In this case there could still be a cost of inadequate action if PATSB with smaller net benefit, say, was being compared to PATGB with a greater net benefit.

The design of an action, and inaction in respect of it, needs to consider what the action is intended to address. For example, the objective of the action may be to address a single problem such as the effect of HIV/AIDS on children, or multiple problems concerning children. Thus, for a given population of children one could ask: (i) what is the cost of failing to address a single problem such as the effect of HIV/AIDS on the children? (ii) what is the cost of failing to deal with multiple problems concerning these children?

The first question could focus on any single problem, which here we have taken to be the implications of HIV/AIDS for children. However, the influence of different pre-existing factors, such as poverty, can affect the magnitude of this problem. For example, both poverty and HIV/AIDS have adverse implications for children's educational attainment. If a child's family is so poor that her educational status cannot get any worse, there is no scope for HIV/AIDS to lead to further deterioration. In this case, the child's educational situation may not improve from an intervention that addresses only HIV/AIDS; a reduction in poverty may be necessary. Hence the educational cost of not undertaking the HIV/AIDS intervention may be zero.

If, however, we do not restrict the action to interventions addressing only HIV/AIDS, the benefits of action can be large. With a broader scope for policy intervention which includes the reduction of both poverty and HIV/AIDS, the action can lead to an improvement in children's educational status. Hence the cost of failing to deal with multiple problems concerning children (e.g. HIV/AIDS and poverty) will be different from the cost of failing to deal with a single problem (e.g. HIV/AIDS). In dealing with multiple problems, the counterfactual action will tend to consist of a set of interventions that address the determinants of the different problems.

The identification of a counterfactual action is a major step in the process of defining and measuring the cost of inaction. In certain situations this step of the process may already have been taken. Where there is a determinate plan of action to achieve an agreed goal, the counterfactual is simply that plan. For example, almost every country in the world has signed the Convention on the Rights of the Child. Many countries have developed plans of action designed to lead to the fulfillment of the commitments to which they have agreed. If these plans are not implemented there will be a cost of inaction. In such situations there is less of a need to identify other actions as counterfactuals—except insofar as the latter entail a lower implementation cost. In that case the identified plan of action to achieve the agreed goal is not cost-effective, but the cost of inaction can still be measured relative to it.

In summary, the cost of inaction depends on the counterfactual action that is chosen against which the cost is assessed. The counterfactual action can be based on interventions that generate greater gross benefits but have a high cost of implementation, or smaller benefits with a lower cost of implementation. Also, the counterfactual action can be based on a single intervention or on multiple interventions across sectors. Finally, in situations where there is an agreed goal and plan of action to achieve the goal, the counterfactual is already given. If this plan is not implemented, costs of inaction will arise and can be estimated.

2.4. Which costs?

The perspective adopted by the evaluator will determine the costs that are included in calculating the cost of inaction. Indeed the evaluator's perspective is central in determining what is included in any benefit-cost or cost-effectiveness analysis.[1] In assessing the consequences of inaction, we need to consider the costs that are experienced by different persons and institutions at different points in time. Moreover, costs that fall on one agent may lead to secondary costs which are borne by other agents. The evaluator needs to consider a range of costs, monetary and non-monetary, and the different agents and institutions that bear these costs. As an example, the agents or institutions might be the following: children, families; community members; and the broader society and economy.

Given the initial problem of children affected by HIV/AIDS, the cost of inaction will fall directly on children in terms of their health and development. Such costs may arise from infection, the loss of care-givers, and reduced family income. The costs borne by children do not typically end with them. For example, child HIV infection carries costs for the family, in terms of greater expenditure and time spent in providing care. Families experiencing such costs may draw on support networks within the community for financial or human resources, which extend the costs beyond the family. Families may also make demands on publicly-provided services financed by local, state or central government. Other social costs may arise from failing to deal adequately with the consequences of the initial problem. For example, children who have suffered from neglect following the loss of their primary care-giver may be more prone to anti-social behaviors such as drug abuse, crime, etc. The costs borne by people consist not only of financial costs but also emotional and other psychological costs. The inclusion of costs falling beyond the child, family, and community allows consideration of broader social and economic costs.

The example of children affected by HIV/AIDS shows how initial costs experienced by children can lead to secondary costs faced by other agents or institutions. It also indicates how consequences in the current time period can have cost implications in subsequent periods. Hence estimation of the cost of inaction needs to consider the consequences for different agents and institutions across different time periods. Table 2.2 lists the consequences of children affected by HIV/AIDS for different agents/institutions and time periods.

In evaluating the costs of inaction across time periods, there are at least three issues that require attention: the appropriate time horizon for considering costs; the discount rate for comparing monetary costs in different time periods; the estimation of non-monetary costs in each time period.

The time horizon and discount rate selected to aggregate monetary costs over time can have a large effect on the measured costs of inaction. The costs of inaction can be borne over a long period of time, and may even continue inter-generationally—as some researchers have suggested in the case of neglect in children's nutrition, health and education. Some non-monetary costs that occur in the future should not be discounted, such as future lives lost in comparison to current lives lost.[2] However, the choice of time horizon does

THE COST OF INACTION: CONCEPT AND CONTENT 19

Table 2.2. Children affected by HIV/AIDS: Consequences for agents/ institutions by time period

Agents/institutions	Short-term consequences	Medium- and long-term consequences
Children	HIV infection Illness Withdrawal from school to provide care for ill family members Death	Reduced educational attainment Reduced earning potential Lower health status (physical and mental)
Family	Emotional suffering Time providing care Monetary costs of care	Economic insecurity
Community members	Reduced access to healthcare services due to increase in demand	Increase in anti-social behavior
Broader society and economy	Financing costly HIV/ AIDS treatment Financial cost of replacement care for children	Increase in crime Shrinkage of fiscal space

affect the measurement of both the monetary and non-monetary costs of inaction.

Many costs lend themselves to quantification in monetary terms, e.g. budgetary and out-of-pocket expenditures. There are other costs that can be quantified but are not easily monetized—for example, illness and death of children and their families, and social costs such as violent crime. There are still other costs that cannot be quantified even in non-monetary terms— e.g. pain, suffering, and emotional distress. In cases where costs cannot be reduced to a monetary figure and aggregated to yield a total overall cost, we need to consider alternative approaches to assessing the costs of inaction. Rather than identifying and calculating only those costs that can be monetized, we can quantify certain costs by using non-monetary scales, e.g.

for malnutrition, morbidity, lives lost, etc. Indeed, it may not even be appropriate to reduce costs such as illness suffered or lives lost to monetary values. The costs that are quantified in different spaces can be presented as the elements of a multidimensional vector. The non-quantifiable (and non-quantified) costs can be listed separately in a table. This approach allows the retention of information useful to policymakers in a summary form without reducing all costs to a single monetary aggregate—often through the use of questionable value judgements. Policymakers need such information in considering the many value judgements and trade-offs involved in assessing the costs of inaction.

2.5. Defining and measuring the cost of inaction

As mentioned at the beginning of this chapter, not all negative events can be considered to be costs of inaction. Only those negative events that are preventable by taking some action or set of actions can count as consequences of 'inaction'. Of the subset of negative events that can be prevented by an action, a 'cost' may be said to arise from not undertaking the action. However, different actions will in general prevent different negative consequences in this subset. The 'cost' of not undertaking one action that prevents some negative consequences will be different from the 'cost' of not undertaking another action that prevents different negative consequences. Hence each action will generally imply a different 'cost of inaction'. The cost of inaction can in principle be assessed against any (counterfactual) action that could have avoided some of the negative consequences that are of concern.

In this chapter we have also discussed different approaches to choosing actions against which to measure the cost of inaction—ranging from limited or full benefit-cost analysis to cost-effectiveness analysis. The counterfactual action may be given exogenously (or suggested by a concerned party), but the question still arises of defining and measuring the cost of inaction. In other words, how do we characterize the loss from not undertaking an action?

The action will have both constitutive and consequential benefits (avoiding the negative consequences of not undertaking it), and it will have a cost of implementation. The *net benefit* of the action is the sum of its constitutive and consequential benefits minus the cost of implementation. It is this net benefit that is lost if the action is not implemented. *We define the cost of inaction as the net benefit foregone by not undertaking an action.*

Each action has different constitutive and consequential benefits (negative consequences avoided) and different costs of implementation. Hence the net benefit of each action will generally be different—i.e., each action will have a different cost of inaction.

To summarize, the problem of the 'cost of inaction' is not simply that by doing nothing (commonly understood as 'inaction'), negative consequences will arise. The problem is one of not doing *something* that will avoid these negative consequences. Then the question arises as to *what* thing should be done to avoid these negative consequences. This recognition leads to wanting to do the thing that results in the largest net benefit—measured as the costs of the negative consequences avoided by doing it, plus its constitutive (positive) benefits, minus the cost of doing it. Of course, other actions may result in large net benefits, which are estimated in the same way. But the cost of inaction has to be assessed in relation to some specific action. This (counterfactual) action could be one that has the largest net benefit if our purpose is normative, or some other action that has been proposed if the purpose is descriptive.

This chapter has attempted to examine alternative ways in which the 'cost of inaction' can be conceptualized. Defining the cost of inaction requires us to: (1) choose the criterion for determining desirable or optimal actions; (2) identify a specific (counterfactual) action with respect to which the cost of inaction is evaluated; and (3) select the costs that are to be included in the analysis.

In discussing counterfactual actions, we considered both the gross benefit of an action and sets of actions that are drawn from multiple sectors. With regard to inclusion of costs, a distinction was made between different types of cost, the agents or institutions that bear the costs, and the time period over which the costs are borne.

With alternative approaches to identifying counterfactual actions, and their benefits and costs, both monetary and non-monetary, there are many possibilities for defining and measuring the cost of inaction. In this chapter we have attempted to clarify some basic concepts, and have settled on a broad-based approach to the definition and measurement of the cost of inaction.

References

1. Sen A. Control areas and accounting prices: An approach to economic evaluation. *Economic Journal* 1972; 82(325):486–501.
2. Anand S, Sen A. Human development and economic sustainability. *World Development* 2000; 28(12):2029-2049.

CHAPTER 3

Rwanda country background

3.1. Introduction

In this chapter we provide a concise country background for Rwanda. This includes a brief description of the country's geography and population, recent history, political and administrative system, economy, and its health and education system. These features shape the social interventions that may be considered feasible and desirable. In considering responses to children affected by poverty and HIV/AIDS, the situation faced by households with children needs to be identified and recognized.

3.2. Geography and population

Rwanda is a small landlocked country in eastern Africa with a land area of only 26,338 square kilometers. It shares borders with the Democratic Republic of Congo (DRC) (formerly Zaïre), Uganda, Tanzania, and Burundi.[1] On the one hand, its small size limits the domestic market and makes integration into world markets critical. On the other, lack of access to the sea and long distances from major markets result in high costs of trade. The costs of external trade are augmented by the country's poor transport infrastructure.[2]

Rwanda is the most densely populated country in sub-Saharan Africa.[1] In 2010 its population was 10.6 million.[3] The total fertility rate is high; it was estimated to be 5.4 in 2009.[3] The population is also very young; in 2010 an estimated 43% of the population was under 16 years of age.[3] Between 2005 and 2010, the urban population grew at an average annual rate of 4.4%, and in 2010 19% of the total population was urban.[3] The genocide and war resulted in an imbalanced sex ratio. Since then the situation has been improving — the number of men per 100 women increased from 87 in 2001 to 90 in 2006, and to 94 in 2009.[4,5]

The country had approximately 1.9 million households in 2006, and average household size was 5 persons. The proportion of female-headed households in 2006 was 23.8%, down from 27.6% in 2001. Three out of four female heads of household were widows. The proportion of child-headed households in 2006 was 0.7%, down from 1.3% in 2001; this decrease is attributed mainly to the aging of children who became heads of household during the genocide.[4]

3.3. History
3.3.1. Pre-colonial Rwanda
Pre-colonial Rwanda was a highly organized kingdom ruled by a centralized administration, the head of which was the king. Before the arrival of German colonists in 1899, Rwandans had lived in relative peace for the previous 400 years.[6] During this time the Tutsis, who made up less than 15% of the population, established themselves as a feudal ruling class over the Hutus. Under colonial rule, first by Germans and then by Belgians, the Tutsis and Hutus were identified as separate ethnic groups. With a limited number of their own people on the ground, the German colonialists relied on Tutsis as the ruling aristocracy to enforce control, thereby entrenching Tutsi dominance over Hutus.[7] After World War I, the League of Nations declared the transfer of Rwanda from Germany to a protectorate of Belgium.[8] The Belgians deepened ethnic divisions, and issued identity cards which specified the tribe to which a holder belonged.[7] By the time the country won its independence from Belgium in 1962, the Belgian policy of proxy rule that had favored the Tutsi led to tensions between Hutus and Tutsis.[8] The situation became more complicated when, in early 1960, Belgium changed its policy and started to favor Hutus — appointing Hutu chiefs to replace Tutsis. On 1 July 1962, Rwanda became independent and Grégoire Kayibanda, a Hutu devoted to making Tutsis subordinate and establishing hegemony of the Hutu, became the leader of the government.[7]

Faced with discrimination, and at times violent persecution, many Tutsis fled the country. The refugees organized themselves, and an armed conflict began in 1990 between the Hutu-dominated government and the Tutsi Rwandan Patriotic Front (RPF).[7] As a result of the conflict, social-sector spending fell from 35% of government expenditure in 1985 to 20% in 1992, while defense and administration expenditure grew from 45% to 64%. As social-sector expenditures fell, the need for social services increased because the population living below the poverty line rose: from 38% in 1986 to more than 53% in 1992. By the early 1990s, Rwanda was one of the ten poorest countries in the world.[9]

When Hutu President Habyarimana signed the Arusha Accords with RPF in March 1993, tensions between the Hutus and Tutsis appeared to be subsiding. For a country then bankrupt and without sufficient food, the Arusha Accords were intended to ensure both continued donor funding and the establishment of a transitional democratic government that included the Tutsi as well as the Hutu. Hutu extremists, however, adamantly opposed the plan.[7]

3.3.2. The genocide

In April 1994, President Habyarimana was assassinated, an event that initiated a premeditated genocide. Tensions between the Hutu and Tutsi, fanned by propaganda and organized militia, erupted into mass killing of Tutsis and moderate Hutus.[10] To end the genocide, RPF launched a full-scale invasion from Uganda and eventually took control of the country. When RPF declared the war to be over on 18 July 1994, at least 800,000 people had been killed in a period of approximately 100 days. Every aspect of the government and infrastructure were affected by the genocide. Hospitals, schools and government offices were destroyed or looted, and the police system had become dysfunctional. The infrastructure necessary for electricity, water and telephones was destroyed.[7] A year's harvest was lost, and the country's human resources were decimated.[7,11] For example, the number of doctors working in the country fell from 253 in 1988 to 117 after the genocide; and by 1999 there were still only 148 physicians.[12] An estimated two million people fled the country and another one million were internally displaced.[1] Among those who left were the Hutu-dominated army who fled into neighboring Zaïre (DRC).

The genocide and the subsequent war had significant negative consequences for children. An estimated 21% of children (1.26 million) lost one or both parents during the genocide or as a result of increased mortality from disease.[13,14]

3.3.3. Post-genocide

On 19 July 1994, RPF organized a government comprised of representatives of all the major parties. The one party prohibited from involvement in the new government was the *Mouvement Revolutionnaire Nationale pour le Developpement,* the party responsible for the coordination and execution of the genocide. The new leaders were President Pasteur Bizimungu, a moderate Hutu who had opposed the genocide, and Vice President Paul Kagame, a Tutsi and leader of RPF.[7] After falling out with the ruling RPF, President Bizimungu resigned from the presidency in 2000 and was replaced by then Vice President, Paul Kagame.[15]

The government adopted a new constitution in 2003 that eliminated reference to ethnicity, and prepared for presidential and legislative elections in August and September of that year. On 25 August 2003, incumbent Paul Kagame was elected president for a seven-year term with 95% of the vote. Legislative elections were held between September and October 2003; they were considered orderly and fair despite some irregularities.[1]

Between 1994 and 1996, many refugee camps in Zaïre (now DRC) fell under the control of Hutu extremists. After attacks by Hutu militias on local Zaïrian Tutsis in 1995, Zaïre attempted — but failed — to force Hutu refugees to return to Rwanda. To end raids into Rwanda by Hutu militia based in the refugee camps, and to allow refugees to return home, Rwandan troops entered Zaïre in 1996 and attacked the Hutu-militia dominated camps. Hutu militias fled the camps and moved deeper into Zaïre. The Rwandan troops joined forces with Zaïrian rebels to give chase to the Hutu militia. With the support of Rwandan troops, the Zaïrian rebels were able to depose Zaïre's President, Mobutu Sese Seko.[16]

By 2000 more than three million refugees had returned to Rwanda.[17] Many returnees were suspected of involvement in the genocide. In 2001, the government set up Gacaca, a dispute-resolution system to process the large number of genocide-related cases. Under this system, those facing lesser charges were put on trial in their communities, while the formal courts tried those who were thought to bear the greatest responsibility for the genocide.[18] As of June 2009, the *Gacaca* courts had tried over 1.5 million cases and had some 4,000 pending.[19] Amnesty International expressed concerns in 2007 that poorly-qualified and corrupt *Gacaca* judges were fueling public distrust of the system.[10]

3.4. Current political and administrative system

Rwanda is a constitutional republic with executive, legislative and judicial branches.[20] The executive branch consists of three parts: the President, who acts as head of state; the Prime Minister, who acts as head of government; and the Cabinet, which is comprised of the Council of Ministers. The President appoints the Prime Minister and the Cabinet members.[21] The legislative branch consists of an 80-seat Chamber of Deputies and a 26-seat Senate.[10] The Chamber of Deputies, or lower house, consists of 53 directly-elected members, 24 women chosen by local councils, two deputies chosen by a youth council, and one representative from a federation for the disabled.[10] The Senate, or upper house, consists of 12 members elected by local councils, eight members appointed by the President, four members chosen by a forum of political parties, and two representatives from universities. All members of the Chamber of Deputies serve five-year terms, and all Senate members serve eight-year terms.[10] The judicial system is comprised of the Supreme Court, high courts of the Republic, provincial courts, district courts, and mediation committees.[21] Universal suffrage is granted to citizens over 18 years of age.[1]

Administratively, Rwanda is divided into Kigali City and North, South, East, and West Provinces.[21] The Provinces are divided into a total of 30 Districts, and the Districts are subdivided into Sectors (416), Cells (2,150), and Villages (14,975).[22]

The country adopted a new constitution in 2003. The new constitution stipulates that the largest political party cannot occupy more than half of the Cabinet seats, and that the President, Prime Minister, and President of the Chamber of Deputies cannot belong to the same party.[10] The constitution grants broad powers to the President, who can serve up to two seven-year terms, can declare a state of emergency, and can dissolve the Chamber of Deputies.[10,11] The constitution also requires that women occupy at least 30% of the seats in both the Chamber of Deputies and the Senate. After the 2008 legislative elections, women now occupy 45 out of the 80 seats (56%) in the Chamber of Deputies.[1] Rwanda holds the world record for the highest percentage of women in the national parliament.[23] This high percentage may well influence the policies that are proposed by the government in respect of children and families.

The strong drive for national unity has discouraged political pluralism, causing many opposition parties to take views similar to those of the government. Parties based on ethnicity or religion, and parties identified with the 1994 genocide, have been banned. The ruling RPF party maintains control over political life. The situation is, however, slowly changing as restrictions on political debate are being relaxed.[10]

A strong president and ruling party can hinder open public debate, which can limit the degree to which controversial policies are discussed. On the other hand, the government has shown a clear commitment to economic and human development and to identifying the best ways to achieve these ends. The apparent support for the poor suggests that pro-poor policies, which perhaps would not be considered elsewhere, can be carried out in Rwanda.

3.5. Economy
3.5.1. The national economy
The economy was decimated by the genocide and subsequent civil war. In 1994, the conflict led to a 40% decline in GDP.[1] Economic growth recovered after the genocide, with an average increase in real GDP of 10.8% per year between 1996 and 2000. Growth slowed slightly between 2001 and 2006, averaging 6.4% per year.[22] During the global financial crisis, the country has managed to maintain an above-average growth rate relative to its neighbors. Despite recent growth, GDP per capita remains low. In 2010 GDP per capita was US$530 in current prices, and PPP$1,155 in current international dollars.[3]

Other macroeconomic indicators have been improving recently. The trade gap has narrowed, due to both higher international prices for major exports and an increase in export volumes. Agricultural products account for approximately 50% of exports, and minerals for 28% of exports. Coffee and tea exports benefited from increases in both international prices and export volumes. Mineral exports benefited from increases in international prices.[24]

Economic growth has boosted government revenue receipts, which has allowed for expansion of public spending.[25] The human and social development sectors (health, education and social protection; and youth, culture and sports) continued to receive the main share (31.1%) of government spending. The overall fiscal deficit (excluding grants) is expected to be 13.8% of GDP in 2010/11. Donor inflows are a significant source of state budget financing.[24] The World Bank has noted that the country is highly dependent on foreign aid, and attention must be paid to the stability of such funding.[25] The government is taking steps to decrease dependency on donor funding.[24]

Despite recent improvements, government debt remains a concern. The country's participation in the Heavily Indebted Poor Countries (HIPC) Initiative and the Multilateral Debt Relief Initiative reduced its external debt to 15% of GDP in 2006, from 71% in 2005 and 90% in 2003.[24] However, the December 2007 Rwanda-Joint International Monetary Fund and World Bank Debt Sustainability Analysis indicated that the country is still at a high risk of "debt distress"[a] due to reduced concessional financing and insufficient export growth. The World Bank estimated that if the government maintains moderate domestic financing and repays pre-genocide debt, its public-debt-to-GDP ratio will rise from 15% in 2007 to stabilize at about 20% of GDP in the long term.[25]

3.5.2. Poverty

UNDP's 2009 Human Poverty Index places Rwanda 100 out of 135 countries for which the statistic was computed.[27] Income inequality is high and rising: the Gini coefficient increased from 0.467 in 2000 to 0.531 in 2005.[22] Low GDP per capita and high levels of inequality account for some 56.9% of the population living below the national income poverty line in 2005; the poverty line in 2005 was US$162[b] (RWF90,000) per adult equivalent per year.[4] Moreover, 37% of Rwandans lived in extreme income poverty in 2005, i.e., below US$114 (RWF63,500) per adult equivalent per year — the minimum food expenditure required to meet an intake of 2,100 kilocalories per day.[25] The extreme poverty line is defined as the level of expenditure "below which households could not even afford the basic food consumption basket, even without spending anything on non-food items."[28] A 2008 study estimates that 83% of children, or two million, can be considered vulnerable because of poverty or living conditions.[14]

Progress has been made in the reduction of poverty, but much more remains to be done. Between 2000/01 and 2005/06, national income poverty declined from 60.4% to 56.9%, rural poverty declined from 66% to 62%, and poverty in Kigali declined by 3 percentage points to 20%.[25] Although the proportion of people living in poverty has decreased, the absolute number of poor people has increased since 2000/01 because of rapid population growth.[22] The World Bank estimates that the economy needs at least 8% annual growth to reduce poverty levels significantly. Based on this estimate, the predicted growth of 6% for the period 2007–27 will be inadequate.[25]

The high poverty rate of 56.9% in Rwanda in 2005/6 shows some regional variation within the country. Almost 92% of the country's poor (and 93% of the country's extremely poor) population lives in rural areas. Table 3.1 summarizes the poverty rates in the City of Kigali and in each of the four provinces, which are largely rural. Kigali has, as expected, much lower rates of poverty and of extreme poverty. The poverty headcounts in the provinces are fairly similar, with the exception of Eastern Province which has a markedly lower poverty rate than the other three provinces.[4]

Table 3.1. Regional variation in poverty, 2005/06

Province	Poverty headcount 2005/06 (%)	Extreme poverty headcount 2005/06 (%)
City of Kigali	20.2	11.1
Southern Province	67.2	47.2
Western Province	62.0	40.9
Northern Province	62.7	40.8
Eastern Province	50.4	28.7
National	**56.9**	**37.0**

Source: National Institute of Statistics of Rwanda. *EICV Poverty Analysis for Rwanda's Economic Development and Poverty Reduction Strategy*. Kigali, Rwanda: NISR, 2007.

Vulnerability of the population can be assessed in terms of its food security. Data from 2006 show that over half (52%) of the rural population is considered to be food insecure or highly vulnerable.[c] A further 26% of the rural population is considered moderately vulnerable to food insecurity, leaving only 22% of the rural population as food secure.[29] It should also be emphasized that food security is heavily dependent on local agriculture, as 90% of the food consumed is produced domestically.[25] To supplement domestic production, the country imports approximately 130,000 tons of food annually. Food imports consist mainly of edible oil, wheat, sugar, rice, beans, maize, cooking bananas, and dairy products.[30]

Food insecurity frequently results in child malnutrition — approximately 52% of children under five are stunted, and 18% are underweight. Malnutrition and stunting are associated with the wealth indicator estimated from the Demographic and Health Survey (DHS) 2005.[31] Among families in the lowest wealth quintile (i.e., the poorest 20% of Rwandans in 2005), 31% of children below five years of age were underweight, whereas only 10% were underweight among families in the highest wealth quintile (the richest 20% of Rwandans).[32]

Poverty is linked to agricultural output: the majority of adults are either employed within the agriculture sector or derive their livelihood from farming. Although the percentage of the total population that engages in subsistence farming has decreased from 85% in 2000/01 to 71% in 2005/06, the proportion remains extremely high. Poverty is highest among households whose main source of income is agricultural wage labor; over 90% of such households were considered poor in 2005/06.[4]

Key factors in reducing poverty include increasing agricultural productivity and incomes, diversifying sources of livelihood away from agriculture, and reducing population growth.[25] However, the country currently lacks opportunities for rural non-farm employment, which poses a barrier to diversification.[4]

The government has implemented a number of policies to reduce poverty and its impact on children. Central among these policies is the Vision 2020 *Umurenge* Program (VUP). Vision 2020 is a comprehensive plan that, by the year 2020, aspires to transform Rwanda into a middle-income country with per capita income of US$900 (at constant 2000 prices when the Program was formulated), a poverty rate of 30%, and life expectancy at birth of 55 years.[33,34] The Program aims to reduce poverty and increase the productive capacity of the rural poor through a combination of public works, income generation cooperatives, credit packages, and direct support.[35]

VUP is designed to respond differently to households depending on their availability of land and labor. The Program first targets the poorest households and then categorizes them based on their endowments of land and labor. Households with land and working-age adults are offered credit packages. Households with working-age adults but no land are given the opportunity to participate in public works programs. Households with neither land nor labor qualify for direct support, in the form of healthcare services, education, and cash grants. VUP is implemented by the government and supported by the UK Department for International Development (DfID) and other development partners and non-governmental organizations (NGOs). VUP was initiated in 30 *Imirenge* (Sectors) in March 2008.[36]

In addition to VUP, the government has sought to address poverty by increasing agricultural production. Interventions in this area include efforts to increase the proportion of land available for farming, improvement of irrigation and other farming techniques, and establishment of farming cooperatives. Interventions aimed at improving population health and strengthening the education system can also be considered as poverty reduction efforts. Such interventions are discussed in the health and education sections of this chapter.

3.6. Energy, water and sanitation

Electricity consumption per capita in 2004 (at 31 kilowatt-hours) was the fifth lowest in the world.[37] As of 2005, only 4% of the population had an electricity connection.[38] Although electricity production has increased, limited access remains a problem: in 2009 only 6% of the population had access to electricity.[39] The government aims to increase access to electricity to 35% of the population by 2020.[22]

The supply of firewood is limited, with the country having lost more than half its forest cover between 1990 and 2005. Yet almost all of its rural population (95.5%) still depends on firewood for cooking. As a result, children spend many hours each week fetching firewood for cooking. Further deforestation as well as water scarcity will require children to walk longer distances—risking their safety and possibly decreasing their participation in school.[40]

According to DHS 2005, only 27.4% of the population had sustainable access to improved water sources.[32] Notwithstanding efforts since 2001 to provide new water networks, the proportion of households that use safe sources of water for drinking remained unchanged between 2001 and 2006.[44] In Kigali, the proportion of households with access to safe water decreased by 6.4 percentage points (from 88% to 81.6%) between 2001 and 2006, as supply did not keep pace with urbanization.[40]

A minority of the population reports using improved sanitation facilities.[6,41] The situation is gradually improving: for example, the proportion of households using ventilated improved pit latrines increased fourfold from 7% in 2000 to 28% in 2005. But as of 2005, only 1% of households used flush toilets.[32] The government has dedicated 1% of GDP to water and sanitation management, which is higher than the average share of GDP allocated to water and sanitation in sub-Saharan Africa (0.5% of GDP in 2007).[40]

3.7. Health

3.7.1. Overview of population health

Life expectancy at birth is low. In 2009, it was only 49 and 52 years for men and women, respectively.[38] In 2010 the infant mortality rate was 59 per 1,000 live births and the under-five mortality rate (U5MR) 91 deaths per 1,000 live births.[3] U5MR varies by stratum, mothers' education and household wealth. According to DHS 2005, it is 1.6 times higher in rural than in urban areas, and four times higher among mothers with no education (174 per 1,000 in 2005) than among mothers with secondary education or more (43 deaths per 1,000). In the lowest wealth quintile U5MR (161 per 1,000) is nearly twice as high as it is in the highest wealth quintile (84 per 1,000). Mortality rates have declined significantly in recent years and are now below their pre-genocide levels.[32] Between 2000 and 2010, infant mortality fell from 106 deaths per 1,000 live births to 59 deaths per 1,000 live births, and U5MR fell from 177 deaths per 1,000 live births to 91 deaths per 1,000 live births.[3]

In 2006, malaria was a leading cause of morbidity and mortality in Rwanda; it was associated with 37% of outpatient visits and 41% of hospital deaths. Of these deaths, 42% occurred among children under five years of age. The government and its partners have taken a number of steps to prevent and treat malaria. As a result, by 2007, the share of malaria in hospital deaths fell sharply from 41% to 15%. The program was particularly successful at protecting children: in 2006, of the 41% of in-hospital deaths from malaria, 42% were of children; in 2007, of the 15% of in-hospital deaths from malaria, 22% were of children. This suggests that child deaths declined more rapidly than adult deaths.[12]

The dramatic improvement in just one year is due to the national integrated malaria campaign of 2006. During the campaign more than 1.4 million long-lasting insecticide nets were distributed and artemisinin-based combination therapy (ACT) was offered in all government and government-assisted health facilities. According to the 2007 Malaria Indicator Survey (MIS), 54% of households owned at least one insecticide-treated net, a three-fold increase since 2005. During 2005–07 the proportion of children under five and pregnant women who slept under insecticide-treated nets increased almost five-fold to 60%. The 2007 Rwanda Service Provision Assessment (RSPA) found that 93% of all health facilities offered malaria treatment services. About 90% of health facilities offering malaria services had anti-malarial medicines on the day they were surveyed; however, 42% of health facilities had been out of stock of some anti-malarial medicine during the previous six months.[32]

Pneumonia and other acute respiratory infections (ARI) are also leading causes of mortality among children under five. In 2007, the prevalence of ARI among these children was reported to be 15%. Children 6–11 months old showed the highest prevalence of ARI (22%) and were the group most often brought for treatment to health facilities. RSPA 2007 reports that only 13% of children who needed antibiotics for symptoms of ARI received them.[42]

Tuberculosis (TB) is also a major health problem in Rwanda. In 2004 there were an estimated 660 cases per 100,000 persons. TB-related mortality was 102 per 100,000 persons in 2004, up from 55 per 100,000 persons in 2000. The increase in mortality is likely to be the result of HIV-TB co-infection. In 2007, the Ministry of Health reported an 86% success rate for TB treatment. To help prevent the spread of TB, Bacillus Calmette-Guérin (BCG) vaccination is provided at birth; officially the vaccine is mandatory but it is unclear what sanctions are instituted if parents refuse to have their children vaccinated.[42]

In 2008 diarrhea was the cause of 11.3% of hospital deaths, making it the third highest cause of hospital deaths behind malaria and pulmonary infections.[43] In 2007, 14% of children had diarrhea, with the highest prevalence among children aged 6–11 months (23%) and 12–23 months (22%). Oral rehydration therapy (ORT) is the most common treatment for diarrhea. Although 39% of children under five who need ORT receive some form of it, an estimated 42% of children do not receive any treatment for diarrhea.[44]

DHS 2005 reported a very high maternal mortality rate of 750 maternal deaths per 100,000 births — almost 8 women for every 1,000 children born.[32] The majority of these deaths are due to obstetric complications such as hemorrhage, sepsis, and eclampsia.[42] Anemia is also a significant problem among women, with 35% of all pregnant women (and 33% of all women) being iron deficient.[32] Estimates suggest that anemia contributes to 11% of maternal deaths.[42]

Of particular importance for children's health is immunization. According to WHO and UNICEF, immunization coverage in 2008 was 93% for TB, 97% for diphtheria, pertussis and tetanus (DPT), 97% for polio, and 92% for measles.[45] The Expanded Program on Immunization (EPI) recommends that all children by the age of 12 months receive vaccinations for TB, DPT, polio, and measles.[42] A pentavalent vaccine (DPT-HepB-Hib) was introduced in 2002, and coverage in 2007 was estimated to be 97%.[45] Although immunization coverage is high for individual vaccines (in the 90%-plus range), a smaller percentage of children complete all vaccinations (TB, DPT, polio and measles) within the recommended time frame. RSPA 2007 reports that among fully-vaccinated children, 74% received all vaccinations in the first 12 months and 80% received all vaccinations by 23 months of age; hence 20% received all vaccinations only after (or in) month 24.[42]

3.7.2. HIV/AIDS
HIV/AIDS prevalence

Estimates of HIV prevalence in Rwanda have varied considerably since the virus was first discovered in the country. The first national survey, conducted in 1986, reported adult HIV prevalence of 17.8% in urban areas and 1.3% in rural areas. In 1991 adult prevalence was estimated to be 27% in

urban areas, 8.5% in semi-urban areas, and 2.2% rural areas.[32] HIV surveillance resumed after the 1994 genocide, with a new surveillance system established in 1996. Data gathered from 10 sentinel sites found a rise in infection rates in 1996 compared to 1991. In 1996, adult prevalence was estimated
to be 27% among urban residents, 13% among semi-urban residents, and
6.9% among rural residents.[32]

In 1997 adult prevalence was estimated to be 11.1% overall — 10.8% for
men and 11.3% for women. In 2002, the national sentinel surveillance system expanded to 24 sites, allowing for the estimation of more precise information on prevalence. The 2002 data showed much lower rates, with adult
prevalence varying between 7.0% and 8.5% in urban areas and between 2.6%
and 3.6% in rural areas. Data from 2003 showed almost the same rates.[32]

UNAIDS and WHO estimated that HIV prevalence in 2007 among 15–49
year-old adults was 2.8% and the total number of people living with HIV
was approximately 150,000.[46] The 2007 estimates suggest that 19,000 children below the age of 14 years are HIV-positive and 220,000 children are
thought to have lost their parents to AIDS.[41] According to WHO estimates,
HIV/AIDS was the leading cause of death in Rwanda in 2002, accounting for
18% of deaths in that year.[47]

DHS 2005 data show that 35–39 year-old women had an HIV prevalence of 6.9% and were the female age-group with the highest prevalence.
Women in the 40–44 year and 30–34 year age-groups had the second- and
third-highest female prevalence of 6.3% and 5.9%, respectively. The male
age-group with the highest prevalence was the 40–44 year group with a 7.1%
prevalence, followed by the 45–49 year group with 5.3% prevalence.[32]

Response to HIV/AIDS

The country's response to HIV/AIDS began in 1987 with the creation of
the National Program for HIV/AIDS Control (Programme Nationale de
Lutte contre le SIDA, or PNLS). In 2000 PNLS was divided into two new
organizations based at the Ministry of Health (MOH): the National AIDS
Control Commission (Commission Nationale de Lutte contre le SIDA, or
CNLS), which is the coordinator of multi-sectoral responses, and responsible for national policy development, partnerships, monitoring and evaluation; and the Treatment and Research AIDS Center (TRAC).[43]

In January 2006 the government decentralized its management of the
HIV/AIDS response to the district level. Since this restructuring, CNLS has
served as a coordinating body for the 30 District AIDS Control Committees,
which are responsible for translating national policy into local programs
and for developing an annual action plan for their district's HIV-related
activities.[43] In 2007 TRAC merged with the National Malaria Control Program and the National Tuberculosis and Leprosy Control Program to create

TRAC Plus, whose mission is to promote action in response to epidemics of infectious diseases.[48]

The responses to HIV/AIDS have been characterized by strong leadership, high-level political support, and a systematic process for mobilizing local authorities to adhere to national standards. The 2009–2012 National Strategic Plan (NSP) on HIV and AIDS is fully harmonized with both the 2008–2012 Economic Development and Poverty Reduction Strategy (EDPRS) and the 2009–2012 Health Sector Strategic Plan.[43]

HIV/AIDS testing, treatment and prevention services have been rolled out in both urban and rural areas. In 2008, 75.4% of health facilities offered voluntary counseling and testing (VCT), but only 20.2% of the targeted population had been tested.[49] The number of facilities offering PMTCT services has increased from 28% (120 out of 420 sites) in 2005 to 76% (362 out of 476 sites) in 2009. The percentage of HIV-positive pregnant women who receive ART in PMTCT programs has increased from 53.7% in 2005 to 95% in 2009. At the end of 2008, the transmission rate among 18-month old children born to HIV-positive mothers was estimated to be 6.9%.[50] Notwithstanding the PMTCT successes, in 2008 only 43% of all hospitals and health centers offered the full package of HIV services, which include VCT, PMTCT and ART.[49] Only 43% of health facilities offered ART programs in 2008, and 62% and 66% of eligible adults and children, respectively, received ART.[49]

Targets outlined in the 2009–2012 NSP consist of ambitious medical, public health, and social goals. These goals include halving HIV incidence between 2009 and 2012, reducing HIV morbidity and mortality significantly, and ensuring equal opportunities for people infected and affected by HIV. NSP also places increased emphasis on testing for sero-discordant couples and for partners of pregnant women. Increased prevention efforts are planned for high-risk groups such as sex workers, truck drivers, prisoners and homosexuals.[51]

Between 2007 and 2008 total HIV spending increased by 33%, from US$74.6 million in 2007 to US$110.8 million in 2008. The US government, through the President's Emergency Plan for AIDS Relief (PEPFAR), remained the major financial contributor to HIV responses in the country — it contributed 58% and 54% of total spending in 2007 and 2008, respectively. The Rwandan government itself contributed 8% and 6% of such spending in 2007 and 2008, respectively, with the rest being made up by agencies such as the Global Fund to fight AIDS, TB and Malaria (GFATM).[51]

The government is not the only entity involved in responding to children and adults living with HIV/AIDS. A large number of international and national NGOs have programs designed to benefit these groups. Also, a number of community-level responses to HIV/AIDS have emerged. Support from the government and NGOs has been important in helping to maintain and grow these community responses. There are 116 NGOs working on HIV/AIDS in Rwanda, of which 37 are local, 46 are national, and 33 are international. The country has more than 1,400 local community-based organizations (CBOs) and associations: 1,227 associations of People Living with HIV/AIDS, 107 faith-based groups, and 183 associations for disabled people. Despite the large number of local groups, many high-risk groups are not well covered; these groups include out-of-school youth and young girls who are rape victims.[52]

3.7.3. Health infrastructure and financing

Progress in health typically requires a range of actions in different sectors. Anti-poverty measures and actions in the education sector are effective ways to address the social determinants of health. But healthcare is also critical in affecting people's health. The state of the health infrastructure will thus be an important area in identifying interventions to improve health.

Following the 1978 Alma Ata declaration on primary healthcare, the Government of Rwanda committed itself to the development of a basic healthcare system that offered primary care to the entire population. After the WHO Africa Regional Committee meeting in 1985, the government adopted a health development strategy based on decentralized management and provision of care at the district level.[42] Before the 1994 genocide, health services were, in principle, free to all; after the genocide, publicly-provided health services were weak, mainly because a large part of the health infrastructure was destroyed.[12] After peace was re-established, the Ministry of Health (MOH) launched a health-sector reform initiative, which was announced in 1995 and adopted in 1996. This initiative sought to improve the health of the population by building a national healthcare system providing quality services that were accessible to the majority of people. In March 2005, the government adopted the Health Sector Policy and the Health Sector Strategic Plan (HSSP) 2005–2009. This policy and plan sought to assist the government's efforts to improve health and well-being of the population, increase productivity, and reduce poverty.[42]

Administration of the health sector comprises three tiers. The highest administrative tier is responsible for developing health policy. The second tier is the district administration. There are 30 administrative districts. Each district has at least one district hospital and several primary healthcare facilities. The lowest tier consists of the primary healthcare facilities, which include health centers, health posts, and dispensaries. These are the most decentralized administrative units.[42]

In addition to public health facilities, there are government-assisted facilities that are operated by various religious and non-profit organizations. They have the same functions, responsibilities, and management structures as the public facilities but are not managed and operated by the government. Government-assisted facilities are registered with and receive assistance from the government. In 2007, 25% of the first- and second-level health facilities were government-assisted. In terms of private healthcare, there were 373 private health facilities in 2007; of these, 72 were operated by physicians, and the remaining 301 were operated by nurses. More than 70% of these facilities were located in or around Kigali City. The MOH also provides guidance on ways in which practitioners of traditional medicine can operate alongside government health services.[42]

The government has tried to ensure that health centers are accessible to the population. A health center is considered accessible if it can be reached within 1.5 hours by foot. In 2007, 85% of the population lived within this accessible distance.[42]

RSPA 2007 found that only 44% of health facilities offered the full range of basic services (all health facilities are expected to offer these services). Among health facilities, health centers and polyclinics were most likely to offer the full range of services, and about 60% did on the day they were surveyed. More than half (58%) of government health facilities offer the full range of services, whereas only 45% of government-assisted facilities offer them. According to RSPA, none of the private, NGO or community facilities offered all the basic services. Facility-based 24-hour childbirth services are available in 93% of hospitals and 88% of health centers. The RSPA 2007 survey found that treatment for sexually-transmitted infections (STIs) is available almost universally, with 95% of facilities offering STI services.[42] In 2007 family-planning services were available in 73% of facilities, antenatal services in 80% of facilities, and child immunization in 75% of facilities.[42]

DHS 2005 data show that during their pregnancy 95% of women visit an antenatal clinic (ANC) at least once, 68% attend either two or three times, and 13% visit four or more times. According to DHS 2005, women came for their first ANC visit when they were 6.4 months into their pregnancy on average, which is quite far into gestation.[53] Apart from concerns related to frequency and timing of visits, the quality of ANC services also needs to be considered: only about 10% of health facilities that offer ANC services have the full package of medicines to manage the common complications of pregnancy.[42]

Although ANC visits are fairly common, delivery in a health facility or in the presence of a health professional is relatively rare. In 2007 only 38% of children were born in the presence of a health professional or a trained traditional birth attendant (TBA), whereas 43% of women delivered with an untrained TBA. The remaining women delivered either alone or with the help of a relative.[42]

The country's health sector is clearly under-resourced. In 2003 annual health expenditure per capita was only US$13.5.[38] The government is making a concerted effort to scale-up public expenditure on health. Between 2005 and 2009, health expenditure per capita has increased more than twofold, from US$20 to US$48.[38] The increased expenditure has been, in part, a result of international support. In 2007, 52% of health-sector funding came from international partners, and 48% from the national budget.[42]

Despite increased funding, healthcare infrastructure and personnel remain scarce. In 2007 there were only 16 hospital beds per 10,000 population. The density of health workers is also very low; in 2004 the country had only 4 nurses and midwives per 10,000 persons. WHO estimates that in 2005 there were just 432 physicians in the whole country — a density of less than 1 doctor per 10,000 persons.[31]

MOH directly employs 62% of all public-sector health personnel. The remaining 38% of public-sector personnel are paid through other means such as direct contracts with government health centers (24%) or through NGOs, volunteer organizations, or local government (14%).[42]

Currently, the health system is partly funded through user fees. There are some exemptions available for poor patients; but these exemptions or discounts can result in budget shortages if the health facilities are not otherwise reimbursed. In addition to government funding and user fees, about 75% of health facilities report some type of external funding or reimbursement for client services such as payments from employers of patients, private insurance, charities, or government social insurance systems.[42]

Rwanda is a leader among low-income countries on the African continent in its implementation of an extensive health insurance scheme. This is known as *Mutuelles de Santé* (or *Mutuelles*). Financial costs and the quality of healthcare have kept many poor people from utilizing health services. Hence the government designed and implemented the *Mutuelles* program to reduce financial barriers to access healthcare, bolster the budgets of health facilities, and improve quality of services.[42] The scheme was piloted in 1999 and became national policy in 2004. Heavily subsidized by MOH and donors, membership requires an annual payment and provides access to essential healthcare.[43] The Minimum Package of Activities (MPA) in *Mutuelles* covers all services and drugs provided at health centers including pre- and postnatal care, vaccinations, family planning, minor surgical operations, and essential and generic drugs. Health insurance subscribers are entitled to subsidized preventive care through MPA.[53] The insurance enables access to primary care and HIV services and drugs for an annual fee, which in 2009 was less than US$2 (RWF1,000) per person.[43] By June 2008 an estimated 78% of the population was covered by *Mutuelles*.[52] The government is dedicated to increasing the coverage of *Mutuelles* still further. To this end, VUP funds *Mutuelles* for people enrolled in the poverty reduction program.[54]

3.8. Education

3.8.1. Current state

The government has prioritized universal primary education in an effort to reach the UN Millennium Development Goals (MDGs) and the targets set in its national poverty reduction strategy — Vision 2020. Between 2001 and 2005, net primary-school enrollment increased from 75% to 87% among girls and from 73% to 84% among boys, and the country is on track to achieve the MDG for universal primary education (MDG2).[55,56] However, as of 2007, the primary-school completion rate was only 52%, and the completion rate was lower for girls (41%) than for boys (59%).[33] There are also marked disparities in education outcomes between urban and rural areas. In rural areas 31% of the population report never having received any schooling, compared to 19.4% of the population in urban areas. Of urban residents 4.5% report that they have completed secondary school, compared to 0.6% of rural residents.[32]

Apart from low primary-school completion rates, data from 2007 show that only 54% of those completing primary school moved on to secondary school.[25] As a result of low completion and transition rates, secondary-school enrollment remains low. During 2003–08, the gross secondary-school enrollment rate was 19% for boys and 17% girls.[57] It is estimated that in 2005 0.7 million children (of age 7–18 years) were out of school and out of vocational training programs.

Between 2001 and 2005, teacher training increased the number of qualified teachers by 45%.[22] Efforts to train and recruit teachers, however, have not matched increases in student enrollment, and the student-teacher ratio in primary school has increased from 58 in 2002 to 71 in 2007.[25] The country has one of the highest pupil-teacher ratios in sub-Saharan Africa.

3.8.2. Interventions to improve early childhood development

The Ministry of Education (MINEDUC) has outlined a number of strategies to extend the provision of early childhood development (ECD) services. It intends to establish community-based ECD centers which are provided with materials, equipment and training. Furthermore, MINEDUC intends to support the National Curriculum Development Center so that the Center can design a relevant integrated curriculum for all ECD facilities. MINEDUC also plans to recruit and train ECD teachers, and incentivize the private sector to continue their provision of ECD services.[58]

Apart from MINEDUC, other government agencies — such as Ministry of Gender and Family Promotion, MOH, Ministry of Finance and Economic Planning, and Ministry of Local Government — are contributing financially to the development of ECD programs. NGOs such as CARE have also implemented a number of ECD interventions.[59]

3.8.3. Interventions to improve primary and secondary education

In 2003 MINEDUC began to implement the fee-free education policy which enables children to attend primary school without paying school fees.[60] In 2008 it initiated the Nine-Year Basic Education Program, which extended fee-free education to include the first three years of secondary school, or *tronc commun*. This policy aims to reduce primary-school dropouts and improve the transition rate from primary to secondary school.[22]

The government plans to increase the number of trained teachers to deal with increasing enrollment and also to improve the quality of education. It has set targets for 2012 that include a pupil-teacher ratio of 47 and the establishment of a Teacher Service Commission, an organization that is intended to increase teacher motivation and retention.[61] To achieve the target pupil-teacher ratio, the government plans to increase the number of primary-school teachers from 30,637 in 2006 to 41,883 in 2012, the number of secondary-school teachers from 7,818 in 2006 to 15,712 in 2012, and technical-education teachers from 119 in 2006 to 550 in 2012.[61]

In collaboration with the World Food Programme (WFP) the government offers school meals in some primary schools.[62] Other education sector reforms enacted within the last five years include changing the language of instruction from French to English, reducing the number of subject options offered in school (i.e., children take the same number of subjects, but from a smaller range of options), and encouraging teachers to specialize in specific subjects.[56] In addition to these initiatives, an alternative educational framework has been developed to complement formal education. This framework is composed of three elements: General Education Programs, which include catch-up programs; Livelihood Skills Development Programs, which teach specific skills to avoid HIV/AIDS and address structural causes of transmission; and Outreach Programs. Proponents advocate that this alternative education subsystem, which targets children outside the formal school system, should be considered an integral part of national basic education.[63]

3.9. Government coordination of interventions

In general, the government's strategies and policies towards children are supportive and progressive. But children still face many barriers to healthy development. For example, a 2007 study estimated that 83.3% of children corresponded to the government's definition of Orphans and Vulnerable Children (OVC), a statistic that underscores the country's level of poverty and social insecurity.[14]

For healthy development of children, complementary interventions may often be needed. For example, education interventions may work better if complemented by interventions that improve children's health. Recognizing that children have a range of needs, the government has developed guidelines for those providing support to OVC. These guidelines are referred to as the Minimum Package for Care, Protection, and Support and were developed to streamline and harmonize a comprehensive response to OVC. The Minimum Package outlines the basic level and type of care that a child should receive. This includes access to basic healthcare services, prevention of mother-to-child-transmission (PMTCT) of HIV, antiretroviral therapy (ART) for infected children and their parents, food assistance, emergency nutritional support for malnourished children, support for school fees and supplies, prevention of all forms of abuse, and economic security interventions.[64] The Minimum Package strives to encourage responses to both immediate and longer-term needs of OVC.[64] The government hopes to ensure that children receive age- and gender-appropriate support.[64] The Minimum Package sets a high standard, but few children receive the full package. According a progress report submitted to GFATM in 2007, implementing NGOs were only able to reach 12% of OVC in 2006 with one or more of the elements of the package such as basic health, food assistance and education support.[65]

The government and its partners have developed policies and implemented a range of interventions to improve the health and education of children. Policies are in place, but fully implementing these interventions is hindered by a lack of appropriately qualified people or by a lack of funding. It appears that there is political will to address poverty and improve the lives of children, but the scale of the problem relative to the resources available is such that many people will continue to live in difficult circumstances for the foreseeable future.

3.10. Conclusion

In 1994 Rwanda suffered a catastrophe of unimaginable proportions. The genocide and civil war not only caused great pain and suffering in that year, but devastated the economy and capacity of the state to offer public services. As a result, poverty increased, people's health deteriorated, and children dropped out of school.

Since 1994 the government-led program of reconstruction has resulted in high rates of economic growth, better social services and political and economic stability. While the situation has improved, it is still grave. More than half the population still lives in poverty, and health and education indicators have only recently begun to surpass their pre-1994 levels. It appears that the social and economic situation will keep improving as the government continues to emphasize both social services and economic growth.

Identifying inaction in the Rwandan context is not easy. Certainly there are many actions which would improve the lives of people in the country. The question is which of them can feasibly be implemented in addition to what is already being done. Resources are limited, and qualified staff are over-extended. Identifying inaction in Rwanda is the subject matter of the next chapter.

ANNEX

Annex 3A. Rwanda — Basic statistics

Indicator	Rwanda	Year	SSA	Year
POPULATION				
Total population (million)	10.0	2009	840.3	2009
Population age 0–14 (% of total)	42	2009	43	2009
Life expectancy at birth (years)	51	2009	53	2009
Female life expectancy at birth (years)	52	2009	54	2009
Male life expectancy at birth (years)	49	2009	51	2009
Crude birth rate (per 1,000 persons)	41	2009	38	2009
Crude death rate (per 1,000 persons)	14	2009	14	2009
Infant mortality rate (per 1,000 live births)	70	2009	81	2009
Under-5 mortality rate (per 1,000 live births)	111	2009	130	2009
ECONOMY				
GDP (current US$ billion)	5.2	2009	956.4	2009
GDP per capita (current US$)	522	2009	1,138	2009
GDP per capita at PPP (current international $)	1,136	2009	2,162	2009
GNI (current US$ billion)	5.2	2009	910.6	2009
GNI per capita, Atlas method (current US$)	490	2009	1,103	2009
GNI per capita at PPP (current international $)	1,130	2009	2,065	2009
Agriculture (value added) as % of GDP	34.2	2009	13	2009
Industry (value added) as % of GDP	14.5	2009	30	2009
Services, etc. (value added) as % of GDP	51.3	2009	57	2009
Trade as % of GDP	40.9	2009	63	2009
National poverty ratio (% of national population below national poverty line)[f]	59	2006	—	—
Rural poverty ratio (% of rural population below rural poverty line)	64.2	2006	—	—
Urban poverty ratio (% of urban population below urban poverty line)	23.2	2006	—	—
IDA grants (current US$ million)[g]	103.3	2009	—	—
Net official development assistance received (current US$ million)	934.4	2009	—	—

continued

Annex 3A. Rwanda — Basic statistics (*continued*)

Indicator	Rwanda	Year	SSA	Year
Net ODA received (% of GNI)[h]	18	2009	—	—
HEALTH				
Health expenditure, public (% of GDP)	3.9	2009	4	2009
Health expenditure, private (% of GDP)	5.1	2009	3	2009
Community health workers per 1,000 population	1.41	2004	—	
Nurses and midwives per 1,000 population	0.45	2005	1	2009
Physicians per 1,000 population	0.02	2005	0.19	2009
Hospital beds per 1,000 population	1.6	2007	—	
NUTRITION				
Exclusive breastfeeding (% of children under 6 months)	88.4	2005	33	2009
Low-birth weight babies (% of births)	6.3	2005	14	2009
Stunting prevalence, height-for-age (% of children under 5)	51.7	2005	42	2009
Underweight prevalence, weight-for-age (% of children under 5)	18	2005	25	2009
Prevalence of undernourishment (% of population)[i]	34	2007	26	2007
Depth of hunger (kilocalories per person per day)[j]	310	2007	256	2007
INFRASTRUCTURE				
Roads, total network (km)	14,008	2004	—	—
Roads, paved (% of total roads)	19.0	2004	—	—
Road density (kms of road per 100 sq. km. of land area)	53.0	2004	—	—
Internet users (per 100 persons)	4.5	2009	—	—
Mobile cellular subscriptions (per 100 persons)	24.3	2009	9	2009
Telephone lines (per 100 persons)	44	2009	37	2009

continued

Annex 3A. Rwanda — Basic statistics (*continued*)

Indicator	Rwanda	Year	SSA	Year
EDUCATION				
Public spending on education as % of GDP	4.1	2008	4	2008
Public spending on education as % of government expenditure	20.4	2008	19	2008
Expenditure per primary-school student as % of GDP per capita	8.2	2008		
Expenditure per secondary-school student as % of GDP per capita	34.3	2008	—	—
Expenditure per tertiary student as % of GDP per capita	222.8	2008	—	—
Gross primary-school enrollment (%)	150.7	2009	—	—
Gross female primary-school enrollment (%)	151.4	2009	—	—
Gross male primary-school enrollment (%)	149.8	2009	—	—
Net primary-school enrollment (%)	95.9	2008	—	—
Net female primary-school enrollment (%)	97	2008	—	—
Net male primary-school enrollment (%)	94.7	2008	—	—
Gross secondary-school enrollment (%)	26.7	2009	—	—
Gross female secondary-school enrollment (%)	26	2009	—	—
Gross male secondary-school enrollment (%)	27.5	2009	—	—
Adult literacy rate (% of persons age 15 and above)	70.7	2009	—	—
Primary-school completion rate (%)	54	2008	62	2006
Female primary-school completion rate (%)	55.9	2008	57	2006
Male primary-school completion rate (%)	52	2008	67	2006

Note: '—' denotes not available.

Source: *World Development Indicators 2011.*

Endnotes

a.   A country is in "debt distress" when at least one of the following three conditions hold: (i) the sum of interest and principal arrears is large relative to the stock of outstanding debt; (ii) it receives debt relief in the form of rescheduling and/or debt reduction from the Paris Club of bilateral creditors; (iii) it receives substantial balance of payments support from the IMF under its non-concessional Standby Arrangements or Extended Fund Facilities.[26]

b.   The US$ value is based on the 2005 exchange rate reported by the National Bank of Rwanda.

c.   The World Food Programme defines "food insecurity" as "poor or borderline food consumption and very weak food access; or weak or very weak access and poor consumption."[29]

d.   'Safe sources of water' are defined as public water fountains or standpipes, protected springs, purchased tap water, or water supplied by a public utility.

e.   According to WHO criteria, 'improved sanitation facilities' include connection to public sewers, connection to septic systems, pour-flush latrines, simple pit latrines, and ventilated improved pit latrines. Service or bucket latrines, public latrines, and open latrines are not considered improved sanitation facilities.

f.   Although *World Development Indicators 2011* and the National Institute of Statistics of Rwanda (NISR) use the same data and the same national poverty line, their estimates of poverty are slightly different. We use the NISR estimate of 56.9%, as does the World Bank elsewhere.[25]

g.   IDA grants are net disbursements of grants from the International Development Association (IDA).

h.   Net official development assistance (ODA) consists of disbursements of loans made on concessional terms (net of repayments of principal) and grants by official agencies of members of the Development Assistance Committee (DAC), by multilateral institutions, and by non-DAC countries to promote economic development and welfare in countries and territories in the DAC list of ODA recipients. It includes loans with a grant element of at least 25 percent (calculated at a rate of discount of 10 percent).

i.   Prevalence of undernourishment refers to the percentage of the population whose food intake is insufficient to meet dietary energy requirements.

j.   The depth of hunger is the average shortfall in kilocalories for malnourished people below the minimum dietary energy needed to maintain body weight and undertake light activity. It is considered low when it is less than 200 kilocalories per person per day, and high when it is more than 300 kilocalories per person per day.

References

1. United States Department of State. *Background Note: Rwanda.* Washington, DC: US Department of State, Bureau of African Affairs, 2009.
2. Bigsten A, Isaksson AS. *Growth and Poverty in Rwanda: Evaluating the EDPRS 2008–2012.* Country Economic Report 2008:3. Stockholm, Sweden: Swedish International Development Cooperation Agency, Department for Policy and Methodology, 2008.
3. World Bank. *World Development Indicators 2011.* Washington, DC: World Bank, 2011.
4. National Institute of Statistics of Rwanda. *EICV Poverty Analysis for Rwanda's Economic Development and Poverty Reduction Strategy.* Kigali, Rwanda: NISR, 2007.
5. UN. Rwanda-United Nations data: A world of information. Geneva, Switzerland: United Nations Statistics Division, 2009. http://data.un.org/CountryProfile.aspx?crName=Rwanda. Accessed November 30, 2011.
6. Rwanda Development Gateway. Pre-Colonial Rwanda. About History. Kigali, Rwanda: RDG, 2005. http://www.rwandagateway.org/spip.php?article2. Accessed November 30, 2011.
7. Meredith M. *The Fate of Africa: A History of Fifty Years of Independence.* New York, NY: Public Affairs, 2006.
8. Rwanda Development Gateway. Colonial Rwanda. About History. Kigali, Rwanda: RDG, 2005. http://www.rwandagateway.org/spip.php?article4. Accessed November 11, 2011.
9. World Bank. *Rwanda Poverty Reduction and Sustainable Growth.* Washington, DC: World Bank, Department of Poverty Reduction & Equity, 1994.
10. Freedom House. Freedom in the World 2008 — Rwanda. Washington, DC: Freedom House, 2008. http://www.freedomhouse.org/template.cfm?page=363&year=2008&country=7476. Accessed November 11, 2011.
11. UNCTAD, ICC. *An Investment Guide to Rwanda: Opportunities and Conditions* (UNCTAD/ITE/IIA/2006/3). New York, NY and Geneva, Switzerland: United Nations Conference on Trade and Development (UNCTAD) and International Chamber of Commerce (ICC), 2006.
12. National Institute of Statistics, Rwanda Ministry of Health, Macro International Inc. *Rwanda Service Provision Assessment Survey 2001.* Kigali, Rwanda and Calverton, MD: NIS, RMH, and Macro International Inc., 2003.
13. Rwanda Ministry of Gender and Family Promotion. *Monitoring and Evaluation System for Strategic Plan of Action for Orphans and Other Vulnerable Children.* Kigali, Rwanda: Government of Rwanda, 2009.
14. Rwanda Prime Minister's Office. *A Situation Analysis of Orphans and Other Vulnerable Children in Rwanda.* Kigali, Rwanda: Government of Rwanda, 2008.

15. BBC News. From president to prison. London, UK: British Broadcasting Corporation (BBC), 2004. http://news.bbc.co.uk/2/hi/africa/3728807.stm. Accessed November 30, 2011.

16. BBC News. Rwanda profile. London, UK: British Broadcasting Corporation (BBC), 2011. http://news.bbc.co.uk/2/hi/africa/country_profiles/1070329.stm. Accessed November 30, 2011.

17. Hovy B. *Rwanda: 2002 UNHCR Statistical Yearbook.* Geneva, Switzerland: UNHCR, Division of Operational Support, Population Data Unit, 2002.

18. Wolters S. *The Gacaca Process: Eradicating the Culture of Impunity in Rwanda.* Pretoria, South Africa: Institute for Security Studies, 2005.

19. IRIN. Rwanda: Jury still out on effectiveness of 'Gacaca' courts. Kigali, Rwanda: IRIN, 2009. http://irinnews.org/Report.aspx?ReportID=84954. Accessed November 30, 2011.

20. United States Department of State. *2008 Human Rights Report: Rwanda.* Washington, DC: US Department of State, 2009.

21. Musiime E. Rwanda's Legal System and Legal Materials. GlobaLex. New York, NY: New York University School of Law, Hauser Global Law School Program, 2007.

22. Rwanda Ministry of Finance and Economic Planning. *Economic Development and Poverty Reduction Strategy 2008–2012.* Kigali, Rwanda: Government of Rwanda, 2007.

23. BBC News. Women to rule Rwanda parliament. London, UK: British Broadcasting Corporation (BBC), 2008. http://news.bbc.co.uk/2/hi/7620816.stm. Accessed November 30, 2011.

24. African Development Bank, Organization for Economic Co-operation and Development. *Rwanda: African Economic Outlook.* Abidjan, Côte d'Ivoire: ADB and OECD, 2007.

25. World Bank. *Country Assistance Strategy for the Republic of Rwanda for the Period FY09–FY12.* Washington, DC: World Bank, 2008.

26. Kraay A, Nehru V. When is external debt sustainable? *World Bank Economic Review* 2006; 20(3):341–365.

27. UNDP. *Human Development Report 2009 — Rwanda.* Country Fact Sheets. New York, NY: UNDP, 2009.

28. McKay A, Greenwell G. *Methods Used for Poverty Analysis in Rwanda.* Kigali, Rwanda: NISR, 2007.

29. World Food Programme. *Rwanda: Comprehensive Food Security and Vulnerability Analysis.* Rome, Italy: WFP, 2006.

30. Morris ML, Drake L, Ezemenari K, Diao X. Promoting sustainable pro-poor growth in Rwandan agriculture: What are the policy options? Selected Paper 173011. Annual Meeting of American Agricultural Economics Association. Portland, OR: 2007.

31. World Health Organization. WHO Statistical Information System: Rwanda.WHO, 2008. http://apps.who.int/whosis/data/Search.jsp. Accessed November 11, 2011.

32. National Institute of Statistics, Rwanda Ministry of Health, Macro International Inc. *Rwanda Demographic and Health Survey 2005*. Kigali, Rwanda and Calverton, MD: NIS, RMH, and Macro International Inc., 2006.

33. National Institute of Statistics of Rwanda. *Millennium Development Goals: Toward Sustainable Social and Economic Growth*. Country Report 2007. Kigali, Rwanda: NISR, 2007.

34. Rwanda Ministry of Finance and Economic Planning. *Rwanda Vision 2020*. Kigali, Rwanda: Government of Rwanda, 2000.

35. EDPRS Flagship Program. *Vision 2020 Umurenge: An Integrated Local Development Program to Accelerate Poverty Eradication, Rural Growth, and Social Protection*. Kigali, Rwanda: Government of Rwanda, 2007.

36. Devereux S. The Vision 2020 Umurenge Programme: A pathway to sustainable livelihoods for rural Rwandans? Annual IPAR Research Conference. Kigali, Rwanda: 2011.

37. UNDP. *Fighting Climate Change: Human Solidarity in a Divided World*. Human Development Report 2007/2008. New York, NY: UNDP, 2007.

38. World Bank. Data — Rwanda.World Bank, 2011. http://data.worldbank.org/country/rwanda. Accessed November 27, 2011.

39. Rwanda Ministry of Infrastructure. Electricity. mininfra.gov.rw/index.php?option=com_content&task=view&id=114&Itemid=142. Accessed December 28, 2011.

40. UNDP. *Turning Vision 2020 into Reality: From Recovery to Sustainable Human Development*. National Human Development Report. Rwanda 2007. Kigali, Rwanda: UNDP, 2007.

41. UNICEF. *State of the World's Children 2009: Maternal and Newborn Health*. New York, NY: UNICEF, 2008.

42. National Institute of Statistics, Rwanda Ministry of Health, and Macro International Inc. *Rwanda Service Provision Assessment Survey 2007*. Kigali, Rwanda and Calverton, MD: NIS, RMH, and Macro International, Inc., 2008.

43. National AIDS Control Commission. *National Strategic Plan on HIV and AIDS 2009–2012*. Kigali, Rwanda: Rwanda Ministry of Health, 2009.

44. National Institute of Statistics of Rwanda, Rwanda Ministry of Health, and Macro International Inc. *Rwanda Interim Demographic and Health Survey 2007–08*. DHS Final Reports. FR215. Kigali, Rwanda and Calverton, Maryland: USAID, UNDP, 2009.

45. WHO, UNICEF. *Review of National Immunization Coverage*. Geneva, Switzerland: WHO and UNICEF, 2008.

46. UNAIDS, WHO. *Epidemiological Fact Sheets on HIV and AIDS, 2008 Update.* Geneva, Switzerland: UNAIDS and WHO, 2008.

47. WHO. Country Health System Fact Sheet 2006: Rwanda. Geneva, Switzerland: WHO, 2006. http://www.afro.who.int/home/countries/fact_sheets/rwanda.pdf. Accessed December 19, 2011.

48. Healthy Futures. Trac Plus, Ministry of Health, Kigali, Rwanda — (TRAC Plus). 2011. http://www.healthyfutures.eu/index.php?option=com_k2&view=item&layout=item&id=103&Itemid=240. Accessed November 16, 2011.

49. Mugabo J. Rwanda achievements and challenges towards universal access to HIV prevention and care and treatment services in health sector. 5th Annual National Pediatric Conference on Children Infected and Affected by HIV and AIDS. Kigali, Rwanda: 2009.

50. Tsague L. Quality PMTCT services for all: Towards an HIV free generation. 5th Annual National Pediatric Conference on Children Infected and Affected by HIV. Kigali, Rwanda: 2009.

51. Rwanda National AIDS Control Commission. *Country Progress Report January 2008–December 2009.* United Nations General Assembly Special Session on HIV and AIDS. Kigali, Rwanda: Government of Rwanda, 2010.

52. Rwanda National Country Coordinating Mechanism. *Strengthening Civil Society to Scale Up HIV and AIDS Prevention, Care, and Support and Impact Mitigation Programs Towards Universal Access in Rwanda.* Proposal Form. Round 8. Kigali, Rwanda: Global Fund, 2008.

53. Joint Learning Network. Rwanda: Mutuelles de Santé. 2011. http://www.jointlearningnetwork.org/content/mutuelles-de-santé. Accessed November 12, 2011.

54. Rwanda Ministry of Health. *Health Sector Strategic Plan: July 2009–June 2012.* Kigali, Rwanda: Rwanda Ministry of Health, 2009.

55. UNICEF. *Revised Country Program Document, Rwanda 2008–2012.* New York, NY: UNICEF, 2007.

56. World Bank. *Rwanda: Education For All — Fast Track Initiative.* Washington, DC: World Bank, 2009.

57. UNICEF. *Rwanda: Statistics.* New York, NY: UNICEF, 2010. http://www.unicef.org/infobycountry/rwanda_statistics.html. Accessed November 30, 2011.

58. Rwanda Ministry of Education. *Education Sector Strategic Plan 2006–2010.* Kigali, Rwanda: Government of Rwanda, 2006.

59. CARE, USAID, Hope for African Children Initiative. *Promoting Early Childhood for OVC in Resource Constrained Settings: The 5x5 Model.* Promising Practices. Atlanta, GA: CARE, 2006.

60. Taton V, Nabongo C, Chiejine I, Kamuragiye A. *Investing in Rwanda: Ef-

fective Choices for Orphans and Girls in Primary Education. New York, NY: UNICEF, 2007.

61. Rwanda Ministry of Education. *Education Sector Strategic Plan 2008–2012.* Kigali, Rwanda: Government of Rwanda, 2008.

62. World Food Programme. *Projects for Executive Board Approval. Executive Board Second Regular Session.* Development Project Rwanda. 20677.0. Rome, Italy, 2007.

63. Obura AP. *Planning a Systemic Education Response to the Needs of Orphans and Other Vulnerable Children in Rwanda.* Kigali, Rwanda: Ministry of Education, Science, Technology and Scientific Research, 2005.

64. Binagwaho A, Karekezi A, Rwakunda A. *HIV/AIDS in Rwanda: Documenting Progress in HIV Response 2003–2007 — Minimum Package of Services for OVC Rwanda Experience.* Kigali, Rwanda: National AIDS Control Commission, 2007.

65. Rwanda National Country Coordinating Mechanism. *Towards Universal Access to Integrated HIV/AIDS Services in Rwanda.* Proposal form — Round 7. Kigali, Rwanda: Global Fund, 2007.

CHAPTER 4

Priority areas in Rwanda

4.1. Introduction

In order to identify priority areas we conducted a situation analysis and an in-country consultation. The situation analysis comprised a review of Rwanda's economic and social background and its current policies. Following this, we conducted key-informant interviews in the country. This process led to the identification of five priority areas: (1) prevention of HIV among adolescents; (2) income poverty reduction; (3) promotion of early childhood development (ECD); (4) expansion of education; and (5) reduction of child malnutrition.

Government and civil society organizations have responded vigorously to the country's HIV/AIDS epidemic. As a result, HIV prevalence has fallen. To sustain and extend the gain, it is necessary to continue efforts towards reducing the spread of HIV. An important part of an HIV-reduction response is to focus prevention efforts on adolescents. Reducing the incidence of HIV within this age-group benefits not only members of the group, but future generations too. HIV is typically introduced into the adolescent age-group when young girls are infected through sex with older men. If this inter-generational transmission can be prevented, or at least reduced, it will protect both the girls and boys of this generation and the next. If girls are not infected they will not be able to infect boys. If boys are not infected, they will not be able to infect young women once they have grown up.

High rates of income poverty underlie many of the difficulties experienced by children. Poverty affects children's nutritional status, health, access to education, and their families' ability to deal with crises — such as illness or death among adult members. Reducing poverty strengthens a family's ability to support its children, which leads to numerous benefits.

Interventions aimed at promoting ECD have been shown to have substantial short- and long-term benefits. Efforts are already underway in this area in Rwanda, but more can certainly be done. It is difficult to reverse the negative consequences that follow when ECD is neglected or ignored — it is far better to act early.

Education is beneficial in and of itself, but it also has instrumental value. Increasing school enrollment has the potential to lead to a wide range of benefits over the longer term. Rwanda has experienced a rapid increase in primary-school enrollment. But if the full benefits of this increase are to be realized, steps need to be taken to enhance the supply and quality of secondary education.

Child nutrition is recognized by both the government and civil society as a priority area. While efforts are already underway to address malnutrition, further steps can and should be taken. Given the importance of nutrition in child health, well-being and development, this is a critical area.

4.2. Prevention of HIV among adolescents

An increase in adolescents' knowledge of HIV/AIDS is part of the ongoing efforts of the government and its partners to reduce HIV transmission. Comprehensive knowledge[a] of HIV among youth increased from 9% in 2000 to 15% in 2006.[1] Estimates from 2005 suggest that among persons aged 15–24 years, 51% of women and 54% of men correctly identified ways of preventing the sexual transmission of HIV and rejected major misconceptions about its transmission.[2] Furthermore, knowledge of at least one of the three main methods of HIV prevention (abstinence, faithfulness to one uninfected partner, and condom use) increased from 71% in 2000 to 83% in 2006.[1] The percentage of adolescents receiving HIV-testing, however, remains low. As of 2006, only 13% of females aged 15–24 years and 11% of males aged 15–24 years had ever been tested.[3] Efforts are being made to address this issue: more than a third (38%) of those tested in the TRAC 2007 outreach were aged 18–25 years.[1]

The Ministry of Education (MINEDUC) has included HIV/AIDS information in school textbooks and has encouraged peer education in secondary-school anti-AIDS clubs. National mass-media campaigns, involving radio and billboards, are used to communicate HIV/AIDS-prevention messages and to promote the purchase and use of condoms.[4] The government is taking steps to offer complete HIV services — which include voluntary counseling and testing (VCT), PMTCT and ART — in all 500 health facilities in the country by 2012. However, it should be noted that by 2009, only 2.1% of facilities (7 out of 334) with HIV-testing equipment offered services specifically designed to provide HIV counseling and testing to youth.[3]

As male circumcision reduces the risk of female-to-male transmission of HIV, the government is taking steps to increase the proportion of men who are circumcised. According to the 2009–2012 National Strategic Plan for

HIV and AIDS, in 2007 only 15% of males aged 15–59 years were circumcised. In 2007, only 21% of health facilities had staff capable of performing male circumcision. The government aims to increase this number to 80% of health facilities capable of performing this service by 2012.[3] During 2010–11 the government has been involved in the development and testing of a new simple-to-use device for adult male circumcision, and is planning to use it widely. Moreover, from 2012 onwards, the government expects to have 50% of newborn males circumcised.

While there is a high level of awareness of HIV/AIDS, it is less common for individuals to have comprehensive knowledge.[1] This would seem to suggest that additional actions aimed at improving knowledge may be desirable. However, information about HIV prevention may not, on its own, be enough to change behavior and reduce the incidence of new HIV infections among young people. Young people will also need support to develop skills — such as negotiating safe sex — which will help to protect them against infection. Such support could be provided through practical lessons that discuss strategies to avoid HIV transmission.[5] But other factors also influence risk behavior of young people, including negative aspects of the social context which shape the behavior, e.g. poverty.

4.2.1. Integration of HIV/AIDS information into the school curriculum

A number of studies have shown that incorporating HIV-prevention messages and sex education into school curricula can improve adolescents' knowledge about ways of avoiding HIV. In some instances, this improved knowledge has led to reduced risk behavior among adolescents. The evidence on the effectiveness of school-curriculum interventions is sufficient to recommend their widespread implementation.[6] In Rwanda, efforts to include HIV/AIDS information in school curricula are already underway.[4,7,8] However, during the consultation process, some respondents expressed concern that the current education material was overly focused on biological information and not on the development of prevention skills. Respondents argued that the curriculum did not cover relevant social issues, such as gender-based violence, which contribute to the spread of HIV. The suggestion was made that CNLS (Commission Nationale de Lutte contre le SIDA, i.e., the National AIDS Control Commission) should play a more active role in curriculum development so as to improve the quality of the course material.

In widening the focus of the curriculum, the skills and resources required for implementation need to be considered. In regard to life-skills education, teachers without specialized training may be uncomfortable teaching sensitive subjects. It has been suggested that the sensitivity of issues such as sex or condom use may compromise unprepared teachers' relationship with students. Health workers or local experts can be brought in to provide these lessons, as they are more knowledgeable and better able to address sensitive issues.[6]

Ensuring that the HIV curriculum is expanded to include a greater focus on decision-making, prevention skills and social issues is an important area of action to consider. Of course, the impact of this action may be limited by the capacity of the already-strained school system. Introducing a new expanded curriculum would have greater impact if it occurred along with an improvement in the education system. For example, the curriculum would be more effective if it was part of an intervention to improve teacher training, increase the number of classrooms, and reduce class size. Improving the HIV/AIDS curriculum as a stand-alone intervention may not have much effect on risk behavior, but curriculum development as part of a set of actions that includes strengthening the education system may well be effective and desirable.

Any intervention that seeks to change risk behaviors will be limited in its impact if the materials necessary to bring about the change are not available. Promoting condom use, for example, will have little impact if condoms are difficult to obtain. Similarly, encouraging HIV and STI testing will have little impact if young people have difficulty in accessing a testing facility.

4.2.2. Promotion of condom use

According to the 2009–2012 National Strategic Plan (NSP) on HIV and AIDS, access to condoms remains patchy, even for high-risk groups. The Rwanda Service Provision Assessment (RSPA) Survey 2007 found that only two-thirds of the health facilities in Kigali City had condoms available on the day surveyed. Of facilities that provide STI treatment, 15% did not have condoms available on the day of the survey.[3]

The government aims to make condoms more widely available in health facilities and other sites. For out-of-school youth, the government plans to make condoms available through peer educators. Community-based distribution initiatives are also planned to make condoms available at high-risk "hotspots" and to target groups at risk. In 2008, 15 million condoms per annum were available for distribution; in 2012 the government hopes to make 26 million condoms available for distribution.[3] According to DHS 2005, only 37% of women and 73% of men aged 15–24 years reported they knew of a place to purchase or obtain condoms.[2] By 2012, the government aims to increase these percentages to 60% for women and 80% for men.[3]

Promoting condom use has been shown to be effective in preventing HIV, especially when combined with other interventions. For example, the 70% decrease in HIV prevalence in Uganda was linked, in part, to increased condom use.[5] A Population Services International (PSI) program that aimed to change youth behavior through social marketing of condoms in Cameroon, Madagascar and Rwanda appears to have increased adolescents' use of HIV-counseling and -testing services. It also increased knowledge of proper condom use and awareness of locations to obtain them, and the belief that family and friends support condom use.[9]

Condom promotion is already underway, and there are plans for major expansion. Although many respondents believed that condom promotion was a problem area, this should become less of a concern if plans are implemented. If plans are not implemented, then failure to make condoms available will certainly be an important area of inaction.

4.2.3. Youth-friendly health services

Many respondents commented that additional efforts are needed to ensure that youth feel comfortable in accessing health services. This concern stretched not only to HIV-specific services such as VCT but also related services such as STI testing and treatment, and family planning. Respondents also noted that youth-friendly services (YFS) would enable HIV-infected adolescents to seek treatment more easily. Respondents had different views on the best way to provide such services. Some argued in favor of school clinics; others advocated the inclusion of basic health services within youth clubs. Still others made a case for specialist adolescent health clinics. Finally, some respondents argued for making existing health services more youth friendly.

NSP 2009–2012 details steps to increase the availability and accessibility of high-quality STI treatment by providing youth-friendly STI screening and referral services.[3] There are plans for reaching out to homeless youth, with specific programs for substance users and adolescent mothers.[3] The National Youth Council has been tasked with establishing youth-friendly centers that serve as focal points where youth can access a range of services.[10] Although these centers will not provide medical services, they will encourage young people to seek appropriate healthcare.

A number of reasons have been identified for adolescents not accessing health services. These include restricted information and testing, negative community perceptions, concerns among youth about being seen at a clinic, and judgemental provider attitudes. Providing YFS may help overcome some accessibility and utilization issues, but not others. A study in Zambia found that the use of family-planning services is correlated more strongly with the level of community support for youth to access these services than with clinics' "youth-friendliness".[11] Similarly, a WHO 2006 review of HIV-prevention interventions for adolescents argues that merely providing a clinical service in a youth center will not guarantee high levels of use.[12] This concern was echoed by respondents in Rwanda. They cited the need to reduce stigma in the community, improve training of healthcare personnel, and facilitate discussion of sensitive adolescent health issues within the family.

One possibility raised by a number of respondents is to address stigma by working with religious and other local leaders. There is evidence that such interventions can be successful provided they are appropriately planned and monitored, and the leaders are compensated for their time and effort.[13] For example, in 1992 the Islamic Medical Association of Uganda designed an HIV-prevention intervention that involved Islamic imams in prevention efforts. After two years of the program, members of the community reported a significant increase in knowledge of HIV/AIDS infection and transmission, an increase in condom use, and a decrease in the number of sexual partners.[14]

Interventions designed to improve parent-child communication do not appear promising. Studies of such programs have not found evidence of a positive effect on children's sexual or contraceptive behavior. Parent-child communication about sexuality improves during the program, but is not sustained after it ends.[15] Given this evidence, WHO does not recommend widespread HIV-prevention efforts delivered through family or traditional networks until the initiatives have been evaluated further.[13]

It appears that knowledge about HIV/AIDS, availability of condoms, life-skills training, and access to health services may not be sufficient to reduce the prevalence of HIV. These interventions are focused on the individual and do not consider the influence of factors that shape risk but are beyond the individual's control. Examining these factors and responses to them is important if significant areas of inaction are to be identified.

4.2.4. Promoting school attendance of girls

The enrollment of a girl in school is associated with a lower risk of contracting HIV.[5] Girls who have completed secondary education are at lower risk of HIV infection than girls who have only finished primary school. This occurs because on average they start to have sex at a later age, and when they do they practice safer sex.[16]

The government recognizes the importance of promoting girls' education. The Cabinet has developed and approved a girls' education policy, which emphasizes school achievement, performance in national exams at all levels, and science and technology. A National Task Force for the coordination of girls' education was established in 2005. The 2008–2012 Education Sector Strategic Plan (ESSP) aims to implement a number of programs to improve girls' school attendance, including the building of additional sanitation facilities. In accordance with the Nine-Year Basic Education Program initiated in 2008, the government has extended fee-free education to cover both primary schooling and the first three years of secondary school.[7]

Notwithstanding existing efforts and success in promoting girls' education, much more needs to be done to improve primary-school completion rates and secondary-school enrollment rates, for both girls and boys. Although net primary-school enrollment reached 96% in 2008, the primary-school completion rate was only 54% in that year.[17] According to 2009 data, secondary-school enrollment was only 27% for boys and 26% for girls.[17] A number of actions can be undertaken to improve school enrollment of girls, and these are discussed below. (Section 4.5.1 discusses actions to increase enrollment of both girls and boys.)

4.2.5. Reducing the cost of sending children to school

Dropping out of school is often attributed to private costs of school attendance such as expenditure on uniforms and school supplies. Uniforms are the largest single educational expense, accounting for 42% of education expenditure by households. Books and stationery together constitute another 37% of education expenditure.[18] Many households withdraw their children from primary school due to the cost of uniforms, textbooks and school lunches.[18] Costs are more of a barrier to enrollment in secondary school than in primary school, because of fees charged at the secondary level.[7]

During the country consultation, several respondents reported that education costs were a major hindrance to school enrollment and retention — particularly of girls. They emphasized the importance of addressing the problem of children dropping out at the end of primary school. Respondents supported interventions which provide school materials to both primary- and secondary-school children, and also suggested the removal of secondary-school fees. They took different views on whether such interventions should be provided universally or targeted at children from poor households.

A study conducted in Kenya in 2007 found that reducing the private cost of education to families, by providing school uniforms for children, reduced not only dropout rates but also teen marriage and childbearing.[19] In 1993, the World Bank and the Government of Bangladesh launched a Female Secondary School Assistance Project to increase girls' secondary-school enrollment and decrease dropout rates. The program funded the tuition fees of girls entering secondary school and provided them with a monthly stipend conditional on maintaining a 75% school attendance rate and a score of at least 45% in annual school exams, and also remaining unmarried. Water and sanitation facilities were provided at school, the quality of teacher training was improved, and the management capacity of the Ministry of Education was strengthened. Female enrollment in Bangladesh increased from 30% in 1994 to 54% in 2000.[20]

There is increasing use of conditional cash transfers (CCTs) as a way of helping families with the costs of educating children in their care. For example, the PROGRESA program in Mexico provides CCTs to rural households on condition that their children attend school and the family visits local health centers regularly. The conditional cash transfers for secondary-school attendance were higher for girls than for boys. PROGRESA is said to have helped increase girls' secondary-school enrollment by 9 percentage points from a baseline rate of 67%.[21]

4.2.6. School-feeding

School-feeding can also be a powerful tool to increase school enrollment and retention, and children's nutrition. For example, a school-feeding intervention in Pakistan which provided free lunches in 4,035 girls' schools in 29 of the country's poorest districts led to a 40% increase in school enrollment. Further benefits in terms of nutrition, education and female empowerment were also noted as supplementary outcomes of the intervention: for instance, wasting declined by almost half.[22] The World Food Programme (WFP) argues that school-feeding programs help poor children attend school, stay in school, and learn while they are there — especially when these programs are targeted at girls.[23] Rwanda already has a school-feeding program, but its coverage is low and there is room for expansion. School-feeding will be discussed again in relation to child nutrition in section 4.6.5.

4.2.7. Improving school sanitation facilities

In a study of 500 Rwandan girls, half of them reported missing school during menstruation.[24] Such absence from school leads to fragmented education and higher dropout rates. Female teachers may also abstain from school when menstruating due to a lack of sanitation facilities.[25] A UNICEF evaluation of the African Girls' Education Initiative in Uganda found that the provision of water and separate latrines for girls improved adolescent girls' school attendance. Previously these girls had been missing three to four days of school every month.[26]

A related problem is that many girls cannot afford sanitary pads in Rwanda. As of 2009, the price of sanitary pads was high, partly because of the value-added tax on this product. Rwanda is one of the few East African countries that retains a tax on sanitary pads.[24] Aside from removing the tax, there are other ways to reduce the price of this item. The Makapads project in Uganda, begun in 2003, manufactures sanitary pads from locally available materials that are much cheaper: this has made the pads more affordable.[27]

The interventions mentioned above have the potential to improve school enrollment. Covering the cost of school books and uniforms (for all or for a target population), CCTs, school-feeding, and improved sanitary facilities are all actions of special interest. However, it is important to recognize that the impact of these actions may be limited because of the poor condition of the education infrastructure and the relatively small number of appropriately qualified teachers. Increasing enrollment without at the same time strengthening the school system will limit the benefits of school attendance. Strengthening the education system in several complementary respects is likely to constitute a set of actions with very high returns. Improving the school system is one example of how interventions that are not directly linked to HIV prevention can play an important role in HIV-prevention efforts.

4.2.8. Prevention of HIV among adolescents: Actions of special interest

Integration of HIV/AIDS education into the national school curriculum is of special interest. Similarly, YFS is of special interest if combined with actions to address stigma in the community. An action that provides direct support to families so that they start or continue to send girls to school is also of special interest.

4.3. Income poverty reduction

Household poverty has serious negative consequences for children's nutrition, health and education. National income poverty rates have declined, but still remain very high. Moreover, rapid population growth has resulted in an increase in the absolute number of people living in poverty.[10]

The government is implementing a number of poverty reduction policies. Central among these policies is the Vision 2020 *Umurenge* Program (VUP), which aims to reduce poverty by increasing the productive capacity of the rural poor through a combination of public works, cooperatives, credit packages and direct support. The VUP program is implemented by the government and is supported by the United Kingdom Department for International Development (DfID) in conjunction with other development partners and NGOs. Implementation of the program began with a small-scale pilot intervention in March 2008.[28]

The design of VUP involves providing assistance to households according to their access to land and availability of labor. The program first identifies households that are the poorest and then categorizes them based on their endowments of land and labor. Households with land and with adults able to work are offered credit packages. Households with no land but with adults able to work are given the opportunity of employment in public works programs (PWPs). Households with neither land nor labor are provided with direct support.[28]

The public works program began in July 2008 and enrolled over 17,500 households in its first year of operation.[29] The types of project undertaken include watershed management and terracing, among others. The budget for each program consists of salaries as well as material and administrative costs.

Worker salaries are set below the market wage for unskilled labor in the region. The salary scale and total budget are based on local labor costs and product prices, and the former is then published in the local newspaper.[28]

The credit package involves a contract between the targeted households and the VUP management team. The contract specifies activities for which the use of credit is permissible. Households that are party to the contract are enrolled in the VUP Insurance Scheme (VUPIS), which facilitates credit approval from local microfinance institutions. VUPIS can reschedule or pay off debt depending on circumstances. Because the insurance reduces risk for local microfinance institutions, they are more likely to lend to households that are part of VUPIS. Adult men and women — including pregnant or lactating women and female heads of household — may apply for credit packages. Landless persons are not allowed to access credit, as it is assumed they do not have the assets to generate the return to pay back the loan.[28]

Targeted beneficiaries who are unable to participate in public works because they lack labor, or who are unable to obtain credit because they are landless, are eligible to receive direct support. Direct support is officially unconditional, but recipients are expected to participate in skill-acquisition or handicraft and social-service activities. Disabled persons, child-headed households, elders, genocide survivors, people living with HIV/AIDS (PLWHA), street children, refugees and returned exiles are among the vulnerable groups eligible to receive direct support. In addition to cash transfers, direct support includes provision of community childcare centers, child nutrition programs, and adult literacy and numeracy classes.[28]

VUP is an impressive program, but given the high levels of poverty additional actions are necessary. Although almost all respondents agreed that poverty reduction was a priority, they differed in terms of the actions they believed would be affordable and socially acceptable. Contrasting views were also expressed with regard to the likely psychological impact on beneficiaries of different types of support.

In-kind transfers were suggested because of their perceived simplicity and social acceptability; those against them focused on high cost and inflexibility. Many respondents argued in favor of interventions that support families to develop income-generating activities (IGAs). Other respondents were in favor of microcredit as a way to support business development. IGAs and microcredit received the most support, but some respondents doubted that these interventions could be successful on a large scale. They agreed that IGA interventions should be implemented by NGOs, but argued that the government should implement direct cash transfer (CT) programs. These respondents stated that CT programs are relatively simple and easy for the government to scale-up quickly. Direct CTs, however, brought the debate back to their long-term sustainability and hence viability. Many respondents voiced concerns that CTs promote dependency and would be socially unacceptable. Some stated that if cash were distributed, it should be done only through PWPs.

4.3.1. In-kind transfers

Common examples of in-kind transfers are food, housing, school supplies and clothing. Some respondents argued that in-kind transfers were preferable to other interventions because they were more likely to be socially acceptable. They also stated that a strength of in-kind transfers, compared with income-generating activities (IGAs), is that they are relatively simple to implement. In-kind transfers are beneficial even if the recipient lacks business skills and good health. Respondents also suggested that program administrators of in-kind transfers, unlike IGA program administrators, do not require high levels of technical training.

Most respondents agreed that in-kind transfers are a useful short-term response to a crisis. However, concerns were expressed about the sustainability and scale of such programs, and whether they could adjust to the changing consumption needs of families — families may be short of food in one period, and in another they may face difficulty paying school fees. These concerns appeared to lead many respondents to focus on IGAs as a more flexible and sustainable approach. The income from IGAs can be spent on whatever the family needs in each period.

4.3.2. Promoting income-generating activities

The idea of supporting families to develop small business enterprises that lead to sustained higher incomes is appealing. Many respondents argued in favor of interventions that aim to achieve this end. Two types of intervention were mentioned: IGAs and microcredit. Both of these interventions aim to support the development of microenterprises. The difference is that microcredit relies on the provision of financial loans, while IGA interventions work more closely with beneficiaries and include a range of activities such as enhancing skills and transferring productive assets. In this sub-section we focus on the potential of IGAs, while the next sub-section considers the possibility of expanding microcredit.

Interventions that promote the development of IGAs have been carried out in a number of countries in Asia, Africa, and Latin America. In many of these settings, a historic reliance on subsistence agriculture has been identified as a constraint on income growth of poor families. In this context, the aim of IGA promotion is not only to increase income, but also to diversify its sources and reduce its volatility.[30] Rural households in Rwanda need to diversify their income sources given that such a high proportion of them rely on subsistence agriculture which is vulnerable to weather and other risks.

The design of IGA interventions needs to take account of the socio-economic background of potential beneficiaries. For example, if people have been affected by a sudden event such as a natural disaster or war, they may in some instances only need short-term support to get back on their feet; in other instances they will need long-term support. Consider the IGA intervention of the United Nations High Commissioner for Refugees (UNHCR) for Afghan refugees in Pakistan. Surveys had shown that many refugees were skilled artisans who had fled their homes because of the conflict, but had left their work tools behind. The program, Assistance to Skilled Afghan Refugees, provided free tools to enable artisans to work in Pakistan. UNHCR estimated that daily income levels for beneficiaries increased threefold as a result of this initiative and average per capita income was raised above the poverty line. A major factor in the program's success was that those who had completed the program could be gainfully employed because they had prior experience of the trade and there was a demand for their services.[31]

Programs similar to this UNHCR one have led some to suggest that IGA interventions tend to benefit those who have had some prior training.[32] People who are not trained in a trade which they are supposed to start practicing, or have no prior experience in running their own business, will draw limited benefit from these programs. If programs are to benefit such people, skills-development activities will have to be included as part of the IGA intervention. Other considerations may also affect the success of such interventions in the case of extremely poor families. IGA interventions typically involve a lag between the start of the program and the time that participants begin to receive higher incomes. It may be difficult for extremely poor families, who are struggling to meet their daily survival needs, to resist the opportunity of selling income-generating assets to satisfy immediate consumption needs. For example, if families are struggling to feed their children, they may sell the tools or livestock given to them as part of an IGA intervention — to enable consumption in the short term.

Efforts have been made to design IGA programs which benefit families that would not normally be able to wait for the income return from developing an IGA. A prominent example is the FXB-Village Program, which is an intervention designed to support children and families who live in extreme poverty in areas historically affected by HIV/AIDS. The FXB-Village Program runs for three years and has been implemented in Rwanda, Burundi, Uganda, Thailand and India, among other countries. Working with local community leaders to target the most vulnerable households, the program provides each participating household with a package of material support and skill-building assistance. Families receive psychosocial support, information, and advice on child protection services that are available in their region. Critically, the intervention also provides families with nutritional support, and assistance in accessing health and education services. By providing such basic support the program alleviates some of the immediate pressures on households and allows them to develop individual and group IGAs. Without such material support vulnerable families would find it difficult to invest time in activities that benefit them only after a lag. The support to families is gradually scaled back over the three-year period as they are expected increasingly to meet their needs through income from IGAs. Evaluations of the FXB-Village Program have shown that children and families benefit substantially from the comprehensive intervention. Children in FXB-Villages enroll in and attend school at higher rates than do their peers. Evaluations suggest that 67% of households in rural areas and 96% of households in urban areas progress from extreme poverty to self-sufficiency within the three-year period of the intervention and are able to maintain and increase incomes thereafter.[33]

A concern that is often raised in relation to IGA interventions is the difficulty that individual participants can have in marketing their products or skills — particularly if they are located in poor or isolated areas.[34] One way to address this is to support group IGAs. For example, the FXB-Village and other IGA programs in Rwanda encourage the formation of cooperatives of 50 or more people. The higher levels of production make it worthwhile for retailers in cities and towns to travel to make purchases from these cooperatives located in rural areas.

At the consultative meeting, respondents expressed concern that although successful at the local level, scaling-up IGA programs to the national level may be difficult. Key factors in ensuring IGA success include the ability of the NGO or implementing organization to work with families in designing IGAs that suit the family and the market.[34] Some respondents argued that the close support required to tailor IGAs to the circumstances of individual families would be impossible to replicate on a national scale.

Although the difficulty of running a national-level IGA program must be taken into consideration, the limited duration of the intervention makes it less of a problem than it appears. As support is not offered for an indefinite period — three years in the case of the FXB-Village Program — providers of the intervention can move from one community to the next. A national program that provides close support simultaneously to a large proportion of the population may not be feasible, but a smaller program moving from community to community (every three years) may be possible and effective. This does, however, mean that there would be delays before some families receive assistance. To circumvent this problem, it may be worth considering the possibility of combining a national cash transfer program with an IGA intervention that supports participants on a rolling basis. The CT program would provide immediate support to address the most extreme forms of poverty among households not (yet) covered by the IGA program, while the latter helps selected families lift themselves out of poverty permanently.

There are clearly a number of arguments in favor of IGA interventions, yet some potential pitfalls and limitations need to be considered. Households that are highly labor-constrained may not be able to benefit, e.g. when adult members are very ill or old. Poorly-designed IGA interventions have in the past been seen to create dependency on the international donor providing the goods, materials and training — rather than promoting sustainable enterprises. Examples of such dependency have been observed in IGA programs for Mozambican refugees.[35] The creation of dependency is more likely to occur when the IGA is capital-intensive or reliant on international sales. IGAs which require high levels of capital and training, but for which a market does not exist, can end up generating little income in relation to the costs of implementation. In such situations IGAs are not likely to be a cost-effective way of reducing poverty. Avoiding these pitfalls and being aware of the limitations emphasizes the need for well-designed IGAs and well-trained implementers.

4.3.3. Promoting microfinance

Microfinance was suggested by some respondents as an alternative to IGA programs. Microfinance institutions provide poor households with access to financial resources and services. They allow households to borrow and save in reliable and convenient forms, and can offer health, life, and disability insurance.[36]

The underlying concept is that improved access to credit can provide the poor with the financial resources to partake in activities that result in increased incomes. Access to credit can also help impoverished families to smooth consumption by allowing them to borrow instead of cutting family expenditure.[37] However, such consumption smoothing can cause problems in the long term if families are left with high levels of debt.

Microfinance has been seen to have had success in some countries — e.g., Indonesia and Sri Lanka.[38] A number of microcredit initiatives have been evaluated, including programs of the Grameen Bank and Bangladesh Rural Advancement Committee (BRAC). Evidence suggests an increase in household consumption (above the amount of the loan) for families that participated in these programs, and a significantly greater increase in household consumption when the borrowers were female.[37]

Concerns have been voiced with regard to microfinance in general (microcredit, microsavings, and microinsurance) and with microcredit in particular. Some researchers have suggested that borrowing families may use child labor to help repay loans, possibly at the expense of school attendance.[39] Concerns have also been raised that increasing access to credit for poor families may lead to unmanageable debt because families spend the loan on consumption or on unprofitable business activities. Such debt may lead people to take out new loans simply to pay off older ones.[40] Spiraling debt can be highly stressful. A rise in the number of suicides in rural Andhra Pradesh in India has been linked with people being unable to repay their accumulated debts from microloans. Many of these issues were also mentioned by respondents during the consultation in Rwanda. Of particular concern was the possibility that ventures might fail and leave participants in a worse situation with no income to pay off their loans.

4.3.4. Cash transfers

Many see the provision of regular small cash transfers (CTs) to poor families as an important intervention capable of reducing the impact on children of poverty and HIV/AIDS. The evidence that CTs positively affect children's wellbeing is clear.[32] Notwithstanding this evidence, respondents held mixed views on the appropriateness of CTs in Rwanda.

CTs have been seen to reduce poverty, and more than a dozen countries in southern and eastern Africa have implemented or are piloting CT programs. Currently, Rwanda is piloting a CT program in conjunction with development partners including DfID and the World Bank. CTs help families secure a basic level of consumption and reduce fluctuations in income, thus helping to avert the sale of assets during crises. CTs are also used to cover transport costs and user fees to access services. Sometimes the cash transfer is invested in productive assets or job search, both of which can lead to higher incomes.[32]

CTs can take many different forms. CT targeting typically involves consideration of poverty, and can include consideration of age — for example, through provision of old-age pensions or child-support grants. Poverty and age considerations are often combined, e.g. with means-tested old-age pensions. Furthermore, some cash transfer programs have conditions, while others do not. CT programs also vary in terms of the amounts that are transferred. In Zambia, for example, the amount of transfer in the Social Cash Transfer Scheme is US$10 per household per month, with an additional US$2.50 if the household has children. In Mozambique, the monthly transfer is between US$3 and US$6, depending on household size.[32]

Recently, conditional cash transfers (CCTs) have grown in popularity, particularly in Latin America. These programs are typically targeted at poor households and the cash is often paid to mothers. In addition to cash, some programs include in-kind transfers, such as nutritional supplements or school supplies for children.[41] The amount of cash paid may vary according to the age and gender of the child, and the transfer may be a one-off payment or paid in installments. As a condition of these transfers, recipients agree to undertake specific actions such as enrolling their child in school, attending pre- and postnatal healthcare clinics, and ensuring their child gets vaccinated. CCT programs reduce poverty, and improve health and education outcomes as a result of increased utilization of healthcare and school attendance.[32]

Colombia's CCT program, *Familias en accion*, provided an average transfer of US$20 per family per month and had a large impact on impoverished households. Reducing poverty through CCTs can improve outcomes for children. For example, the PROGRESA CCT program in Mexico provided a transfer of US$13 per family per month, which was equivalent to 20% of mean household expenditure of the poor households that were targeted. The CCT decreased school dropout rates and encouraged transition to secondary school. Moreover, mothers who had been receiving benefits for 12 months reported significantly lower illness among children aged 0–5 years. CCTs in Mexico have also been linked with a decreased occurrence of stunting.[32]

While CCTs have received a great deal of attention recently, other types of cash transfers also appear to be effective. The old-age pension program in South Africa has led to an improvement in the health and nutrition of children, especially of girls.[42] While the intervention is not designed to benefit children, it does so because many children live in households that include pensioners. The Child Support Grant in South Africa has shown similar positive impacts. For example, households that receive the grant are more likely to enroll their children in school than otherwise similar households that do not receive the grant.[43]

Although the positive impact of CTs has been demonstrated in a variety of contexts, a number of respondents expressed concerns. At the consultative meeting many respondents suggested that a CT program would not be sustainable due to its high recurrent costs. A common argument was that CTs would encourage dependency, and respondents argued that CT beneficiaries would lose their spirit of self-reliance. Although the dependency argument was more common, some respondents suggested that the opposite may in fact be occurring. These respondents claimed that through the VUP cash transfer intervention, instead of families losing self-reliance they were putting aside the transfers to set up IGAs. Another frequently raised concern was that CTs would not be socially acceptable, and respondents argued that CTs would therefore not be politically feasible. Other respondents countered this argument by emphasizing that VUP already included a CT component which appeared to be acceptable to the public.

4.3.5. Public works programs

Public works programs (PWPs) support poor households by providing payment in-cash or in-kind in return for labor. These programs can be targeted at poor households in general or towards specific groups such as HIV-affected households. Initiatives for households affected by HIV/AIDS can be tailored to be less physically demanding.[32] PWPs have been used as a general response to poverty. India, for example, has used PWPs since the early 1950s to provide employment opportunities during the agricultural slack season or in conditions of drought.[44]

PWPs were mentioned by a number of respondents as a way to make cash payments more socially acceptable. Respondents also pointed to potential benefits for the community, because public works can be directed to developing community assets. Despite concerns that PWPs favor healthy men of working age, respondents argued that the program could be adapted to accommodate ill, elderly and female persons.

A number of PWPs have been designed to benefit women, but they have not always managed to achieve their goals. One program which includes features intended to ensure that women are able to benefit is the Maharashtra Employment Guarantee Scheme (MEGS) in India. The scheme provides jobs within 5 kilometers of a woman's residence and pays an equal wage to men and women. In this program, almost half of all participants were women.[44] In a program in South Africa that included efforts to involve women less than a quarter (23%) of participants were female.[44]

PWPs need not be short-term and can be used on a semi-permanent basis. This allows participants the option to opt in or out depending on whether work is available elsewhere. As a result these programs perform an insurance function. For example, the National Rural Employment Guarantee Act in India mandates all state governments to provide at least 100 days of guaranteed wage employment to adults who are willing to work at the set wage.[44]

PWPs have been shown to benefit participants in a variety of ways. In the Productive Safety Net Program in Ethiopia, 60% of beneficiaries were found less likely to sell assets to buy food, and 30% enrolled more of their children in school.[44] Almost half of those surveyed reported an increased utilization of healthcare facilities, and they attributed these changes to participation in the program.[44]

In addition to short-term relief for beneficiaries, PWPs can offer training that helps participants to find permanent work elsewhere or to become self-employed. The Expanded PWP in South Africa, for example, provides training beyond the skills needed for the job, thus preparing workers for longer-term employment or self-employment. For instance, manual laborers working on road projects are offered training in unrelated building skills such as bricklaying.[44]

PWPs not only assist those employed but also generate outputs, such as improved public infrastructure or school buildings, which benefit the entire community. These programs can create or maintain infrastructure such as roads, bridges, schools, health centers and sewage systems. Other possible projects include developing irrigation systems, cleaning roads and other public facilities, and offering social services such as daycare. These social assets can make a significant difference to communities. For instance, a project in Zambia that improved a road network resulted in increased access to markets for 37% of people in the area.[44]

In examining the possibility of PWPs, evidence suggests that three key issues of implementation must be considered: ensuring a regular flow of funds from central government to implementing agencies; ensuring that there are adequate funds in program budgets for non-wage expenses such as building materials; and managerial capacity. If these issues can be addressed, public works programs are certainly of special interest.

4.3.6. Income poverty reduction: Actions of special interest

Poverty reduction leads to improvements in nutrition, school attendance, healthcare utilization, and effectiveness of medical treatment. Given the significance of income poverty reduction and the variety of interventions involved in addressing it on a national scale, a number of actions are of special interest.

Public works interventions are socially acceptable and supported by evidence, so they warrant further analysis. The level of interest in IGAs, and evidence that when combined with other family support they can respond to immediate and long-term family needs, makes them of special interest. Given the evidence on effectiveness of conditional cash transfers in achieving improvements in school attendance and healthcare utilization, they too are considered to be of special interest.

4.4. Early childhood development

Early childhood development (ECD) programs are designed to improve the capacity of young children (aged 0–5 years) to develop. As children develop, they undergo a series of physical, cognitive and emotional changes. Numerous studies have demonstrated that ECD programs can help support children's development, with important short- and long-term implications.[45] The rapid brain development that occurs in early life is susceptible to environmental influences. Positive stable human relationships are crucial to proper child development, and stress and abuse during early life can impair healthy brain development.[46] ECD programs are particularly beneficial for children's education: they lead to decreased likelihood of grade repetition, dropping out of school, and the need for special education.[47]

Enrollment in preschool is increasing. ESSP 2006–2010 states that MIN-EDUC will act as a coordinator of ECD interventions, and encourage the private sector, communities and civil society to take on the task of providing

ECD services.[48] To support service providers, the Experimental Resource Center for Preschool Activities, sets national standards for ECD services and develops appropriate teaching materials.[49]

The NGO sector has implemented a number of ECD programs in Rwanda. For example, CARE piloted an ECD program in 2006 which also includes interventions directed at the caregiver and family, the community, and policymakers at district and community levels. CARE's intervention includes food and nutrition support, child development programs, economic strengthening of families, health promotion, and child rights and protection.[50]

In the context of an HIV epidemic, ECD services take on a special role as they help to reduce the impact on children of difficult household circumstances. The Joint Learning Initiative on Children and HIV/AIDS (JLICA) notes that successful ECD interventions can help children affected by HIV/AIDS — through protecting their health and improving their social and economic outcomes in later life.[51] ECD programs can be particularly important when children are living in poverty and do not have access to healthcare and other social services.[51]

A variety of approaches are available to expand ECD services in Rwanda. These include the establishment of centers, in-house care, and home visitation. Studies of each of these approaches have linked them to positive outcomes for children. It should be noted that the ECD services discussed here have a rather narrow focus. They are concerned mainly with early education and less with other aspects such as healthy pregnancies and child nutrition and health.

4.4.1. ECD centers

ECD centers employ trained staff to work in formal facilities. The benefits of such centers have been studied elsewhere in the world, for example in Nepal. In Nepal, ECD centers run by local women help children to develop learning skills.[52] The centers make use of low-cost teaching materials and provide children with an opportunity to engage in directed activities as well as free play. Children who participate in these centers are better prepared for school. Once at school, children exposed to ECD are more successful in year-end examinations: 81% of ECD children passed grade 1 compared with 61% of non-ECD students. In grade 2, 94% of ECD children passed the year-end examination compared with 68% of children not exposed to ECD. Nationally, 36.5% of grade 1 children repeated the year, but only 5.5% of the ECD group did.[52]

ECD centers could certainly benefit children in Rwanda. Their cost, however, may limit the number of centers that can be established. Unlike home-based care and home-visitation programs, ECD centers require a dedicated building and staff and as a result are more expensive.

4.4.2. *Home-based ECD care*

Home-based programs are seen as a lower-cost option that is still effective. Home-based care (HBC) involves the provision of ECD services to groups of children at the home of an ECD service provider. Such programs are in place in a number of different countries. For example, Bolivia has a large-scale home-based ECD and nutrition program called *Proyecto Integral de Desarrollo Infantil* (PIDI). PIDI offers daycare, nutritional support, and educational services to children in poor urban areas. Children aged 6 months to 6 years are placed in groups of 15 to be cared for in homes located in their neighborhoods. Local women selected by the community serve as home daycare workers. These women work in groups of two or three to provide integrated child development services — including recreational activities, nutritional assistance, growth monitoring, and referral of children to other services as needed. The objectives of PIDI are to improve children's health and early cognitive and social development by providing them with nourishment, supervision and stimulation.[47] Tests were administered to children enrolled in PIDI on bulk motor skills (e.g. balancing and walking), fine motor skills (ability to manipulate small objects), language skills, and psychosocial skills. Results show that the program increased children's test scores by 5% on average.[53]

Similar to center-based care, home-based care (HBC) programs have been shown to have a positive effect on a range of child development indicators. If such programs are implemented in settings where HIV is common, training must be provided that includes components related to the care of HIV-positive children and children affected by ill-health and death from HIV/AIDS in their families. Although HBC programs do not require the investment and maintenance of infrastructure associated with a center, the two program designs do share a common limitation. Both HBC programs and ECD centers require children to be brought to a site for care. This requirement may be demanding in rural areas where most of the Rwandan population lives. Interventions that reach out to families, such as home visitation, may be more appropriate than center-based or home-based care.

4.4.3. *Home visitation for ECD*

Home-visitation programs employ trained individuals to conduct family visits. During these visits, the trained individuals provide information on topics such as early education and nutrition. Visits may also include monitoring children's development and referral to other services. A number of ECD home-visitation programs have been shown to have positive effects on child development.[54] In Jamaica, the Roving Caregivers Program trains volunteers to demonstrate to and teach parents child-stimulation activities and child-rearing practices. The program also holds sessions focusing on parenting skills, especially for teen mothers. The results of this program confirm an improvement in child development.[55]

Home-visitation programs can reach families in rural areas. Families do not have to meet transportation costs or take as much time off work as they would if they had to access center-based services.[51] Home-visitation programs seek to improve child outcomes by improving the knowledge base of the child's primary caregiver.

4.4.4. Early childhood development: Actions of special interest

A stressful living environment for children at an early age, associated with material deprivation and lack of positive attention, can have major negative implications for children's development. Interventions in the early years of children's lives can help prevent developmental problems and can lead to many benefits for them and wider society.

A set of actions combining home-based care and home visits is of special interest. It would be too expensive to establish ECD centers in all areas. However, it would be useful to establish ECD centers as training centers in selected areas.

4.5. Education

Education is crucial to the development of both children and society. Attending school reduces children's chances of engaging in risky sexual behavior.[56] More highly educated individuals can protect themselves better against HIV, because they are more likely to understand modes of transmission and the link with high-risk behaviors. Educated individuals also tend to be more confident and hence more comfortable discussing condom use with their partner.[57]

The government has made universal primary education a priority and net enrollment reached 96% in 2008.[17,58] The World Bank reported that Rwanda is on track to achieve MDG2 for universal primary education.[59] Despite high enrollment, the primary-school completion rate was only 54% in 2008.[17] Of those completing primary school, the transition rate to secondary school was low; only 54% of children who finished primary school in 2007 enrolled in secondary school.[17]

4.5.1. Promoting secondary-school attendance

A number of actions can promote children's school attendance. Some of these were discussed in relation to girls' attendance in section 4.2.4. These interventions can be extended to benefit boys as well.

Many respondents emphasized the importance of increasing the number of qualified teachers and investing in school infrastructure. Education expenditure was, however, 4.1% of Gross National Income (GNI) in 2009, which is higher than the sub-Saharan average of 3.6%.[17] Thus the government may find it difficult to increase spending further. The negative consequences of not investing more in training teachers and building schools, however, may be greater than the costs of doing so. Of particular concern is the need to invest in secondary-school infrastructure and in teacher-training. Primary-school enrollment has increased rapidly in recent years and many more children are now completing this level of education. Secondary school places, however, are scarce. Moreover, the disparity in enrollment between the rich and the poor is pronounced in secondary school: secondary-school enrollment is 10 times higher for children from the highest wealth quintile (26%) compared to the lowest wealth quintile (2.6%).[60]

In the Education Sector Strategic Plan (ESSP) 2008–2012, the government has already outlined ambitious targets for secondary-school expansion, particularly with regard to lower-secondary school.[7] The government plans to increase gross enrollment in the first three years of secondary school from 24% in 2006 to 55% in 2012. Upper-secondary school enrollment is planned to increase from 13% in 2006 to 19% in 2012.[7]

The increases in primary-school enrollment have been so large that further expansion of the secondary-school system will be required if the current transition rate from primary to secondary school is to be maintained. Expansion of the secondary education system will require building more schools and training more teachers. Certainly, both teacher-training and infrastructure development are of special interest for further analysis.

4.5.2. Vocational training

The importance of school education was not doubted by respondents, but a number argued that alternative forms of education should be considered. Specifically, they indicated an interest in promoting vocational training, an action the government is already pursuing.

According to ESSP 2008–2012, students can transition to vocational schools after completing *tronc commun* (i.e., lower-secondary school) or upon graduation from upper-secondary school.[7] The government hopes to increase the number of students who receive vocational training, which will better prepare adolescents to enter the world of work. In order to accomplish this goal, the government plans to increase the number of vocational teachers and to provide additional training to current teachers. It intends to open five vocational training centers, one per province, for such training.[10] It should be noted that as of 2007 vocational education accounted for only 1% of the education sector's annual budget. Furthermore, ESSP 2008–2012 plans to allocate only 2% of the education budget to vocational training in 2012.[7]

International evidence on vocational training is mixed. A review of studies on post-program employment and earnings of graduates noted that 78%

of vocational training programs report a positive impact on these fronts. However, questions have been raised about the extent to which benefits (i.e., subsequent increases in the earnings of participants relative to control groups) outweigh program costs.[61]

Given the amount of attention vocational training is receiving in government plans, this area cannot be considered one of inaction. Although vocational training is being offered, these services may be difficult to access for children living in poverty. Children in poverty may find it difficult to pay fees and meet other costs associated with attending vocational training, such as transport and material costs. Actions such as covering fees, providing materials, and offering meals at training centers could be considered.

4.5.3. Education: Actions of special interest

Strengthening the education system is a goal of the government. The recent increases in primary-school enrollment are likely to lead to demand for secondary-school places being higher than the planned supply. Expanding the secondary-school system to the level necessary to maintain current transition rates from primary to secondary school is clearly an action of special interest.

4.6. Nutrition

Malnutrition is thought to be an underlying factor in approximately 60% of the illnesses that cause deaths among children in Rwanda.[62] The most prominent types of malnutrition in the country include protein-energy malnutrition and micronutrient deficiency. Such malnutrition has contributed to high infant and child mortality. In 2005, an estimated 22% of children under five were underweight and 45% of children under five were stunted (defined as more than two standard deviations below median height-for-age of the reference population). Rural areas were more affected by stunting than urban areas — 47.3% compared to 33.1%.[62]

The country's population suffers from a variety of micronutrient deficiencies. Iron deficiency contributes to maternal mortality, and to low birthweight and reduced attention span and scholastic achievement among children. Data from 2005 show that anemia affects 48% of children: 22% of children have mild anemia, 18% are moderately anemic, and 8% are severely anemic. Overall, 27% of women were anemic in 2005: 15% had mild anemia, 8% were moderately anemic, and 4% were severely anemic. It is thought that a prominent cause of anemia is a diet based on cereals and root vegetables, such as potatoes and cassava, which are poor sources of iron. The general population also suffers from Vitamin A deficiency, and 7% of pregnant women have night blindness.[62]

Many households in Rwanda cannot secure sufficient food to satisfy their nutritional needs. In 2005 an estimated 7% of households reported having only one meal a day, and only 3% three meals a day.[62] High poverty rates and large household size contribute to malnutrition.[62,63] As of 2005/06, approximately 37% of the population lived in extreme poverty and could not afford a food basket with the minimum requirement of 2,100 kcal per day.[63] Meat is consumed by only 29% of children, and cow's milk is consumed by only 12% of children.[62]

Although breastfeeding is common practice in Rwanda, the Ministry of Health reports that infants are not exclusively breastfed as recommended. Infants who are breastfeeding are often also given pared-down portions of family meals consisting of cassava or cereal-based porridge.[62]

The government recognizes the importance of responding to these concerns, and plans to implement a number of actions to improve nutrition. The 2005 National Nutrition Policy included interventions for the promotion of optimum feeding of infants and young children; scaling-up community-based nutrition programs; food fortification; prevention and management of malnutrition and related diseases; nutritional support to PLWHA and their families; and awareness campaigns to bring about dietary behavior change.[62] The Ministry of Health (MOH) promotes exclusive breast-feeding for infants from birth to 6 months. This recommendation includes infants born to HIV-positive mothers who cannot meet the UNAIDS-recommended conditions for formula feeding. The Ministry encourages breast-feeding by establishing support groups at the community level. The government is implementing a national code for marketing substitutes to breast milk as well as developing a national strategy on infant and child feeding in the context of HIV/AIDS. Among other measures, all breast-feeding women who work in the public and private sectors will receive paid periods of maternity leave, and dedicated breast-feeding space will be provided in the workplace and public areas.[62]

The Community Based Nutrition Program (CBNP) aims to help communities access nutritional services. The government is conducting training, promoting under-five growth monitoring, and organizing educational programs which include micronutrient supplementation, de-worming and health education. CBNP also encourages social mobilization activities that promote the identification, development and use of safe water sources, personal and environmental hygiene, use of insecticide-treated mosquito nets, family planning, HIV/AIDS prevention, and membership of *Mutuelles*.[62]

With the exception of iodized salt, fortified foods are not commonly consumed in Rwanda. MOH is commissioning studies on the technical and financial feasibility of fortifying local foods, and is developing national standards for their fortification.[62]

The government aims to increase food availability at the national, community and household levels. Strategies to this end include promoting the production and consumption of local foods that are rich in micronutrients, developing guidelines on healthy dietary practices, and improving post-harvest food processing and preservation techniques.[62] The government plans to expand its mass-media campaigns to discourage unhealthy diets and promote healthy lifestyles. These campaigns attempt to convey relevant messages to healthcare professionals, community health workers, teachers, churches, CBOs and NGOs.[62]

Although the government is already taking a number of steps to address malnutrition, it is worth considering what else can be done. Almost all respondents felt that existing efforts should be greatly strengthened given the country's poor nutrition indicators. Respondents held varying opinions about the interventions that would be most effective in dealing with malnutrition. Some respondents argued in favor of providing at-risk families with direct nutritional support in the form of food baskets. Others argued that this approach would not be sustainable and that household food production should be increased through kitchen gardens. Some interviewees highlighted the link between poverty and malnutrition, and advocated interventions designed to increase the income of families (e.g. through IGAs) instead of providing direct nutritional support. Other interviewees suggested that school-feeding programs should be promoted rather than interventions that utilize the family as the entry point to improve child nutrition.

Some respondents did not believe that the prevailing malnutrition problem is simply a result of lack of food; they identified poor education on nutrition as a major cause. Although programs on nutrition education are desirable, lack of knowledge about appropriate nutrition is obviously not the only contributor to malnutrition. We know that almost 40% of the population lives below the extreme poverty line corresponding to a minimum food requirement of 2,100 kilocalories per adult per day. For this group an increase in food consumption is a necessary condition for alleviating malnutrition.

4.6.1. Direct provision of food to families

Evidence suggests that food rations can prevent weight loss and nutritional supplements can help rehabilitate malnourished children.[32] In-kind food transfers are appealing for a number of reasons. First, they are more politically acceptable than other forms of direct support.[64] Secondly, as poor families spend a high percentage of their income on food, reducing food expenditure will release a significant portion of the family budget for services such as education and healthcare.[64] However, there are concerns that such programs may be difficult to sustain given the large administrative costs associated with their implementation.[32]

4.6.2. Kitchen, school and community gardens

Interventions which promote the cultivation of kitchen gardens can lead to increases in household consumption, especially of fruits and vegetables. Moreover, surplus production can be sold to generate additional household income. Gardens can also be used to benefit community groups. For example, HIV-positive self-help groups can benefit from community gardens, and school gardens can increase food consumption among school children.[32]

A number of concerns have been raised with respect to the effectiveness of interventions which promote the cultivation of food gardens. First, food does not become available to the family (or community or school) until fairly long after planting. This delay may require kitchen garden interventions to be combined, at least in the short term, with other food-support measures that have a more immediate impact. Secondly, kitchen gardens involve an opportunity cost for participants, as time spent tending the garden is no longer available for other activities. Thirdly, such interventions may encourage child labor. These issues, however, can often be addressed through better design. However well designed they are, kitchen gardens cannot be the only response as they cannot be cultivated by those who are physically unable to work because of ill-health or old age.

4.6.3. Cash transfers

Families can use money from cash transfers (CTs) to purchase food. Evidence suggests that in many conditional and unconditional CT schemes, the majority of the transfer goes towards the purchase of food.[32] In some cases, CTs can be a more efficient means of increasing food consumption than direct food transfers. CTs may be more efficient than in-kind food transfers when food is available for purchase locally, and administrative costs are lower for CTs than for in-kind transfers. Cash also allows the family to decide what type of food they wish to obtain.[64]

When considering CT schemes to enhance nutrition in a community, the capacity of surrounding markets to meet the resulting increase in food demand must be investigated.[64] Cash does provide more flexibility to the family than in-kind support, but it also exposes families to the risks associated with supply shortages if local markets cannot keep pace with increased demand and food prices rise. This risk suggests that when food supplies in a region are limited, in-kind food transfers may be more appropriate than CTs.[64]

Compared to in-kind food transfers, CTs allow families the flexibility to use the transfer for food only when they feel it is appropriate. They may choose to spend on food when household food production is low, but when food production is high, the transfer can be spent on other goods and services such as education and healthcare. An evaluation of an intervention in

Malawi showed that 70% to 80% of the cash transfers were spent on food during food shortages in December and February, but only 30% of the transfers were spent on food in April after the maize harvest had begun.[32]

The evidence that CTs can be used as a response to malnutrition also justifies other interventions which seek to increase household incomes. For example, IGAs or public works programs could also provide the family with money to purchase food.

4.6.4. School-feeding

A study by the Ministry of Gender and Family Promotion and WFP argues that school-feeding may be the most effective approach to responding to chronic malnutrition among children in the country.[65] Many respondents agreed with this position, and went on to emphasize that other positive outcomes would flow from a school-feeding intervention. These outcomes include higher school attendance and an improved capacity for learning.[66]

Evidence of school-feeding programs on nutritional status has been gathered in several countries. Many studies have demonstrated that school-feeding programs in primary school improve the nutritional status of enrolled children. Programs have been shown to increase children's daily energy consumption, and improve their anthropometric indicators such as height-for-age z-scores and body mass index (BMI).[66,67] Children in Peru who received breakfast at school showed increased energy and protein intake, and improved iron levels.[67] A randomized trial in rural Jamaica found that children receiving a school breakfast gained 0.25 centimeters in height during 8 months of intervention, compared to a control group.[55] Food consumption at school has been linked to improved nutritional outcomes in other countries too. For example, results from a school-feeding program in Bangladesh showed an increase in BMI of participating primary-school children.[68] A Ugandan study found benefits not only for school children, but also for their preschool siblings. It was thought that families directed food to preschool siblings as older children were now able to receive food at school, or these preschool siblings went to school with the older children to access food there.[69]

School-feeding not only improves nutritional outcomes but also has a positive impact on school enrollment and attendance. For example, a school-feeding program in Bangladesh increased net enrollment by 9.6 percentage points from a baseline of 65%.[68] There is also evidence that for malnourished children school-feeding improves school attendance, concentration, and test scores.[70]

School-feeding is clearly an intervention with great potential. Recognizing this potential, the government has already been working with the World Food Programme (WFP) to provide school meals in areas they have identified as being food insecure. In the joint WFP/Government program, daily food supplements for children include 30 grams of beans, 100 grams of maize meal, 8 grams of vegetable oil, and 3 grams of salt — adding up to a total of 532 kilocalories per day. Of the food given to children in these programs, 20% is acquired locally, 40% regionally, and 40% internationally. WFP plans to increase the purchase of local foods when domestic production capacity improves.[71] Initially, WFP planned to feed 142,100 boys and 147,900 girls, or a total of 290,000 children, for 180 days each year. In 2009, WFP increased the number of beneficiaries to 350,000 children to account for increased enrollment in primary school following the removal of school fees for the first nine years of schooling.[71,72] These beneficiaries will be supported through the year 2012.[71] The government is currently considering alternative ways to expand school-feeding. These include expanding the WFP intervention to other areas. They also include supporting the development of school gardens and encouraging community participation. Although there are proposals to expand the school-feeding program, it is still important to examine the costs of not expanding it. Such an analysis would provide more detailed information regarding the scale to which the intervention should be expanded. For this reason, school-feeding is certainly an action of special interest.

4.6.5. Nutrition: Actions of special interest

The logistical support necessary to provide in-kind food transfers to families is costly and may be difficult to sustain on an on-going basis.[32] However, such an intervention would provide immediate benefit. Given that some other actions involve a lag before nutritional benefits are realized, direct support is of special interest as an emergency response. In the longer term, IGAs and PWPs are likely to be more cost-effective than food transfers in improving children's nutritional status.

In addition to in-kind support to families, child nutrition can be addressed through the school system. Expanding the current school-feeding intervention is certainly of special interest. School-feeding not only affects children's nutritional status but helps keep them in school, and has been proven effective in a variety of contexts.

4.7. Conclusion

The government, along with its international and civil society partners, is doing much to support children affected by HIV/AIDS and poverty. However, given the severity of the situation, there is certainly more that can be done. Based on a review of the literature and interviews with key informants in the country, we identified a number of actions of special interest relating to adolescent HIV prevention, income poverty reduction, ECD, education, and nutrition.

We have selected three interventions for further analysis. The interventions were selected because they appear to be desirable, and help to illustrate the application and range of the COI method. The three interventions selected for further analysis are: (i) a scaled-up FXB intervention; (ii) expansion of secondary schooling; and (iii) school-feeding. The FXB intervention is an integrated poverty reduction action which seeks to support extremely poor families in multiple and complementary ways. The implementation of such an action forms part of an integrated response to three priority areas — income poverty reduction, education and nutrition. The FXB action was selected partly because we observed it closely through field visits and the implementing organization (FXBI) allowed us access to detailed design, cost and output data. The action to expand secondary schooling is primarily a response to the education priority area. If school construction is done through public works, the intervention would also have an effect on income poverty reduction. Moreover, keeping girls in school will help with HIV prevention. The expansion of secondary schooling involves implementing a couple of complementary actions: constructing schools, and training and deploying teachers. Finally, school-feeding is a response to both the nutrition and education priority areas.

Endnote
a. 'Comprehensive knowledge' is defined as correctly identifying ways of preventing the sexual transmission of HIV and rejecting major misconceptions about its transmission.

References
1. Treatment and Research AIDS Center. *Rapport Annuel du Trac 2007*. Kigali, Rwanda: Treatment and Research AIDS Center, 2008.
2. National Institute of Statistics, Rwanda Ministry of Health, Macro International Inc. *Rwanda Demographic and Health Survey 2005*. Kigali, Rwanda and Calverton, MD: NIS, RMH, and Macro International Inc., 2006.
3. Rwanda Ministry of Health. *National Strategic Plan on HIV and AIDS 2009–2012*. Office of the President, National AIDS Control Commission. Kigali, Rwanda, 2009.
4. Government of Rwanda. *Rwanda National Policy on Condoms*. Kigali, Rwanda: Government of Rwanda, 2005.
5. Coates T, Richter L, Caceres C. Behavioral strategies to reduce HIV transmission: How to make them work better. *Lancet* 2008; 372(9639):669–684.
6. Kirby D, Obasi A, Laris BA. The effectiveness of sex education and HIV education interventions in schools in developing countries. *World*

Health Organization Technical Report Series 2006; 938:103–150.

7. Rwanda Ministry of Education. *Education Sector Strategic Plan 2008–2012.* Kigali, Rwanda: Government of Rwanda, 2008.

8. Global Fund to Fight AIDS, Tuberculosis and Malaria. *Rwanda RWN-102-G01-C-00.* Grant Performance Report. External Print Version. Kigali, Rwanda: Global Fund, 2010.

9. Neukom J, Ashford L. *Changing Youth Behavior through Social Marketing: Program Experiences and Research Findings from Cameroon, Madagascar and Rwanda.* Washington, DC: PRB and PSI, 2002.

10. Rwanda Ministry of Finance and Economic Planning. *Economic Development and Poverty Reduction Strategy 2008–2012.* Kigali, Rwanda: Government of Rwanda, 2007.

11. Mmari KN, Magnani RJ. Does making clinic-based reproductive health services more youth-friendly increase service use by adolescents? Evidence from Lusaka, Zambia. *Journal of Adolescent Health* 2003; 33(4):259–270.

12. Dicks B, Ferguson J, Chandra-Mouli V. Review of the evidence for interventions to increase young people's use of health-services in developing countries. In: Ross DA, Dick B, Ferguson J, eds. *Preventing HIV/AIDS in Young People: A Systematic Review of the Evidence from Developing Countries.* Geneva, Switzerland: WHO, 2006.

13. Maticka-Tyndale E, Brouillard-Coylea C. The effectiveness of community interventions targeting HIV and AIDS prevention at young people in developing countries. *World Health Organization Technical Report Series* 2006; 938:243–285.

14. Kagimu M. Evaluation of the effectiveness of AIDS health education interventions in the Muslim community in Uganda. *AIDS Education and Prevention* 1998; 7:10–21.

15. Kirby D, Laris BA, Rolleri L. HIV transmission and prevention in adolescents. In: Peiperl L and Volverding P, ed. *HIV InSite Knowledge Base.* San Francisco, CA: UCSF, 2002.

16. Hargreaves J, Boler T. *Girl Power: The Impact of Girls' Education on HIV and Sexual Behavior.* London, UK: ActionAid International, 2006.

17. World Bank. *World Development Indicators 2011.* Washington, DC: World Bank, 2011.

18. Taton V, Nabongo C, Chiejine I, Kamuragiye A. *Investing in Rwanda: Effective Choices for Orphans and Girls in Primary Education.* New York, NY: UNICEF, 2007.

19. United Nations Global Coalition on Women and AIDS. *Research Dossier: HIV Prevention for Girls and Young Women in Kenya.* London, UK, 2007.

20. World Bank. *Bangladesh: Female Secondary School Assistance Project*

II. World Bank, Human Development Sector Unit, South Asia Region, 2008.

21. Schultz TP. *School Subsidies for the Poor: Evaluating a Mexican Strategy for Reducing Poverty.* FCND Discussion Paper No. 102. Washington, DC: International Food Policy Research Institute, Food Consumption and Nutrition Division, 2001.

22. Pappas G, Agha A, Rafique G, Khan KS, Badruddin SH, Peermohamed H. Community-based approaches to combating malnutrition and poor education among girls in resource-poor settings: Report of a large scale intervention in Pakistan. *Rural and Remote Health* 2008; 8(3):820.

23. World Food Programme. *School Feeding Works for Girls' Education.* Rome, Italy: WFP, 2001.

24. Kang'Ong'Oi R. Sanitary pads too expensive. The Newtimes 2009; (June 11, 2009). http://www.newtimes.co.rw/index.php?issue=13923&article=1708&week=24. Accessed December 27, 2011.

25. Kayiggwa P. Rwanda: Adolescents missing school during menstruation call for sanitary pads. The Newtimes 2007. http://allafrica.com/stories/200710120286.html. Accessed December 27, 2011.

26. Chapman DW, Kyeyune R, Lokkesmoe K. *Evaluation of the African Girls Education Initiative Country Case Study: Uganda.* New York, NY: UNICEF, 2003.

27. Insigoma J. Makapads: Makere University makes affordable sanitary pads. 2006; (December 16, 2006). http://www.ugpulse.com/business/makapads-makerere-university-makes-affordable-sanitary-pads/549/ug.aspx. Accessed December 27, 2011.

28. Devereux S. The Vision 2020 Umurenge Programme: A pathway to sustainable livelihoods for rural Rwandans? Annual IPAR Research Conference. Kigali, Rwanda: 2011.

29. United Kingdom Department for International Development. Cash protection for Rwanda's poor. London, UK: Department for International Development, 2009. http://reliefweb.int/node/305842. Accessed January 7, 2011.

30. Davis B, Winters P, Carletto G, Covarrubias K, Quinones E, Zezza A, Stamoulis K, Bonomi G, DiGiuseppe S. *Rural Income Generating Activities: A Cross Country Comparison.* Rome, Italy: United Nations Food and Agriculture Organization, Agricultural and Development Economics Division, 2007.

31. Knudsen AJ, Halvorsen K. Income-generating programs in Pakistan and Malawi: A comparative review. *Journal of Refugee Studies* 1997; 10(4):462–475.

32. Adato M, Basset L. What is the Potential of Cash Transfers to Strengthen Families Affected by HIV and AIDS? A Review of the Evidence on Im-

pacts and Key Policy Debates. Joint Learning Initiative on Children and HIV/AIDS. JLICA Learning Group 1: Strengthening Families. Washington, DC: International Food Policy Research Institute, Food Consumption and Nutrition Division, 2008.

33. Desmond C. Evaluation Report: FXB-Village Model Income Generation Sustainability. Geneva, Switzerland: FXB International, 2007.

34. Mead DC, Liedholm C. The dynamics of micro and small enterprises in developing countries. *World Development* 1998; 26(1):61–74.

35. Wilson KB. *Internally Displaced, Refugees and Returnees From and in Mozambique.* Studies on Emergencies and Disaster Relief. Uppsala, Sweden: Nordic Africa Institute, 1994.

36. James-Wilson D, Torres V, van Bastelaer T, Yamba B, Parrott L. *Economic Strengthening for Vulnerable Children: Principles of Program Design and Technical Recommendations for Effective Field Interventions.* Washington, DC: USAID, Save the Children and Academy for Educational Development, 2008.

37. Weiss J, Montgomery H. *Great Expectations: Microfinance and Poverty Reduction in Asia and Latin America.* Paper No. 15. Tokyo, Japan: ADB Institute, 2005.

38. Quinones B, Remenyi J. *Microfinance and Poverty Alleviation: Case Studies from Asia and the Pacific.* London, UK: Routledge, 2000.

39. Marcus R, Porter B, Harper C. *Money Matters: Understanding Microfinance.* London, UK: Save the Children, 1999.

40. ILO. Women in the Informal Sector and their Access to Microfinance. The Inter-Parliamentary Union Annual Conference. Windhoek, Namibia: ILO, 1998.

41. Adato M, Basset L. *Conditional Cash Transfer Programs: A "Magic Bullet" for Reducing Poverty.* Washington, DC: International Food Policy Research Institute, 2007.

42. Duflo E. Child health and household resources in South Africa: Evidence from the old age pension program. *American Economic Review* 2000; 90(2):393–398.

43. Case A, Hosegood V, Lund F. *The Reach and Impact of Child Support Grants: Evidence from KwaZulu-Natal.* Princeton, NJ: Princeton University, Woodrow Wilson School of Public and International Affairs, Center for Health and Wellbeing, 2004.

44. Del Ninno C, Subbarao K, Milazzo A. *How to Make Public Works Work: A Review of the Experiences.* Social Protection Discussion Papers. No. 0905. Washington, DC: World Bank, Social Protection and Labor, 2009.

45. Shonkoff JP, Phillips DA. Healthy development through intervention. In: Shonkoff JP, Phillips DA, eds. *From Neurons to Neighborhoods: The Science of Early Child Development.* Washington, DC: National Academy

Press, 2000.

46. Shonkoff JP, Phillips DA. Rethinking nature and nurture. In: Shonkoff JP, Phillips DA, eds. *From Neurons to Neighborhoods: The Science of Early Child Development*. Washington, DC: National Academy Press, 2000.

47. World Bank. Early Childhood Development Program Evaluations. Washington, DC: World Bank, 2009. http://web.worldbank.org/WBSITE/EXTERNAL/TOPICS/EXTCY/EXTECD/0,,contentMDK:20207792~menuPK:528428~pagePK:148956~piPK:216618~theSitePK:344939,00.html. Accessed January 9, 2012.

48. Rwanda Ministry of Education. *Education Sector Strategic Plan 2006–2010*. Kigali, Rwanda: Government of Rwanda, 2008.

49. Rwanda Ministry of Education. *Education Sector Policy*. Kigali, Rwanda: Government of Rwanda, 2003.

50. CARE, USAID, Hope for African Children Initiative. *Promoting Early Childhood for OVC in Resource Constrained Settings: the 5x5 Model*. Promising Practices. Atlanta, GA: CARE, 2006.

51. Kim J, Mungherera L, Belfer M. Integration and Expansion of Prevention of Mother-to-Child Transmission of HIV and Early Childhood Intervention Services. Joint Learning Initiative on Children and HIV/AIDS. JLICA Learning Group 3: Expanding Access to Services and Protecting Human Rights. Boston, MA: Harvard University, FXB Center, 2008.

52. Save the Children. *What's the Difference? An ECD Impact Study from Nepal*. Kathmandu, Nepal: Save the Children, 2003.

53. Behrman JR, Chen Y, Todd P. *The Impact of the Bolivian Integrated "PIDI" Preschool Program*. Philadelphia, PA: University of Pennsylvania, 2000.

54. Engle PL, Black MM, Behrman JR, Cabral de Mello M, Gertler PJ, Kapiriri L, Martorell R, Young ME. Strategies to avoid the loss of developmental potential in more than 200 million children in the developing world. *Lancet* 2007; 369(9557):229–242.

55. Powell CA, Walker SP, Chang SM, Grantham-McGregor SM. Nutrition and education: A randomized trial of the effects of breakfast in rural primary school children. *American Journal of Clinical Nutrition* 1998; 68(4):873–879.

56. Baingana F, Fuller A, Guyer AL. The Implementation Gap in Services for Children Affected by HIV/AIDS. Joint Learning Initiative on Children and HIV/AIDS. JLICA Learning Group 3: Expanding Access to Services and Protecting Human Rights. Boston, MA: Harvard University, FXB Center, 2008.

57. Jukes M, Simmons S, Fawzi MCS, Bundy D. Educational Access and HIV Prevention: Making the Case for Education as a Health Priority in Sub-Saharan Africa. Joint Learning Initiative on Children and HIV/AIDS.

JLICA Learning Group 3: Expanding Access to Services and Protecting Human Rights. Boston, MA: Harvard University, FXB Center, 2008.

58. Rwanda National Institute of Statistics. *Millennium Development Goals: Toward Sustainable Social and Economic Growth, Country Report 2007.* Kigali, Rwanda: NIS, 2007.

59. World Bank. *Rwanda: Education For All — Fast Track Initiative.* Washington, DC: World Bank, 2009.

60. National Institute of Statistics of Rwanda, Rwanda Ministry of Health, and Macro International Inc. *Rwanda Interim Demographic and Health Survey 2007–08.* DHS Final Reports. FR215. Kigali, Rwanda and Calverton, Maryland: USAID, UNDP, 2009.

61. Betcherman G, Godfrey M, Puerto S, Rother F, Stravreska A. *A Review of Interventions to Support Young Workers: Findings of the Youth Employment Inventory.* SP Discussion Paper No. 0715. Washington, DC: World Bank, Social Protection and Labor, 2007.

62. Rwanda Ministry of Health. *National Nutrition Policy.* Kigali, Rwanda: Government of Rwanda, 2005.

63. National Institute of Statistics of Rwanda. *EICV Poverty Analysis for Rwanda's Economic Development and Poverty Reduction Strategy.* Kigali, Rwanda: NISR, 2007.

64. Gentilini U. *Cash and Food Transfers: A Primer.* Rome, Italy: World Food Programme, 2007.

65. Rwanda Prime Minister's Office. *A Situation Analysis of Orphans and Other Vulnerable Children in Rwanda.* Kigali, Rwanda: Government of Rwanda, 2008.

66. Kristjansson B, Petticrew M, MacDonald B, Krasevec J, Janzen L, Greenhalgh T, Wells GA, MacGowan J, Farmer AP, Shea B, Mayhew A, Tugwell P, Welch V. School feeding for improving the physical and psychosocial health of disadvantaged students. *Cochrane Database of Systematic Reviews* 2009; 1(CD004676):1–138.

67. Adelman S, Gilligan DO, Lehrer K. *How Effective are Food for Education Programs? A Critical Assessment of the Evidence from Developing Countries.* Food Policy Series 9. Washington, DC: International Food Policy Research Institute, 2008.

68. Ahmed AU. *The Impact of Feeding Children in School: Evidence from Bangladesh.* Washington, DC: International Food Policy Research Institute, 2004.

69. Adelman S, Alderman H, Gilligan DO, Konde-Lule J. *The Impact of Alternative Food for Education Programs on Child Nutrition in Northern Uganda.* Washington, DC: International Food Policy Research Institute, 2008.

70. Taras H. Nutrition and student performance at school. *Journal of School*

Health 2005; 75(6):199–213.

71. World Food Programme. *Food Assistance Support for Education.* Rwanda Development Project 10677.0. Rome, Italy: WFP, 2007.

72. World Food Programme. *Budget Increase to Development Activities.* Rwanda Development Project 10677.0. Rome, Italy: WFP, 2011.

CHAPTER 5

Scaled-up FXB intervention: An integrated approach to poverty reduction

5.1. Background

Rwanda is one of the most densely populated countries in Africa, and the 20th poorest country in the world.[1] Its population declined from 7.15 million in 1990 to 5.5 million in 1994, owing to the genocide and associated exodus of refugees. But in recent years the population has been growing, and is estimated to be 10.6 million in 2010. The country's economy was devastated by the genocide and subsequent civil war. The conflict led to a 40% decline in GDP in the year 1994.[2] GDP per capita in 2005 international dollars decreased from PPP$812 to PPP$431 between 1993 and 1994.[3] After the genocide there was an economic recovery which resulted in real GDP growth that averaged 10.8% per year between 1996 and 2000. Growth slowed between 2001 and 2006, averaging 6.4% per year. As a result of growth since the war, GDP per capita (in 2005 international dollars) rose to PPP$971 in 2009, and was PPP$1,155 (in current international dollars) in 2010.[3]

Despite the pro-poor policies of the government and rapid economic growth, poverty rates have remained high. In 2005/06 an estimated 57% of the population was living below the national poverty line. In 2000/01 the poverty rate was 60%; thus between 2000/01 and 2005/06 there was only a three percentage point decline. Between 2000/01 and 2005/06, the proportion of people living in extreme poverty (i.e., those whose income is insufficient to meet just the minimum food requirement of 2,100 kilocalories per day) declined from 41% to 37%. The persistence of high poverty, despite rapidly increasing GDP per capita, is partly attributable to high and rising inequality. The Gini coefficient rose from 0.29 in 1985 to 0.47 in 2001, and to 0.51 in 2006.[4]

Poverty adversely affects households' ability to care for their children. A 2008 study estimated that 83% of children (i.e., about two million children) were vulnerable because of poverty or living conditions.[5] In-country consultation with the government, NGOs, multi- and bi-lateral organizations, and a review of the current socio-economic situation, have led to the identification of four actions which could be undertaken to reduce poverty and improve children's welfare. The four poverty-reduction actions identified were: promotion of income-generating activities (IGAs), provision of microfinance, the undertaking of public works, and expansion of cash transfers.

IGA interventions were emphasized during in-country consultations, particularly by NGOs. However, implementing interventions which seek to promote IGAs without considering complementary needs is likely to meet with only limited success — especially when the target population is extremely poor. When living in extreme poverty with immediate consumption needs not met, it is difficult to invest time and effort in activities that lead to increased consumption only after some delay: all effort is spent in activities that help to meet immediate needs. An *integrated* poverty reduction intervention involving basic capability enhancement — with IGAs as one among other complementary actions — is likely to be more successful. FXB International is an NGO that provides such an integrated intervention in Rwanda through its FXB-Village Program. The intervention examined in this chapter is a scaled-up FXB (SFXB) intervention.

5.2. Description of intervention

The intervention analyzed here is a set of integrated poverty reduction actions which aim to enhance people's basic capabilities. An important action in this intervention is the promotion of IGAs. The set of complementary actions is designed to respond to households' immediate basic needs, while preparing and supporting them to develop their IGAs or microenterprises. The intervention includes efforts to assist households to recover from health, consumption, and other shocks; to learn what business opportunities are available to them; and to establish their own microenterprises. The intervention combines short-term support for nutrition, education, sanitation and health, and subsequent support for microenterprise development. Microenterprise development involves the provision of training and some initial capital to households, and assistance in accessing the services of existing microfinance institutions. The goal of microenterprise development is to help households lift themselves out of poverty and sustain incomes at a higher level. Higher incomes lead to numerous consequential benefits, including improvements in children's health and education.

SFXB is targeted at ultra-poor households with children. Successful targeting requires properly-designed selection criteria implemented with the help of the local community. Once households are recruited into the program, they receive three types of support: a basic support package (BSP); an asset transfer (AT) and microfinance support (MFS); and psychosocial support and training. After three years of intensive assistance and training, households graduate from the program. See Annex 5A for a detailed description of this intervention, whose design is based on the FXB-Village Program of FXB International in Rwanda.

5.3. Estimation of costs and benefits

The costs and benefits of the intervention are examined for a cohort of 2,000 households enrolling in the program in 2012. The design of SFXB requires that staff pay close individual attention to beneficiaries and continue to maintain personal contact. Given this need, the program design has households grouped into clusters of 80 households — as in the FXB-Village Program. There are thus 25 different clusters for the cohort of 2,000 households. The costs associated with providing services are incurred during the three years following enrollment. The benefits accrue not only while a household is enrolled in the program but on an ongoing basis in the future. Although costs are incurred only in the first three years, a period of 30 years is considered for the calculation of increased household incomes and a period of 15 years for benefits to children's health and education. All monetary costs and benefits are measured in constant 2012 US$.

5.3.1. Resource requirements and costs

Resource requirements and costs of providing services to 2,000 households (approximately 10,000 persons) are estimated by use of budgetary data from the existing FXB-Village Program, which provides these services in Rwanda to clusters of 80 households each. With 2,000 households recruited into the program in 25 clusters, the human and physical resource requirements in the first three years will be: 134 staff, 25 vehicles, and 32 offices. Annual staff costs include salaries and staff training. Annual vehicle costs are calculated through annuitization of the capital investment, and include running costs such as fuel and maintenance. Office costs are based on annual rental rates for such space.

Many categories of SFXB staff require to have received some tertiary education prior to their employment — viz. at least two years of post-secondary schooling. Professional staff with such tertiary education include unit managers (6), social workers (25), nurse counselors (25), bookkeepers (6), procurement and distribution officers (26), and other professional staff (9). Other staffing categories include drivers (25) and office security guards (13). Table 5.1 summarizes coverage of the program and its associated resource requirements.

Table 5.1. SFXB program coverage and resource requirements

SFXB program coverage and inputs	Year 1 2012	Year 2 2013	Year 3 2014
Program coverage			
Number of supported households	2,000	2,000	2,000
Number of supported persons	10,000	10,000	10,000
Staff (number)	**134**	**134**	**134**
Professionals as % of total	88	88	88
Other staff as % of total	12	12	12
Vehicles and offices			
Vehicles (number)	25	25	25
Office rooms (number)	32	32	32

Total costs can be classified into two major categories: costs of direct support and costs of implementation. Direct support costs are defined as the value of goods and materials provided to households by SFXB; implementation costs are defined as the costs of delivering these goods and providing complementary services such as psychosocial support and training. Direct support costs consist of transfers to households through BSP (in the form of food, healthcare, education, housing, water and sanitation), and asset transfers (ATs). Implementation costs consist of staff salaries, staff training costs, vehicle expenditure, non-salary recurrent expenditure, and administrative overhead. Implementation costs account for more than half of the total costs.

Average total cost per household is expected to decline from US$900 in year 1 (2012) to US$600 in year 3 (2014). This decline occurs because the level of BSP is larger in year 1 than in years 2 and 3. Table 5.2 provides details of SFXB costs for a cohort of 2,000 households. Costs for a *single* cluster of 80 households are provided in table 5C.1 in Annex 5C.

The present value (PV) in 2012 US$ of the total costs of the intervention over the 3-year period at a discount rate of 3% per annum is US$4.5 million.

5.3.2. Methods and assumptions for estimation of benefits

We consider both the constitutive and the consequential benefits which arise from this intervention. Constitutive benefits consist of increases in household income brought about by the program, both before and after graduation. Constitutive benefits also include non-income benefits to households while they are enrolled in the program, such as improved school attendance of children and fewer deaths among children under five. Among

Table 5.2. SFXB cost estimates for 2,000 households (2012 US$ thousand)

	Year 1 2012	Year 2 2013	Year 3 2014
Direct transfers (2012 US$ thousand)			
Basic support package	782	319	222
Asset transfer	0	270	0
Implementation cost (2012 US$ thousand)			
Salaries	615	627	640
Staff training	9	0	0
Vehicle expenditure	133	133	133
Non-salary recurrent expenditure	171	171	171
Beneficiary training (venue and materials)	11	11	11
Administrative overhead	79	60	23
Total cost (2012 US$ thousand)	**1,799**	**1,592**	**1,200**
Implementation cost as % of total cost	57	63	82
Total cost per household (2012 US$)	**900**	**796**	**600**

constitutive benefits that are quantifiable, we have chosen a subset to provide a summary. For example, years of schooling is used as a summary measure of child education benefits, and under-five mortality as a summary measure of child health benefits. Constitutive benefits that are not quantifiable are not reported here, and hence we understate the total constitutive benefits of the intervention.

Consequential benefits occur largely after graduation and consist of further health and education benefits that result from higher household incomes in the future. The benefits also include other capability enhancements.

The quantified constitutive benefits are calculated by comparing with- and without-intervention estimates of school enrollment and under-five mortality. With-intervention estimates of school enrollment and under-five mortality are based on information provided by FXB-Village Program staff and a review of program data. Without-intervention estimates of school enrollment and under-five mortality are based on data for extremely poor households extracted from DHS 2005.

Increases in income as a result of the intervention consist of increases in income both during the program period (years 1–3) and after graduation from the program (years 4–30). Increases in income during the program are taken to be the value of in-kind transfers through BSP and that of the initial capital transfer. To estimate the increase in incomes of households after graduation, we need to predict the level of incomes in year 4 and the growth rates of income for years 4–30, all measured at 2012 prices. This time path of incomes needs to be compared with the time path of incomes for these households if they had not enrolled in the program. For graduates of the program, the levels of household income in year 4 are based on evaluation data from the FXB-Village Program currently operating in Rwanda.[6]

Aggregate household income is taken to grow at the same rate as that projected for real GDP in years 4–30. For this period we project GDP per capita to grow at the same rate as it did during 2005–9. The incomes of households at different income levels, however, are not all taken to grow at the same rate as aggregate household income. For the period 2000/01–2005/06 for which household income (expenditure) data are available, we know that the incomes of non-poor households grew much faster than those of poor households. To forecast household incomes in the future, we posit a linear relationship between household income growth and household income level, constraining aggregate household income to grow at the same rate as GDP. This generates the required formula to predict household income levels in years 5–30 from their levels in year 4.

In order to calculate the consequential benefits arising from higher incomes, we estimate a relationship between the outcomes of interest (school enrollment and under-five mortality) and household income. The consequences for school enrollment and under-five mortality can then be forecast from the income levels for each year of the projection.

The consequences for health and education are projected for 15 years, whereas household income itself is projected for 30 years. To estimate health and education consequences requires information on the age composition of children in the household. It is not clear how this might change over the 30-year projection period, but we assume that the average age composition of children remains essentially stable in years 1–15. This is tantamount to assuming that aging of children in, and departure of children from, households is balanced by new births. To predict age composition of households beyond 15 years requires demographic modeling that is beyond the scope of this study. Hence, the longer-run (years 16–30) effects of household income on health and education are not included, leading to an underestimation of total consequential benefits. We project household income for 30 years on the assumption that, even if composition changes, higher incomes will continue to accrue to these households.

Estimating constitutive education and health benefits
Constitutive education and health benefits are calculated by taking the

differences in school enrollment and under-five mortality that occur in years 1–3 *with-* and *without-*program implementation. The program is targeted at households in extreme poverty, specifically at those in quintile 1 of the income distribution. We assume that 90% of households enrolled in SFXB are drawn from quintile 1 of the income distribution and 10% from quintile.[2] Although data are not available on school enrollment and under-five mortality by income quintile, DHS 2005 provides such information by wealth quintile,[a] and we assume that the income and wealth quintiles contain effectively the same households.

For program households, outcomes for school enrollment and under-five mortality in years 1–3 are based on information provided by FXB-Village Program staff and a comparison of their estimates with levels of enrollment and under-five mortality observed among better-off households in DHS 2005. For non-program households, we use a weighted average of these outcomes for DHS 2005 quintiles 1 (90%) and 2 (10%) — adjusted for improvements in education since 2005. Without-intervention outcomes are subtracted from with-intervention outcomes to provide the magnitude of improvement resulting from the intervention.

Estimating the increase in income of households during years 1–3

The increase in income of households during the period of enrollment in the program (years 1–3) is taken to be the value of direct transfers to them. During years 1–3 households receive BSP and an asset transfer. These transfers serve to increase the income of households and are included as constitutive benefits of the intervention.

Estimating increases in income after graduation

The projection of incomes after graduation (years 4–30) is based on suppositions concerning the success of household (and group) IGAs/microenterprises. The projection of incomes *without* intervention is based on the level of household income in year 4 and its rate of growth during years 4–30.

We first explain how the time path of incomes *with* intervention is computed. This involves four steps concerning: (A) the level of household income at graduation; (B) the rate of business failure in the years immediately following graduation (years 4–6); (C) the rate of business setbacks and its impact on income (years 7–30); and (D) the relationship between income level and income growth rate.

A. Based on the results of the FXB-Village Program in Rwanda, we assume that at graduation (end of year 3) 70% of households will move above the poverty line and 30% will remain below it.[6] An evaluation of the FXB-Village Program found that the intervention led to 67% and 96% of participating households in rural and urban areas, respectively, moving above the poverty line by the of year 3. Over 90% of Rwanda's poor live in rural areas; therefore, we assume that at least 90% of enrolled households will be from rural areas—leading to a weighted average of 70% above the poverty line at graduation. The poverty line is specified in terms of household expenditure per equivalent adult in 2012 US$. Program households who cross the poverty line are assumed to be uniformly distributed in the expenditure interval defined by the 20% of households immediately above this line. The upper endpoint of this interval was calculated using expenditure data from the 2005/06 *Enquête Intégrale sur les Conditions de Vie des ménages de Rwanda* (EICV) expressed in 2012 US$. The expenditure level corresponding to the upper endpoint of this interval turns out to be 1.6 times the poverty line. The 30% of program households who remain below the poverty line are assumed to be uniformly distributed below it.

B. The early life of a microenterprise or IGA is generally considered to be a risky period.[7,8] For this reason we take account of possible failure of microenterprises and IGAs once intensive support is withdrawn at graduation. Although data on the general rate of microenterprise failures are available for the East Africa region, no information is available on the specific failure rate of microenterprises following a period of intensive support and training. We assume that during the first three years following graduation (years 4–6) a total of 10% of microenterprises and IGAs will fail. We take such failure to mean that these households fall back *below* the poverty line.

C. Once microenterprises survive years 4–6, businesses are not likely to fail completely but may suffer periodic setbacks. We assume that 3% of microenterprises suffer a setback in year 7 and that this rate declines linearly to 1% in year 30. By a business setback we mean a once-for-all negative shock which leads to a 30% decline in income in the year of the setback; thereafter, however, we assume that household incomes continue to rise at a normal rate. Of course, instead of setbacks some microenterprises may enjoy extraordinary successes, but we do not take this possibility into account.

D. Although aggregate household income in years 4–30 has been taken to grow at the same rate as GDP, increasing inequality in Rwanda suggests that non-poor households experience higher rates of income growth than poor households. Forecasting future income levels thus requires an estimate of the differential income growth rate of households at different income levels. The relationship between income growth rate and income level was estimated from trends in historical data and assumptions about the effect of pro-poor government policies.

EICV 2005/06 and the EICV 2000/01 provide information on household expenditure but not on household income. We use data on household expenditure as a proxy for household income. This is a reasonable supposition for most households in the survey, because we do not expect any significant saving except by the richest of households. A comparison of disaggregated household expenditure data from 2000/01 and 2005/06 shows that expenditures of households above the poverty line increased much faster than expenditures of households below the poverty line. If this trend continues, we expect the growth rate of household expenditure to be a monotonic increasing function of the level of household expenditure.

We estimate this function from primary data for EICV 2005/06 and from published information for EICV 2000/01. For EICV 2000/01 we do not have access to the primary data, and the published information provides only the average expenditure of poor households. By using GDP data for 2000, we can impute the average expenditure of non-poor households in 2000/01. For 2005/06 we are able to calculate directly the average expenditure of both poor and non-poor households. Thus, after correcting for inflation, we know the growth rate of real expenditure between 2000/01 and 2005/06 for both poor and non-poor households. To reflect the higher growth rate of GDP per capita observed between 2005 and 2009 (5.1% per annum) compared to the period 2000–05 (3.4% per annum), we raise the growth rate of expenditure of both poor and non-poor households by a factor of 1.5 (i.e., 5.1/3.4). Finally, to account for the fact that recent government policies are likely to have increased the income growth rate of households below the poverty line,[b] one percentage point is added to the income growth rate of the poor and an appropriate reduction is made to the income growth rate of the non-poor so that the growth rate of aggregate income (of the poor and non-poor combined) remains equal to that of GDP. A straight line is then joined through these two points to provide the relationship between the growth rate and the level of household expenditure (income).

This function is applied to levels of household income in year 4 (step A) to forecast incomes in years 5–30. These forecasts are adjusted for the possibility of microenterprise failures (step B) and setbacks (step C) to provide the time path of incomes *with* intervention.

We now explain how the time path of incomes *without* intervention is computed. This involves two steps concerning: (i) the income levels of households in year 1 if they are not enrolled in the program; and (ii) their income growth rates in order to forecast income levels for years 2–30.

i. Our targeting assumption is that 90% of program households are drawn uniformly from quintile 1 of the income/expenditure distribution and 10% from quintile 2. To determine their income levels in year 1, we need estimates of the endpoints of the income intervals corresponding to quintiles 1 and 2, respectively. We use the EICV 2005/06 expenditure data to provide these endpoints for the year 2005/06. The expenditure endpoints in 2005/06 are projected to 2012 levels (at 2005 prices) by applying the linear function described above. Finally, these estimates are converted to 2012 US$ to account for inflation between 2005/06 and 2012. The expenditure of households selected from each quintile is assumed to be uniformly distributed within that quintile. This provides an estimate of expenditure (income) for year 1 of the projection, i.e., 2012.

ii. Income levels for years 2–30 are projected by applying recursively the linear function linking the growth rate of household income to the level of household income.

One final adjustment is made to incomes *with-* and *without-*intervention to account for the fact that income data are obtained from household surveys, which typically underestimate true household incomes (expenditures). For example, compared to national accounts data, average household income (expenditure) measured through surveys can be 40–50% lower.[9] It is thus regarded as reasonable by some to adjust survey estimates up towards the corresponding national accounts figures.[10] The survey expenditure estimates can be scaled — partially or fully — to the level of average Household Final Consumption Expenditure (HFCE) in the national accounts. The expenditure data from EICV 2005/06 yield a mean household expenditure which is 58% of average HFCE in the national accounts. We adopt a scaling factor denoted by λ, where $\lambda = 0$ implies no scaling and $\lambda = 1$ implies scaling the survey mean all the way up to the HFCE mean. We choose a value of $\lambda = 0.5$, and examine the implications of applying $\lambda = 0$ or $\lambda = 1$ in sensitivity analysis in section 5.3.3.

Together the above steps allow us to estimate a time path of incomes *with-* and *without-*intervention. Subtracting one from the other provides a forecast of the time path of the *increase* in incomes that result from the intervention.

Estimating consequential benefits

Consequential benefits occur mainly after graduation and consist of child health and education benefits that result from higher household incomes in the future. Four steps are involved in calculating the magnitude of these benefits which concern: (1) data on child outcomes classified by household income and other determinants; (2) regression analysis to isolate the effect of changes in household income on child outcomes; (3) predicting child outcomes with- and without-intervention; and (4) non-income effects arising from the intensive training and support received during the program period.

1. We do not have data on child health and education classified directly by

household income. EICV 2005/06 contains expenditure (income) information, but no data on child health and education outcomes. DHS 2005 does contain information on socioeconomic variables, including health and education, but does not include income (expenditure) data. However, from the asset index compiled using DHS data on consumer durables, we can group households into wealth quintiles. To create a link between child outcomes and income by quintile, we first match the expenditure quintiles of EICV to the wealth quintiles of DHS, i.e., we assume that the DHS wealth quintiles and the EICV expenditure quintiles comprise the same households. We then convert the household expenditure quintiles into income intervals by calculating the lower and upper expenditure endpoints that correspond to these quintiles. Thus we have a linking of data on child outcomes and absolute expenditure (income) intervals.

2. Child outcomes depend on both income and other household characteristics, such as adult education, household size, etc. To isolate the effects of changes in household income on education outcomes, we estimate regression equations using the DHS 2005 unit record data. The dependent variables are primary- or secondary-school enrollment of a child, and the independent variables are the following: average number of years of completed education of adults in the household, gender and age of household head, household size, urban/rural location, age and gender of child, orphan status of child, relationship of child to household head, and household income interval. Logit regressions provide the probability of school enrollment conditional on values of the independent variables (the results are reported in table 5B.4 in Annex 5B). For all independent variables except household income, we assign to households enrolled in the program the average value of the variable for quintile 1 (income interval 1). The probability of school enrollment among households with these characteristics then becomes a function only of their household income.

   This method is applied to the three education outcomes: age-appropriate primary-school enrollment, over-age primary-school enrollment, and secondary-school enrollment. Child health outcomes are summarized by under-five mortality, but we do not use this method to isolate the effects of household income. Instead, we simply assign the under-five mortality associated with the income interval to which a household belongs, without holding other determinants of under-five mortality constant at the average level for households in quintile 1.

3. Given the procedure outlined above, child outcomes are a function only of household income in the case of both school enrollment and under-five mortality. The predicted income of a household is used to place it in one of the five income intervals. This allows us to estimate school enroll-

ment and under-five mortality from household income for each year of the 15-year projection period, with and without intervention.

4. The intensive training and support received during the program is likely to help improve education outcomes independently of any increase in household incomes. This non-income effect is taken into account as follows. We first calculate the probability of school enrollment conditional on the income interval into which a household moves after the intervention, i.e., as in step (3). This probability is then adjusted upwards to reflect the effects of the training received while enrolled in the program. Informed by discussion with FXB-Village Program staff, we have adjusted the probability of over-age primary-school enrollment by a factor of 1.1 and of secondary-school enrollment by a factor of 2.0.

Together, the above four steps allow us to forecast school enrollment and under-five mortality *with* and *without* intervention. Subtracting one from the other provides a prediction of the *increase* in quantified consequential benefits that result from the intervention. See Annex 5B for further details on the methods and assumptions used to estimate constitutive and consequential benefits.

5.3.3. Constitutive benefits
Quantified constitutive benefits
The constitutive benefits of SFXB are the increased incomes of extremely poor households and their improved child health and education outcomes. Using the methods described above, we estimate that SFXB will lead to a present value of *increased* household incomes over a 30-year period, discounted at 3% per annum, of US$21.2 million. The present value of the total costs of SFXB is US$4.5 million. Thus the *net present value* (NPV) of the financial benefits and costs of SFXB is US$16.7 million.

Approximately 70% of households are estimated to move out of poverty at graduation (end of year 3).[c] Because of early failures of some IGAs and microenterprises, the percentage of households above the poverty line falls from 70% in year 4 to (a minimum of) 62% in year 6, but by year 15 it recovers to 70% as a result of subsequent income growth. On average, between years 4 and 15, 67% of households are above the poverty line income as a result of the intervention. (After year 20 some households will move out of poverty simply on account of the income growth assumed for everyone without intervention.)

The constitutive benefits for child health and education occur in years 1–3 during enrollment in the program. The number of years of primary-school education for children of appropriate age increase by 7%; given that primary-school enrollment for the age-appropriate group of children is already high, there is not much room for improvement. The number of years of primary-school education for over-age children almost double (a 1.8-fold increase), there being significant room for improvement for this group. The number of years of secondary-school education increase more than 3-fold; there is considerable room for improvement here because very few children from extremely poor households attend secondary school. The constitutive benefits relating to child health are estimated to be a 14% lower under-five mortality rate (132 deaths per 1,000 live births rather than 154 deaths per 1,000). With a cohort of 2,000 households, this improvement in under-five mortality will lead to 23 fewer instances of under-five deaths during the three years of basic support. The decrease in mortality is only one indication of the health benefits of SFXB. There are health benefits other than reduced mortality on account of improved nutrition and access to medical care. Preliminary results from the FXB-Village monitoring and evaluation system suggest that the incidence of hunger and diarrhea decreases as a result of the intervention: the percentage of households going a whole day without food falls from 91% at enrollment to 7% in year 1 to 1% in year 3. Similarly, diarrhea prevalence among under-fives falls from 30% at enrollment to no reported cases from year 2 onwards.[11]

The quantified constitutive benefits for the cohort of 2,000 households are summarized in table 5.3. Results for a single cluster of 80 households (the unit in the FXB-Village Program) are provided in Annex 5C.

5.3.4. Consequential benefits

The consequential benefits of this intervention occur primarily after households graduate from the program. To the extent possible, we have attempted to quantify these benefits. There are consequential benefits that we have identified but not quantified, and these are discussed below.

Quantified consequential benefits

The consequential benefits of the intervention are the post-program improvements in child health and education attributable to the intervention. Table 5.3 summarizes these benefits for years 4–15. Unlike income forecasts that are made for 30 years, child health and education benefits are restricted to a period of 15 years because of our limited knowledge of long-term changes in household composition. During years 4–15, the number of years of education for children of primary-school age is expected to increase by a modest 1%. The number of years of primary-school education for over-age children is expected to increase by 134%. Finally, the number of years of secondary education for children is expected to increase by 241%. During years 4–15, *without* SFXB the under-five mortality rate will be 149 deaths per 1,000 live births. *With* SFXB it is expected to be 139 deaths per 1,000 live

Table 5.3. Quantified constitutive and consequential benefits of SFXB

CONSTITUTIVE BENEFITS	
Poverty reduction at graduation	
% of households moved out of poverty	70
Number of persons moved out of poverty	7,000
Present value of increased incomes in years 1–30 (2012 US$ million)	**21.2**
During program (years 1–3)	1.3
Post-program (years 4–30)	19.9
% increase in years of primary education (years 1–3)	
Age-appropriate	7
Over-age	84
% increase in years of secondary education (years 1–3)	212
% decline in under-five mortality (years 1–3)	14
CONSEQUENTIAL BENEFITS (YEARS 4–15)	
% increase in years of primary education	
Age-appropriate	1
Over-age	134
% increase in years of secondary education	241
% decline in under-five mortality	6
FINANCIAL BENEFITS/COSTS (YEARS 1–30)	
PV of increased incomes in years 1–30 (2012 US$ million)	**21.2**
PV of total costs (2012 US$ million)	**4.5**
NPV of increased incomes in years 1–30 (2012 US$ million)	**16.7**

births, i.e., 6% lower. This lower rate implies 38 fewer instances of under-five mortality among children in the cohort of 2,000 households.

Non-quantified consequential benefits

Some consequential benefits cannot be quantified easily, either due to data limitations or because of the nature of the benefit. In table 5.4 we have identified some of the non-quantified consequential benefits that result from the quantified constitutive and consequential benefits, and the path-

Table 5.4. Non-quantified consequential benefits of SFXB

Quantified benefit leading to non-quantified consequential benefit	Pathway to consequential benefit	Non-quantified consequential benefit
Increased household income from basic support package and earnings from IGAs and microenterprises	1. Improved nutritional intake among children 2. Improved nutrition among adults 3. Improved access to education and health services 4. Employment creation through IGAs and microenterprises 5. Multiplier impact on income of the community	• Lower rates of absenteeism and grade repetition (1, 3) • Improved cognitive ability and school performance (1) • Improved child health through improvement in children's ability to resist infectious diseases (1, 3) • Better quality of life (1, 2, 3) • Improved adult productivity (2, 3) • Employment of community members (4) • Increase in community income (5)
Increased years of primary and secondary education	1. Reduced HIV risk behavior 2. Increased labor productivity in the future 3. Secondary education increases the probability of formal-sector employment 4. Improved health-seeking behaviors 5. Increased adoption of modern family planning in the future	• Decline in HIV incidence (1) • Higher future earnings (2, 3) • Improved maternal health in the future (4, 5) • Decline in fertility (5)

continued

Table 5.4. Non-quantified consequential benefits of SFXB *(continued)*

Quantified benefit leading to non-quantified consequential benefit	Pathway to consequential benefit	Non-quantified consequential benefit
Reduced under-five mortality	1. More children alive 2. Reduced suffering and distress for families 3. Less time spent caring for dying children	• Improved family well-being (1, 2) • Increased time available for other productive activities (3)

ways through which these non-quantified benefits arise. Empirical evidence from published sources has been used to ascertain the causal pathways, and is discussed in the text.

Non-quantified consequential benefits resulting from increased household income

Income is expected to be higher for SFXB households as a result of both direct transfers and increased earnings from IGAs or microenterprises. Higher income levels lead to a number of consequential benefits that we have not quantified. With an increase in income, households are able to spend more on food with a resultant improvement in their members' nutritional status. There is evidence that improvement in children's nutrition leads to improved school attendance and cognitive ability, and a better quality of life.[12] Given that 50% of Rwandan children under five years of age are stunted and 20% are underweight,[13] there is much scope for improvement in children's nutritional status. Better nutrition also has benefits for adults — for example, in improving productivity and quality of life.

Increases in household income also lead to improved access to health services, through families being better able to meet the costs of healthcare.[14] Increased access to healthcare is likely to lead to improved child and adult health.[15]

Some IGAs and microenterprises require the employment of non-family members. In this case IGAs can help to create employment among members of the local community.

An increase in the incomes of participating households can, through a multiplier effect, lead to an increase in incomes of other community members. For example, there is evidence of income-multiplier effects in cash-transfer programs when the cash is invested in income-generating activities.[16,17]

Non-quantified consequential benefits resulting from increases in primary and secondary education

SFXB leads to both constitutive and consequential benefits in terms of education. The constitutive benefits arise from SFXB support of school enrollment in years 1–3 of the program, and the consequential benefits arise from increases in household income in years 4–15 which lead to higher enrollment. In turn, the increases in primary and secondary education lead to a number of consequential benefits — higher future earnings, reduced fertility, and improved health. According to a World Bank report, the private returns to primary and secondary education in Rwanda are high.[18] Also, according to a study in Kenya, secondary education improves the chances of getting a formal-sector job.[19]

Increased primary and secondary education leads to improved health and lower fertility in later life. Higher levels of girls' education positively influence their health-seeking behavior and adoption of modern contraceptive methods. For example, Wirth et al. find that 42% of Ethiopian women with secondary education had skilled birth attendants present during childbirth, compared to 10% and 3% for those with primary and no education, respectively.[20] Similarly, women with secondary education were 2.6 times more likely to receive antenatal care than women with no education.[21] Empirical evidence from elsewhere in the world suggests that improved education is associated with better maternal health, less early marriage, more frequent adoption of modern contraceptives, and lower fertility rates.[19,20,22,23]

Non-quantified consequential benefits resulting from reductions in under-five mortality

Child deaths cause suffering and distress in families; their reduction leads to improved family well-being. Deaths of children are generally correlated with illness among children. Fewer child deaths mean that less time is spent by adults in caring for dying and ill children. This leaves more time available to adults for other productive activities.

5.3.5. Sensitivity analysis

A number of assumptions have been made to estimate the impact of SFXB on incomes over a 30-year period and on health and education over a 15-year period. Information on the short-term outcomes of this intervention is available through FXB-Village Program staff and an impact evaluation study, but data relating to longer-term impacts have not been assembled as yet. Given the limited availability of data and length of the projection period, we consider the effects of varying the key assumptions made, i.e., we conduct a sensitivity analysis.

The longer-term impacts of SFXB are driven primarily by income gains in years 4–30 after enrollment in the program. The income increases will in turn affect consequential health and education outcomes which are a function of income. We therefore focus attention on the sensitivity of increased incomes in years 4–30 to key assumptions made. We summarize income gains over time by the present value (PV) of increased incomes in years 4–30 discounted at 3% per annum. The changes in the PV of increased incomes provide a direct indication of changes to a quantified constitutive benefit; they also provide an indirect indication of changes to consequential health and education benefits. Table 5.5 shows how the PV of increased incomes in years 4–30 is affected by changes in central assumptions.

The *net present value* (NPV) of increased incomes in years 1–30 requires adding to the PV of increased incomes post-program the PV of increased incomes in years 1–3 (US$1.3 million) and subtracting the PV of total costs (US$4.5 million) — see table 5.3. This results in a fixed absolute amount of US$3.2 million that must be subtracted from the PV of increased incomes in years 4–30 to calculate the NPV of increased incomes in years 1–30. Hence the percentage impact of a change in an assumption will be larger for NPV of increased incomes in years 1–30 than for the PV of increased incomes in years 4–30.

1. Our targeting assumption is that 90% of program households are selected from quintile 1 of the income/expenditure distribution and 10% from quintile 2. If *all* households were selected from quintile 1, the PV of increased incomes would be 5% larger; if 80% were selected from quintile 1 and 20% from quintile 2, the PV of increased incomes would be 5% smaller. For every 10 percentage point decrease in the proportion of households selected from quintile 1 (with the remainder selected from quintile 2), the PV is 5% smaller.

2. We have assumed that as a result of BSP, asset transfers and IGA/micro-enterprise development, 70% of households move above the poverty line by the end of year 3. For reasons mentioned in Annex 5B this percentage is likely to be an *underestimate*. If, as an alternative, we assume that 90% move above the poverty line by the end of year 3, the PV of increased incomes will be 22% larger. A 20-point increase (decrease) in this percentage raises (lowers) the PV of increased incomes by 22%.

3. We have assumed that the 70% of households who move above the poverty line at graduation will be distributed uniformly in the income interval corresponding to 1 quintile immediately above the line. If instead we assume that they are distributed uniformly in the income interval corresponding to 1.5 quintiles above the poverty line, the PV of increased incomes will be 135% higher. If the assumption is changed from 1 quintile to 0.5 quintile above the line, the PV of increased incomes will be 24% lower. The reason for this asymmetric variation is that the upper

Table 5.5. Sensitivity of PV of increased incomes in years 4–30 to changes in central assumptions

Central assumption	Alternative assumption 1	Change in PV using assumption 1	Alternative assumption 2	Change in PV using assumption 2
(1) 90% of households enrolled from quintile 1	100% enrolled	+5%	80% enrolled	–5%
(2) 70% of households move above the poverty line by end of year 3	90% move above poverty line	+22%	50% move above poverty line	–22%
(3) Distribution of households at graduation (year 4) in income interval corresponding to 1 quintile above the poverty line	1.5 quintiles above the poverty line	+135%	0.5 quintile above the poverty line	–24%
(4) 10% of IGAs/microenterprises fail within 3 years after graduation (in years 4–6)	5% fail	+4%	15% fail	–4%
(5) 3% of businesses suffer a setback in year 7, and thereafter the annual rate of business setbacks declines linearly to 1% in year 30	1% in each of years 7–30	+13%	5% in year 7, declining linearly to 1% in year 30	–12%
(6) Once-for-all decrease of 30% in household income as a result of a business setback	Once-for-all 10% decrease	+15%	Once-for-all 50% decrease	–13%
(7) Annual growth rate of GDP per capita in years 1–30 equal to annual growth rate during 2005–09	Annual growth rate 20% higher	+30%	Annual growth rate 20% lower	–18%
(8) $\lambda = 0.5$	$\lambda = 1$	+27%	$\lambda = 0$	–27%

endpoint of the income interval corresponding to a higher percentile increases disproportionately with the percentile. Thus the upper endpoint of the income interval corresponding to 0.5 quintile immediately above the poverty line is a factor of 1.2 times the poverty line; that corresponding to 1 quintile is a factor of 1.6 times the poverty line; and that corresponding to 1.5 quintiles is a factor of 3.2 times the poverty line.

4. We have assumed that 10% of IGAs/microenterprises fail in years 4–6. If the assumed failure rate is reduced to 5%, the PV of the increased incomes rises by 4%; if the failure rate is raised to 15%, the PV of increased incomes falls by 4%.

5. We have assumed that 3% of businesses suffer a setback in year 7, and thereafter the annual rate of business setbacks declines linearly to 1% in year 30. By a business setback we mean a once-for-all negative shock that leads to a 30% decrease in household income in the year of the setback. If instead the rate of business setbacks is assumed to be 1% in *each* of years 7–30, then the PV of increased incomes rises by 13%. If the rate of business setbacks is 5% (instead of 3%) in year 7, and thereafter the rate declines linearly from 5% to 1% in year 30, the PV of increased incomes falls by 12%.

6. We have assumed that a business setback leads to a once-for-all decrease of 30% in household income in the year of the setback. If instead a business setback leads to a once-for-all decrease of 10% in household income, then the PV of increased incomes will be 15% higher; if it leads to a once-for-all decrease of 50% in household income, then the PV of increased incomes will be 13% lower.

7. We have assumed that GDP per capita in years 1–30 will grow at the annual rate observed during 2005–09, i.e., at 5.1% per annum. If the annual growth rate of GDP per capita in years 1–30 is 20% higher, i.e., it is 6.1% per annum, then the PV of increased incomes will be 30% larger; if the annual growth rate is 20% lower, then the PV of increased incomes will be 18% smaller.

8. We have used household survey data to estimate the incomes of households above (and below) the poverty line, by assuming that households are distributed uniformly in the income interval corresponding to 1 quintile immediately above the line (and distributed uniformly below it). The boundaries of the income interval were calculated directly from EICV 2005/06 survey data on household expenditures. However, it is known that household expenditure (and income) from surveys typically underestimate true household expenditure (income). The correction for this underestimation is made by adjusting survey estimates up towards the corresponding national accounts figures. We have used a scaling factor of λ = 0.5 to adjust all EICV household expenditures up by half the difference

between average Household Final Consumption Expenditure (HFCE) in the national accounts and mean survey expenditure. If instead we assume $\lambda = 1$ (full adjustment), the PV of increased incomes rises by 27%; if we assume $\lambda = 0$ (no adjustment) the PV of increased incomes falls by 27%.

The value used for λ affects estimates of household income, but not the consequential health and education benefits — which are based on the *quintile* to which a household belongs. Although income increases lead to reduced under-five mortality, there are sharply diminishing returns in the relationship: under-five mortality is much larger in quintile 1 than in quintile 2 (or in higher quintiles). Therefore, estimates of under-five deaths avoided by higher incomes are sensitive to the proportions in which enrolled households are drawn from quintiles 1 and 2, respectively. If *all* households are drawn from quintile 1 (and none from quintile 2), the number of under-five deaths avoided as a result of the SFXB intervention will be 10% greater.

Consequential benefits also arise from non-income effects of the intervention. The training and encouragement that adults receive during the program will continue to affect their motivation to send children to school after graduation. Even small effects of training can dominate the consequential education benefits when education outcomes do not vary significantly with income, as in the case of enrollment of over-age children in primary school. For example, if households who have been through the program are just 10% more likely to send their over-age children to primary school, the number of years of primary education received by these children will be several-fold larger.

We have conducted sensitivity analysis on the results of the SFXB intervention because of the need to make assumptions given limited data on impacts. The exercise helps us to identify variables and assumptions that have a significant effect on outcomes. For evaluation in the future we believe there is a clear need for more comprehensive data on the impacts of this type of intervention.

5.4. Summary and conclusion

The costs of implementing SFXB for 2,000 households (25 clusters of 80 households each) are incurred during the three years of direct support, i.e., years 1–3. The present value of the total costs of the intervention in 2012 US$ over the 3-year period is US$4.5 million.

Two types of constitutive benefit result from this investment: immediate gains in health and education for children in enrolled households (years 1–3); and increases in household income during years 1–30 (in-kind transfers in years 1–3 and income increases from IGAs/microenterprises in years 4–30). During years 1–3, the intensive support is expected to lead to a 7% increase in years of primary education for children of primary-school age, and an 84% increase in years of primary education for over–age children. Furthermore, during years 1-3, there is expected to be a 212% increase in years of secondary education, and a 14% decline in under-five mortality (see table 5.3).

On the income side, we estimate that the intervention results in a present value of increased household incomes in years 1–30 of US$21.2 million. With the present value of costs of the program at US$4.5 million, the *net present value* of increased incomes from the intervention is US$16.7 million.

A number of consequential benefits arise from the increased incomes, and from the training and encouragement received during the program. The quantified consequential benefits in years 4–15 include increases in years of primary and secondary schooling, e.g. a 241% increase in years of secondary education. Quantified consequential benefits in years 4–15 also include a 6% reduction in under-five mortality.

The analysis undertaken in this chapter highlights a number of considerations in implementing a program of this type. To maximize both income and non-income benefits it is important to enroll the poorest households. But the evaluation of such a program should not consist simply in terms of its success in reducing poverty: it should include the potentially large income gains of those who move above the poverty line. Some consequential outcomes may not be very sensitive to increases in income, and there may be need for support and training that focuses specifically on improving such outcomes. Thus if discrimination against girls leads to very few girls attending school, independent of household income, then support and training should focus on informing adults of the importance of girls' education.

The implementation of an intervention of this type requires skilled staff. If such an intervention is to be scaled-up, and the supply of qualified staff is inadequate, investment in training appropriately skilled staff will be needed. Scaling-up may also require special attention to ensure that service standards are maintained with expansion.

SFXB is based on a rationale of family-strengthening, and involves a set of complementary actions designed to enhance capabilities in a sustainable manner. The set of actions is intended not only to provide short-term support but to help change the course of people's lives. Hence, the intervention is an *investment* and should be evaluated accordingly — in relation to its benefits over the long term. If the benefits are counted only for the period of intensive support (years 1–3), the magnitude of total benefits of the intervention will be seriously underestimated.

The SFXB intervention package consists of a set of contemporaneous and complementary actions. For extremely poor households, BSP, training and psychosocial support are a prerequisite for IGA or microenterprise development. Owing to the complementary nature of the actions, it is not possible to attribute the results of an action undertaken in one dimension to that dimension alone. Thus, the income increases that result from the SFXB program cannot be attributed solely to asset transfers or IGA/microenterprise training: they arise from the package as a whole. We believe that a singular focus on IGA/microenterprise investment is unlikely to lead to similar impacts on income, let alone on health and education outcomes. Understanding the importance of complementarity is critical to the design of SFXB.

ANNEX
Annex 5A. Description of intervention

Intervention: A set of complementary actions intended to enhance human capabilities. SFXB is designed to assist households to minimize the impact of extreme income and human poverty in the short term, and to establish IGAs/microenterprises to lift themselves out of poverty and sustain incomes at higher levels in the long term.

Goal: The goal of the intervention is to improve the well-being of families living in extreme poverty by providing short-term direct support and promoting long-term expansion of capabilities and income.

Components of support: The program enrolls households for a three-year period of intensive support. In these three years households are provided with complementary services in different areas including nutrition, psychosocial support, housing, healthcare, etc. The types of support are described below and the timing of these services is shown in figure 5A.1.

- **Basic support package (BSP)**: As part of capability enhancement, households are supported with in-kind transfers to ensure that basic nutrition, education, healthcare, and water and sanitation needs are met for three

Figure 5A.1. SFXB intervention timeline

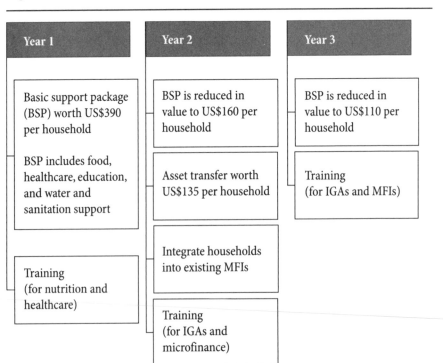

years. The value of BSP is scaled back gradually over the three years as households become self-sufficient.

Two services are provided to facilitate access to the capital needed to develop IGAs or microenterprises:

- *Asset transfer (AT)*: During year 2 of the program, each household receives an in-kind transfer of productive assets worth approximately US$135 in money value.
- *Microfinance support (MFS)*: This support is designed to promote the integration of households into existing institutions that provide loans, such as saving and credit cooperatives (SACCOs), *Banque Populaire du Rwanda* (BPR), MFIs, and NGOs. To advance integration of extremely poor households into the existing microfinance system, the program encourages savings and helps households to open bank accounts.

- **Training**: Households receive monthly training during years 1–3. Topics covered in training sessions include nutrition, healthcare, entrepreneurship and microfinance. In year 1 households participate in training that focuses on child nutrition and healthcare. The training in years 2 and 3 focuses on entrepreneurship and microfinance support.

Selection of households: The program seeks to enroll ultra-poor households. Efforts are made to select the poorest households, in particular those from quintile 1 of the income/expenditure distribution. Community and local government support structures are used to identify eligible households.

Annex 5B. Assumptions and data

Program coverage and cost estimation: Projections of program coverage and costs are based on the following assumptions regarding household size and composition, and data on input costs.

Coverage and household size
- *Selection of households*: It is assumed that 90% of households are recruited from quintile 1 of the income/expenditure distribution, and 10% of households from quintile 2.

Household size and composition
- Based on DHS 2005 data, the average household size of enrolled households is assumed to be 5 persons.
- 1.5 adults per household are assumed to be actively involved in the program's income-generating activities.[24]
- The average age composition of households is assumed to remain constant over the 15-year projection period considered for health and education benefits.

Table 5B.1. SFXB households per worker by type of worker

Type of worker	SFXB households per worker
Unit manager	320
Social worker	80
Nurse/Counselor	80
Child rights promotion officer	640
HIV prevention officer	640
Bookkeeper	320
Center security guard	160
Procurement officer	160
Distribution officer	160
Microfinance advisor	640
Driver	80

Table 5B.2. Annual salary by type of worker

Type of worker	Annual salary (2012 US$)
Unit manager	8,400
Social worker	6,000
Nurse/Counselor	6,000
Child rights promotion officer	6,000
HIV prevention officer	6,000
Bookkeeper	6,000
Center security guard	1,500
Procurement officer	6,000
Distribution officer	6,000
Credit counselor	6,000
Driver	1,800

Cost information
- *Basic support package (BSP)*: The cost of basic support per household is assumed to be US$390 in year 1, US$160 in year 2, and US$110 in year 3. The cost of BSP takes account of support for: food and nutrition; health (insurance, treatment, mosquito nets, etc.); school uniforms and fees; sanitation; and water purification. Basic support continues until the end of year 3. Data on the cost of BSP are taken from the budget of the FXB-Village Program in Rwanda.

Table 5B.3. Unit cost per annum of recurrent expenditure by item

Item description	Unit cost per annum (2012 US$)
Vehicle insurance and taxes	350
Vehicle maintenance	1,800
Fuel expenses	3,900
Office rental	960
Office utilities	120
Supplies	360
Communication and telephones	600

- *Beneficiary training*: Based on FXB-Village Program records and budgetary information, it is assumed that about 50 adults participate in each monthly training session, and each session costs US$15 for materials and the training venue.
- *Asset transfer (AT)*: The average value of AT is assumed to be US$135 per household. This is the average amount provided for micro-projects in the FXB-Village Program. BRAC's program of targeting the ultra-poor in Bangladesh provides an asset transfer of US$150 per household.[25]
- *Staff*: The estimate of staff requirements is based on beneficiary-to-staff ratios of the FXB-Village Program in Rwanda.
  - Salary assumptions are based on a review of NGO budgets of similar programs in Rwanda. Salaries are assumed to increase at the rate of 2% per year for calculation of costs over the three-year period.
  - It is assumed that staff are trained for three days on the mission and strategy of SFXB, and are paid during training. Training materials are assumed to cost US$15 per staff member being trained.
  - Attrition of staff is assumed to occur at the rate of 5% per year. This assumption is based on reported attrition rates among health workers in neighboring Kenya.[26]

Vehicles and office rooms
- It is assumed that for every unit manager four vehicles are needed by staff under his/her supervision. The ratio of vehicles to unit managers is taken from the FXB-Village Program in Rwanda. The useful life of a vehicle is assumed to be 10 years.
- It is assumed that one office room is shared among three professional staff members. The staff-to-office room ratio is based on the assumption that staff members spend much of their time in the field.

Table 5B.4. Logit regressions of age-appropriate and over-age enrollment in primary school, and of enrollment in secondary school

Variables	Enrolled in primary school (age-appropriate)		Enrolled in primary school (over-age)		Enrolled in secondary school	
	Coefficient	Standard error	Coefficient	Standard error	Coefficient	Standard error
Quintile2 (yes=1)	0.227*	0.095	0.190	0.112	1.254*	0.503
Quintile3 (yes=1)	0.143	0.098	0.057	0.115	1.220*	0.478
Quintile4 (yes=1)	0.174	0.098	0.254*	0.107	1.436*	0.480
Quintile5 (yes=1)	0.682*	0.121	0.358*	0.127	2.824*	0.483
Location dummy (urban=1/rural=0)	0.195*	0.098	−0.041	0.107	0.706*	0.189
Gender of household head (HHH) (female=1)	−0.103	0.086	−0.131	0.107	−0.310	0.191
HHH age (years)	0.006	0.003	0.007*	0.003	0.007	0.006
Child age (years)	0.227*	0.018	−0.653	0.032	0.299*	0.069
Child gender (male=1)	−0.124*	0.061	0.048	0.076	0.001	0.134
Household size (number of members)	−0.009	0.017	0.081*	0.018	0.026	0.034
Only mother alive (yes=1)	0.272	0.161	−0.009	0.184	−0.111	0.241
Only father alive (yes=1)	−0.093	0.210	−0.134	0.206	−0.308	0.388
Both parents alive (yes=1)	0.094	0.227	0.252	0.250	0.132	0.398
Average number of years of completed education for adults in the household	0.147*	0.019	0.117*	0.022	0.232*	0.043
Close relative of HHH (child or spouse=1)	0.174	0.128	0.226	0.146	0.228	0.266
Not a relative of HHH (yes=1)	−1.101*	0.157	−1.175*	0.162	−0.573*	0.273
Constant	−1.384	0.294	8.999	0.565	−10.382	1.342
Number of observations	9,507		4,178		4,582	

* Significant at the 5% level

- Unit costs of recurrent expenditure on vehicles and office rooms are based on a review of the FXB-Village Program budget and are summarized in table 5B.3.

Other costs
- An administrative overhead is included at 10% of the value of direct transfers.
- The present value of costs in constant 2012 US$ is calculated by applying a discount rate of 3% per annum.

Benefits estimation
- *Household income:* The methods used to forecast household income in the projection period are described in the main text.
- *Program success rate*: 70% of households are assumed to move above the poverty line upon graduation from the program. The 70% success rate is based on an impact evaluation study of the FXB-Village Program.[6] The canvassing of household incomes in this study was based primarily on cash earnings, i.e., cash income earned through market transactions. Production for own consumption, which is often a large component of rural IGAs, was not counted as part of household income. Because such in-kind (non-cash) income was not imputed in the impact evaluation study, the post-program incomes of rural households (especially) will have been underestimated. Hence the program success rate of 70 % of households moving out of poverty is likely to be an *underestimate*.
- *Primary- and secondary-school eligibility and enrollment probabilities*: The estimates of the proportion of children eligible for primary- and secondary-school enrollment are based on household age composition by quintile obtained from DHS 2005. Baseline data on enrollment are taken from DHS 2005, and the rate of increase in national enrollment since 2005 has been applied to each quintile.
  - DHS 2005 data show that 24% of individuals in quintile 1 are primary school-age children, and that 83% of these children attend primary school. It is assumed that in the absence of the intervention this enrollment rate will increase by 1% per annum until it reaches 99%.
  - DHS 2005 data show that 11% of individuals in quintile 1 are children who are *above* primary-school age but have not yet completed primary school. All these children are assumed to be eligible to attend primary school, even though only 58% of these over-age children are currently enrolled. It is assumed that in the absence of the intervention the enrollment rate of such children will increase by 0.5% per year.
  - DHS 2005 data show that only 0.5% of individuals from quintile 1 are children who have completed primary school and are therefore eligible for enrollment in secondary school.

- *Non-income outcomes while enrolled in the program:* Enrollment assumptions for children in years 1–3 of the program and receiving BSP are based on information provided by FXB-Village Program staff and a review of this information.
  - It is assumed that 95% of primary school-age children in SFXB will enroll in primary school. This enrollment rate is assumed to increase at 1% per annum.
  - It is assumed that 95% of children who are above primary-school age but have not completed primary school, will enroll in primary school. This enrollment rate is assumed to increase at 0.5% per annum.
  - It is assumed that 20% of secondary school-age children who have completed primary school will enroll in secondary school in year 1 of the program, 40% in year 2, and 60% in year 3.
  - It is assumed that while enrolled in the program, households face an under-five mortality rate (U5MR) of 132 per 1,000 live births. This U5MR is the rate among households in quintile 3 of the DHS 2005 wealth distribution.
  - The present value of increased incomes is estimated by applying a discount rate of 3% per annum to future monetary values expressed in 2012 US$.

Regression results

To isolate the effects of changes in household income on education outcomes, regression equations have been estimated using DHS 2005 unit record data. The dependent variables are primary or secondary school enrollment, and the independent variables are as follows: average number of years of completed education of adults in the household, gender and age of household head, household size, urban/rural location, gender and age of child, orphan status of child, relationship of child to household head, and household wealth quintile. Logit regressions provide the probability of school enrollment conditional on values of the independent variables. For households enrolled in the program we assign the *average* values for quintile 1 for all independent variables except household income. The probability of school enrollment among households with these characteristics is then simply a function of household income. The regression results are summarized in table 5B.4 below.

Annex 5C. Results for a single cluster of 80 households: the FXB-Village Program

The results in the main text are presented for a cohort of 2,000 households (25 clusters of 80 households each). Given the need for staff and beneficiaries to develop a close working relationship, it is necessary for staff to work in clusters of households; in the FXB-Village Program each cluster contains 80 households. The following tables present the costs and quantified benefits for a single cluster of 80 households. They comprise the benefit-cost calculations for the implementation unit of the FXB-Village Program. (The figures presented in the text for a cohort of 2,000 households are a multiple of 25 of those shown here for a single cluster of 80 households.)

Table 5C.1 presents estimates of program coverage, staff and vehicle requirements for a single cluster of 80 households. The 5 staff include 3 full-time staff who work in a single cluster (i.e., a social worker, a nurse and a logistical support person) and 2 full-time equivalent staff. The 2 full-time equivalent staff are made up of fractions of the time of the unit manager and other staff involved in administrative and logistical support across clusters.

Table 5C.2 presents the cost estimates for a single cluster of 80 households during the three years of program implementation.

Table 5C.3 presents the quantified constitutive and consequential benefits associated with a single cluster of 80 households.

Table 5C.1. Program coverage and resource requirements for a single cluster of 80 households

Program coverage and inputs	Year 1 2012	Year 2 2013	Year 3 2014
Program coverage			
Number of supported households	80	80	80
Number of supported persons	400	400	400
Staff (number)	5	5	5
Professionals as % of total	88	88	88
Other staff as % of total	12	12	12
Vehicles and offices			
Vehicles (number)	1	1	1
Office rooms (number)	1	1	1

Table 5C.2. Cost estimates for a single cluster of 80 households (2012 US$ thousand)

Itemized cost	Year 1 2012	Year 2 2013	Year 3 2014
Direct transfers (2012 US$ thousand)			
Basic support package	31.3	12.8	8.9
Asset transfer	0	10.8	0
Implementation cost (2012 US$ thousand)			
Salaries	24.6	25.1	25.6
Staff training	0.4	0.0	0.0
Capital expenditure	5.3	5.3	5.3
Non-salary recurrent expenditure	6.8	6.8	6.8
Beneficiary training (venue and materials)	0.4	0.4	0.4
Administrative overhead	3.2	2.4	0.9
Total cost (2012 US$ thousand)	**72.0**	**63.7**	**48.0**
Implementation cost as % of total cost	57	63	82
Total cost per household (2012 US$)	**900**	**796**	**600**

Table 5C.3. Quantified constitutive and consequential benefits for a single cluster of 80 households

CONSTITUTIVE BENEFITS	
Poverty reduction at graduation	
% of households moved out of poverty	70
Number of persons moved out of poverty	280
Present value of increased incomes in years 1–30	
(2012 US$ thousand)	**849**
During program (years 1–3)	53
Post-program (years 4–30)	796
% increase in years of primary education (years 1–3)	
Age-appropriate	7
Over-age	84
% increase in years of secondary education (years 1–3)	212
% decline in under-five mortality (years 1–3)	14
CONSEQUENTIAL BENEFITS (YEARS 4–15)	
% increase in years of primary education	
Age-appropriate	1
Over-age	134
% increase in years of secondary education	241
% decline in under-five mortality	6
FINANCIAL BENEFITS/COSTS (YEARS 1–30)	
PV of increased incomes in years 1–30 (2012 US$ thousand)	**849**
PV of total costs (2012 US$ thousand)	**179**
NPV of increased incomes in years 1–30 (2012 US$ thousand)	**670**

Endnotes

a. The wealth quintiles are derived from an asset index calculated using principal component analysis on household data on consumer durables. For details, see http://www.measuredhs.com/topics/wealth/methodology.cfm.

b. Recent efforts by the government to enable income growth among poor households have included microcredit promotion, public works, cash transfers and health insurance.

c. The figure of 70% moving out of poverty at the end of year 3 is likely to be an underestimate — see Annex 5B.

References

1. World Bank. *Rwanda at a Glance.* Washington, DC: World Bank, 2008.

2. United States Department of State. *Background Note: Rwanda.* Washington, DC: US Department of State, Bureau of African Affairs, 2009.

3. World Bank. *World Development Indicators 2011.* Washington, DC: World Bank, 2011.

4. National Institute of Statistics of Rwanda. *EICV Poverty Analysis for Rwanda's Economic Development and Poverty Reduction Strategy.* Kigali, Rwanda: NISR, 2007.

5. UNICEF. *New Study Finds over 2 Million Vulnerable Children in Rwanda.* New York, NY: UNICEF, 2008.

6. Desmond C. Evaluation Report: FXB-Village Model Income Generation Sustainability. Geneva, Switzerland: FXB International, 2007.

7. Walter T, Rosa P, Barabas S, Balunywa W, Serwanga A, Namatovu R, Kyejjusa S. Global Entrepreneurship Monitor: GEM Uganda 2004 Executive Report. Kampala, Uganda: Makerere University, Business School, 2004.

8. SBP Business Environment Specialists. *Small Business Development in South Africa: Time to Re-assess.* Johannesburg, South Africa: SBP Business Environment Specialists, 2009.

9. Deaton A. Measuring poverty in a growing world (or measuring growth in a poor world). In: Anand S, Segal P, Stiglitz JE, eds. *Debates on the Measurement of Global Poverty.* Oxford, UK: Oxford University Press, 2010.

10. Bhalla S. Raising the standard: The war on global poverty. In: Anand S, Segal P, Stiglitz JE, eds. *Debates on the Measurement of Global Poverty.* Oxford, UK: Oxford University Press, 2010.

11. FXB Center for Health and Human Rights. Some Key Improvements Across 3 Years of the FXB-Village Network. Boston, MA: Harvard University, FXB Center, 2011.

12. Taras H. Nutrition and student performance at school. *Journal of School Health* 2005; 75(6):199-213.

13. WHO. *World Health Statistics 2009*. Geneva, Switzerland: WHO, 2009.
14. Adato M, Basset L. What is the Potential of Cash Transfers to Strengthen Families Affected by HIV and AIDS? A Review of the Evidence on Impacts and Key Policy Debates. Joint Learning Initiative on Children and HIV/AIDS (JLICA). JLICA Learning Group 1. Washington, DC: International Food Policy Research Institute, Food Consumption and Nutrition Division, 2008.
15. Habyarimana J, Mbakile B, Pop-Eleches C. The Impact of HIV/AIDS and ARV Treatment on Worker Absenteeism: Implications for African Firms. New York, NY: Columbia University, Department of Economics, 2009.
16. Sadoulet E, de Janvry A, Davis B. Cash Transfer Programs with Income Multipliers: PROCAMPO in Mexico. Washington, DC: International Food Policy Research Institute, Food Consumption and Nutrition Division, 2001.
17. Woller G, Parsons R. Assessing the community economic impact of microfinance institutions. *Journal of Developmental Entrepreneurship* 2002; 7(2):133–148.
18. World Bank. *Education in Rwanda: Rebalancing Resources to Accelerate Post-conflict Development and Poverty Reduction*. Washington, DC: World Bank, 2004.
19. Ozier O. The Impact of Secondary Schooling in Kenya: A Regression Discontinuity Analysis. Berkeley, CA: University of California, Berkeley, Department of Economics, 2010.
20. Wirth M, Balk D, Delamonica E, Storeygard A, Sacks E, Minujin A. Setting the stage for equity-sensitive monitoring of the maternal and child health MDGs. *Bulletin of the World Health Organization* 2006; 84(7):519–527.
21. International Institute for Applied Systems Analysis. *Economic Growth in Developing Countries: Education Proves Key*. Policy Brief. Laxenburg, Austria: IIASA, 2008.
22. Kravdal Ø. Education and fertility in sub–Saharan Africa: Individual and community effects. *Demography* 2002; 39(2):233-250.
23. Verspoor AM, with the SEIA team. *At the Crossroads: Choices for Secondary Education in Sub-Saharan Africa*. Washington, DC: World Bank, 2008.
24. UNFPA. *Rwanda Steps Up to the Challenge of Universal Reproductive Health Care*. New York, NY: UNFPA, 2010.
25. Ahmed SM. Capability development among the ultra-poor in Bangladesh: A case study. *Journal of Health and Population Nutrition* 2009; 27(4):528–535.
26. Chankova S, Muchiri S, Kombe G. Health workforce attrition in the public sector in Kenya: A look at the reasons. *Human Resources for Health* 2009; 7(58):1–8.

CHAPTER 6

Expanding secondary
education in Rwanda

6.1. Background

In an effort to reach the UN Millennium Development Goals (MDGs) and the targets set in Vision 2020, the government has prioritized universal primary education.[1] Between 2001 and 2005, net primary-school enrollment increased from 75% to 87% among girls and from 73% to 84% among boys.[2] Given such progress, the World Bank has indicated that Rwanda is on track to achieve the MDG for universal primary education (MDG2).[3] Despite these successes in enrollment, there remain shortfalls in primary education. Thus, as of 2008, the primary-school completion rate was only 54%, and the completion rate in 2007 was lower for girls (41%) than for boys (59%).[1,4]

The situation in respect of secondary education is worse. Only 54% of those completing primary school moved on to secondary school in 2007.[5] This implies that only about one-quarter of children who enroll in grade 1 go on to secondary school. In 2009 the gross secondary-school enrollment rate was 27% for boys and 26% for girls.[4,6]

Household income influences school attendance of children. According to DHS 2005, 92% of children from the highest wealth quintile were attending primary school, compared to 79% of children from the lowest wealth quintile. The disparity between rich and poor in secondary education is more pronounced: secondary-school enrollment is 10 times higher for children from the highest wealth quintile (26%) compared with the lowest wealth quintile (2.6%).[7]

Education is critical to the development of children. If children are denied the opportunity to attend school, their probability of engaging in risk behaviors and facing a life of poverty is greater.[8] For children who are affected by HIV/AIDS or poverty at home, schools provide a degree of security and stability. Moreover, education can help to improve children's health in both the short and the long term. For example, educated individuals are more likely to understand how HIV is spread and how AIDS can be treated. Such understanding may lead to a reduction in risky sexual behaviors and improved adherence to HIV/AIDS treatments including antiretrovirals.[9]

The government has formulated plans to expand access to secondary education which are described in its Education Sector Strategic Plan 2008–2012 (ESSP).[10] For the purposes of this chapter we assume that all the government's planned expansions of secondary education between 2008 and 2012 will be implemented by 2012; we have no data on the state of implementation. Against this baseline we examine an intervention that expands access *beyond* the ESSP 2008–2012 plan targets. We are uncertain what the government is proposing to do after 2012, but this intervention is designed to exploit the gains that have been achieved in primary-school enrollment in the country. The government itself is likely to increase the provision of secondary education after 2012, and could thus seize some of the net benefits deriving from the intervention described below.

6.2. Description of intervention

The expanded secondary schooling (ESS) intervention aims to increase the number of students enrolling in and completing secondary school by expanding the supply of secondary-school places over the next 20 years from 2012 to 2031. ESS will expand the supply of secondary-school places to meet the demand arising from increased numbers of primary-school graduates assuming that transition rates from primary to secondary school remain at their current levels. The additional demand for secondary-school places will necessitate the construction of many more schools and the training of many more teachers than is currently planned in the government's ESSP 2008–2012. Between 2012 and 2031, ESS involves the construction of 1,000 secondary schools and the training and deployment of 130,000 secondary-school teachers. The construction of these schools and the training and deployment of these teachers are part of the set of complementary actions examined in this chapter. Annex 6A provides a detailed description of the ESS intervention.

6.3. Estimation of costs and benefits

The costs and benefits of ESS are estimated by projecting enrollment under two scenarios. The first scenario is based on the government's published education sector plans. Under this scenario, the number of secondary-school places for the entire projection period from 2012 to 2031 is assumed to remain *constant* at the 2012 target level specified in ESSP. Of course, the government may expand the provision of secondary education beyond the

ESSP 2012 level, but the first scenario assumes constancy given that we are not aware of the government's post-2012 plans. In the second scenario *with* ESS, the number of secondary-school places is increased compared to the first scenario. The expansion is designed to accommodate the increasing numbers of primary-school graduates who are expected to transition to secondary school if current transition rates are maintained — between primary and lower-secondary school and between lower-secondary and upper-secondary school.

Enrollment under ESS for the projection period 2012–31 is forecast as follows. For 2012 we take enrollment to be that targeted in ESSP 2008–12 for 2012. For subsequent years enrollment is calculated from grade 1 enrollment forecasts in the future (from population projections of the number of seven-year olds) and rates at which children progress to higher grades (which depend on assumed repetition and dropout rates). See Annex 6B for more details.

The difference in annual enrollment between these two scenarios provides the information needed to estimate the costs and benefits of ESS. The additional number of children enrolled, together with assumed pupil-teacher ratios and class sizes, are used to estimate the additional number of teachers to be trained and deployed, and the additional number of schools to be constructed. The costs of ESS are then calculated from unit costs of training, teacher salaries, non-salary running costs, and school construction. Details of the assumptions and unit costs are provided in Annex 6B.

The constitutive benefits of ESS are taken to be the increases in secondary-school enrollment and graduation. The quantified consequential benefits include increases in the lifetime incomes of ESS students, and future reductions in under-five mortality, fertility and maternal mortality. These benefits are estimated using relationships observed elsewhere in the world between these outcomes and years of schooling. Details of the assumptions made to estimate the benefits are provided in Annex 6B.

6.3.1. Program coverage and cost

The ESS intervention consists of building schools and training and deploying secondary-school teachers. Over the 20-year projection period 2012–31, an additional 2.5 million children will enroll in secondary school as a result of ESS. For selected years, table 6.1 summarizes the additional number of children who will attend secondary school due to ESS. The table also shows the additional number of teachers and schools required, and the costs associated with providing secondary education to these children. See table 6C.1 in Annex 6C for detailed estimates by year of the number of teachers that need to be trained and schools constructed, along with their respective costs.

Table 6.1. ESS students, teachers, schools, and associated costs: Selected years

Year	2012	2016	2021	2026	2031
Number of ESS students enrolled (1,000s)	24	532	626	553	658
Lower secondary	0	300	145	204	244
Upper secondary	24	232	481	349	414
Number of ESS teachers	879	17,799	21,782	18,931	22,519
Lower secondary	0	9,529	4,615	6,480	7,747
Upper secondary	879	8,270	17,167	12,451	14,772
Number of ESS schools built	172	45	0	58	0
Total cost (2012 US$ million)	61.5	151.0	142.7	157.3	150.2
Capital expenditure	56.6	57.6	3.5	36.2	0.0
School construction	18.7	5.5	0.0	9.6	0.0
Teacher training	37.9	52.1	3.5	26.6	0.0
Recurrent expenditure	4.9	93.4	139.2	121.2	150.2
Teacher salaries	1.9	37.2	53.3	50.0	65.6
Non-salary running costs	3.0	56.2	85.9	71.2	84.6
Total cost per student (2012 US$ million)	2,597	284	228	285	228

During 2012–31 ESS will require more than 130,000 secondary-school teachers to be trained and deployed. Approximately 32,000 of these will be for lower-secondary level, also known as *tronc commun*, and 98,000 will be for upper-secondary level. Prior to deployment, *tronc commun* teachers receive two years of post-secondary school training, while upper-secondary school teachers receive four years of such training.

The government's drive to increase primary-school enrollment has led to gross enrollment rates higher than 100% — as much as 142% in 2008.[10] This has occurred because older children who previously did not complete, or even begin, primary school started to attend it after access was increased. Gross enrollment rates in excess of 100% will not continue indefinitely. As the system stabilizes and net enrollment approaches 100%, a decreasing proportion of over-age children will not have been to primary school. Hence gross enrollment will eventually fall to 100%. As a result, grade cohorts will start to shrink after a while — the number of children enrolled in a particular grade in one year will be smaller than the number enrolled in the same grade in the previous year. This shrinkage — associated with lower rates of over-age enrollment — will be offset at some point by growth in the population of school-age children. For example, in years 1–8 of the projection period 2012–31, the grade 1 cohort will shrink in size as enrollment of over-age children falls; in years 9–20 it will increase in size as a result of population growth.

The education system must expand to meet the needs of gross enrollment higher than 100%, after which it will contract with the shrinking of grade cohorts. The expansion has occurred in primary school, and will occur in secondary school if ESS is implemented. These effects are reflected in the projection of numbers of lower- and upper-secondary school students in table 6.1 and table 6C.1 in Annex 6C.

The total number of secondary-school teachers required by ESS will need to increase from 879 in 2012 to 21,782 in 2021 (table 6.1). As grade cohorts shrink, the number of teachers required will decrease — to 18,931 in 2026. With growth in the population of school-age children, the number of teachers required will again increase — to 22,519 in 2031. See table 6C.1 in Annex 6C for year-by-year estimates of teacher requirements.

ESS entails the construction of approximately 1,000 additional secondary schools between 2012 and 2031. On average each school will have 15 classrooms. Schools are to be equipped with proper sanitation facilities, with separate latrines for girls and boys. The lack of adequate sanitation services has been identified as a deterrent to school attendance, especially among girls.[10] The costs of school construction are included in the year in which they are incurred. As the school buildings will stand and continue to be used after the end of the ESS projection period 2012–31, this method of attributing capital costs overstates the costs of ESS relative to the benefits we estimate. We do not estimate the benefits of education received by those who attend these schools after 2031.

The average total cost per year of ESS over the 20-year period 2012–31 is approximately US$142 million (see table 6C.1 in Annex 6C). The present value of total costs over 2012–31, discounted at 3% per annum, amounts to US$2.1 billion.

6.3.2. Constitutive benefits

Education has both intrinsic and instrumental value. Education directly enhances multiple human capabilities, and is a means to other objectives such as higher income.[11] The constitutive benefits of ESS are measured in terms of increased schooling. Benefits arising from the instrumental value of education are classified as consequential benefits, and are discussed in the next sub-section. Table 6.2 summarizes the constitutive benefits of ESS for selected years.

The constitutive benefits of ESS are the increases in enrollment in, and completion of, secondary school. ESS will enable an additional 24,000 children to enroll in secondary school in 2012, rising to 658,000 in 2031. Over the period 2012–31, ESS will lead to an annual average of 450,000 additional children being enrolled in secondary school. This amounts to an average increase in the secondary-school enrollment rate over the period of 28 percentage points.

These increases in enrollment will lead to increases in the number of years of education received and of secondary-school graduates. The estimation of years of education and completion of secondary schooling will depend on dropout rates, which we assume to be the target rates in ESSP for 2012.

Overall, ESS will lead to an additional 9.1 million years of secondary education received by children over the 20-year period 2012–31. Between 2012 and 2031 an annual average of 84,000 children per year will graduate from secondary school, or a cumulative total during 2012–31 of 1.7 million children (see table 6C.2 in Annex 6C).

6.3.3. Consequential benefits

More years of secondary education lead to a variety of consequential benefits. Some of these benefits, such as individual income increases, are

Table 6.2. Constitutive benefits of ESS: Selected years

Year	2012	2016	2021	2026	2031
Number of ESS students enrolled (1,000s)	24	532	626	553	658
Number of ESS secondary-school graduates (1,000s)	0	59	142	94	114
ESS enrollment as % of children of secondary-school age	2	34	34	26	29
ESS enrollment as % of children of lower secondary-school age	0	36	15	18	21
ESS enrollment as % of children of upper secondary-school age	3	32	55	34	36

realized only after students join the labor market. Other benefits may be realized later — e.g. the decline in under-five mortality of children born to ESS students. This sub-section discusses the long-term benefits that arise from ESS.

Quantified consequential benefits

Available data allow for the quantification of four consequential benefits: the increase in individual incomes; future reduction in under-five deaths; future decline in fertility; and future reduction in maternal mortality. Table 6.3 summarizes these consequential benefits.

Increase in individual incomes

The increase in individual incomes of ESS students requires us to compare the incomes of those who obtain secondary education through ESS with the incomes of those who complete primary school but do not go on to secondary school. Based on a review of returns to education in Africa, we assume that the increase in individual income per year of secondary schooling in Rwanda is 14%.[12] As we do not have information on the baseline income of those who only complete primary school, we estimate it by applying available data on the return to primary schooling to the wages of a person with no primary education. The assumptions underlying the calculations are discussed in Annex 6B.

Using a discount rate of 3% per annum, the present value of the increase in lifetime incomes (over 30 years) of those who receive secondary education through ESS, compared to those who only complete primary school, is estimated to be US$6.0 billion. As mentioned earlier, the present value of total costs of ESS at a 3% discount rate is US$2.1 billion. This yields a net present value of financial returns from ESS of US$3.9 billion.

If a discount rate of 5% per annum is used instead of 3% per annum, the present value of the increase in incomes falls to US$2.7 billion, and that of total costs to US$1.8 billion. Hence with a 5% discount rate, the net present value of financial returns decreases to US$0.9 billion.

Table 6.3. Quantified consequential benefits of ESS over students' lifetimes

Present value of increased lifetime incomes (2012 US$ million)	6,021
Future under-five deaths avoided (number of children)	154,000
Future maternal deaths avoided (number of women)	9,000
Decline in TFR among ESS-educated women (%)	33

The estimates of increases in future incomes are based on years of secondary education received, which have been calculated assuming ESSP dropout rates. It should be noted that the ESSP dropout rates are simply targets for 2012, not rates observed in the data. Indeed, the rates observed in the latest available data from 2007 are much higher.[10] If the ESSP targets are *not* reached and current (2007) dropout rates continue, then fewer children will stay on in secondary school and years of secondary education received will be lower. Hence increases in future incomes of ESS students will be lower. If current dropout rates persist, the present value of the increase in lifetime incomes discounted at 3% per annum falls from US$6.0 billion to US$3.6 billion, and the net present value of financial returns from US$3.9 billion to US$2.1 billion.

The income of a person with education is estimated from the baseline income of a person without education by applying the appropriate rates of return to years of education received. As in chapter 5 (section 5.3.2) this baseline income is assumed to grow over time at a rate associated with the growth rate of GDP per capita. The future growth rate assumed for GDP per capita is the observed growth rate between 2005 and 2009. If, instead, we assume that the future growth rate of GDP per capita will be the growth rate observed between 2000 and 2005, then the present value of the increase in future incomes discounted at 3% per annum falls from US$6.0 billion to US$4.8 billion, and the net present value from US$3.9 billion to US$2.7 billion.

Our estimation of increases in future incomes is based on a rate-of-return of 14.0% per year of secondary education.[12] This figure is the average rate-of-return to secondary education for young adults in seven African countries. The World Bank has published estimates of rates of return to education in Rwanda based on data from 2000.[13,14] The rate-of-return reported for secondary education is 21.3%, which is much higher than is likely to be applicable to ESS graduates in the period 2012–31. When the data were collected in 2000, only a small fraction (less than 8%) of the workforce in Rwanda had any secondary education.[14] Moreover, given the skilled labor shortages stemming from the genocide, employers were bidding up wages in order to attract professionals back into the country.[14] These factors would have contributed to the very high estimate found for the year 2000. Since then, as the supply of secondary-educated workers has increased, returns to education will have fallen. The expansion of secondary schooling envisaged under ESS will increase the supply of educated workers substantially, and add further downward pressure to the rate-of-return to secondary education.

Future reduction in under-five mortality

A mother's education is a significant determinant of the probability of survival of her child. It is known that mothers with secondary or higher education are more likely to utilize healthcare facilities for their children.[15,16] Educated mothers are also more likely to be knowledgeable about disease prevention and cure.[16] Hence, the expansion of secondary education through ESS is likely to reduce the under-five mortality rate. To calculate the reduction in under-five mortality we use estimates from the World Bank on the relationship between rates of under-five mortality and years of schooling.[17] We estimate that women who receive secondary education through ESS will have 31 fewer deaths per 1,000 live births compared to women who only complete primary school. The reduction in under-five mortality resulting from the intervention will amount to 154,000 fewer child deaths in the future.

Future reduction in maternal mortality

Women with secondary education are more likely to access and utilize health services, and to use modern contraceptive methods. The utilization of such health services can help to reduce maternal mortality. A study in Ethiopia, for example, found that 42% of women with secondary education had skilled birth attendants present during delivery, compared to 10% and 3% of women with primary and no education, respectively.[18] Similarly, women with secondary education were three times more likely to receive antenatal care than women with no education.[18] A decrease in maternal deaths can be expected from improvements in access to these health services. A World Bank study estimates that one additional year of schooling for each of 1,000 women will lead to two fewer maternal deaths among them.[17] On the basis of this estimate, it is predicted that the increase in secondary education through ESS will lead to 9,000 fewer maternal deaths in the future.

Future decline in fertility

Education is associated with delayed marriage and with adoption of modern contraceptive methods, both of which help to lower fertility.[13,18,19,20] Thus an expansion of secondary schooling in Rwanda is likely to reduce the total fertility rate (TFR) among women who receive such education. It is estimated that, compared to women who only complete primary school, the average reduction in TFR for women who receive secondary education through ESS will be 1.1 births (i.e., a 33% reduction).

Non-quantified consequential benefits

We are unable to quantify all consequential benefits of ESS, but we can identify and describe some of these non-quantified benefits. The pathways through which such consequential benefits arise are based on results of studies conducted elsewhere in the world. Table 6.4 summarizes the non-quantified consequential benefits that may be expected to arise from ESS.

Table 6.4. Non-quantified consequential benefits of ESS

Quantified benefit leading to non-quantified benefit	Pathway to non-quantified consequential benefit	Non-quantified consequential benefit
Expansion of secondary education	1. Education helps children to understand and apply anti-HIV messages 2. Education empowers girls and helps them negotiate safer sex 3. Children of more educated adults are more likely to use condoms 4. Educated mothers better understand the importance of breast-feeding 5. More educated labor force 6. Educated parents are more likely to send their children to school	• Reduction in HIV/AIDS risk behavior and incidence (1, 2, 3) • Reduction in child malnutrition (4) • Economic growth (5) • Next generation better educated (6)
Reduction in maternal mortality	1. The presence of mothers is critical for child development, health and education	• Improved child development and well-being (1)
Reduced fertility	1. Lower fertility enables families to spend more per child on nutrition, health and education	• Better child health and nutritional outcomes (1)

Consequential benefits of expansion of secondary education

Expansion of secondary education is likely to reduce HIV/AIDS risk behavior, promote exclusive breastfeeding, contribute to economic growth, and increase education of the next generation. We describe below how expansion of secondary education can result in the aforementioned benefits.

- **Reduced HIV/AIDS risk behavior**: Education tends to increase young people's mobility, which can raise their risk of HIV infection. At the same time, education can provide them with information, skills and bargaining power which reduces the risk. The net impact depends on the level of education received. The influence of primary schooling alone is debatable, but there is general agreement on the protective effects of completing secondary or higher-level education. Compared to girls with only primary schooling, those who complete secondary schooling are found to have a lower risk of HIV infection. Secondary education is associated with more frequent condom use and fewer sexual partners. Education also empowers girls and helps them negotiate safer sex. There is also an inter-generational benefit as more educated parents influence condom use by their daughters.[21]
- **Breastfeeding**: Exclusive breastfeeding is considered the ideal way to feed infants and very young children. It supports children's growth and development, and helps to protect them against diseases.[22,23] Maternal education has a significant impact on mothers' breastfeeding choices: mothers with low levels of literacy are less likely to breastfeed exclusively.[24,25] The reduced mortality associated with breastfeeding is already captured through quantification of the decline in under-five mortality, but there are other health benefits of breastfeeding such as reduction in child malnutrition.
- **Economic growth**: Investments in secondary education have been shown to have a positive and statistically significant association with GDP growth.[26] Education leads to a more productive labor force. Increased lifetime incomes of ESS students have already been quantified, but education also has externalities that lead to economic growth beyond the increase in these individuals' incomes.
- **Educated parents are more likely to send their children to school**: Educating children in this generation is likely to increase levels of education in the next generation. More educated parents are more likely to send their children to school.

Consequential benefits arising from reductions in maternal mortality
We have quantified the expected reduction in future maternal deaths as a result of ESS (table 6.3), but there are also other benefits arising from lower maternal mortality. Maternal deaths have an adverse effect on child nutrition, health and education outcomes.[27] Thus a reduction in maternal mortality is likely to lead to improved child development and well-being.

Consequential benefits arising from reductions in total fertility
Expansion of secondary education in Rwanda is likely to lead to a lower

total fertility rate (quantified in table 6.3). Lower fertility enables families to invest more per child in their children's nutrition, health and education.[28] It has been found that children who have fewer siblings have lower rates of malnutrition.[29] Hence lower fertility is expected to lead to better child health and nutritional outcomes.

Consequential benefits of school construction

ESS involves the construction of approximately 1,000 new schools during 2012–31. This school construction program will employ thousands of un-skilled workers. The increase in incomes of workers is likely to contribute to a reduction of income poverty.[30] School construction under ESS can be in-cluded as part of the public works intervention of the Vision 2020 *Umurenge* Program (see chapter 4).

6.3.4. Demand-side factors

We have assumed that the expanded supply of schools and teachers under ESS will lead to higher levels of enrollment in, and completion of, secondary education. In other words, we are assuming that there is sufficient unmet demand for secondary education. There are demand-side factors which de-ter families from sending children to secondary school — such as high op-portunity costs of attending school, fees charged in upper-secondary school, and the cost of school materials and uniforms. The Ministry of Education in Rwanda acknowledges the existence of these factors,[10] but details of how it intends to address the problem are not available.

Our enrollment projections recognize that demand-side factors contrib-ute to the current low transition rate in Rwanda of 60% from primary to lower-secondary school.[10] Our projections of enrollment in table 6.1 (and the tables in Annex 6C) are based on the transition rate *remaining* at this level, not increasing. As explained in section 6.3.1, the increase in enrollment in secondary school occurs simply because larger numbers of children com-plete primary school. Keeping the transition rate constant over the projec-tion period is tantamount to assuming that demand-side factors will remain unchanged.

6.4. Summary and conclusion

The Government of Rwanda has successfully increased enrollment in primary school and has started to expand enrollment in secondary school. Enrollment in secondary school is, however, still low and further expansion is warranted. Some expansion will occur if the government is able to achieve the targets set in its Education Sector Strategic Plan (ESSP) 2008–2012. However, if the government does not increase secondary-education targets beyond those it has set for 2012, there will be large costs of inaction.

The results reported in this chapter compare ESS with maintaining secondary-school places at the target levels set for 2012 in ESSP. The ESS intervention is designed to provide additional secondary-school places at levels that allow children to continue to transition from primary to secondary school at *current* rates. If ESS is implemented, an annual average of 450,000 more children will be able to attend secondary school during the period 2012–31. This implies an average increase in the gross secondary-school enrollment rate over the period of 28 percentage points. Between 2012 and 2031, approximately 1.7 million more children will complete secondary school. Quantified consequential benefits of ESS include a US$6.0 billion increase in the present value of future incomes, 154,000 fewer under-five deaths in the future, 9,000 fewer maternal deaths in the future, and a 33% reduction in TFR among ESS-educated women. In addition to these quantified benefits there are numerous non-quantified benefits which have been identified and described.

The constitutive and consequential benefits of ESS are large, as are its costs of implementation. The present value of the total costs of ESS over the period 2012–31 is US$2.1 billion. The intervention will have significant budgetary implications if it were to be funded entirely by the Government of Rwanda. ESSP 2008–2012 projects the recurrent costs of secondary education to be RWF29 billion in 2012,[10] equivalent to US$49 million (at 2011 exchange rates). Expansion of secondary education as proposed in ESS will require a recurrent expenditure of US$4.9 million in 2012, US$93.4 million in 2016, and US$139.2 million in 2021. Thereafter, recurrent expenditure will be approximately US$130 million per year until 2031 (see table 6.1 and table 6C.1 in Annex 6C).

The Ministry of Education's projected capital expenditure for secondary schools is RWF10 billion, or US$17 million, for 2012. ESS requires capital expenditure on school construction and teacher training of US$56.6 million in 2012, US$57.6 million in 2016, and US$3.5 million in 2021. Thereafter, capital expenditure averages at US$22 million per annum (see table 6C.1 in Annex 6C). Thus, the capital expenditure required for ESS is much larger than the 2012 capital budget of the Ministry.

The Ministry's recurrent and capital expenditure budget already indicates a financing gap in 2011 of RWF45.3 billion, or US$75 million.[10] The expansion of secondary education through ESS may put unsustainable pressure on an over-stretched government budget. The government could attempt to recover some of the costs by raising fees for upper-secondary school. But this may compromise the effectiveness of the program, as fees are likely to constrain demand for schooling. The government could also seek to share costs with local communities by asking them to meet a portion of the costs associated with school construction.

The government may be in a fiscal position to finance some, though not necessarily all, of the ESS intervention. The international community may be willing to finance the remaining part of the ESS program. However, if funding is not found and secondary education in Rwanda is not expanded, there will be large costs of inaction.

ANNEX
Annex 6A. Description of intervention

Intervention: To build schools and train teachers to expand the supply of secondary education. The intervention is designed to meet the increased demand for secondary schooling that arises from increases in primary-school enrollment.

Context: The government has adopted a policy of free education for all grades of primary school and for the lower grades of secondary school. Net primary-school enrollment is estimated to be as high as 96% (in 2008), and strategies are in place to increase it to 100% by 2012.[4,10] Enrollment in secondary school, however, is very low with net enrollment at only 29% (in 2009).[4]

The set of actions: ESS involves supply-side actions to increase access to secondary education through the construction of new schools and the expansion of teacher training and deployment. During 2012–31, the program involves constructing 1,000 new secondary schools and training 130,000 new secondary-school teachers. To reduce absenteeism and dropout among girls, the schools are to be equipped with proper sanitation and hygiene facilities.

Annex 6B. Assumptions and methods

Enrollment, teacher training and school construction: The following assumptions have been made to estimate ESS school enrollment, and number of teachers and schools.

- **National intake ratio for grade 1:** The national intake ratio for grade 1 is defined as the total number enrolled in grade 1 divided by the total number of seven-year old children. We estimate the national intake ratio for grade 1 in 2012 to be 1.12 by linear extrapolation of the intake ratios in 2010 and 2011. This value is used to predict grade 1 enrollment in 2012 based on the number of seven-year olds in Rwanda (from UN population data). The ratio is assumed to decline by 10% in 2013 as the backlog in enrollment of over-age pupils is cleared. Thereafter this ratio is set equal to 0.99.

- **Repetition and dropout rates:** The repetition and year-end dropout rates in our projections are the ESSP targets for these rates in 2012. In 2007 the average dropout rate in primary school was 10%.[10] The ESSP has a target average dropout rate of 5% for 2012, and a target repetition rate of 7%.

- **Future dropout rates in the absence of ESS:** The success of government policies in expanding primary-school enrollment is leading to larger numbers of children finishing primary school. If ESS is not implemented, current dropout rates at the end of primary school (grade 6) and lower-secondary school (grade 9) will increase because all children will not be accommodated in secondary school. In this case, dropout rates will be 54% higher at the end of primary school, and 62% higher at the end of lower-secondary school.

- **Pupil-teacher ratio:** According to ESSP 2008–2012, the pupil-teacher ratio in lower-secondary school (*tronc commun*) is targeted to be 32 in 2012.[10] In our projections we assume that the pupil-teacher ratio for lower-secondary school will be 32. The pupil-teacher ratio in upper-secondary school was 26 in 2006.[10] In our projections we assume that the pupil-teacher ratio in upper-secondary school will increase to 28 in 2016 and remain constant thereafter. Note that the pupil-teacher ratio is not the same as the average class size. The average class size is the pupil-teacher ratio divided by the average 'teaching load'.

- **Teaching load:** The teaching load is the proportion of the school day that a teacher spends teaching pupils, as opposed to time spent in preparation, marking and administration. Primary-school teachers typically spend more of the school day teaching than do secondary-school teachers. Secondary-school teachers often have low teaching loads — particularly those teaching more specialized subjects such as mathematics and science. In South Africa, which has a much more established secondary education system than Rwanda, the teaching load for secondary-school teachers is 0.87.[31] The teaching load is likely to be lower in Rwanda than in South Africa, and lower in upper-secondary school (where there is more teacher specialization) than in lower-secondary school. Accordingly, we assume that lower-secondary and upper-secondary school teachers spend 0.8 and 0.75, respectively, of the school day in teaching. In our projections it is assumed that the organization of the school system will improve over time, and that in five years (2016) the teaching load will increase to 0.9 and 0.8, respectively, for lower- and upper-secondary school.

- **Teacher attrition rates:** We have no data on teacher attrition rates in Rwanda. Based on data from Tanzania, Chad and Benin, we assume attrition rates among secondary-school teachers to be 5% per annum.[32] Attrition is included even in year 1; thus in table 6C.1 the number of teachers recruited in year 1 (2012) is 5% higher than the number needed in that year.

- **School size:** The average number of students in a secondary school is assumed to be 450. This assumption determines the number of schools that will be required given the projected increase in secondary-school enrollment as a result of ESS.

Cost estimation: The following assumptions are made to estimate the costs of the teachers and schools required under ESS.

- **Teacher salaries:** Based on monthly salary information of school teachers in Rwanda, it is assumed that in 2012 lower- and upper-secondary school teachers will receive an annual salary of US$1,700 and US$2,040, respectively.[33] Their salaries are assumed to increase at 1% per annum in real terms between 2012 and 2031. This is 1 percentage point lower than the rate assumed in chapter 5, because teachers are employees of government subject to tighter budgets.
- **Non-salary running costs:** Non-salary running costs include materials and utilities. The Ministry of Education reports that annual non-salary running costs in lower- and upper-secondary school are US$72 and US$122 per student, respectively.[34] We use these values for 2012, and for subsequent years assume that they increase at 1% and 2% per annum, respectively, for lower- and upper-secondary school.
- **Teacher-training costs:** Teacher-training costs are based on lower-secondary school teachers being trained for two years after completing their secondary education and upper-secondary school teachers receiving four years of post-secondary education. The unit cost per person of one year of teacher training is assumed to be US$3,700. This estimate is based on the costs of teacher training in Rwanda in 2003,[35] adjusted to 2012 prices. We assume that teacher-training costs increase by 1% per year between 2012 and 2031.
- **School construction costs:** School construction costs are based on the number of classrooms that need to be constructed. Given an average school size of 450 students and an average class size of 30 students, a typical secondary school will have 15 classrooms. From World Bank data for African countries, we assume it will cost approximately US$7,000 to construct a classroom in 2012.[36,37] In addition to classroom construction costs, we add a cost for building latrine facilities of US$1,000 per classroom; this figure is based on latrine construction costs in Senegal, Uganda and Zambia.[37] Construction costs in 2012 US$ are assumed to increase at 3% per year over the period 2012–31.
- **Discount rate:** The discount rate used to calculate present value of costs is 3% per annum.

Estimation of benefits: Our projections of secondary-school enrollment, repetition and dropout provide us with estimates of the constitutive benefits of ESS, viz. school enrollment and graduation. The assumptions needed to estimate other quantified benefits are discussed below.

- **Private income returns to education:** On the basis of a 2009 review, rates of return to primary and secondary education are available for a number of African countries.[12] The rates we apply for Rwanda are taken from this review: 8.9% per year for primary schooling (an average across

4 African countries) and 14% per year for secondary schooling (an average across 7 African countries).[12] Estimates of private rates of return to education in Rwanda are available in a World Bank study, which reports them to be 13.2% and 21.3%, respectively, per year of primary and secondary education.[13] For reasons explained in the text, these rates are likely to be too high for projections of income gains of ESS students in 2012–31. We consider it more appropriate to use the African averages from the 2009 review.

- **Increase in lifetime incomes:** To calculate the increase in incomes resulting from secondary education, we need a base wage for individuals who have completed primary education. This was not available for Rwanda, so we had to estimate it. We estimated it by applying the rate-of-return to primary education to the wage of a person with no education. The daily wage of a person with no education was taken to be US$0.4 in 2012 on the basis of key-informant interviews. To this wage we apply the assumed rate-of-return to primary education of 8.9% per year of primary schooling to provide the income of individuals who have completed primary education. Then the increase in private incomes from secondary education is calculated by applying the rate-of-return to secondary education of 14% for the years of secondary schooling received to the base wage of an individual who has completed primary education. To calculate the cost of attending secondary school, we assume that students forego their daily wage while at school and pay for school materials and uniforms at a cost of US$100 per year.

- **The present value of increase in lifetime incomes** is calculated using a discount rate of 3% per annum.

- **Reductions in under-five mortality rate (U5MR):** According to the National Institute of Statistics of Rwanda, the U5MR for children born to mothers with no education was 210 per 1,000 live births in 2005.[38] (More recent estimates of U5MR are available at the population level, but not for mothers with different levels of education.) On the basis of estimates by the World Bank, we assume that U5MR declines by 7% for each additional year of education received by a mother.[17]

- **Reduction in total fertility rate (TFR):** The TFR in Rwanda in 2005 was estimated to be 5.4.[6] Among mothers with no education, TFR is estimated at 6.9.[38] On the basis of estimates by the World Bank, we assume that each additional year of female education reduces TFR by 10%.[17]

Annex 6C. Costs and constitutive benefits of ESS during 2012–31
See: Table 6C.1. ESS program coverage and cost estimates: 2012–31
See: Table 6C.2. Quantified constitutive benefits of ESS: 2012–31

Table 6C.1. ESS program coverage and cost estimates: 2012–31

Year	2012	2013	2014	2015	2016	2017	2018	2019	2020	2021
Number of ESS students enrolled (1,000s)	**24**	**114**	**253**	**396**	**532**	**621**	**668**	**683**	**665**	**626**
Lower secondary	0	37	105	200	300	336	308	238	176	145
Upper secondary	24	77	148	196	232	285	361	445	489	481
Number of ESS teachers	**879**	**4,003**	**8,697**	**13,353**	**17,799**	**20,829**	**22,644**	**23,435**	**23,036**	**21,782**
Lower-secondary teachers	0	1,173	3,342	6,360	9,529	10,655	9,768	7,546	5,576	4,615
Upper-secondary teachers	879	2,830	5,355	6,993	8,270	10,174	12,876	15,889	17,460	17,167
Number of ESS teachers recruited (laid-off)	**923**	**3,324**	**5,129**	**5,324**	**5,336**	**4,073**	**2,947**	**1,963**	**752**	**(164)**
Lower-secondary teachers.	0	1,232	2,336	3,337	3,645	1,660	(399)	(1,845)	(1,691)	(730)
Upper-secondary teachers	923	2,092	2,793	1,987	1,691	2,413	3,346	3,808	2,443	566
Number of ESS schools built	**172**	**134**	**91**	**46**	**45**	**91**	**32**	**0**	**0**	**0**
Total cost (2012 US$ million)	**61.5**	**91.6**	**119.5**	**139.8**	**151.0**	**164.1**	**158.2**	**149.6**	**143.1**	**142.7**
Capital expenditure	**56.6**	**70.5**	**73.8**	**69.8**	**57.6**	**51.8**	**30.5**	**10.3**	**0.0**	**3.5**
School construction	18.7	15.0	10.6	5.4	5.5	11.5	4.2	0.0	0.0	0.0
Teacher training										
Lower secondary	13.5	21.6	26.9	20.6	5.0	0.0	0.0	0.0	0.0	3.5
Upper secondary	24.4	33.9	36.3	43.8	47.2	40.3	26.4	10.3	0.0	0.0
Recurrent expenditure	**4.9**	**21.1**	**45.7**	**70.0**	**93.4**	**112.3**	**127.7**	**139.4**	**143.1**	**139.2**
Teacher salaries										
Lower secondary	0.0	2.1	6.1	11.9	18.2	20.8	19.5	15.3	11.6	9.8
Upper secondary	1.9	6.1	11.8	15.7	19.0	23.8	30.8	38.7	43.4	43.5
Non-salary running costs	3.0	12.8	27.8	42.3	56.2	67.7	77.5	85.3	88.1	85.9
Total cost per student (2012 US$)	**2,597**	**802**	**472**	**353**	**284**	**265**	**237**	**219**	**215**	**228**

continued

Table 6C.1. ESS program coverage and cost estimates: 2012–31 (continued)

Year	2022	2023	2024	2025	2026	2027	2028	2029	2030	2031
Number of ESS students enrolled (1,000s)	**576**	**536**	**519**	**531**	**553**	**580**	**604**	**626**	**644**	**658**
Lower secondary	144	157	172	190	204	217	227	234	241	244
Upper secondary	432	379	348	341	349	363	377	391	403	414
Number of ESS teachers	**20,001**	**18,522**	**17,859**	**18,198**	**18,931**	**19,844**	**20,687**	**21,410**	**22,050**	**22,519**
Lower-secondary teachers	4,576	4,973	5,445	6,020	6,480	6,892	7,206	7,441	7,649	7,747
Upper-secondary teachers	15,425	13,549	12,414	12,178	12,451	12,952	13,481	13,969	14,401	14,772
Number of ESS teachers recruited (laid-off)	**(782)**	**(552)**	**230**	**1,247**	**1,681**	**1,905**	**1,877**	**1,793**	**1,742**	**1,596**
Lower-secondary teachers	189	646	744	875	785	757	674	607	590	486
Upper-secondary teachers	(971)	(1,198)	(514)	372	896	1,148	1,203	1,186	1,152	1,110
Number of ESS schools built	**0**	**0**	**21**	**49**	**58**	**55**	**47**	**41**	**30**	**0**
Total cost (2012 US$ million)	**137.3**	**134.2**	**139.5**	**149.5**	**157.3**	**163.2**	**163.2**	**162.6**	**158.8**	**150.2**
Capital expenditure	**9.1**	**16.0**	**25.8**	**33.6**	**36.2**	**35.3**	**28.8**	**22.4**	**13.1**	**0.0**
School construction	0.0	0.0	3.3	8.0	9.6	9.3	8.3	7.4	5.9	0.0
Teacher training										
Lower secondary	5.8	6.8	7.1	6.6	6.2	5.6	5.3	4.8	2.2	0.0
Upper secondary	3.3	9.1	15.4	19.0	20.3	20.4	15.3	10.1	5.0	0.0
Recurrent expenditure	**128.2**	**118.3**	**113.7**	**115.9**	**121.2**	**127.9**	**134.4**	**140.3**	**145.7**	**150.2**
Teacher salaries										
Lower secondary	9.9	10.9	12.2	13.8	15.1	16.4	17.5	18.4	19.3	20.0
Upper secondary	39.9	35.8	33.4	33.4	34.9	37.0	39.3	41.5	43.7	45.7
Non-salary running costs	78.4	71.6	68.1	68.7	71.2	74.4	77.6	80.3	82.7	84.6
Total cost per student (2012 US$)	**238**	**250**	**269**	**282**	**285**	**281**	**270**	**260**	**247**	**228**

Table 6C.2. Quantified constitutive benefits of ESS: 2012–31

Year	2012	2013	2014	2015	2016	2017	2018	2019	2020	2021
Number of ESS students enrolled (1,000s)	24	114	253	396	532	621	668	683	665	626
Number of ESS secondary-school graduates (1,000s)	0	0	15	39	58	60	70	97	122	142
ESS enrollment as % of children of secondary-school age	2	8	17	26	34	39	40	39	37	34
ESS enrollment as % of children of lower secondary-school age	0	5	14	25	36	39	35	26	19	15
ESS enrollment as % of children of upper secondary-school age	3	11	21	27	32	38	46	54	57	55

continued

Table 6C.2. Quantified constitutive benefits of ESS: 2012–31 (*continued*)

Year	2022	2023	2024	2025	2026	2027	2028	2029	2030	2031
Number of ESS students enrolled (1,000s)	576	536	519	531	553	580	604	626	644	658
Number of ESS secondary-school graduates (1,000s)	140	122	104	95	94	97	101	106	110	114
ESS enrollment as % of children of secondary-school age	30	27	25	25	26	26	27	28	28	29
ESS enrollment as % of children of lower secondary-school age	14	15	16	17	18	19	20	20	21	21
ESS enrollment as % of children of upper secondary-school age	48	40	36	34	34	34	35	35	36	36

References

1. Rwanda National Institute of Statistics. *Millennium Development Goals: Toward Sustainable Social and Economic Growth, Country Report 2007.* Kigali, Rwanda: NIS, 2007.
2. UNICEF. *Revised Country Program Document, Rwanda 2008–2012.* New York, NY: UNICEF, 2007.
3. World Bank. *Rwanda: Education For All — Fast Track Initiative.* Washington, DC: World Bank, 2009.
4. World Bank. *World Development Indicators 2011.* Washington, DC: World Bank, 2011.
5. World Bank. *Country Assistance Strategy for the Republic of Rwanda for the Period FY09–FY12.* Washington, DC: World Bank, 2008.
6. UNICEF. *Rwanda: Statistics.* New York, NY: UNICEF, 2010. http://www.unicef.org/infobycountry/rwanda_statistics.html. Accessed November 30, 2011.
7. Rwanda Ministry of Finance and Economic Planning. *Economic Development and Poverty Reduction Strategy 2008–2012.* Kigali, Rwanda: Government of Rwanda, 2007.
8. Baingana F, Fuller A, Guyer AL. The Implementation Gap in Services for Children Affected by HIV/AIDS. JLICA Learning Group 3. Boston, MA: Harvard University, FXB Center, 2008.
9. Jukes M, Simmons S, Fawzi MCS, Bundy D. Educational Access and HIV Prevention: Making the Case for Education as a Health Priority in Sub-Saharan Africa. JLICA Learning Group 3. Boston, MA: Harvard University, FXB Center, 2008.
10. Rwanda Ministry of Education. *Education Sector Strategic Plan 2008–2012.* Kigali, Rwanda: Government of Rwanda, 2008.
11. Sen A. *Development as Freedom.* New York, NY: Anchor Books, 1999.
12. Colclough C, Kingdon G, Patrinos H. *The Pattern of Returns to Education and its Implications.* Policy Brief No. 4. Cambridge, UK: Research Consortium on Education and Poverty, 2009.
13. Verspoor AM, with the SEIA Team. *At the Crossroads: Choices for Secondary Education in Sub-Saharan Africa.* Washington, DC: World Bank, 2008.
14. World Bank. *Education in Rwanda: Rebalancing Resources to Accelerate Post-Conflict Development and Poverty Reduction.* Washington, DC: World Bank, 2004.
15. Ogunjuyigbe PO. Under-five mortality in Nigeria: Perception and attitudes of the Yorubas towards the existence of 'Abiku'. *Demographic Research* 2004; 11(2):43–56.
16. Cleland JC, Ginneken JKV. Maternal education and child survival in developing countries: the search for pathways of influence. *Social Science and Medicine* 1988; 2(12):1357–1368.

17. Abu-Ghaida D, Klasen S. *The Economic and Human Development Costs of Missing the Millennium Development Goal on Gender Equity*. Washington, DC: World Bank, 2004.

18. Wirth M, Balk D, Delamonica E, Storeygard A, Sacks E, Minujin A. Setting the stage for equity-sensitive monitoring of the maternal and child health MDGs. *Bulletin of the World Health Organization* 2006; 84(7):519–527.

19. Kravdal Ø. Education and fertility in sub-Saharan Africa: Individual and community effects. *Demography* 2002; 39(2):233–250.

20. Ozier O. The Impact of Secondary Schooling in Kenya: A Regression Discontinuity Analysis. Berkeley, CA: University of California, Berkeley, Department of Economics, 2010.

21. Hargreaves J, Boler T. *Girl Power: The Impact of Girls' Education on HIV and Sexual Behavior*. London, UK: ActionAid International, 2006.

22. Rwanda Ministry of Health. *National Guidelines for Food and Nutritional Support and Care for People Living with HIV/AIDS in Rwanda*. Kigali, Rwanda: Government of Rwanda, 2007.

23. WHO. *Nutrition for Health and Development*. Executive Board 128th Session, Provisional agenda item 4.15. Geneva, Switzerland: WHO, 2010.

24. Fredrickson DD, Washington RL, Pham N, Jackson T, Wiltshire J, Jecha L. Reading grade levels and health behaviors of parents at child clinics. *Kansas Medicine* 1995; 96(3):127–129.

25. Kaufman H, Skipper B, Small L, Terry T, McGrew M. Effect of literacy on breast-feeding outcomes. *Southern Medical Journal* 2001; 94(3):293–296.

26. Gyimah-Brempong K, Paddison O, Mitiku W. Higher education and economic growth in Africa. *Journal of Development Studies* 2006; 42(3):502–529.

27. Kirigia JM, Oluwole D, Mwabu GM, Gatwiri D, Kainyu LH. Effects of maternal mortality on GDP in the WHO African region. *African Journal of Health Sciences* 2006; 13(1-2):86–95.

28. Serra R. *The Demographic Context and its Implications for Childhood Poverty*. CHIP Report No. 5. London, UK: Childhood Poverty Research and Policy Centre, 2004.

29. Kravdal Ø, Kodzi I. Children's stunting in sub-Saharan Africa: Is there an externality effect of high fertility? *Demographic Research* 2011; 25(18):565–594.

30. Del Ninno C, Subbarao K, Milazzo A. *How to Make Public Works Work: A Review of the Experiences*. Social Protection Discussion Papers. No. 0905. Washington, DC: World Bank, Social Protection and Labor, 2009.

31. Crouch L. *Turbulence or Orderly Change? Teaching Supply and Demand in the Age of AIDS*. Pretoria, South Africa: Department of Education, Republic of South Africa, 2001.

32. Mulkeen A, Chapman DW, DeJaeghere JG, Leu E. *Recruiting, Retaining, and Retraining Secondary School Teachers and Principals in Sub-Saharan Africa*. Washington, DC: World Bank, Africa Region Human Development Department, 2007.

33. Rwanda Ministry of Education. *Rwanda Education Sector: Long-Term Strategy and Financing Framework 2006–2015 (LTSFF)*. Kigali, Rwanda: Ministry of Education, 2006.

34. Rwanda Ministry of Education. *Education Sector Strategic Plan 2006–2010*. Kigali, Rwanda: Government of Rwanda, 2006.

35. Richardson AM. *Comparative Cost Analysis in Distance Teacher Education*. Kigali, Rwanda: Kigali Institute of Education, Distance Training Office, 2006.

36. World Bank. *Education for All: Building the Schools*. Washington, DC: World Bank, 2003.

37. Theunynck S. *School Construction Strategies for Universal Primary Education in Africa: Should Communities be Empowered to Build their Schools?* Washington, DC: World Bank, 2009.

38. National Institute of Statistics, Rwanda Ministry of Health, Macro International Inc. *Rwanda Demographic and Health Survey 2005*. Kigali, Rwanda and Calverton, MD: NIS, RMH, and Macro International Inc., 2006.

CHAPTER 7

A school-feeding program in Rwanda

7.1. Background

Many families in Rwanda cannot secure access to sufficient food and, as a result, 34% of the country's population is undernourished.[1] Low levels of food consumption are particularly serious for children. Some 23% of children below the age of five are underweight,[2] and 52% of them are stunted.[3] The prevalence of stunting increases with age, from 8% among children under 6 months to 55% for children aged 12 months.[4] Protein-energy malnutrition and micronutrient deficiency — especially iron deficiency — are common among children. The Ministry of Health has identified severe protein-energy malnutrition as one of the leading causes of morbidity among children under five years of age. Food insecurity, large household size, and poor feeding practices are cited by the Ministry as the major causes of malnutrition.[5]

The Government of Rwanda and UNICEF have highlighted school-feeding as an effective approach to deal with chronic malnutrition among children in the country.[6] In addition to improving nutrition, school meals can result in positive educational outcomes — such as better attendance and capacity to learn at school. The World Food Programme (WFP) argues that school-feeding programs are an incentive for poor children, particularly girls, to go to and stay in school, and improve their capacity to learn.[7] The government, in collaboration with WFP, is already providing school-feeding in areas it has identified as food insecure. WFP had planned to phase out its support of the school-feeding program and transfer full responsibility for it to the government by 2012.[8] This plan was revised in 2011 and WFP now intends to increase the number of children provided with school meals by 30% while it prepares the government and communities to assume responsibility for the program.[9]

Aside from its collaboration with WFP, the government is involved in other interventions to expand school-feeding and deal with child malnutrition. One of these interventions is the School Garden Project which encourages schools to grow food locally. As schools expand their capacity to produce food, financial and in-kind support for school-feeding will gradually be scaled back from these schools and diverted to other schools to start or expand their school-feeding programs. The government has also tasked mayors to assume responsibility for malnutrition in their districts, and is rewarding those who develop innovative and effective responses. These new initiatives are likely to help reduce child malnutrition.

Although a school-feeding program already exists, and there are government plans to extend coverage, many children are not covered and will not be covered in the near future. We examine the costs and benefits of expanding school-feeding from its current coverage of 14% of children enrolled in primary and lower-secondary school under the Government/WFP program to a coverage of 50% of children. This will more than triple the size of the existing program.

7.2. Description of intervention

The intervention we consider in this chapter is an expanded school-feeding program (ESFP) for a 10-year period from 2012 to 2021. The current Government/WFP program reaches 14% of children enrolled in primary and lower-secondary schools, whereas ESFP is designed to increase coverage from 14% to 50% of these children. ESFP is designed to scale up school-feeding at a linear rate from 14% in 2012 to 50% in 2021. The program will first be expanded in those geographic areas identified as high priority in terms of their degree of poverty.

ESFP will provide children with one meal a day to improve their nutritional status and their attendance at school. Children will receive a cooked meal five days a week for 180 school days of the year.[10] In line with the government's School Garden Project,[11] the community will be requested to play an active role in the program's design and implementation, and in time to assume responsibility for ESFP in local schools. Annex 7A provides a detailed description of the intervention.

7.3. Estimation of costs and benefits
7.3.1. Program coverage and cost

The coverage estimates of ESFP over time are based on expanding the WFP program from its current level of 14% of children in primary and lower-secondary school to 50% of children. The ESFP design is based on this expansion occurring over a 10-year period from 2012 to 2021, and its cost estimates are based on the unit per-child costs of the current WFP program.

To reach the target coverage of 50% of children by 2021 from the 2012 baseline of 14%, the intervention involves increasing the coverage of primary and lower-secondary school children by 3.6 percentage points each year until 2021. In 2021 ESFP will provide school meals to 1.29 million children. The majority of recipients will be children at primary school. However, as national enrollment in secondary school increases, a larger proportion of children receiving meals will be from lower-secondary school. The increases in the number of children receiving school meals through ESFP are summarized in table 7.1, and details are provided in table 7C.1 in Annex 7C.

ESFP is expected to benefit not only the children who receive meals at school, but also their preschool siblings. We use data on household composition from the Demographic and Health Survey (DHS) 2005 to calculate the ratio of preschool siblings to children enrolled in primary or lower-secondary school in ESFP target areas. From these data we calculate that there are 85 preschool siblings for every 100 primary or lower-secondary school children in the target areas. For selected years, table 7.1 shows the number of preschool siblings of children receiving school meals through ESFP. Table 7C.1 in Annex 7C provides details for each year of the period 2012–21.

We estimate the annual cost of ESFP by applying a per-child cost of school-feeding to the number of children covered in each year. From WFP data on per-child costs, we take the annual cost per child to be US$42. Based on WFP budgets, food inputs (ingredients) account for approximately 50% of costs, with transportation (international and domestic), meal preparation, and administration accounting for the balance.

The implementation costs of ESFP are significant. As the coverage of the program expands, the annual cost of ESFP will increase from US$4 million in 2012 to US$54 million in 2021 (all figures in 2012 US$). During 2012–21 the average annual cost of ESFP is US$28.2 million, and the present value of total costs over the period, discounted at 3% per annum, is US$236.2 million. Table 7.1 summarizes the costs of ESFP for selected years, and table 7C.1 in Annex 7C provides details of the costs for each year of the period.

7.3.2. Benefits

ESFP will lead to both constitutive and consequential benefits. The constitutive benefits are the improved nutrition and education outcomes for primary and lower-secondary school children who receive meals. Unfortunately, we are unable to quantify the nutritional benefits for children receiving school meals. We have *no* information on the nutritional status of children who are above five years of age in Rwanda (whether or not they are receiving school meals) — and hence no baseline from which to quantify any improvement. Information on stunting and wasting is available from DHS 2005 only for children below five years of age.[4] Anthropometric data for

Table 7.1. ESFP coverage and costs (2012 US$ million): Selected years

Year	2012	2016	2021
Number of children receiving school meals through ESFP (1,000s)	98	603	1,288
Primary-school children	89	489	895
Lower secondary-school children	9	115	392
Number of preschool siblings of children receiving school meals through ESFP (1,000s)	83	514	1,097
Total cost of ESFP (2012 US$ million)	4.1	25.1	53.7
Food costs	1.9	11.9	25.5
International transport	0.5	2.9	6.1
Within-country transport, storage and handling	0.6	3.7	7.9
Other direct operational costs	0.3	1.8	3.8
Direct support costs	0.5	3.2	6.8
Overhead cost	0.3	1.6	3.5

school-age children would have allowed us to estimate the nutritional gains for children who receive meals as part of ESFP. Studies from other countries on the nutritional impact of school-feeding programs show significant improvements in children's anthropometric indicators such as height-for-age z-scores, weight-for-age z-scores, and Body Mass Index (BMI).[12-14] For example, in Bangladesh the average gain in BMI from one year of school-feeding was 0.62 points (a 4.3% increase),[12] and in Jamaica the average gain in height from eight months of school-feeding was 0.25 centimeters.[14]

One constitutive benefit of ESFP that we are able to quantify is higher school enrollment. Other educational benefits — such as improved test scores and concentration of children while at school — are not quantified due to lack of information. We discuss these later.

The consequential benefits of school-feeding include an increase in the number of upper-secondary school graduates. ESFP will lead to more children remaining in and completing lower-secondary school, as a result of which they are more likely to enroll in and complete upper-secondary school. As mentioned earlier, there are also likely to be consequential nutritional benefits of school-feeding for the preschool siblings of children who receive school meals, because households tend to reallocate freed food resources in favor of younger siblings.[15] The increase in the number of secondary-school graduates and improved nutritional outcomes for preschool siblings have been quantified. Other consequential benefits have not been quantified, but are discussed later.

The constitutive benefits of ESFP that we can quantify are increased enrollment in and completion of primary and lower-secondary school. To estimate these benefits we need to predict the impact of ESFP on enrollment and on grade repetition, which determine rates of school completion. No data are available for Rwanda on the impact of school-feeding on enrollment, so we have resorted to data from other countries on increased enrollment resulting from school-feeding programs.[12,16,17] Applying the results of these studies, we can calculate the percentage of children out-of-school who would be expected to enroll in school if a school-feeding program were introduced. We apply this percentage to children out-of-school in the targeted regions of Rwanda.

We assume that ESFP will succeed in targeting school-feeding to poor regions. In order to calculate its impact, we need information on the size of the out-of-school population of children in these regions. We assume that 70% of children in the targeted regions are from national wealth quintiles 1 and 2, and 30% are from higher quintiles; this information is combined with DHS 2005 data on out-of-school children by wealth quintile. This allows us to estimate the size of the population of school-age children who are out of school in the targeted regions.

School-feeding is also likely to lead to a reduction in grade repetition. We do not have data on the magnitude of the effect, and make the assumption that the rate of grade repetition (percentage of children repeating a grade) declines by the same factor as the percentage of out-of-school children declines due to higher school enrollment resulting from ESFP. Studies show that school-feeding programs improve school attendance and test scores.[12,17] Sustained attentiveness and concentration in class, along with improvement in test scores, are some of the constitutive benefits of ESFP. Although we do not have the data to quantify these benefits, they are to some extent captured in our estimates of reduction in grade repetition and increase in school completion.

Two consequential benefits of ESFP have been quantified, viz. increase in the number of children graduating from upper-secondary school, and reduction in stunting among preschool siblings of children who receive school meals. The number of upper-secondary school graduates is estimated from the additional number who complete lower-secondary school as a result of ESFP, and the current transition rates to and through upper-secondary school in Rwanda.

School-feeding programs have been shown to benefit the preschool siblings of children receiving school meals.[15] This may occur through a reallocation of food within the household away from children who receive food

at school towards preschool siblings who stay at home.[13] Some studies, however, suggest that the food consumed by children at school is additional to
their normal intake within the household — in which case there will be less
of an effect on nutrition of preschool siblings.[12]

We use data from a similar intervention in Uganda to estimate the reduction in stunting among preschool siblings of children who receive meals
at school.[15] The authors of the Uganda study suggest that the benefit arises
either from reallocation within the household or from preschool siblings
turning up to school at meal times to get food provided to the children at
school. Whatever the pathway, we assume that similar benefits to those observed in Uganda will be experienced in Rwanda.

The impact of ESFP on preschool siblings (age 0 to 5) of children receiving meals at school is estimated through the percentage decline in stunting.
We construct a distribution of height-for-age Z-scores (HAZ) for children
0–5 years old in the ESFP target regions using DHS 2005 data, which allows
us to calculate the percentage falling below the cut-off that defines stunting (two standard deviations below the WHO Child Growth Standards median).[18] The Ugandan study provides an estimate of the *average* impact of
school-feeding on HAZ scores of preschool siblings. The impact of ESFP
in Rwanda is then calculated by shifting the HAZ distribution constructed
for target regions to the right by the *average* change in HAZ observed in
Uganda. This allows us to calculate the new percentage falling below the
fixed cut-off. The percentage decline in stunting is applied to the number of
preschool siblings of children receiving school meals through ESFP in each
year (see table 7.1 and table 7C.1 in Annex 7C). This provides the annual
number of cases of stunting avoided among preschool siblings.

Quantified constitutive benefits

ESFP will lead to an increasing number of additional children enrolled in
school as the coverage of school-feeding expands. It is estimated that 970 additional children will enroll in school in 2012, which will increase to 109,505
in 2016 and to 445,537 in 2021. The increases in school enrollment come
predominantly from increased enrollment in primary school. As the children in primary school proceed to higher grades, increased enrollment in
lower-secondary school will rise. Table 7.2 summarizes the increases in primary and lower-secondary school enrollment for selected years. Table 7C.2
in Annex 7C presents year-by-year estimates of additional enrollment for
the period 2012–21.

Despite improvements in primary-school enrollment in recent years as a
result of government initiatives, the rates of primary-school completion and
transition to secondary school remain low.[19] We expect primary- and lower-
secondary school completion rates to improve with the implementation of

Table 7.2. Quantified constitutive benefits of ESFP: Selected years

Year	2012	2016	2021
Number of additional children enrolled in school	**969**	**109,506**	**445,537**
Primary school	969	92,769	279,570
Lower-secondary school	0	16,737	165,967
Number of additional children completing school			
Primary school	0	10,999	61,923
Lower-secondary school	0	1,608	31,028

ESFP. Providing meals at school is likely to increase regular school attendance and, by avoiding intermittent hunger, to improve learning outcomes. We estimate that in 2016 some 11,000 additional children will complete primary school and 1,600 additional children will complete lower-secondary school. The numbers of additional children completing primary and lower-secondary school will increase over time, and reach almost 93,000 in 2021. For selected years, table 7.2 summarizes the effects of ESFP on numbers of children completing primary and lower-secondary school. Year-by-year estimates are provided in table 7C.2 in Annex 7C.

Unquantified constitutive benefits

Several constitutive benefits could not be quantified because of lack of data, or the benefit being unquantifiable. In particular, we were unable to quantify the improvement in nutritional status of children receiving meals at school. Nonetheless, the evidence concerning unquantified benefits is significant and we consider it below. Table 7.3 summarizes the unquantified constitutive benefits resulting from ESFP and the pathways to these benefits.

Improvement in the nutritional status of children who receive school meals

A number of studies have documented the positive contribution of school-feeding programs to the nutritional status of children. A 2008 review of the literature on the nutritional impact of school-meal programs concludes that they increase children's daily energy consumption and improve their anthropometric indicators such as BMI and height-for-age z-scores.[20] A 2009 Cochrane review of evidence on school-feeding programs in low-income countries also finds that children receiving school meals have better nutritional status relative to control groups, resulting in gains in both weight and height.[13] A randomized trial conducted in rural Jamaica to identify the

Table 7.3. Unquantified constitutive benefits of ESFP

ESFP action	Pathway to unquantified constitutive benefit	Unquantified constitutive benefit
Provide school meals	1. School meals improve nutrition 2. School meals encourage daily school attendance 3. Better nutrition can improve cognitive function 4. School meals reduce intermittent hunger	• Improved nutritional outcomes (1) • Improved school attendance (2, 3, 4) • Improved test scores (3, 4) • Children concentrate better in class (3, 4)

impact of school breakfasts finds that children receiving breakfast gained 0.25 centimeters in height during 8 months of intervention compared to the control group.[14] An evaluation of a school-feeding program in Bangladesh finds that the program increased the average BMI of beneficiary children by 0.62 points (a 4.3% increase) compared to the average BMI of children in the control group.[12]

In Rwanda such constitutive benefits of a school-feeding program cannot be quantified owing to lack of data. But it should be clear from the extensive evidence, including the Cochrane review, that ESFP is likely to improve the nutritional status of children who receive meals at school.

Improvement in school attendance

Studies evaluating school-meal programs in low-income countries have underscored the improvement in attendance as a result of school meals.[12,13,21] The pathways to improved attendance include the direct attraction of free meals, and the impact of school meals on reduction in illness.[13,22] Improvements in attendance lead to longer exposure to learning and mental stimulation, and hence to improved academic performance.[13] ESFP should thus help to improve academic performance through its influence on school attendance. Some of these effects are captured in increases in primary and lower-secondary school completion, which are quantified and discussed above.

Cognitive function and test scores

The nutritional status of children affects their performance at school through its effect on cognitive function and, in cases of short-term hunger, on their ability to concentrate and perform complex tasks.[13,23,24] Empirical evidence regarding the impact of school-feeding programs on learning outcomes as measured by test scores is typically positive. In Jamaica it has been observed that school breakfasts improve verbal fluency among undernourished children,[25] and improve arithmetic test scores.[14] Many studies have found positive impacts, particularly when recipient children have been malnourished.[12,14,15,23-25] A comprehensive review has concluded that school meals consistently improve school performance of students who are undernourished.[17] Given the high prevalence of malnutrition in Rwanda,[2] it is reasonable to expect that expansion of school-feeding will lead to improved cognitive function and test scores.

Reduction in essential micronutrient deficiencies in children

Deficiency of vitamins and micronutrients (such as iron) is common among Rwandan children.[5] Fortification of school meals is generally considered to be a least-cost approach to reduce vitamin and micronutrient deficiencies among school children.[26] ESFP needs to ensure that fortified foods are included among those provided in school meals.

Improved behavior and playground activity

A study conducted in Kenya reports that children who received school meals exhibited higher levels of playground activity, and pro-social as opposed to anti-social behavior. In tasks that involved playing leadership roles and initiating social interactions, these children outperformed children who were not given school meals.[13]

Quantified consequential benefits

The consequential benefits of ESFP that we have quantified are fewer cases of stunting among preschool siblings, and increased numbers of children graduating from secondary school because they have been able to complete lower-secondary school. Table 7.4 summarizes these quantified consequential benefits for selected years. Table 7C.3 in Annex 7C provides the year-by-year figures.

Reduction in stunting among preschool siblings

Evaluations of school-feeding programs show that such programs have consequential benefits for the preschool siblings of children who receive meals at school.[15,27] Assuming similar benefits occur in Rwanda, ESFP will reduce the incidence of stunting among preschool children. To be clear, we are not suggesting that stunting will be reversed, but that ESFP will avert cases of stunting before they occur. The younger a child is when their sib-

Table 7.4. Quantified consequential benefits of ESFP: Selected years

Year	2012	2016	2021
Cases of stunting avoided among preschool siblings	10,109	23,750	38,924
Number of additional children graduating from upper-secondary school	0	35	5,173

ling starts to receive school meals, the greater the possibility of avoiding the child's growth being stunted.

We estimate that in year 1 of the intervention (2012), 10,109 cases of stunting among children under five will be averted. As coverage of ESFP expands, more cases of stunting will be avoided. In 2021, there will be 38,924 fewer cases of stunting among preschool siblings.

Upper-secondary school graduation

Because a greater number of children will complete primary and lower-secondary school as a result of ESFP, more children are expected to progress to upper-secondary school. This in turn will increase the number of children graduating from upper-secondary school. Over the period 2012–21 it is estimated that an additional 9,600 children will graduate from upper-secondary school as a result of ESFP.

Non-quantified consequential benefits

In addition to the consequential benefits we have quantified, several other consequential benefits flow from ESFP that are not quantified. These benefits are summarized in table 7.5 and discussed below.

Consequential benefits from increased school enrollment

School-feeding increases enrollment in and performance at school. The evidence suggests that improvements in educational attainment improve the health of the next generation, reduce HIV prevalence, and bring about better economic outcomes. Improved access to education for women leads to improvements in child nutrition through its impact on breastfeeding practices and other pathways.[28,29] It is also suggested that education reduces HIV/AIDS risk behavior,[30] lowers rates of youth pregnancy,[31] and increases the future economic productivity of the labor force.[32,33] Thus, ESFP can have an important effect on future health and education outcomes, and hence on economic growth.

Table 7.5. Non-quantified consequential benefits of ESFP

Quantified benefit leading to consequential benefit	Pathway to consequential benefit	Non-quantified consequential benefit
Increased school enrollment and completion	1. Schooling reduces HIV risk behavior 2. Educated girls more likely to negotiate safer sex 3. Education helps to reduce fertility 4. More educated future labor force 5. Children not available for work while they are at school	• Reduction in HIV/AIDS prevalence (1, 2) • Economic growth (3, 4) • Reduction in child labor (5)
Reduced stunting among preschoolers	1. Better-nourished children start school earlier 2. Better-nourished preschoolers perform better at school	• Improved education outcomes (1, 2)

Consequential benefits from girls' education

School-feeding programs are likely to increase girls' enrollment in and performance at school.[34] Better educational attainment of girls plays a vital role in improving their lives as women because educated girls have greater access to the labor market, have fewer children,[31,35-37] face lower maternal mortality, and are in a better position to protect themselves from HIV/AIDS.[34] Despite the existing gender parity in current primary-school enrollment rates in Rwanda, there is a significant gender gap in completion rates.[38] ESFP will help to retain girls through primary school — leading to multiple benefits.

Reduction in child labor

Increased enrollment through ESFP is likely to reduce the participation of children in household work and farm activities.[23] A review of evidence on school-feeding programs reports that such programs tend to protect children from the risk of both formal and informal child labor.[34] An evaluation of a school-feeding program in Burkina Faso suggests that although the program did not eliminate child labor, it led to it becoming less burdensome; children did not do farm work during the day but performed less demanding domestic tasks after school hours.[24] It is estimated that 27% of Rwandan children aged 5–14 years engage in labor activities related to subsistence agriculture, tea and sugarcane farming, domestic service, and so on.[39] ESFP should help to reduce the incidence of child labor.

Long-term benefits of better nutrition of preschool siblings

Expansion of ESFP is likely to benefit the preschool siblings of children receiving meals at school. This can contribute to reducing extreme forms of malnutrition such as stunting. Improvements in child nutrition are valuable not only for their own sake, but because of the further consequential benefits to which they lead. A number of studies, in both developing and developed countries, suggest that childhood malnutrition has adverse effects on health and education outcomes in adulthood.[40-42] Longitudinal data from rural Zimbabwe show that reductions in stunting among preschool children enable children to start school earlier and to complete more years of schooling. These children also end up taller as adults.[40-42] Similarly, a study in rural Tanzania found that well-nourished children have a significantly higher chance of completing primary school.[41] Better-nourished children in the Philippines enter school earlier and learn more effectively, leading to a superior academic performance.[42]

7.4. Summary and conclusion

School-feeding programs have been proven to be effective in a variety of contexts. The government recognizes the potential of school-feeding, and in partnership with WFP is already implementing such a program. The current Government/WFP program is, however, relatively small in scale and there is much scope for expansion. Expanding the school-feeding program will improve the nutritional status of children who receive meals. Unfortunately we have not been able to quantify this nutritional benefit for lack of data, but there is strong evidence that it occurs. In addition to nutritional benefits, ESFP will help to increase school enrollment and children's ability to concentrate and learn while at school. Both the nutritional and educational benefits are constitutive benefits of school-feeding.

ESFP will also lead to a range of consequential benefits. For example, more children will attend upper-secondary school which is not covered by ESFP. School meals help to keep children at school, which makes it more likely that they proceed to the next level of schooling — in this case upper-secondary school. We estimate that during the 10-year period 2012–21 an additional 9,600 children will go on to complete upper-secondary school as a result of ESFP.

Consequential benefits accrue not only to children who receive meals, but also to their preschool siblings. The first five years of a child's life are critical, and there are long-term consequences of being malnourished in this period. Even though there is some positive effect for preschoolers from school meals received by their siblings, efforts to address this problem directly are important.

ESFP will increase coverage of school-feeding from 14% to 50% over a 10-year period from 2012 to 2021. Increasing coverage beyond 50% will lead to further constitutive and consequential benefits. However, the benefits will increase at a diminishing rate because ESFP targets poor areas first. As coverage expands and less poor areas are included, the benefits to children from school-feeding get smaller.

While there are clear benefits to expanding the scale of the existing Government/WFP school-feeding program, it is difficult to determine the appropriate level of coverage for ESFP. The government has identified school-feeding as a priority, but questions of financing the expansion and its appropriate scale need to be discussed among national policymakers and their development partners. It is hoped that the analysis presented here will inform these discussions.

ANNEX
Annex 7A. Description of intervention

Intervention: The intervention will expand the coverage of the existing school-feeding program from 14% of children in primary and lower-secondary school to 50% over a 10-year period from 2012 to 2021. It will be implemented in the poorest areas first, and then in other parts of the country. The target coverage of 50% is to be achieved in 2021.

Goal: The intervention has the dual objectives of improving the nutritional status of school children and improving their educational outcomes.

Context: Food insecurity is a major threat to children's well-being in Rwanda. And despite improvements in primary-school enrollment, retention in and subsequent completion of primary and secondary education remain low.[19] Expanding the current school-feeding program has the potential to improve children's nutritional status and reduce the impact of undernutrition on school attendance and completion.[6,15]

Design: ESFP will provide one meal a day for children in primary and lower-secondary schools located in areas that have been targeted as poor. Children will receive cooked meals for five days a week in each week of the school year, which amounts to 180 days in the calendar year. The types of meal served will conform to local conditions, eating habits and preferences. To improve nutritional and learning outcomes, the food will be fortified with vitamins and minerals in which Rwandan children are deficient.[43] Professional management will ensure that school-meal ingredients continue uninterrupted throughout the school year. The caloric content of the school meal will be 30% to 45% of children's daily requirement (i.e., 555 to 830 kilocalories per school meal).[23]

Procurement: School-feeding programs have the option of buying food from international, national and local markets. Wherever possible, ESFP will rely on national or local purchase of foodstuffs. African governments and the New Partnership for Africa's Development (NEPAD) recommend that school-feeding programs utilize national food supply and production. Buying food locally or nationally benefits small-scale farmers by expanding their market opportunities.[44,45] The government, through its School Garden Project, has already begun to support and develop local production and community participation.[11]

Targeting: Geographic targeting will be used to prioritize areas with high levels of poverty. Regional data on poverty rates will be used to identify the poorest areas. The program will provide school meals to all children in primary and lower-secondary schools in the intervention areas.

Annex 7B. Methods and assumptions
Cost estimation

Cost estimation is based on information from the current school-meals program in Rwanda implemented by the government and WFP. The annual cost of school meals provided through ESFP is taken to be US$41.67 per child, which is the annual per-child cost of the Government/WFP school-feeding program in Rwanda. The total cost of ESFP is calculated by multiplying this unit cost by the number of children covered. Total costs are disaggregated into six categories reported by WFP,[8] and shown in table 7B.1 .

Table 7B.1. Disaggregation of total cost of ESFP by category

Category of cost	% of total cost
Food costs	47
International transport	11
Within-country transport, storage and handling	15
Other direct operational costs	7
Direct support costs	13
Overhead cost	7

Program coverage and targeting

- **Coverage**: The current Government/WFP school-feeding program provides meals to 350,000 children,[10] i.e., to 14% of children enrolled in primary and lower-secondary schools. ESFP is a 10-year program over the period 2012-21 that will linearly increase coverage from 14% of children in primary and lower-secondary school in 2012 to 50% in 2021.
- **Targeting**: The current Government/WFP school-feeding program and ESFP both target poorer areas. The regional focus is intended to achieve disproportionate coverage of children from poor households (DHS 2005 wealth quintiles 1 and 2). We assume that 70% of children who receive meals under ESFP will be from national wealth quintiles 1 and 2, and the remaining 30% from higher quintiles.

Estimation of benefits

- **Education benefits:** The impact of ESFP on school enrollment and completion is estimated by using DHS 2005 baseline data for Rwanda and information on the impact of school-feeding programs from other countries. The impact on school enrollment is based on evidence from a school-meals program in Bangladesh — which increased net enrollment by 9.6 percentage points.[12] In the Bangladesh study, enrollment in the control group *without* school-feeding was 65%. Given that 35% of children were out of school, the increase of 9.6 percentage points implies that 27% of children (9.6/35) who were out of school in Bangladesh became enrolled in school as a result of the intervention. To calculate the impact of ESFP on school enrollment in Rwanda, we applied this same percentage of 27% to children out-of-school in targeted areas. We use DHS 2005 data by wealth quintile as above to estimate the size of the out-of-school population of children in targeted areas.

In order to estimate school completion as a result of ESFP, we need to know the impact on grade repetition rates. To our knowledge, there is no study which estimates the impact of school-feeding programs on grade repetition rates. However, there is well-documented evidence for malnourished children which shows significant positive impacts of school-feeding on attendance, concentration and test scores.[12,17] We assume that improvements in attendance and test scores will translate into reduced grade repetition rates for children from households in quintiles 1 and 2 only, i.e., for children from extremely poor households. For these children, we assume that grade repetition rates will decrease by 27% as a result of ESFP.
See chapter 6 for sources of information relating to baseline enrollment rates, dropout rates and repetition rates.

- **Nutrition benefits**: The impact of ESFP on stunting of preschool siblings is based on evidence from a randomized trial in Northern Uganda.[15] The current rates of stunting among under-fives in Rwanda are obtained from DHS 2005. We use the Ugandan data to estimate the difference that school-feeding will make to the nutritional status of preschool siblings, measured in terms of improved HAZ scores, and we use DHS 2005 data to estimate the difference that these improved HAZ scores will make to rates of stunting.

In Uganda it is found that preschool siblings of children who receive school meals have height-for-age Z-scores that are 0.363 standard deviations higher than children from the control group.[15] DHS 2005 data provide us with the distribution of height-for-age Z-scores of children under-five in Rwanda, by wealth quintile. From this we calculate the HAZ distribution for ESFP target areas, under the assumption that 70% of children are from national wealth quintiles 1 and 2, and 30% are from higher quintiles. The cut-off that identifies stunting is two standard deviations below the WHO Child Growth Standards median. Applying the cut-off to the HAZ distribution for ESFP target areas, we can estimate the percentage of children who are stunted. To estimate the impact of ESFP, we shift the HAZ distribution for ESFP target areas to the right by the average increase in HAZ observed in Uganda (0.363 standard deviations) and calculate the new percentage falling below the cut-off. In other words, this calculation assumes that all preschool children under five in target areas benefit from ESFP by the same absolute amount of 0.363 standard deviations.

Annex 7C. ESFP coverage, costs, and benefits

Table 7C.1. ESFP coverage and costs: 2012–21

Year	2012	2013	2014	2015	2016	2017	2018	2019	2020	2021
Number of children receiving school meals through ESFP	97,649	210,616	335,029	467,318	603,271	739,428	873,794	1,011,759	1,150,141	1,287,574
Primary school	89,038	187,433	289,414	390,816	488,719	575,903	652,487	728,806	808,923	895,285
Lower-secondary school	8,611	23,183	45,615	76,502	114,552	163,525	221,307	282,953	341,218	392,289
Number of preschool siblings of children receiving school meals through ESFP	83,201	179,452	285,455	398,170	514,006	630,016	744,501	862,051	979,958	1,097,056
Total cost of ESFP (2012 US$ million)	4.07	8.78	13.96	19.47	25.14	30.81	36.41	42.16	47.93	53.65
Food costs	1.93	4.16	6.62	9.24	11.93	14.62	17.27	20.00	22.74	25.45
International transport	0.46	1.00	1.59	2.22	2.86	3.51	4.15	4.80	5.46	6.11
Within-country transport, storage and handling	0.60	1.30	2.07	2.88	3.72	4.56	5.39	6.24	7.09	7.94
Other direct operational costs	0.29	0.63	1.00	1.39	1.80	2.21	2.61	3.02	3.43	3.84
Direct support costs	0.52	1.11	1.77	2.47	3.18	3.90	4.61	5.34	6.07	6.79
Overhead cost	0.27	0.57	0.91	1.27	1.64	2.02	2.38	2.76	3.14	3.51

Table 7C.2. Quantified constitutive benefits of ESFP: 2012–21

Year	2012	2013	2014	2015	2016	2017	2018	2019	2020	2021
Number of additional children enrolled in school	969	8,466	27,350	60,665	109,506	172,948	235,653	304,635	375,589	445,537
Primary school	969	8,001	24,926	53,319	92,769	138,959	175,934	212,166	246,818	279,570
Lower-secondary school	0	465	2,424	7,346	16,737	33,989	59,719	92,469	128,771	165,967
Number of additional children completing primary school	0	425	1,846	4,790	10,999	19,430	29,201	39,896	51,027	61,923
Number of additional children completing lower-secondary school	0	14	111	544	1,608	3,702	7,189	13,525	21,936	31,028

Table 7C.3. Quantified consequential benefits of ESFP: 2012–21

Year	2012	2013	2014	2015	2016	2017	2018	2019	2020	2021
Cases of stunting avoided among preschool siblings	10,109	13,716	17,240	20,631	23,750	26,586	29,219	32,855	36,011	38,924
Number of additional children graduating from upper-secondary school	0	0	0	7	35	132	449	1,206	2,682	5,173

References

1. World Food Programme. *The State of Food Insecurity in the World: Addressing Food Insecurity in Protracted Crises*. Rome, Italy: Food and Agriculture Organization of the United Nations, 2010.

2. UNICEF. *State of the World's Children 2009: Maternal and Newborn Health*. New York, NY: UNICEF, 2008.

3. WHO. *WHO Statistical Information System: Rwanda*. Geneva, Switzerland: WHO, 2008.

4. National Institute of Statistics, Rwanda Ministry of Health, Macro International Inc. *Rwanda Demographic and Health Survey 2005*. Kigali, Rwanda and Calverton, MD: NIS, RMH, and Macro International Inc., 2006.

5. Rwanda Ministry of Health. *National Nutrition Policy*. Kigali, Rwanda: Government of Rwanda, 2005.

6. Rwanda Prime Minister's Office. *A Situation Analysis of Orphans and Other Vulnerable Children in Rwanda*. Kigali, Rwanda: Government of Rwanda, 2008.

7. World Food Programme. *School Feeding Works for Girls' Education*. Rome, Italy: WFP, 2001.

8. World Food Programme. *Budget Review for the Approval of Regional Director*. Rwanda Development Project 10677.0. Budget Revision No. 08. Rome, Italy: WFP, 2007.

9. World Food Programme. *Budget Increase to Development Activities*. Rwanda Development Project 10677.0. Rome, Italy: WFP, 2011.

10. World Food Programme. *Food Assistance Support for Education*. Rwanda Development Project 10677.0. Rome, Italy: WFP, 2007.

11. Ndahiro A, Codjia G. *School Garden in Rwanda*. Rome, Italy: Food and Agriculture Organization of the United Nations, 2006.

12. Ahmed AU. *The Impact of Feeding Children in School: Evidence from Bangladesh*. Washington, DC: International Food Policy Research Institute, 2004.

13. Kristjansson B, Petticrew M, MacDonald B, Krasevec J, Janzen L, Greenhalgh T, Wells GA, MacGowan J, Farmer AP, Shea B, Mayhew A, Tugwell P, V W. School feeding for improving the physical and psychosocial health of disadvantaged students. *Cochrane Database of Systematic Reviews* 2009; 1(CD004676):1–138.

14. Powell CA, Walker SP, Chang SM, Grantham-McGregor SM. Nutrition and education: A randomized trial of the effects of breakfast in rural primary school children. *American Journal of Clinical Nutrition* 1998; 68(4):873–879.

15. Adelman S, Alderman H, Gilligan DO, Konde-Lule J. *The Impact of Alternative Food for Education Programs on Child Nutrition in Northern Uganda*. Washington, DC: International Food Policy Research Institute, 2008.

16. Afridi F. The Impact of School Meals on School Participation: Evidence from Rural India. Syracuse, NY: Syracuse University, Department of Economics, 2007.
17. Taras H. Nutrition and student performance at school. *Journal of School Health* 2005; 75(6):199–213.
18. WHO. *World Health Statistics 2011: Indicator Compendium*. Geneva, Switzerland: WHO, 2011.
19. Rwanda Ministry of Education. *Education Sector Strategic Plan 2008–2012*. Kigali, Rwanda: Government of Rwanda, 2008.
20. Adelman S, Gilligan DO, Lehrer K. *How Effective are Food for Education Programs? A Critical Assessment of the Evidence from Developing Countries*. Food Policy Series 9. Washington, DC: International Food Policy Research Institute, 2008.
21. Finan JF, Rashid A, Woel B, Arunga D, Ochola S, Muindi M. *Impact Evaluation of WFP School Feeding Programs in Kenya (1999–2008): A Mixed-Methods Approach*. Rome, Italy: WFP, 2010.
22. World Food Programme. *Summary Report of the Evaluation of School Feeding in Cambodia*. Executive Board, First Regular Session. Rome, Italy: WFP, 2011.
23. Bundy D, Burbano C, Grosh M, Gelli A, Jukes M, Drake L. *Rethinking School Feeding: Social Safety Nets, Child Development and the Education Sector*. Directions in Development. Human Development. Washington, DC: World Bank, 2009.
24. Kazianga H, de Walque D, Alderman H. Educational and Health Impact of Two School Feeding Schemes: Evidence From a Randomized Trial in Rural Burkina Faso. Stillwater, OK: Oklahoma State University, Department of Economics, 2008.
25. Chandler AM, Walker SP, Connolly K, Grantham-McGregor SM. School breakfast improves verbal fluency in undernourished Jamaican children. *Journal of Nutrition* 1995; 125(4):894–900.
26. Rosso JMD. School Feeding Programs: Improving Effectiveness and Increasing the Benefit to Education. A Guide for Program Managers. Oxford, UK: The Partnership for Child Development, 1999.
27. Kazianga H, de Walque D, Alderman H. School Feeding Programs and the Nutrition of Siblings: Evidence from a Randomized Trial in Rural Burkina Faso. Stillwater, OK: Oklahoma State University, Department of Economics, 2009.
28. Fredrickson DD, Washington RL, Pham N, Jackson T, Wiltshire J, Jecha L. Reading grade levels and health behaviors of parents at child clinics. *Kansas Medicine* 1995; 96(3):127–129.
29. Kaufman H, Skipper B, Small L, Terry T, McGrew M. Effect of literacy on breast-feeding outcomes. *Southern Medical Journal* 2001; 94(3):293–296.

30. Hargreaves J, Boler T. *Girl Power: The Impact of Girls' Education on HIV and Sexual Behavior*. London, UK: ActionAid International, 2006.
31. Ozier O. The Impact of Secondary Schooling in Kenya: A Regression Discontinuity Analysis. Berkeley, CA: University of California, Berkeley, Department of Economics, 2010.
32. Barro RJ. Human capital: Growth, history and policy. *American Economic Review* 2001; 91(2):12–17.
33. Gyimah-Brempong K, Paddison O, Mitiku W. Higher education and economic growth in Africa. *Journal of Development Studies* 2006; 42(3):502-529.
34. Molinas L, de la Mothe, M. The multiple impacts of school feeding: a new approach for reaching sustainability. In: Omamo SW, Gentilini U, Sandström S, eds. *Revolution: From Food Aid to Food Assistance: Innovations in Overcoming Hunger*. Rome, Italy: World Food Programme, 2010.
35. Kravdal Ø. Education and fertility in sub-Saharan Africa: Individual and community effects. *Demography* 2002; 39(2):233–250.
36. Verspoor AM, with the SEIA Team. *At the Crossroads: Choices for Secondary Education in Sub-Saharan Africa*. Washington, DC: World Bank, 2008.
37. Wirth M, Balk D, Delamonica E, Storeygard A, Sacks E, Minujin A. Setting the stage for equity-sensitive monitoring of the maternal and child health MDGs. *Bulletin of the World Health Organization* 2006; 84(7):519-527.
38. National Institute of Statistics of Rwanda. *Millennium Development Goals: Toward Sustainable Social and Economic Growth*. Country Report 2007. Kigali, Rwanda: NISR, 2007.
39. United States Department of Labor. *2007 Findings on the Worst Forms of Child Labor – Rwanda*. Washington, DC: United States Department of Labor, 2007.
40. Alderman H, Hoddinott J, Kinsey B. *Long-term Consequences of Early Childhood Malnutrition*. Washington, DC: International Food Policy Research Institute, Food Consumption and Nutrition Division, 2003.
41. Luzi L. *Long-term Impact of Health and Nutrition Status on Education Outcomes for Children in Rural Tanzania*. Florence, Italy: UNICEF, 2010.
42. Glewwe P, Jacoby HG, King EM. Early childhood nutrition and academic achievement: A longitudinal analysis. *Journal of Public Economics* 2001; 81(3):345–368.
43. Allen L, de Benoist B, Dary O, Hurrell R. *Guidelines on Food Fortification with Micronutrients*. Rome, Italy: Food and Agricultural Organization of the United Nations, 2006.
44. Brinkman H-J, Omamo SW, Subran L, Rocchigiani M, Gingerich C, Baissas M, Gelli A, Calef D, Stoppa A, Ahmed A, Sharma M, Morgan

K, Bastja T, Kanemasu Y, Aberman NL. *Home-Grown School Feeding: A Framework to Link School Feeding with Local Agricultural Production.* Rome, Italy: World Food Programme, 2007.

45. USDA Foreign Agricultural Service, Office of Capacity Building and Development. *Assessment of Local Production for School Feeding in Rwanda.* Washington, DC: USDA, 2009.

CHAPTER 8

Angola country background

8.1. Introduction

Angola has come a long way since the end of almost three decades of civil war in 2002, which followed a violent struggle for independence. It has been able to capitalize on its natural resources to stimulate rapid economic growth, even during the world recession. However, if the situation of the majority of the population is to be improved, the government must focus not just on promoting economic growth but also on pursuing a more equitable economic and social development strategy. The living conditions of Angola's 19 million people lag behind neighboring countries with much fewer financial resources.[1] If actions can be proposed and implemented to respond to identified shortcomings, significant improvement is possible. This chapter is the first step in a process of identifying those actions. The chapter provides a socio-economic review of Angola, which will inform the subsequent identification and evaluation of actions.

8.2. Recent history and current political situation

After years of struggle, the people of Angola won independence from Portugal in 1975. The Portuguese administration, and the vast majority of the expatriate population, withdrew rapidly. The subsequent civil war, fought among the three main nationalist movements — the Movimento Popular de Libertação de Angola (MPLA), the União Nacional para a Independência Total de Angola (UNITA), and the Frente Nacional de Libertação de Angola (FNLA) — began shortly after independence and led to widespread social disruption and hundreds of thousands of deaths. During the civil war, the MPLA, led by Agostinho Neto and then by Eduardo dos Santos, and UNITA, led largely by Jonas Savimbi, emerged as the strongest forces.[2] Fueled by natural resource wealth, Angola's civil war became the ground for foreign involvement and proxy wars between competing regimes during the Cold War period. MPLA was backed by Cuba and the USSR and financed through oil resources, whereas UNITA was funded by diamonds and supported mainly by the United States and the Republic of South Africa.[3]

Apart from the conflict between MPLA and UNITA, Cabinda, the enclave in the north of Angola and west of the Democratic Republic of Congo (DRC), has been fighting for separation from Angola since independence.[4] Cabindan separatists, the Front for the Liberation of the Enclave of Cabinda (FLEC), claim that Cabinda was illegally occupied by MPLA following independence from Portugal.[5] As a region with massive reserves of oil, Cabinda has been a highly sought-after and fought-over region in a conflict referred to as Angola's "forgotten war".

MPLA retained control of the government throughout the war, and in the early days of independence showed commitment to the poor with increased social expenditures on education, health, housing, social security, and community services. Education for children, as well as for adults and veterans of the armed forces, was prioritized. The health sector was strengthened by the building of 1,260 health units, the implementation of a free annual vaccination program, and an influx of international doctors, particularly from Cuba.[6] Other social reforms granted much-needed support to working mothers, former guerrillas, and the elderly. However, government funding for these initiatives decreased dramatically in 1977, as a result of growing expectation that international humanitarian organizations would provide such services to Angolans.[6]

Fighting between MPLA and UNITA was halted in 1991 with the signing of the Bicesse peace agreement.[6] During this time, the government revised the constitution, approved multi-party democracy, prioritized civic and human rights, and established the basic principles of a market economy. These freedoms enabled some civil society organizations to begin to develop.[6] Angola's first elections in 1992, at which voter turnout was more than 91% of registered voters, gave dos Santos 49.6% of the vote and Savimbi 40.1%.[6] Although the election was considered by the UN and other external observers to be a fair one, UNITA refused to accept the results and resumed the conflict. The war restarted with unprecedented intensity on both sides and was characterized by widespread human rights abuses that left hundreds of thousands dead and a large proportion of the civilian population displaced.[6]

With resurgence of the war, political control again became heavily concentrated in the office of the President. In January 1999, President dos Santos who was Head of State also became Head of Government, further centralizing power.[6]

During the war the Angolan population suffered directly and indirectly. Substantial neglect and disruption of the health sector led to outbreaks of cholera and yellow fever in the cities, as public sanitation systems collapsed.[6]

The conflict destroyed much of the country's infrastructure, including hospitals, health clinics, roads and schools. Landmines were placed over large parts of the country.[7] The war prompted rapid urbanization, particularly in Luanda from the 1970s to the 1990s.[6] Child soldiers were used on both sides throughout the war.[8] The war also increased violence and discrimination against women, many of whom were raped by soldiers or identified as witches and burned at the stake.[9]

Following sustained government offensives, Savimbi was killed in February 2002, leaving MPLA as the military victors. The civil war formally ended in April 2002 with the signing of the Luena peace memorandum between MPLA and UNITA.[6] Since the peace memorandum, central control over the public and private sectors has remained tight. Power is concentrated in the executive branch of government, which is composed of the President, the Prime Minister, and the Council of Ministers. Each of Angola's 18 provinces is presided over by a Governor appointed by the President. According to Freedom House, over 90% of legislation originates from the executive branch.[10] The current President, Eduardo dos Santos, is expected to seek re-election in the upcoming election which is scheduled for 2012, simultaneously with elections for the National Assembly.[11]

The National Assembly consists of 220 seats, 130 awarded by proportional representation in national elections and the remaining 90 elected by provincial districts. Following Angola's second national parliamentary elections in September 2008, MPLA solidified its stronghold over UNITA and other opposition parties, with MPLA gaining 82% of the vote, UNITA 10% and other opposition parties a combined 8%.[12] MPLA was awarded 191 seats, and UNITA only 16 seats.[12] This marked a notable decline for UNITA, which had won 70 seats in the previous election in 1992.[13] The weakness of opposition to MPLA has decreased the threat of yet another violent political confrontation. However, the diminished opposition decreases MPLA's accountability to the population. For example, the government's budget proposals are not debated publicly, and no discussion is conducted on divergence between budgeted and actual expenditures.[14]

The government has been characterized as lacking transparency, and accusations of corruption are frequently made.[3] Angola is ranked 158 out of 180 countries on Transparency International's Corruption Perception Index.[15] Corruption deters local and foreign investment, and hinders citizens from accessing important social services. For example, teachers and health personnel sometimes charge citizens informal fees — in part because of the limited supply of services and inadequate salaries of employees. Such corruption frequently deters the poorest and neediest people from accessing public services.[16]

The Constitutional Law of 1992 establishes the broad outlines of the judicial structure and delineates the rights and duties of citizens. The legal system is based on Portuguese and customary law. The system is currently weak and fragmented, and is in the process of post-war rebuilding. The President appoints Supreme Court judges to life terms without a procedure that involves parliamentary oversight. The Constitution mandates the establishment of a Constitutional Court, but this has not yet occurred.[10]

There is a large backlog of cases in both the Supreme Court and the criminal courts, causing major delays in hearings.[17] Inadequate training of magistrates, lack of infrastructure, and corruption — all hinder access to, and functioning of, the judicial system.[10] As of 2003, only 23 of the 168 municipal courts were operational.[18] Informal courts tend to be the principal means through which citizens resolve disputes, particularly in rural areas.[17] Rules in these informal courts, however, vary by community and do not provide citizens with the same rights to a fair trial as the formal legal system.[17]

8.3. Economic and social context

The size of Angola's population is estimated to be approximately 19 million in 2010.[1] The population is growing fast with a total fertility rate (TFR) of 5.6; it is thus very young.[1] The Multiple Indicator Cluster Survey (MICS) 2001 showed that by the age of 18 years, 33% of women had already given birth; by the age of 20 years, more than 66% of women had given birth to one or more children. The average age of first marriage was 21.4 years for women and 25 years for men.[19] Estimates based on the Malaria Indicator Survey (MIS) 2006/07 suggest that 46% of the population was under 15 years of age, and 19% was under five years of age. Only 3% of the population was above age 65.[20]

Rapid urbanization occurred during the last 10 years of the war and the first years of peace. The average annual growth rate of the urban population during 1990–2007 was 5.4%.[1] Whereas in the mid-1990s the majority of the population (58%) was rural, by 2007 approximately 55% of the population lived in urban areas.[1] In 2010 the level of urbanization had increased to 59%.[1]

After the war, the country entered a period of reconstruction and rehabilitation marked by significant economic growth fueled by natural resources. The economy is still driven largely by the country's vast resources of oil, diamonds, gold, iron ore, and other minerals — and their related support industries. Fishing, agriculture and lumber production have also seen recent growth, though all remain underdeveloped.[a] Tourism, which is an important sector for Angola's neighbors, is as yet relatively undeveloped. Surging oil prices have led to rapid growth of GDP, which increased from US$19.8 billion in 2004 to US$61.0 billion in 2007 (both in current prices).[1] Despite the economic slowdown in the second half of 2008, Angola's economy continued to grow.[21] In 2008 GDP in current prices was US$84.2 billion.[1] In 2009 the economy contracted, largely because of the OPEC cap on oil production and technical problems that slowed oil extraction, and GDP fell to US$75.5 billion in 2009 in current prices.[1] In 2010 the economy began to recover and GDP reached US$84.4 billion in current prices.[1]

In real terms, GDP per capita increased by 60% (in constant 2005 international dollars) from PPP$3,118 in 2004 to PPP$4,982 in 2007. In 2010, GDP per capita was PPP$5,454 (in 2005 international $).[1]

Crude oil production accounts for between 40% and 50% of GDP, 90% of exports, and 90% of government revenues.[22] As an indication of its magnitude, Angola's oil revenue of US$22.5 billion in 2007 exceeded the total net bilateral overseas development assistance of US$21.5 billion to *all* of sub-Saharan Africa from OECD Development Assistance Committee donors.[23]

Sonangol is the state-owned company that coordinates all business in the oil sector.[24] It is a 51% or more stakeholder in almost all foreign oil ventures in Angola and runs a small refinery.[24] Major foreign partners in the oil industry include Sinopec, Petrobras, Texaco-Chevron, Shell, and ONGC.

Angola is the world's fifth largest diamond producer in terms of value. In 2007 the state-owned diamond company, Endiama, extracted approximately 9.7 million carats of diamonds which yielded US$1.3 billion in revenue. The company is planning to expand production.[25]

Angola has also been able to reduce its debt during the period 2005–08, and had proposed plans to repay its debt to the Paris Club in full by 2010 (it is not clear whether this plan was realized).[26] The country is able to access credit from a variety of international sources. China, Angola's single largest lender, has loaned the country at least US$7 billion since 2004.[27] The World Bank has stated that it will loan Angola US$1 billion between 2009 and 2013 to help the country diversify its economy.[28] Angola severed loan negotiations with the IMF in 2005 due to disagreement on loan conditionality relating to financial transparency.[29]

The large increases in government revenue since 2002 have led to only modest increases in government expenditure on child-related services.[30] Government expenditure has not grown at the same pace as revenue, and fiscal surpluses have increased in recent years. The country's dependence on oil as its primary source of revenue does make government expenditure vulnerable to fluctuations in the price of oil.[26]

In the latter half of the decade 2000–10, Angola has tried to preserve macroeconomic stability through improved fiscal and monetary policies and by reducing dependency on oil revenue by promoting non-oil private sector development.[23] These efforts have improved stability: for example, annual inflation which was 325% in 2000 was down to 14% in 2009.[31] Efforts to reduce inflation further are being made, but capacity constraints are likely to lead to inflation inertia in the near future.[23]

8.3.1. Poverty and food security

Angola suffers from serious inequality and poverty. In 2001, the Gini co-efficient was estimated to be 0.62.[32] In 2009, Angola ranked 143 out of 182 countries on the UNDP's Human Development Index.[33] A large proportion of the population still engages in subsistence agriculture leaving them excluded from the formal economy.[10] Data from MICS 2001 indicated that approximately 70% of the population lived on less than US$2 per day.[19] There is evidence of stunting even among the wealthiest 20% of households. In the top quintile of MICS 2001, a third of children under-five were suffering from moderate or severe stunting.[19]

The UN Food and Agriculture Organization (FAO) estimated that between 2003 and 2005, 46% of the population was undernourished.[b,34] Many factors are responsible for undernourishment in Angola. Food production and transportation have been affected by recurrent floods and droughts, soil depletion, landmines, and poor irrigation and road infrastructure. Food imports, moreover, are constrained by limited port capacity. These factors contribute to what the World Food Programme refers to as food insecurity of households in the country.[c,35]

8.3.2. Housing and access to basic services

In 2001, average household size in Angola was estimated to be 4.8 persons. Urban households tended to be larger than rural households, with an average of 5.1 members compared to 4.3 members. At this time 82% of households had at least one child below the age of 15 years, and 60% of households had a child below the age of 5 years. Over a quarter of households (27%) were headed by women.[19]

Data from MIS 2006/07 show average household size in the country to be 5.7 members, with urban areas having 6.2 members and rural areas 5.1 members. Some 21% of urban households have nine or more members, while only 9% of the rural households are that large. These large urban households live in crowded conditions in cities such as Luanda.[20]

In MIS 2006/07, 50% of all respondents report earth or sand as flooring in their houses; in the rural areas almost 90% of households have earth or sand floors. Nationally, an estimated 35% of households report cement or wood flooring. In the cities, cement or wood is the material for 62% of house floors.[20]

8.3.3. Water and sanitation

Surveys show that less than half (46%) of Angolan households have access to drinking water from an improved source. The situation is better in urban areas where access is 59%, compared to 34% in rural areas. The most common source of drinking water in rural areas (42%) is surface water obtained from lakes and streams.[20]

Data from MIS 2006/07 show that 48% of households have access to an improved sanitation facility, with 18% using a pit latrine with a slab and 17% using a facility that flushes into a septic tank. Just over one-in-five (22%) of Angolans have an unimproved sanitation facility that involves an open pit or a pit latrine without a slab. Over one-quarter (29%) of all households report no toilet facility. In rural areas, the majority of households (54%) report not having a toilet facility.[20]

8.3.4. Electricity and energy

Electricity utilization was rare in 2001, when an estimated 80% of the population did not have access to electricity. Even among households in the top quintile, 15% did not have access to electricity.[19] MIS 2006/07 suggests a somewhat better situation, with just over one-third of the population (38%) reporting access to electricity.[20] According to the 2001 data, the main sources of energy for cooking were firewood (42%), charcoal (41%), and gas (14%).[19]

8.3.5. Security

The country's domestic situation poses a number of security concerns, especially for impoverished women and children. Housing in poor areas, especially in Luanda, is at times insecure, as forced evictions from informal housing have become frequent since the end of the war. Between 2002 and 2006, evictions in and around Luanda have displaced an estimated 20,000 people and destroyed over 3,000 homes.[36]

Civilian crime, though poorly documented, is assumed to be quite common. In part, this can be attributed to the estimated four million weapons currently in civilian possession.[10] Domestic violence is a major problem for women and children. In a survey of 9 municipalities in Luanda province, 78% of girls between the ages 14 and 18 years reported experiencing physical, psychological, or sexual violence.[37] Accusations of child witchcraft have been a growing phenomenon especially against orphaned boys.[10] When these children are accused — often after the death of a family member from HIV/AIDS — they are frequently tortured, beaten, and expelled from their homes onto the streets or into treatment centers.[38]

Human trafficking for prostitution or forced labor is a further problem for women and children. Usually poorer families are targets, as are unaccompanied migrant children. As of June 2009, the government had not investigated, prosecuted or convicted any trafficking offenders.[39]

There is a shortage of social workers in the country. As of December 2008, the Instituto Superior João Paulo II was the only provider of social-work training, and since 2005 only 55 students have graduated as social workers. The shortage of social workers has led to a serious undersupply of child protection services.

The planning of child protection interventions is constrained by a lack of data on the frequency and severity of child abuse. The CRC Implementation Report released in March 2008 stated that Angola had no well-organized system to report or collect reliable data about acts of torture, cruelty, and other maltreatment to which many children are subject in the family, institutions, and community environment.[9]

With more than one-third (35%) of its surface area covered in land mines, Angola is one of the most mined countries in the world.[7] The landmines themselves affect the lives of an estimated 2.2 million people. Of this number 60% are children, and UNICEF suggests that around 80,000 people have been either physically or psychologically affected by mines.[40] Efforts to clear the mines have been underway for some time, but data on the extent to which they have been cleared are not available.[41]

Although the civil war with UNITA has ended, fighting with FLEC has continued in the Cabinda region even after the ceasefire in 2006.[4] FLEC also claims widespread human rights abuses by the military against the rebels in the enclave.[5]

8.4. Health infrastructure and population health

Angola's civil war severely damaged its health infrastructure. Estimates suggest that 65% of the country's health facilities were destroyed during the war from 1975 to 2002.[7] At the end of 2002, 12% of hospitals, 11% of health centers, and 85% of health posts were not operational due to the destruction (or serious deterioration) of physical infrastructure, lack of staff, and inadequate basic equipment.[42] In 2005, access to healthcare was limited to between 30% and 40% of the population, leaving 60% or more without access. Due to the scarcity of clinics, most people are forced to walk long distances to reach a healthcare facility.[43,44] The heaviest fighting during the war occurred in rural areas and the greatest destruction of health infrastructure occurred there. During and immediately after the civil war, Angola's high concentration of land mines inhibited the delivery of services to people, as well as the movement of healthcare workers and materials. The after-effects of war also hindered the delivery of health services because damaged roads, bridges and railways have impeded the movement of health personnel and essential drugs.[44]

The density of doctors in Angola (1 per 10,000 population) is half the average for sub-Saharan Africa (2 per 10,000).[45] By comparison, the density of nurses in Angola (14 per 10,000) is a little above the SSA average (11 nurses per 10,000).[45] During the war, many health professionals took refuge in the provincial capitals. In 2004, 70% of all doctors and 30% of all nurses were living in Luanda.[7] Poor health infrastructure in rural areas is cited as a reason for the continued concentration of health professionals in urban centers.[44] Efforts are, however, underway to rectify the situation.[7]

Under-financing of the health sector has exacerbated the problem of re-constructing and re-establishing health infrastructure after the civil war. In 2002 government health expenditure was only 1.8% of GDP. Since then the situation has improved, and in 2009 government health expenditure was 4.1% of GDP.[1]

Another hindrance to healthcare utilization is the tendency of some health-center staff to charge informal fees for the provision of drugs and services. This practice is sometimes used for personal gain but it is also carried out to generate revenue for the operation of the health facility.[44,46]

Under-financing of the health sector, informal fees and high transport costs all contribute to low utilization of government health services. A 2005 study of the health system found that less than half (42%) of the population use government health services when ill. More than a quarter (26%) use private health facilities, and just over a fifth (21%) resort to self-treatment.[44,46]

The scarcity of drugs within the government health sector further complicates healthcare delivery.[43] Patients are often left with no option but to purchase drugs in the informal market.[44] In the informal market, drugs are often improperly prescribed, are past their expiry dates, or are counterfeit.[44]

The health status of Angolans is among the worst in the world. The low life expectancy at birth of 49 years for males and 52 years for females in 2009 reflects the impact of the country's 27-year civil war, high prevalence of poverty, inadequate primary healthcare, and other factors such as lack of basic education.[1] The under-five mortality rate is extremely high at 161 deaths per 1,000 live births in 2010.[1] Malaria is the leading cause of mortality and morbidity, and threatens the entire population.[43] Angola has an estimated 6 million malaria cases per year, indicating that about one-third of the population is directly affected each year.[7] Malaria accounts for approximately 80% of the demand for healthcare and for 50% of hospital in-patient admissions.[47] Other common causes of mortality and morbidity are acute respiratory infections and diarrheal diseases.[47]

Approximately one-third of households in the country own an insecticide-treated mosquito net. Vulnerable groups such as children and pregnant women sleep under a bednet more often than other household members.[20,48] The most commonly-used drug to treat malaria is chloroquine.[19] But anti-malaria treatments are not always available and only 35% of under-fives who require anti-malarial drugs receive them.[49] This situation contributes to a high level of self-medication, which partly explains why 50% of malaria cases were found to be resistant to chloroquine in 2001.[19]

Maternal mortality has reached excessively high levels. A 2005 UNICEF study estimated the maternal mortality rate to be approximately 1,400 per 100,000 live births. More recent estimates have, however, revised this estimate downward and place the figure at 610 per 100,000 in 2008.[50] Maternal deaths are attributed to common pregnancy problems which are largely untreated. Only 46% of deliveries occur in institutions.[50]

The prevalence of tuberculosis (TB) has increased. WHO estimated TB prevalence to be 285 per 100,000 in 2006, compared to 231 per 100,000 in 1996.[51] In 2007 there were 49,000 new cases of tuberculosis, 9,100 of which occurred among HIV-positive people.[52]

AIDS was first diagnosed in Angola in 1985 but major national efforts to conduct surveillance were hindered until the civil war ended in 2002. The Instituto Nacional de Luta Contra a SIDA has suggested that the spread of HIV/AIDS was slowed by the restricted movement of people during the civil war, both within and outside the country. This may be one reason for Angola having one of the lowest rates of HIV prevalence in southern Africa.[53] Since the war ended, movement has become less restricted and the likelihood of HIV reaching once-isolated communities has increased. Many believe that HIV/AIDS has the potential to spread rapidly, because greater population mobility after the end of the civil war has led to increased travel, trade and contact with neighboring countries — heightening the risks of exposure. It has also been suggested that the large number of displaced people, extreme poverty, and limited female autonomy make the country susceptible to the spread of HIV/AIDS. Since the end of the war, UNAIDS estimates that adult HIV prevalence has increased from 1.7% in 2002 to 2.1% in 2007.[54] Since 2007 adult HIV prevalence is thought to have remained stable at 2.1%.[55]

HIV prevalence varies across different regions of the country: the lowest rates are found in the center of the country and the highest in the border provinces. Proximity to the border with Namibia and Zambia, where adult HIV prevalence is above 15%, accounts for higher prevalence rates in the border regions of Angola.[56] WHO reported that in 2005 HIV prevalence in the border provinces of Cunene and Uíge had reached 9.1% and 4.8%, respectively.[43]

Knowledge about prevention is generally low. In 2005, only 23% of youth surveyed knew about two principal ways to prevent sexual transmission of HIV, and only 9% of mothers with young children knew about mother-to-child transmission.[56]

In 2003, the government created the National Commission to Combat AIDS and Endemic Diseases (Comissão Nacional de Luta Contra o VIH e SIDA). This is a political body coordinated by the President of the Republic and involves the participation of several ministries. The Commission is intended to engage government and civil society organizations in national programs and efforts to prevent HIV/AIDS. To coordinate the activities of these different actors, in 2005 the government created the National Institute for the Fight against HIV and AIDS (Instituto Nacional de Luta Contra o

VIH e SIDA). Currently, the Instituto Nacional de Luta Contra a Sida (INLS) is the lead agency in the country's response to HIV/AIDS, and is charged with the design of policies, norms and training. Specific decisions about logistics and implementation are decentralized to provincial governments and health authorities.[57]

Angola has committed to the United Nations General Assembly Special Session (UNGASS) on HIV/AIDS guidelines. In early 2006, the government declared the Year of Accelerated Action in the Battle against HIV/AIDS. In December 2006, the government launched the National Strategic Plan for Control of Sexually Transmitted Infections and HIV/AIDS 2007-2010.[57] In 2004, the National Assembly passed a comprehensive HIV/AIDS law that promoted the rights of people living with HIV/AIDS (PLWHA), specifying their right to employment, free public healthcare, and confidentiality regarding their HIV status.[56] UNICEF, UNDP and other agencies have been working with the government since 2008 to expand and implement various protocols and guidelines, including treatment for sexually-transmitted infections (STI), voluntary counseling and testing (VCT), prevention of mother-to-child transmission (PMTCT), and promotion of breastfeeding.[58] Despite the general acceptance and practice of male circumcision, there is no official public policy to encourage male circumcision as a means of reducing HIV transmission in female-to-male sexual relations.

In 2005, the Ministry of Social Welfare (Ministério da Assistência e Reinserção Social, or MINARS) and UNICEF commissioned the Center for Scientific Research and Studies and the Catholic University of Angola to produce a Rapid Analysis, Appraisal and Action Plan (RAAAP) on the impact of HIV/AIDS on children and their families. The study group argued that children are vulnerable because of widespread poverty and a lack of institutions to protect their rights. They concluded that these factors exacerbate the impact of HIV/AIDS on children.[59]

8.5. Child health

In 2010 the infant mortality rate in Angola was 98 per 1,000 live births and the under-five mortality rate was 161 per 1,000 live births.[1] These high rates account for the fact that 55% of all deaths in the country are of children under the age of five.[30]

Under-five mortality is caused by malaria, acute diarrheal diseases, acute respiratory infections, measles, and neonatal tetanus. Together, these diseases accounted for 60% of child deaths between 2001 and 2003.[7] MIS 2006/07 found that 20% of children aged 6-59 months had malaria, and that prevalence for rural children was four times higher than for urban children.[20]

MICS 2001 detected little rural-urban disparity in under-five mortality rates. However, rates did vary according to a child's family situation.[19] Compared to children of mothers with no education, children of mothers with secondary or higher education had under-five mortality rates that were 62% lower, and infant mortality rates that were 40% lower.[19] Children from the lowest quintile in 2001 were 40% more likely to die before reaching the age of five than children from the highest quintile.[19]

8.5.1. Malnutrition

A report using MICS 2001 data suggests that malnutrition contributes to half the deaths of under-fives in the country.[19] Chronic malnutrition is common among children under five years of age: an estimated 31% of them are underweight, and 45% suffer from stunting.[50] The risk of malnutrition among children is influenced by their mother's education, socioeconomic status, access to primary healthcare, availability of safe drinking water, and waste disposal practices in the home.[19]

8.5.2. Diarrhea

The UNICEF 2008 report, The State of Africa's Children, estimates that 18% of all under-five deaths in Angola are due to diarrhea. Of these deaths, almost 90% are due to unsafe drinking water, lack of washing water, and poor access to sanitary waste disposal.[60] The treatment for diarrhea in Angola is inadequate. According to UNICEF, in 2001 only 32% of children who had diarrhea received oral rehydration therapy.[60]

8.5.3. Acute respiratory infections (ARIs)

According to MICS 2001, ARIs are one of the main causes of mortality among children. An estimated 8% of children under five years of age were reported to have had an acute respiratory infection in the past two weeks.[19] The main cause of death from ARI is pneumonia, which has higher prevalence and severity among malnourished compared to other children.[42] Mortality rates are associated with pneumonia are high partly because quality diagnosis and standard treatment are not widely available in health units.[42]

8.5.4. Diseases preventable by vaccination

The national Expanded Program on Immunization (EPI) recommends that children be fully vaccinated against DPT (diphtheria, pertussis and tetanus), measles, tuberculosis, yellow fever, and polio before reaching one year of age.[19] In 2003, the government undertook a national campaign against measles and achieved a coverage rate of 96%.[61] After the campaign vaccination coverage rates fell, and in 2007 immunization against measles had fallen to 88% of one-year-old children.[62]

Despite an aggressive vaccination drive in 2003, polio cases resurfaced in 2005. Since then, the number has risen to 29 confirmed polio cases in

2008 — from 8 cases in 2007, 2 in 2006, and 10 in 2005.[61] The government responded with another vaccination drive in 2007, leading to 83% of one-year old children being immunized against polio in that year.[62]

The Hepatitis B vaccine has been integrated into routine immunization schedules since 2006.[61] An estimated 83% of one-year old children in 2009 were immunized against Hepatitis B and Haemophilus influenzae type B (Hib).[62] However, not all necessary vaccines are integrated into the routine immunization schedule, and vaccines for Mumps, Pneumococcal, Rotavirus and Rubella are not included.[61]

In 2007, an estimated 88% of one-year-old children were immunized against tuberculosis.[61] In that year, 99% of one-year-old children received the first dose of DPT and 83% received the final third dose.[62] This percentage receiving the third dose marks a considerable improvement because only one-third of one-year-old children had received the third dose of DPT in 2001.[19] In 2007, 81% of newborn children were protected against tetanus.[62]

8.5.5. Vitamin A deficiency

Vitamin A is important for building resistance to infections such as HIV and malaria. MICS 2001 reported that providing high dose (200,000 IU)[63] vitamin A supplementation to children was associated with a 23% decrease in mortality compared to vitamin A deficient children who did not receive supplementation.[19] According to UNICEF, the rate of coverage for vitamin A supplementation in 2007 was only 36%.[50] Newborns can build up stores of vitamin A through breastfeeding from healthy, well-nourished mothers.[64] Yet 77% of (breastfeeding) mothers' milk was found to be deficient in vitamin A in 2001.[19] While UNICEF and WHO recommend high-dose vitamin A supplementation for women in the post-partum period so that infants receive the necessary amounts, only 21% of post-partum women received vitamin A supplements in 2007.[64] Since 1999, the Expanded Program of Immunization has included a mega-dose of vitamin A. Vitamin A was also given to children aged 9 to 59 months during the National Campaign of Vaccination against Measles in 2003, resulting in 70% of children receiving a mega-dose of vitamin A.[61]

8.6. Education

The state of the education system reflects the impact of the civil war. In 2001, only 56% of primary-school age children were attending primary school.[65] Subsequently enrollment increased rapidly, and by 2005 the gross primary-school enrollment rate was 91%.[30] In 2001, preschool child development services were almost nonexistent, with only 7% of children aged 36–59 months enrolled in an organized education program.[19] Since 2004 increased attention has been paid to children aged 0 to 5 years, with two national forums organized on the care and development of children under 5.[30]

MICS 2001 shows that attendance rates in school are influenced by the wealth quintile to which children belong. In the top quintile, 77% of children attend primary school, whereas only 35% in the bottom quintile do. In the lowest quintile, no females and only 1% of males attend the second level of basic education. Only 56% of children from the lowest quintile complete the first four years of primary education, whereas 89% of the children from the wealthiest quintile do.[19]

MICS 2001 data on education also reflect significant regional variations. The better-performing regions — the Capital and South Regions — showed a 63% attendance rate at primary school, while the worst-performing East Region showed only 44% attendance.[19] Attendance rates in the remaining areas were close to the national average of 56%.[19] It is not surprising that education indicators are much better in the Capital Region, because the education system there suffered less disruption as a result of the civil war. Thus the Capital Region has higher numbers of teachers and more schools still standing than the East Region.[19] It is not surprising that the Capital Region had the highest levels of literacy among women (69%), and the East Region had the lowest (39%).[19]

Educational standards are affected by a number of factors such as overcrowded classes, inadequate school personnel, lack of school materials, and poor school infrastructure.[66] Classrooms are overcrowded in part due to children repeating grades. Repetition is quite common, with the average repetition rate in schools estimated to be over 20%.[30] The vast majority of children do not attend the grade appropriate for their age. MICS 2001 found that 70% of seven-year old children do not attend grade 2 (the grade appropriate for their age) but are still in grade 1, either because they were repeating grade 1 or had started school late. Only 6% of 10- and 11-year olds attend the grade appropriate for their age; 85% of 15-year olds were attending the first six grades of basic education, which should be completed at age 11.[19] In 2001, the government reported an average of 64 students per classroom. In response to this overcrowding, it introduced a system of either two or three shifts of classes per day. These shifts have reduced class size but also significantly reduced the contact between teachers and students.[19]

The civil war destroyed much of the education infrastructure. During the years 1996–99, almost 1,500 school buildings were destroyed in the fighting.[67,68] Lack of infrastructure and limited classroom space have led to the payment of 'fees' to officials to be admitted to school, thereby creating a financial barrier for poorer children.[30] The purchase of textbooks, which are expensive and in limited supply, is another barrier to attending school.[46]

Schools are the site for many health and nutrition initiatives. For example, de-worming tablets are distributed to children through the school system.[69]

In the period 1999–2007, the Ministry of Education in conjunction with the World Food Programme undertook a school-lunch distribution program.[30] Children who are out of school not only miss out on the opportunity of education but also on primary health services and food distribution.

8.7. Policies and programs to improve child well-being

The government has ratified the Convention on the Rights of the Child (CRC), as well as other human rights treaties, viz. the International Covenant on Civil and Political Rights; the International Covenant on Economic, Social and Cultural Rights; and the African Charter on Human and Peoples' Rights. Recently the government also signed the optional protocols to CRC, viz. the Sale of Children; Child Prostitution and Pornography; and the Involvement of Children in Armed Conflict. The government has also signed the International Labour Organization's conventions on the Minimum Age for Admission to Employment and Work, and on the Prohibition and Immediate Action for the Elimination of the Worst Forms of Child Labour. The Constitution also provides a strong national policy framework for the protection and promotion of child well-being.[d]

In practice, however, and in part due to three decades of conflict, implementation of governmental commitments has lagged behind the promise of treaty and national law. For instance, despite recent economic growth, Angola has reportedly allocated insufficient funds for the provision of basic needs of children.[68]

Since the end of the war, the government has taken some steps towards developing its institutional capacity to realize its commitments. It has established the Ministry of Social Assistance and Inclusion (Ministério da Assistência e Reinserção Social, MINARS) and the National Children's Forum (Fórum Nacional Sobre a Criança). MINARS is responsible for the implementation of programs that promote child well-being and development, and the National Children's Forum aims to facilitate coordination among the various ministries and civil society stakeholders to promote children's rights.

In 2007, the government created the National Institute for the Angolan Child (Instituto Nacional da Criança Angolana, INAC) and the National Council on the Child (Conselho Nacional da Criança, CNAC).[71] The National Institute for the Angolan Child is responsible for the promotion of research on the health, education, development and living conditions of children in Angola. The mandate of the National Council on the Child is to serve as a mechanism which coordinates the implementation of programs at the national, regional and local levels. Currently, CNAC includes members from 16 government ministries, the National Institute for the Angolan Child, and civil society representatives.[60]

Beyond coordination, questions remain concerning the effectiveness of many ministries, governmental institutions and government-organized networks. Sceptical observers believe that the government has responded to domestic and international pressure on particular issues (HIV/AIDS, children's rights, the rights of women and families) by creating appropriately named institutions rather than by undertaking meaningful commitments to respond to difficult social problems.

In partnership with UNICEF, WHO and UNFPA, the government has initiated an Accelerated Child Survival and Development Strategy (*Sobrevivência e Desenvolvimento Acelerado da Criança*, SDAC) which is a child well-being plan for the period 2007–13. The government aims, among other things, to improve data collection, to reach MDG targets, and to enable access to health services.[60]

In 2008, as part of efforts to keep children in school, local authorities in several districts assumed control of free school lunches (merenda escolar) from the World Food Programme. The local authorities are now responsible for providing a nutritious snack daily to 1.3 million children throughout the country. The Education Ministry has recently noted that this program, along with social support and healthcare provision through schools, is to be scaled up to all public schools in the country.[72] There are, however, budgetary concerns. The budget for the program has already reached US$90 million and a full scale-up would cost an estimated US$240 million.[73]

Another major governmental initiative on child well-being is the National Strategic Plan for the Accelerated Reduction of Maternal and Child Mortality (*Redução Acelerada de Mortalidade Materno-Infantil*).[42] This initiative is focused on enabling child survival through healthcare and nutritional interventions for pregnant women, mothers, and their children. Its key strategies focus on developing and scaling up integrated care systems for childhood diseases as well as universal coverage of basic health and education interventions. These services will be offered through health facilities, mobile health teams, and community health promoters.

8.8. Conclusion

The above review of the socio-economic situation in Angola highlights large areas of inaction in relation to children affected by poverty and HIV/AIDS. Before moving on to discuss actions that can be proposed in this area, it important to recognize the constraints that the government and other potential actors face. Planning is hindered by lack of data. Implementation is affected by difficulties to do with infrastructure, corruption, and weak property rights.

The war severely damaged the country's education, health and transportation infrastructure. The damage to the health and education infrastructure remains an important constraint to development. The damaged transportation system constrains service delivery — it inhibits children, particularly girls, from attending school due to lack of transport, increased travelling time and cost, and increased dangers of travelling.[74] Damaged transportation systems also inhibit the delivery of essential drugs and services to health service posts.[44] The lack of transportation infrastructure hinders farmers as they try to access agricultural inputs, rebuild their livelihoods, and achieve food security.[75] Inadequate water and sanitation infrastructure affects child malnutrition.[19] The poor state of infrastructure has also deterred investment. In 2006, an Enterprise Survey found that 35.6% of firms identified lack of electricity as the main obstacle to investment in Angola.[76] Since the end of the war, the government has focused heavily on rebuilding destroyed or damaged infrastructure. Many international partners, notably the Chinese government, have been involved in the rebuilding process.[29]

Large increases in government revenue have allowed expenditures on child-related services to increase since 2002.[30] But the country's dependence on oil as its primary source of revenue makes government expenditures susceptible to price fluctuations. For example, President dos Santos has warned that if oil prices fall, spending on reconstruction will be reduced.[26]

Corruption deters both local and foreign investment in Angola, and its citizens from utilizing important social services. For example, in order to gain access to health and education services clients may have to pay bribes to teachers and health personnel.[30,46] Corruption within the government and the judicial system can lead to weak law enforcement and abuses of the law. Over 36% of firms identify crime as a major constraint to business in Angola, as opposed to 22.6% in Africa in general.[76]

Historically, MPLA has been associated with the Mbundu ethnicity, and UNITA has been associated with the Ovimbundu. Suggestions have been made that MPLA discriminated against the Bakongo and the Ovimbundu, two of the largest ethno-linguistic groups in the country.[77] A 2003 study of Angola's regional and ethnic dimensions, however, found no evidence that Ovimbundu-populated areas had been discriminated against in either public healthcare services or food assistance.[78] Rather, the study argued that current economic disparities are likely to be due to past conflict and not current discrimination practices.

In response to the country's common practice of informal land tenure, the government passed a new land law in 2004 that required registration of land ownership within three years of 2004.[10] The law authorizes the government to take possession of land if individuals have not submitted a registration request.[36] The necessary implementing regulations to accompany the law have not been introduced, and evictions have continued after the law was passed.[36]

Angola suffers from a serious lack of data that affects the formulation of public policy. There is uncertainty about basic information such as the size of the national and provincial populations. Inadequate or unreliable data make it more difficult to plan social services such as healthcare and education.

Birth registration is critical to access services. Proof of citizenship is required to enroll in school, and to receive publicly-provided healthcare or other services. In 2001, only 29% of the births of children under five had been registered.[19] Efforts have been made to address this issue, and free birth registration campaigns have been carried out.[79]

All of the above constraints must be considered in identifying interventions to address basic healthcare, poverty and education problems in Angola.

ANNEX
Annex 8A. Angola — Basic statistics

Indicator	Angola	Year	Source	SSA	Year	Source
POPULATION						
Total population (million)	18.5	2010	1	840.3	2009	5
Population under 18 (% of total)	53	2007	2	—	—	—
Population under 5 (% of total)	19	2007	2	—	—	—
Life expectancy at birth (years)	50	2009	5	53	2009	5
Female life expectancy at birth (years)	52	2009	5	54	2009	5
Male life expectancy at birth (years)	49	2009	5	51	2009	5
Crude birth rate (per 1,000 persons)	42	2007	2	38	2009	5
Crude death rate (per 1,000 persons)	16	2007	2	14	2009	5
Infant mortality rate (per 1,000 live births)	115.7	2009	4	81	2009	5
Under-5 mortality rate (per 1,000 live births)	193.5	2009	4	130	2009	5
Total fertility rate	5.6	2007	1	—	—	—
Adolescent fertility rate (per 1,000 girls aged 15-19 years)	121	2011	5	—	—	—
Maternal mortality rate (per 100,000 live births)	610	2005	2	260	2011	5
% of population in urban areas	58	2007	1	37	2009	5
ECONOMY						
GDP (current US$ billion)	75.5	2009	5	956.4	2009	5
GDP per capita (current US$)	4,793	2009	4	1,138	2009	5
Agriculture (value added) as % of GDP	9.9	2007	5	13	2009	5
Industry (value added) as % of GDP	68.4	2007	5	30	2009	5
Services, etc. (value added) as % of GDP	21.7	2007	5	57	2009	5

Indicator	Angola	Year	Source	SSA	Year	Source
HEALTH						
HIV adult prevalence (age 15-49 years)	2.1	2009	6	1.0	2011	5
Number of people living with HIV (1,000s)	200	2009	1	22,000	2007	5
% of youth (age 15-24 years) who have sufficient knowledge[a] of HIV	28.5	2009	4	—	—	—
Contraceptive prevalence rate (% of married or cohabiting women)	6.2	2006	3	—	—	—
Malaria mortality rate (per 100,000 people)	128	2006	3	104	2006	2
% of under-five children who are moderately or severely stunted	45	2007	2	38	2007	1
% of under-five children who are below 2 standard deviations from median weight-for-age of NCHS/WHO reference population	31	2001	2	28	2007	2
HEALTH COVERAGE						
ART coverage among HIV-infected pregnant women for PMTCT (%)	9	2007	3	34	2006	3
% of HIV-infected persons receiving ART	35	2009	3	—	—	—
Doctors per 10,000 population	1	2007	3	1.9	2009	5
Nurses and midwives per 10,000 population	14	2007	3	10	2009	5
Hospital beds per 1,000 population	0.8	2007	3	1.0	2006	3
Children under-five who receive anti-malarial treatment for fever (%)	35	2007	7	36	2006	3
Antenatal care (% women seen at least once)	80	2007	2	72	2007	2
Skilled birth attendance (% of births)	47	2007	2	45	2007	2
Institutional delivery (% of births)	46	2007	2	40	2007	2
Birth registration (% of children under-five)	29	2007	2	30	2007	2

Indicator	Angola	Year	Source	SSA	Year	Source
EDUCATION						
Adult literacy rate (%)	65.6	2009	4	62	2007	2
Male youth literacy rate (%) (males aged 15–24)	76.0	2009	4	90	2007	2
Female youth literacy rate (%) (females aged 15–24)	67.8	2009	4	85	2007	2
Gross male primary-school enrollment	141	2008	5	101	2007	2
Gross female primary-school enrollment	114	2008	5	90	2007	2
Gross male secondary-school enrollment	19	2002	2	36	2007	2
Gross female secondary-school enrollment	11	2002	2	29	2007	2
WATER, SANITATION AND INFRASTRUCTURE						
% of population using improved drinking-water sources	42	2009	4	—	—	—
Urban	57.9	2009	4	—	—	—
Rural	22.8	2009	4	—	—	—
% of population using improved sanitation facilities	59.6	2009	4	—	—	—
Urban	84.6	2009	4	—	—	—
Rural	31.1	2009	4	—	—	—
Access to phones (landlines or mobile) %	33.3	2009	4	—	—	—
Internet users (per 100 persons)	0.3	2009	4	—	—	—
Paved roads as % of total roads	10	2000	4	—	—	—
Access to electricity (% of population)	40.2	2009	4	—	—	—

Sources:
1. USAID. Angola: HIV/AIDS Health Profile. Washington, DC: USAID, 2011.
2. United Nations Children's Fund (UNICEF). State of the World's Children 2009: Maternal and Newborn Health. New York, NY: UNICEF, December 2008.
3. WHO. World Health Statistics 2009. Geneva, Switzerland: World Health Organization, 2009.
4. Instituto Nacional de Estatística (INE). Inquérito Integrado Sobre o Bem-Estar da População (IBEP) 2008-09: Principais Resultados. Luanda, Angola: INE, 2010.
5. World Bank. World Development Indicators 2011. Washington, DC: World Bank, 2011.
6. Republic of Angola. Relatório sobe o Progresso do País para dar Seguimento aos Compromissos da Sessão Especial sobre VIH e SIDA da Assembleia Geral das Nações Unidas. Luanda, Angola: UNAIDS and Instituto Nacional de Luta Contra a SIDA, 2010.
7. World Bank. Millennium Development Goals (MDG) Data on Angola. Washington, DC: World Bank, 2007.

Note: '—' denotes not available.

Endnotes

a. Primary agricultural products include bananas, sugarcane, coffee, sisal, corn, cotton, manioc, tobacco, vegetables, plantains, livestock, and forest products.

b. 'Undernourishment refers to the condition of people whose dietary energy consumption is continuously below a minimum dietary energy requirement for maintaining a healthy life and carrying out a light physical activity with an acceptable minimum body-weight for attained-height'.[1]

c. World Food Programme defines "food insecurity" as "poor or borderline food consumption and very weak food access; or weak or very weak access and poor consumption."[2]

d. See Article 30 of the Constitution Law of the Republic of Angola, adopted by the People's Assembly on August 25, 1992.[3] In addition, Article 21 of the Angolan Constitution provides that "constitutional and legal norms related to fundamental rights shall be interpreted and incorporated in keeping with the Universal Declaration of the Rights of Man, the African Charter on the Rights of Man and Peoples and other international instruments to which Angola has adhered."

e. Sufficient knowledge defined as the ability to correctly identify two ways of preventing the sexual transmission of HIV and can reject two misconceptions about HIV transmission.

References

1. World Bank. *World Development Indicators 2011*. Washington, DC: World Bank, 2011.

2. Chabal P. Transitions in Angola. In: Chabal P, Vidal N, eds. *Angola: The Weight of History*. Chichester, NY: Columbia University Press, 2008.

3. Hodges T. The economic foundations of the patrimonial state. In: Chabal P, Vidal N, eds. *Angola: The Weight of History*. Chichester, NY: Columbia University Press, 2008.

4. Messiant C. The mutation of hegemonic domination. In: Chabal P, Vidal N, eds. *Angola: The Weight of History*. Chichester, NY: Columbia University Press, 2008.

5. Integrated Regional Information Networks (IRIN). Angola: Cabinda, one of Africa's longest, least reported conflicts. Johannesburg, South Africa: IRIN, 2003. http://www.irinnews.org/IndepthMain.aspx?IndepthId=25&ReportId=66282. Accessed November 25, 2011.

6. Vidal N. The Angolan regime and the move to multiparty politics. In: Chabal P, Vidal N, eds. *Angola: The Weight of History* Chichester, NY: Columbia University Press, 2008.

7. World Bank. *Angola: Project Information Document (PID) Appraisal Stage.* Report No. AB4517. Washington, DC: World Bank, 2009.
8. Coalition to Stop the Use of Child Soldiers. *Child Soldiers: Global Report 2008.* London, UK: Coalition to Stop the Use of Child Soldiers, 2008.
9. UN General Assembly. *Convention on the Elimination of All Forms of Discrimination Against Women (CEDAW).* UN Doc No. CEDAW/C/AGO/1–3 New York, NY: UN, 2002.
10. Freedom House. *Angola Country Report.* Washington, DC: Freedom House, 2009.
11. Jornal de Noticias. Presidente de Angola diz que haverá eleições em 2012. Jornal de Notícias 2010. http://jn.sapo.pt/PaginaInicial/Mundo/Interior.aspx?content_id=1487606. Accessed November 24, 2011.
12. BBC News. Landslide for Angola ruling party. London, UK: BBC, 2008 http://news.bbc.co.uk/2/hi/africa/7620504.stm. Accessed November 25, 2011.
13. Center for Systematic Peace. *Polity IV Country Report 2007: Angola.* Vienna, VA: Center for Systematic Peace, 2008.
14. Isaken J, Amundsen I, Wiig A, Abreu C. *Budget, State and People: Budget Process, Civil Society and Transparency in Angola.* Bergen, Norway: Chr. Michelsen Institute, 2007.
15. Transparency International. *2008 Corruption Perceptions Index.* Berlin, Germany: Transparency International, 2008.
16. United Nations in Angola. *Angola: The Post-War Challenges: Common Country Assessment 2002.* Luanda, Angola: United Nations, 2002.
17. U.S. Bureau of Democracy, Human Rights, and Labor. *2008 Human Rights Report: Angola.* Washington, DC: U.S. Bureau of Democracy, Human Rights, and Labor, 2009.
18. U.S. Bureau of Democracy, Human Rights, and Labor. *2004 Human Rights Report: Angola.* Washington, DC: U.S. Bureau of Democracy, Human Rights, and Labor, 2004.
19. Instituto Nacional de Estatistica and UNICEF. *Multiple Indicator Cluster Survey: Assessing the Situation of Angolan Children and Women at the Beginning of the Millennium.* Luanda, Angola: INE and UNICEF, 2003.
20. Consultoria de Serviços e Pesquisas, Consultoria Lda, Consultoria de Gestão e Administração em Saúde - Consaude Lda, Macro International Inc. *Malaria Indicator Survey 2006–2007.* Calverton, MD: Macro International Inc., 2007.
21. International Monetary Fund. *IMF Executive Board Concludes 2008 Article IV Consultation with Angola* (Public Information Notice No. 09/51). Washington, DC: IMF, 2009.

22. World Bank. Angola: Petroleum Sector Non-Lending Technical Assistance. Washington, DC: World Bank, 2009. http://go.worldbank.org/M69ZBBCQO0. Accessed November 25, 2011.

23. International Monetary Fund. *World Economic Outlook Database.* Washington, DC: IMF, 2009.

24. Europa Publications, ed. *Africa South of the Sahara.* London, UK: Routledge, 2003.

25. Almeida H. Angola's Endiama to up diamond production. 2008. http://www.ibtimes.com/articles/20080612/angolas-endiama-to-up-diamond-production.htm. Accessed November 25, 2011.

26. Corkin L. *Angola's Current Economic Prospects: Oil a Curse or a Blessing?* Madrid, Spain: Real Instituto Elcano, 2009.

27. Hanson S. *Angola's Political and Economic Development.* Washington, DC: Council of Foreign Relations, 2008.

28. Reuters. World Bank to loan Angola $1b. TVNZ 2008. http://tvnz.co.nz/content/2321118/4042040.xhtml. Accessed February 6, 2012.

29. Campos I, Vines A. Angola and China: A pragmatic partnership. CSIS Conference on Prospects for Improving U.S.-China-Africa Cooperation. December 5, 2007. Washington, DC: 2008.

30. Republic of Angola. *A World Fit for Children: Actions Undertaken to Meet the Commitments to the United Nations General Assembly Special Session on Children 2002–2006.* Luanda, Angola: Republic of Angola, 2007.

31. World Bank. Country Brief: Angola. Washington, DC: World Bank, 2009. http://go.worldbank.org/6LIK1A3SS0. Accessed November 24, 2011.

32. World Bank. *Angola: Oil, Broad-based Growth, and Equity.* Washington, DC: World Bank, 2007.

33. UNDP. *Human Development Report 2009. Overcoming Barriers: Human Mobility and Development.* New York, NY: Palgrave Macmillan, 2009.

34. UN FAO. Food security statistics: Prevalence of undernourishment in total population. Rome, Italy: UN FAO, 2008. http://www.fao.org/fileadmin/templates/ess/documents/food_security_statistics/PrevalenceUndernourishment_en.xls. Accessed November 24, 2011.

35. World Food Programme. Angola. Rome, Italy: WFP, 2009. http://www.wfp.org/countries/angola. Accessed June 21, 2010.

36. Gagnon G, Kass S. *"They Pushed Down the Houses": Forced Evictions and Insecure Land Tenure for Luanda's Urban Poor.* Vol. 19 (7A). New York, NY: Human Rights Watch, 2008.

37. Committee on the Rights of the Child. *State Report on Angola* (CRC/C/AGO/2-4). Geneva, Switzerland: United Nations, 2008.

38. Integrated Regional Information Networks (IRIN). Angola: 'Witchcraft'

an excuse for child abuse. Luanda, Angola: IRIN, 2006. http://www.irin-news.org/Report.aspx?ReportId=62424. Accessed November 8, 2011.

39. United States Department of State. *Trafficking in Persons Report 2009 – Angola*. Washington, DC: United States Department of State, 2009.

40. Stark-Merklein B. Angolan landmine survivors build a school and look to the future. Luanda, Angola: UNICEF, 2006. http://www.unicef.org/protection/angola_36659.html. Accessed November 24, 2011.

41. Gabelnick T. Angola destroys antipersonnel landmine stocks by 1 January 2007 deadline. Luanda, Angola: UNDP, 2007. http://www.ao.undp.org/News2.htm. Accessed November 8, 2011.

42. Republic of Angola, Ministry of Health, WHO, UNICEF, UNFPA. *Strategic Plan for the Accelerated Reduction of Maternal and Child Mortality in Angola 2004–2008*. Luanda, Angola: Ministry of Health and National Directorate of Public Health, 2004.

43. WHO. *Health Action in Crises: Angola*. Luanda, Angola: WHO, 2005.

44. Connor C, Rajkotia Y, Lin Y-S, Figueiredo P. *Angola Health System Assessment*. Bethesda, MD: USAID and Abt Associates Inc., 2005.

45. WHO. *World Health Statistics 2009*. Geneva, Switzerland: WHO, 2009.

46. United Nations System in Angola. *Angola: The Post-War Challenges: Common Country Assessment 2002*. Luanda, Angola: United Nations, 2002.

47. WHO Regional Office for Africa. *Country Cooperation Strategy: Angola 2002–2005*. Brazzaville, DRC: WHO, 2002.

48. Population Services International. *Angola (2007): Malaria TRaC Study among Caregivers of Children Under Five in Eight Urban Areas*. Second Round. Luanda, Angola: PSI, 2008.

49. World Bank. *Millennium Development Goals (MDG) Data on Angola*. Washington, DC: World Bank, 2007.

50. UNICEF. *State of the World's Children 2009: Maternal and Newborn Health*. New York, NY: UNICEF, 2009.

51. WHO. *Angola*. Geneva, Switzerland: WHO Statistical Information System, 2008.

52. WHO. *TB Country Profile: Angola*. Geneva, Switzerland: WHO, 2009.

53. República de Angola, Instituto Nacional de Luta Contra a SIDA, UN-AIDS. *Relatório de UNGASS 2007*. Luanda, Angola: República de Angola, 2007.

54. UNAIDS. Adult (15-49) HIV prevalence percent by country, 1990–2007. Geneva, Switzerland: UNAIDS and WHO, 2007. http://data.unaids.org/pub/GlobalReport/2008/20080813_gr08_prev1549_1990_2007_en.xls. Accessed November 25, 2011.

55. Republic of Angola. *Relatório sobe o Progresso do País para dar Seguimento aos Compromissos da Sessão Especial sobre VIH e SIDA da As-*

sembleia Geral das Nações Unidas. Luanda, Angola: UNAIDS and Instituto Nacional de Luta Contra a SIDA, 2010.

56. USAID. *HIV/AIDS Health Profile: Angola.* Washington, DC: USAID, 2008.

57. Instituto Nacional de Luta Contra a Sida. *Plano Estratégico Nacional Para o Controlo das Infecções de Transmissão Sexual, VIH e SIDA 2007 a 2010.* Luanda, Angola: INLS, 2006.

58. UNICEF. Angola HIV/AIDS. UNICEF in Action. 2009. http://www. unicef.org/angola/hiv_aids_1343.html. Accessed July 22, 2009.

59. Germain L, Pestana N, D'Abreu NV, Santos R. *Rapid Analysis and Assessment Action Programme (RAAAP).* Luanda, Angola: MINARS, UNICEF, CEIC-UCAN, INLS, and UNAIDS, 2006.

60. UNICEF. Child Survival. The State of Africa's Children. 2008. http:// www.unicef.ca/portal/Secure/Community/502/WCM/PRESS/soac08/ SOAC.pdf. Accessed February 5, 2012.

61. WHO. *Immunization Profile – Angola.* Geneva, Switzerland: WHO, 2009.

62. UNICEF. *Angola – Statistics.* New York, NY: UNICEF, 2009.

63. UNICEF. *Multiple Indicator Cluster Surveys 2: Manual.* New York, NY: UNICEF, 2000.

64. UNICEF. *Vitamin A Supplementation: A Decade of Progress.* New York, NY: UNICEF, 2007.

65. Republic of Angola and UNDP. *Angola: Millennium Goals Report Summary 2005.* Luanda, Angola: Republic of Angola and UNDP, 2005.

66. Women's Refugee Commission. *Global Survey on Education in Emergencies: Angola Country Report.* New York, NY: Women's Refugee Commission, 2003.

67. Allais F. *Children's Work in Angola: An Overview.* Understanding Children's Work Project Working Paper Series. Rome, Italy: UNICEF, 2007.

68. African Child Policy Forum. Country briefs: Angola. The African Report on Child Wellbeing 2008. http://www.africanchild.info/index. php?file=002.pdf. Accessed November 25, 2011.

69. Hvass L. Angola launches third national de-worming campaign in schools. 2008. http://www.unicef.org/infobycountry/angola_45739. html. Accessed November 25, 2011.

70. Republic of Angola. Constitutional Law of the Republic of Angola. International Constitutional Law Project, 2010. http://www.servat.unibe. ch/law/icl/ao00000_.html. Accessed February 3, 2012.

71. Governo de Angola, UNICEF. *Conselho Nacional da Criança: Criação, Atribuições e Estrutura Orgânica 2008–2009.* Luanda, Angola: Governo de Angola, 2008.

72. Angecia Angola Press. School snack lowers dropout trend — Education

Minister. Angecia Angola Press 2009. http://www.portalangop.co.ao/
motix/en_us/noticias/educacao/School-snack-lowers-dropout-trend-
Education-minister,def56ca7-e056-43b2-9043-d0a6408c6334.html.
Accessed December 1, 2011.

73. Angecia Angola Press. Merenda Escolar avaliada em noventa milhões
de dólares ano. 2009. http://portal-demo.angop.ao/motix/pt_pt/noti-
cias/educacao/2009/5/26/Merenda-escolar-avaliada-noventa-milhoes-
dolares-ano,99958cc3-8526-4974-b62f-d293f2f1f385.html. Accessed
February 6, 2012.

74. UNICEF. As Angola rebuilds, tackling the causes of gender inequalities
in schools. 2006. http://www.unicef.org/infobycountry/angola_34422.
html. Accessed November 25, 2011.

75. IFAD. *Enabling the Rural Poor to Overcome Poverty in Angola.* Rome,
Italy: IFAD, 2006.

76. World Bank, Enterprise Surveys. *Enterprise Surveys Country Profile -
Angola 2006.* Washington, DC: World Bank, 2007.

77. Minorities at Risk Project. *Assessment for Ovimbundu in Angola.* College Park, MD: University of Maryland, College Park, Center for International Development and Conflict Management, 2000.

78. Agadjanian V, Prata N. Civil war and child health: regional and ethnic
dimensions of child immunization and malnutrition in Angola. *Social
Science and Medicine* 2003; 56(12):2515–2527.

79. Felton S. With free birth registration, Angola promotes a child's right
to legal identity. Angola. UNICEF, 2010. http://www.unicef.org/infoby-
country/angola_55501.html. Accessed February 3, 2012.

CHAPTER 9

Priority areas in Angola

9.1. Introduction

To identify areas of inaction in relation to children affected by poverty and HIV/AIDS in Angola, we reviewed the country's socio-economic situation and conducted an in-country consultation. Following the review and consultation we identified four priority areas: (1) income poverty reduction; (2) expansion of healthcare services; (3) strengthening the education system; and (4) prevention of HIV/AIDS. In each priority area, we discuss actions identified through the consultation process, and review the international evidence on their effectiveness.

The country has a very high rate of poverty which leads to many negative consequences for individuals and families. Poverty is often both a cause and a consequence of ill-health. The poor are more vulnerable to disease, and sickness can push households into poverty. The reduction of income poverty lowers both the likelihood of illness in households and its negative consequences should it occur. Poverty can lead to children being left out of school or struggling to meet their minimum nutritional needs. Responding to income poverty is crucial as interventions in this area lead to many constitutive and consequential benefits. Among the interventions discussed in this area are: in-kind and cash transfers to the poor, income-generating activities, microcredit programs, employment through public works, and land tenure and distribution.

The poor state of Angola's healthcare system, and the high prevalence of diseases such as malaria, makes the improvement of healthcare a priority for the country. Primary healthcare is of particular concern, given low levels of availability of basic health services. Inaction in relation to primary care will have serious implications for children. The actions discussed in this area include developing a community healthcare system, training doctors and nurses, and task-shifting to level-down health workers.

Education is an important driver of individual and societal development.

It can also serve as an important means to promote the dissemination of health information. The education system in Angola is weak and fragmented. We discuss interventions to expand and improve the education system, including early childhood development (ECD), primary and secondary schooling. We examine the possibility of increasing enrollment in primary and secondary schools, and discuss different approaches to providing ECD services.

The prevalence of HIV in Angola is low, but knowledge about HIV/AIDS among people is limited. HIV-prevention efforts are needed especially in response to high-risk behaviors. Although our focus is on children affected by HIV, prevention for the entire population should be the goal. At this stage, one of the best ways to protect children from HIV is to avoid infection among their parents. We discuss prevention campaigns which involve mass media and those that target specific high-risk groups. We also examine expanding free male circumcision programs in regions of the country where HIV prevalence is high and the rate of male circumcision is low.

9.2. Reduction of income poverty

The country suffers from high levels of inequality and poverty. The Gini coefficient was 0.62 in 2009,[1] and Angola ranked 118 out of 135 countries on the UNDP's Human Poverty Index in 2009.[2] A large proportion of the population still engages in subsistence agriculture, which leaves them excluded from the formal economy.[3] The World Bank estimates that in 2001, 70% of the population lived on less than PPP$2 per day at 2005 international prices.[4]

In 2003, the government proposed the national Strategy to Combat Poverty (*Estratégia de Combate à Pobreza*, or ECP). ECP aims to reduce poverty and accelerate the realization of the Millennium Development Goals (MDGs) and similar objectives adopted by the New Partnership for Africa's Development (NEPAD) and the Southern African Development Community (SADC).[5] As target groups, ECP selected those households that fall below the poverty line and vulnerable groups such as refugees, internally displaced persons (IDPs), former combatants, children and teenagers, and the elderly. The interventions proposed in ECP are to be carried out during the period 2006–15 by the federal government and by provincial and municipal governments.[5] The World Bank, working with the Ministry of Finance and the National Statistics Department, will undertake monitoring and evaluation of ECP. In particular, they have established a set of baseline indicators against which the progress of ECP will be assessed.[6] ECP outlines areas of interventions to address poverty over the long term, such as education and basic infrastructure development. The plan does not consider interventions that aim to reduce income poverty in the short term, which are also clearly needed.

In the following sections we analyze interventions to reduce income poverty in the short and long term. Among them are cash and in-kind transfers, income-generating activities, microcredit programs, employment through public works, and land tenure.

9.2.1. Cash and in-kind transfers to the poor

The possibility of implementing an intervention on conditional cash transfers was discussed in Angola during our consultations. Despite general support for the idea, many organizations interviewed were not clear about how these programs work — in part because such programs are almost non-existent in Angola. The situation is, however, changing and a cash transfer program is being piloted in the country. The World Bank has proposed a voucher scheme to encourage institutional birth deliveries. The program provides vouchers of US$10 to cover transportation costs and an incentive voucher of US$15 upon birth delivery in an institution. The pilot program will be implemented in two municipalities, and provide vouchers for 8,000 deliveries in an institution.

Cash transfer programs have helped to reduce short-term poverty and improve the health and well-being of poor populations in many countries around the world.[7] Conditional cash transfers have important impacts on education, household productivity and labor-force participation. In Ecuador, for example, primary-school enrollment increased by 10 to 13 percentage points as a result of the *Bono de Desarrollo* conditional cash transfer program. The same program was responsible for reducing the incidence of child labor by between 15 and 21 percentage points.[7] Cash transfers can have an impact on the health of both adults and children. The transfers can help to pay for transportation costs and enable visits to health clinics and hospitals.[7] Significant improvements in children's health have resulted from the PROGRESA cash transfer program in Mexico, which is conditional on observed behavior by recipients on health and education. Under PROGRESA, illness rates in the first six months of children's lives were 25% lower than for children in a control group.[8]

Government authorities are aware of the implementation and success of conditional cash transfer programs in other countries, but have argued that "the situation in Angola is different". They have raised concerns that because of the destruction caused by three decades of war, the number of people in need is very high. As a result, the cost to cover all poor people would be too high, and targeting would be difficult because it is hard to identify the poorest. However, government representatives admitted that identification of households for food-basket distribution had already taken place, which was achieved with help of communities. The government distributes food baskets to the elderly and disabled and has proposed paying a minimum wage to these groups. Many of those interviewed expressed reservations about cash transfers, expressing the view that such transfers could make people dependent on the state. Some respondents were also concerned that cash transfers could generate inflationary pressures in areas where the supply of food items is limited.

A number of respondents suggested that implementing in-kind transfers would be politically more acceptable than cash transfers, as state authorities are generally more comfortable supplying materials than money to the poor. It was argued that in-kind transfers were a simple intervention which provided a direct benefit to the poor. For instance, bednet distribution would lead to improved health and a more productive workforce.[9] Respondents mentioned that the government already provides food baskets, but suggested that their distribution needs to be improved. Some respondents advised that in-kind transfers could be in the form of transportation vouchers to ease the cost of travelling to school, health centers or markets.

Food transfers undertaken on a national scale may be logistically difficult. Some interviewees argued that, even if it is potentially beneficial in the short run, food distribution cannot be sustained over the long term. Instead, they argued that specific agricultural policies were needed, including training on basic farming skills and access to seeds and agricultural tools.

9.2.2. Income-generating activities

The promotion of income-generating activities (IGAs) involves assistance to poor families in developing a small-scale business. Cooperatives or group IGAs are somewhat larger initiatives, typically comprising 50 or more people. National and international NGOs working in Angola are already seeking to provide support, training and materials for the development of IGAs.[10] Many respondents suggested that income-generating activities, combined with financial support, could help to reduce poverty in the country.

Access to a market to sell products can be a major constraint. For example, a community in the Bié Province commune of Cassumbi has been producing high-grade honey for years.[11] However, poor roads, distance to a formal market, and a shortage of buyers has prevented this community from making a profit on the production of honey.[11] USAID has funded a community-mapping project to explore the area's resources, and helped the community connect with local businessmen to increase the range of sales and hence incomes.[11]

The informal economy is an important source of employment and income for women in Africa. In sub-Saharan Africa, 84% of women are informally employed, compared to 63% of men.[12] Women enter into micro-entrepreneurship out of economic necessity and a lack of alternative employment options. Many households are dependent on the income that women contribute through these informal economic activities.[12] Women are typically caretakers for children and responsible for household tasks. Because of this, women often choose IGAs that allow them to manage their multiple responsibilities from home. Home-based businesses, however, have restricted possibilities for direct interaction with customers, which constrains their profit and growth opportunities. The occupational and economic options for women are limited by illiteracy, lack of marketable skills, and lack of assets (due to gender discrimination in property and inheritance). Often women have to start their small enterprises with personal savings, or a group of women pool their assets to obtain start-up capital collectively.[12]

Traditionally, women and girls spend more time fetching water compared to men and boys. Water is a prerequisite for food preparation and other household activities in which women are involved. Limited availability of water undermines their efforts at developing IGAs. Investment in improving water supply will help free women's time to undertake IGAs.[12]

Reforms are needed in business regulation to allow for joint registration so that women and men can be equal owners of financial assets, property and household enterprises. These regulations are particularly important in the event of divorce or death when the economic security of women is threatened.

The ability of governments to make informed policy choices is hindered by the absence of data on the size and characteristics of the informal sector. Efforts should be made to correct this as transformation of the informal economy into a dynamic sector will be necessary to reduce poverty.[12]

9.2.3. Microcredit programs

Several organizations interviewed suggested that microcredit programs could help poor families and women improve their lives and the lives of their children. They argued in favor of microcredit programs because they believe that although institutions and infrastructure were destroyed during the war, people have found ways to provide for themselves after the peace accords. To support entrepreneurship, several organizations suggested that the government should expand access to financial institutions in rural areas. Respondents pointed out that some private financial institutions are already present in the capital and main urban centers of the provinces, but these are generally not accessible to the poor.

In addition to expanding financial and banking services within the country, respondents suggested that people would benefit from the provision of microcredit. Microcredit is seen as a way of promoting entrepreneurship and an effective way of helping to reduce household poverty. There are a number of organizations in Angola that have introduced programs to support micro-businesses through the provision of microcredit. Some of them —

CARE, Development Workshop, Adventist Development and Relief Agency (ADRA), and Oikos — have created the Angolan Network to Support Micro-businesses (*Rede Angolana de Apoio ao Sector Micro-empresarial,* or RASME). RASME is part of the Southern Africa Microfinance and Enterprise Capacity Enhancement Facility and provides business networking as well as microcredit to small businesses in Angola.[13]

Microfinance institutions have provided financial services to poor or self-employed individuals and groups. These services provide microcredit loans, but may also include savings or insurance. Through microcredit and savings programs, women and communities are able to start small businesses or micro-enterprises. With appropriate training, communities can take the lead in granting loans, and decide on appropriate interest rates and the use of money earned from interest. The benefits accrue to individuals from an income-generating enterprise, but also to society when communities decide how interest income is to be used — for example, by granting scholarships to girls, or helping those affected by illness. Since 1996 the World Bank has financed microcredit programs and financial services in Bangladesh. These programs were found to have significantly improved the lives of beneficiaries. An assessment carried out in 2001 showed that 99% reported increased income and consumption (especially of food).[14] The same assessment showed that participating households were more likely to send their children to school and improve their housing.[14]

Though microcredit can promote income generation, the damaged road infrastructure and poor telecommunications in Angola may hinder entrepreneurs' ability to access markets, especially in rural areas. Under these circumstances, it is likely that people will use loans to attend to their urgent cash needs but not necessarily to start a new business. In addition, if they over-leverage themselves, vulnerable individuals and families can become impossibly burdened by debt, and in extreme circumstances can be pushed into suicide — as has been witnessed in Andhra Pradesh, India.

9.2.4. Employment through public works

Public works programs help to reduce poverty by directly employing people whose income is below the poverty line. They may be of particular interest in Angola because, in addition to reducing poverty through employment, such programs can contribute to improved infrastructure. For example, the availability and supply of safe water can be increased through public works programs. Currently fewer than half (46%) of all households obtain drinking water from an improved source.[15] Public works programs can also be used to improve sanitation facilities, electricity infrastructure, and other community assets.

Infrastructure is an important factor in affecting health outcomes. A study in Tanzania found that access to safe water during and after childbirth significantly reduced postnatal infections.[16] Improving water and sanitation facilities has been linked to a decline in maternal mortality in many countries.[17]

In public works programs the process of building infrastructure employs people and helps to reduce income poverty. However, during the consultation process respondents pointed out that public works programs do not always employ poor people. Moreover, they cautioned that such programs can be effective only if a household contains at least one able-bodied member.[18]

9.2.5. Land tenure

In order to raise the income of small farmers, farm productivity needs to be improved and the sales of their produce assured. To facilitate this, the government can provide agricultural extension and education services to small farmers, including the dissemination of market information so that farmers can make educated choices on the crops to plant and bring to market. Currently the government's agricultural policy focuses on the promotion of large-scale farming and neglects small- and subsistence-level farming.

Agricultural productivity is influenced significantly by the security of land tenure. Long-term investment by a farmer in improving productivity of a landholding depends on whether the returns will accrue to the farmer. Hence, tenure and its security are critical to investing in land improvement and raising productivity.

Land tenure and land reform have been part of national reconciliation and poverty reduction programs in many countries around the world. Some of Angola's neighboring countries have redistributed land to poor families, initially as part of national reconciliation efforts and then as part of poverty reduction measures. In Namibia, for instance, the National Poverty Reduction Action Programme buys farms in commercial areas for distribution to disadvantaged populations.[19] There may be lessons which can be taken from these efforts to help inform the design of an improved land policy in Angola.

9.2.6. Reduction of income poverty: Actions of special interest

Although relevant, income-generating activities face severe challenges in order to be scaled-up, particularly with regard to infrastructure. Other actions suggested within this priority area, such as cash transfers and provision of microcredit, can be more easily scaled. But there are problems with cash transfers, such as their long-term sustainability and political acceptability, and with microcredit, such as its use to fund consumption rather than investment. Public works may be more acceptable politically and can have large consequential benefits if they are focused on improving infrastructure that is in a state of disrepair or neglect. Public works interventions are thus of special interest. Improving land tenure and distribution may be a politically sensitive action, but it is important for increasing agricultural productivity and reducing rural poverty; hence it is of special interest.

9.3. Expansion of healthcare services

There is a shortage of health facilities and personnel in most parts of the country. People are frequently forced to travel long distances to access healthcare, but transportation is limited and expensive. The government and international donors are directing resources to build some health facilities and clinics. But their number is inadequate and their location is not necessarily appropriate to serve the majority of the population.[20] Moreover, there is a serious shortage of health personnel. For example, there is only 1 doctor per 10,000 population, and doctors are disproportionately located in Luanda.[21]

There are a number of possible actions that can expand healthcare services and improve coverage. We discuss actions to expand healthcare services through training of new health workers, especially community health workers (CHWs), and through task-shifting from doctors to nurses and nurses to CHWs.

9.3.1. Training of health personnel and task-shifting

In Angola, health services are highly vertical and *medicalizados* (medicalized) — a term in Portuguese to describe a system where highly-skilled health staff are required to provide treatment and health services that could be provided by less-skilled staff. Verticalization is, however, impractical in a country that has a shortage of doctors.

Unmet demand for doctors can lead to spillover demand for nurses and pressure on support staff. Angola has recently begun to train specialists albeit on a relatively small scale. Also, since clinical training takes a long time, the supply of qualified specialists has not yet increased. Respondents were worried about the provision of training because they feared that, if done with international partners, the trained personnel could join a "brain drain". Others suggested that there should be more international partnerships and programs to allow medical students to study abroad, e.g. in South Africa or Brazil.

Some respondents suggested that doctors should be required to work in the provinces and rural areas. Training doctors and nurses will have limited impact if newly-qualified staff are not deployed to places where they are most needed. After training, health providers need to be located outside the capital and in the provinces so as to extend care and treatment in rural communities. These providers need to be given incentives to stay in rural areas, in the public sector, and in the country.

Whereas the density of doctors is very low, the density of nurses is higher than the sub-Saharan Africa (SSA) average.[21] Task-shifting that allows nurses to perform the tasks of doctors has increasingly gained support as a means of coping with human resource shortages. The practice of task-shifting is not new to Angola. For example, the country started providing HIV/AIDS treatment using a doctor-centered system but, as noted by the national HIV/AIDS authority, has gradually been using more nurse assistants. Several organizations interviewed mentioned that, despite some early opposition, the government is now more open to the use of nurses to provide health services that have traditionally been the preserve of doctors. Other respondents showed some resistance to task-shifting. They expressed concern that nurses are already overworked and that task-shifting would mean they take up doctors' roles without any salary increases. Ordinary citizens might also resist the change if they perceived the service provided by less-qualified personnel to be of lower standard.

Based on policy advice from WHO, task-shifting has been implemented in many parts of sub-Saharan Africa. In Malawi, nurses decide eligibility for and prescribe antiretroviral (ARV) drugs. Nurses treat opportunistic infections and prescribe ARVs in Botswana, Ethiopia, Uganda and Malawi — thus improving access to treatment and survival.[22] A study comparing HIV/AIDS services provided by medical assistants, nurses and doctors in Malawi found that the quality of HIV care provided by non-physicians was similar to that provided by medical doctors who were HIV experts, and better than that provided by medical doctors who were not HIV experts.[22] Task-shifting is cost-effective — it provides less expensive treatment with comparable results.[23]

The government and health authorities could develop and implement national guidelines, determining specific tasks that are currently reserved for doctors but can be shifted to nurses. Task-shifting where nurses take on certain tasks of doctors also requires specific training for nurses. In addition, nurses need to be recognized and receive appropriate remuneration for the additional workload. Training could at first be undertaken for existing staff and then integrated into the curriculum for new nurses. To guarantee standards, all training needs to be monitored, supervised and evaluated.

9.3.2. Training of community health workers

Training, deploying and supervising community health workers (CHWs) is likely to be a cost-effective means to expanding provision of primary healthcare. CHWs work in local communities and have close contact with the people they serve. In the communities in which they work, CHWs can provide services such as oral rehydration therapy (ORT), distribute bednets, and promote the vaccination of children. They can identify individuals who display signs of serious illness and refer them to community nurses or hospitals. Once patients are referred, CHWs can support the management of infections and encourage adherence to drug regimens.

The deployment of community health workers seems to be accepted in the country, and on a small scale they have practiced in some regions. Respondents emphasized that the deployment of CHWs would ease the burden on patients of traveling long distances to health facilities. In our consultations, communities proposed that health workers should provide a broad range of services which include checking that children have been vaccinated, referring patients to doctors and specialized clinics, and providing basic information about healthcare and nutrition.

The government recognizes the potential of using community health workers. In 2006 it implemented a treatment program for malaria in Huambo province that included training community health workers to supervise and deliver treatment at health facilities.[24] CHW initiatives have tended to be localized and short-lived — and there is no national CHW strategy.

It is also possible to shift tasks currently undertaken by nurses to CHWs. This may be particularly important if nurses are being asked to take on tasks previously carried out by doctors. Available evidence suggests that such task-shifting to CHWs can be effective. Successful patient outcomes have been observed.[22]

Task-shifting requires appropriate training and supervision of CHWs, and the maintenance of high standards of care. CHWs often have low levels of training and knowledge about treatment and therapy. If these services are provided on a volunteer unpaid basis, it will be difficult to maintain standards because turnover is likely to be high. There is no evidence that volunteerism can be sustained for long periods. For CHWs to be effective, a structure is needed to organize their training, employment and supervision. A community healthcare system, which provides a formalized structure for CHWs, may be an appropriate intervention.

9.3.3. Expansion of healthcare services: Actions of special interest

The training of doctors and nurses is of special interest, even though the high cost and long lags are a concern. Task-shifting will have a more immediate impact and is certainly of special interest. CHWs trained to provide a range of primary healthcare services could make a significant impact, particularly if they form part of a community healthcare system. There may be logistical difficulties associated with having to train and retain a large workforce of CHWs, but the potential pay-offs are such that this action is considered to be of special interest.

9.4. Education

Education leads to a range of private and public benefits. Schooling increases individuals' earning capacity, and contributes to improving their and their children's health and well-being. Schooling can also play a role in HIV-prevention efforts. Schools provide an environment where young people can be reached with basic information on HIV transmission. Education programs at schools can also teach skills that help children avoid or reduce risk behaviors.

Despite its clear benefits, the availability and quality of school education remains a problem in Angola. Educational quality is affected by factors such as overcrowded classes, inadequate school personnel, lack of school materials, and poor school infrastructure.[25] Moreover, teacher training is often inadequate and teacher supervision is minimal. In 2001, the government reported an average of 64 students per classroom. In response to this overcrowding, it introduced a system where teachers worked two shifts per school day. The multiple shifts significantly reduced class size but, as each shift was shorter, they also reduced contact hours between teacher and pupil.[26]

In 2001, preschool education was almost non-existent, with only 7% of children aged 36–59 months enrolled in an organized ECD program.[26] Recognizing the importance of ECD, in 2004 the government established a new education system that aimed to increase the availability of preschool education.[27] Provincial governments are supposed to be responsible for providing ECD services. But it is not even clear that a curriculum for ECD has been developed. Although it does not constitute a curriculum, the Ministry of Social Welfare (Ministério da Assistência e Reinserção Social, or MINARS) has produced a series of booklets for families outlining the main stages of child development and providing suggestions of activities to stimulate children's learning.

There is clearly room for improvement in the education sector. Below we present some actions to improve primary and secondary schooling, and ECD services.

9.4.1. Expansion of primary and secondary schooling

A major obstacle to sending and keeping children and adolescents in school is the cost of education. Although all six years of primary school are legally mandated to be free of charge, many children still have to pay formal or informal fees in government schools. Distance and lack of transportation also hinder school enrollment. Most organizations agreed that female adolescents are more vulnerable than male adolescents to dropping out of school.

A number of different actions can be undertaken to keep children in school and to ensure that such efforts benefit girls. A Kenyan project, for example, found that reducing the cost of education by the government paying for school uniforms reduced dropout rates. Stipends for books, uniforms and transportation also improved student retention.[28] School-feeding programs encourage children's enrollment, and help improve nutritional intake and performance at school.[29] Breakfast-deprived children are more likely to suffer attention deficit and fall asleep in class, curtailing the benefit of being in school.[30] Some respondents suggested that adolescents could be retained in the school system for longer if the current school snack program (*merenda escolar*) was extended to high school.

Sanitation and hygiene are cited as major problems for girls' attendance at school. Girls and female teachers often do not attend school during their menstrual periods due to lack of sanitary facilities (toilets and water).[31,32] In Guinea, enrollment rates for girls rose 17% from 1997 to 2002, and dropout rates fell, after improvements in school sanitation.[32] Schools in northeastern Nigeria also showed substantial gains in enrollment after UNICEF and other donors built latrines.[32] Another simple option to improving sanitary conditions is to provide girls with sanitary pads. There are examples of how this can be done cheaply: the Makapads project in Uganda manufactures and distributes sanitary pads that are available at much lower prices than commercially-produced pads.[33]

The training, deployment and supervision of teachers is a problem in Angola. There are too few teachers, who are disproportionately concentrated in urban areas, and rural teachers are often unsupervised because of their location. The government should consider increasing the scale of teacher training as well as providing transportation for supervisors and incentives for teachers to work in rural and remote areas.

9.4.2. Home- and center- based ECD services

Early childhood programs should begin with the provision of services to the mother during pregnancy, such as prenatal care and nutrition. These services should be followed up with support to infants and young children to ensure healthy development. ECD services can be provided through home visitation or daycare at people's homes or in centers.

Home-visiting programs can provide many different education and health services, and have been shown to have a beneficial impact on children.[34] A study conducted in Jamaica investigated the effect of weekly home visits by community health workers for one year. Discussions on parenting issues were held with mothers, and play activities were demonstrated to them. Children from the intervention group showed improvements in development, hearing and speech, and hand and eye coordination. Mothers from the intervention group showed improved knowledge and practices of child rearing.[35]

Home visitation provides information to parents but does not provide daycare for children. Thus home visitation does not free parents' time to undertake other activities. ECD centers do provide daycare, but are expensive. An alternative is home-based care, where a group of children is provided with daycare and ECD services in the home of a community member. This alternative can lead to large benefits without the costs associated with a formal center. For example, Bolivia has a large-scale home-based early childhood development and nutrition program, *Proyecto Integral de Desarrollo Infantil* (PIDI), located in poor urban areas. PIDI offers daycare, nutrition and educational services to children aged 6 months to 6 years.[36] Tests on motor skills, language skills and psychosocial skills were administered to children enrolled in PIDI. Results showed that children aged 37–54 months exhibited an increase in developmental test-score outcomes.[36] The average impact on test scores generally increased as length of participation in the program increased. Positive impacts were larger among children who had participated in the program for at least 13 months. These impacts were nearly twice as high as the overall average impacts.[36] Although no pre-program baseline data were available, the findings suggest a gain in the weight-for-age of children who participated in PIDI for more than seven months.[36]

In situations where cost is not so much of a constraint, formal ECD centers may be considered as an appropriate option. ECD centers have been linked with a range of benefits. For example, children participating in ECD centers are sometimes described by parents and teachers as being well-prepared and enthusiastic about school.[37] The parents of children receiving ECD services are accustomed to an active role in the centers and are more likely to talk to teachers, show an interest in their children's academic progress, raise issues that concern them, and call for accountability from teachers and administrators.[38] ECD-exposed children are often more willing to ask questions about things they do not understand in comparison to children who have not been exposed to ECD.[37] Early childhood centers offer an important venue to improve nutrition, health, and cognitive and social development of children.

There are many approaches to implementing ECD programs which vary from formal centers to home-based approaches. Regardless of the kind of intervention, preschool promotes cognitive development and educational achievement. If quality is assured, all ECD interventions appear to generate similar benefits and there is little to choose between them.[39]

The protracted civil war led to many children reaching adulthood without much education. This affects their well-being and the well-being of their children. Interventions to benefit the current generation of children are of great importance, but this does not mean that the older generation should be neglected. Moreover, one of the best ways to improve children's education may be by supporting adults in their family to provide support to them.

9.4.3. Family-learning programs

Effective family-learning programs can play an important role in supporting child development. The objective of family-learning programs is to improve adult literacy and to educate parents and caregivers on how best to promote the development of children. Such programs benefit adults directly and children indirectly.

Angola already has some ongoing adult education initiatives. These could be extended to include training on child care and development. The government has created the National Institute of Literacy (INA), the National Directory of Adults' Education (DNEA), and the National Institute of Adults' Education (INEDA). The aim of these organizations is to facilitate and coordinate programs on adult education.[40] In 2005, the Ministry of Education launched the National Literacy and Academic Catch-up Strategy (*Estratégia de Alfabetização e Recuperação do Atraso Escolar*). This strategy presents the Ministry's plans to undertake a series of adult literacy programs until the year 2015.[41]

The Ministry of Education also supports NGOs involved in adult education by providing materials and by training teachers and peer educators.[40] UNICEF and UNESCO co-fund projects on adult literacy, especially women's literacy.[40] More recently, other donor agencies such as the Portuguese Agency to Support Development (Instituto Português de Apoio ao Desenvolvimento) have initiated adult literacy projects.[42]

Training on child care and development could be incorporated into existing adult literacy initiatives. International evidence suggests that this type of family-learning approach can be highly beneficial for children. A study was conducted in Turkey to investigate whether educating poor mothers of three- to five-year-olds improved their children's learning ability and if these effects were long lasting.[37] The mothers in the intervention group were involved in an education program that consisted of literacy and numeracy training. Mothers were also trained on the needs of growing children, communication skills, and balancing caretaking and personal time.[37] Children's cognitive development and school performance were monitored. Seven years after the intervention, 86% of the children of the mother-trained group were still in school, compared to 67% of children whose mothers had not undergone training.[37] The children of the mother-trained group also surpassed the control group on cognitive performance. The mother-trained group of children were found to have a more positive outlook on education, and were better integrated socially.[37]

9.4.4. Education: Actions of special interest

All actions suggested under the education priority area require continuous training and supervision of teachers and instructors. Training must be of a high standard as it affects the success of education interventions, especially those aiming to promote ECD. Education actions require significant resources, but lead to large benefits for children. The ECD, primary and secondary sectors are all important and the standard of education offered at each level affects outcomes at that level and beyond. Hence, expansion of the entire education system, including ECD services, and primary and secondary schooling, is of special interest.

9.5. Prevention of HIV

Although the benefits of HIV-prevention interventions in low-prevalence settings are difficult to quantify, they may present an opportunity to avert large numbers of *future* HIV infections. In low-prevalence settings the perception of risk of HIV infection may be underestimated, so that prevention efforts assume added importance.[43]

Since the end of the war, Angola has tried to institute programs and policies designed to prevent HIV infections. A large part of the country's response to HIV/AIDS prevention has been funded by a US$90 million grant from the Global Fund to Fight AIDS, Tuberculosis and Malaria (GFATM), and by a US$21million grant from the World Bank for an HIV/AIDS, Malaria and Tuberculosis Control Project.[44,45] More than half the resources available from the national budget, GFATM, and the World Bank have been used for activities aimed at reducing the incidence of HIV infections through prevention efforts.[45] These efforts have included interventions both for the general population and for targeted high-risk groups. Establishing the appropriate balance between these interventions is difficult because there is limited epidemiological data on the vulnerability of different groups.

Despite prevention efforts, people are poorly informed about HIV/AIDS. In a 2005 study, only 23% of youth surveyed knew of at least two main ways to prevent sexual transmission of HIV. According to the same survey, only 8% of mothers with young children knew about mother-to-child transmission.[46] In 2006, 51.7% of the population in urban areas had knowledge of modes of HIV transmission, but in rural areas only 11.3% had similar knowledge.[47] Respondents suggested that adherence to treatment is also a serious problem, citing reasons such as stigma and lack of understanding of consistent drug use.

There are a number of different interventions that can be undertaken to improve prevention efforts. These include mass media campaigns, prevention campaigns targeted to mobile populations and adolescents, promotion of male circumcision, and condom distribution. These are discussed next.

9.5.1. HIV/AIDS prevention through mass media

HIV-prevention efforts in the country are conducted through multiple channels, such as mass media, the distribution of materials, and workplace education.[48] Respondents noted that these strategies were limited to pockets of populations mainly in urban areas. Some organizations expressed concern about the use of the Portuguese language in information campaigns. Estimates suggest that about 30% of Angolans speak a Bantu language, and not Portuguese, as their first language.[49] Organizations working in the country suggested that information materials need to be translated into local languages so as to be accessible to all. Respondents also expressed concern that prevention and information materials, such as posters and billboards, display people with clothes and fashion accessories outside the reach of the average citizen. In rural areas, these information materials could be sending a message that increases risk behaviors. Respondents suggested that in poor areas, people — especially adolescents and youth — may engage in risky behaviors such as transactional sex to obtain the means to look like the models in the posters and billboards.

General prevention campaigns may not be very effective at reducing the incidence of HIV because they do not target groups at high risk.[43] Therefore, general prevention campaigns alone may be insufficient, even though they have a place in a comprehensive response.[43,50] Mass media campaigns may help promote behavior change and encourage testing among high-risk groups.[51]

9.5.2. HIV prevention among mobile populations and youth

HIV prevalence among migrant workers or mobile populations is usually higher than in the general population.[52] The International Organization for Migration (IOM) recognizes that migrant workers face unique circumstances that often lead to risky behaviors. This is because migrant workers are separated from their partners for extended periods of time. Furthermore, it is difficult to reach mobile populations with initiatives such as testing, condom supply and treatment.[53] Populations are mobile for a variety of reasons apart from migrant work — e.g. the nature of their job, seasonal floods or droughts, and forced eviction through public urbanization programs.[54]

Since the end of the war, the transport system is gradually being restored. Roads in particular have been improved, as have air and sea links. These improvements have made traveling around the country easier. Economic development in urban centers has increased demand for both skilled and unskilled labor, encouraging greater movement of people from rural to urban areas. There is also mobility of people across international borders for trade and work. This increased mobility may lead to the spread of HIV to once-isolated areas. Angola is part of the Regional HIV/AIDS Program for Southern Africa, which seeks to target high-risk populations at border sites.

Despite being part of the initiative, the government's response to HIV/AIDS at the borders seems to be very limited.

The United States Agency for International Development has implemented a regional HIV/AIDS prevention project, called "Corridors of Hope", which focuses on areas near international boundaries in southern Africa. The project addresses the needs of migrant workers and mobile populations near international borders. It identifies interventions and evaluates actions such as selling condoms below market prices and screening sex workers.[55] Experiences gained from this project could help Angola in its efforts to design appropriate interventions.

Youth are another target group for HIV-prevention interventions. Programs that target teenagers and youth are important in Angola, because 70% of the population is under 24 years of age and has little knowledge about HIV prevention.[47] Adolescents and youth are particularly vulnerable to HIV because a large proportion of them engage in sexual intercourse, have concurrent partners, and fail to use condoms correctly or consistently.[56] According to a 2003 KAP study, 37% of young males and 21% of young females had slept with two or more partners in the previous three months.[56] Fewer than half (43%) knew that avoiding several partners was protective against HIV infection, and only one-fifth knew that abstaining from sex altogether was protective.[56] Of young people who had 2–4 partners in the previous three months — a high-risk group — only one in five thought they were at any significant risk of contracting HIV and half of them believed they were at little or no risk.[56] Of those who believed they were at no risk, two-thirds were having unprotected sex with a girlfriend or boyfriend, and half were having unprotected sex with casual partners.[56]

The age at which many people have their first sexual encounter is very low. According to the government, almost one-third (32.3%) of adolescents aged 15–24 years in 2006 had had sex before age 15 and half (49.8%) reported having a non-regular or extra-marital partner in the previous 12 months.[48] A significant proportion of young people in the country initiate sexual activity by age 12.[57]

Teenagers and youth often have little control over resources, a factor that increases engagement in high-risk behaviors such as transactional and intergenerational sex. Transactional sex often involves contact with partners from high-risk groups such as migrant workers and older men.[56] Many respondents suggested that young women get involved with older men for material benefits. Young women who engage in this kind of transactional sex are usually called *catorzinhas* or "fourteeners" — a reference to their age. *Catorzinhas* seem to engage in intergenerational sex in order to acquire high-status items such as cell phones, or to alleviate pressure associated with extreme poverty.

Research suggests that targeting adolescents and youth, as opposed to the general population, has several advantages. For instance, changing behavior and attitudes among teenagers and youth is easier than among adults because the former are still in the process of forming their sexual habits. Often they are also accessible in larger numbers at existing institutions, e.g. schools and youth organizations. Lessons from other low-prevalence countries suggest that youth themselves need to be involved in the delivery of HIV-prevention messages.[58]

Apart from disseminating information about HIV prevention, youth also need to be educated in life-skills-based HIV prevention in primary and secondary schools.[58] Life-skills programs provide practical lessons and strategies on avoiding HIV, and help develop skills among young people to negotiate safe sex.[59] A study among young Zimbabweans found that compared to students who were provided only with information, female students who participated in a skills-based HIV-prevention program were more knowledgeable about condoms and their correct use.[60] They also reported higher condom use.[60]

9.5.3. Free male circumcision

Data show that circumcision reduces the probability of female-to-male HIV transmission in heterosexual relations.[61] Its influence is increased if sexually-transmitted infections are present. Male circumcision is already common in most of Angola with the exception of the southern-most province of Cunene; nationally at least 80% of men are circumcised.[62] Most circumcisions occur as part of a rite of passage for boys.[63] Despite general acceptance of this practice, there is no official public policy to encourage *medical* male circumcision. Substitution of unsafe, unsterile traditional practices with surgically safe circumcision procedures is essential.[61] Circumcision is not mentioned in national policies towards HIV/AIDS, e.g. the National Strategic Plan for the Control of Sexually Transmitted Infections and HIV/AIDS 2007–2010 (Plano Estratégico Nacional, or PEN).

In three randomized control studies undertaken in Africa involving more than 11,000 men, male circumcision was shown to be partially protective in preventing female-to-male HIV transmission. These studies confirmed that male circumcision reduces the risk of HIV acquisition in men by more than half.[51] However, evidence suggests that male circumcision is a less effective method of prevention of HIV transmission for men who have sex with men.[61] Male circumcision has also been regarded as cost-effective. It results in averted infection but requires no ongoing costs in terms of user adherence.[64] According to WHO and UNAIDS, male circumcision should be undertaken only if certain conditions are satisfied. These conditions include a guarantee that consent has been obtained, that sanitary settings are appropriate, and that counseling is available on condom use and safe-sex practices.[62]

Circumcision should be performed as early as possible. Circumcision done before adolescence, particularly in early infancy, has the advantage of being technically easier. Unlike the case with adolescents, infant circumcision does not face the problem of sexual activity occurring during wound-healing.[61]

Providing free universal circumcision at birth may face some resistance. Because male circumcision traditionally serves as a rite-of-passage for male adolescents, it might be considered inappropriate for it to be done at an earlier age. Information campaigns may be necessary to convince families of the benefits of male circumcision at birth. If circumcision takes place at older ages, it is necessary to provide participants with counseling about the need to abstain from sexual intercourse until wound-healing is complete, and to adhere to other risk-reduction behaviors.[61] While a circumcision procedure for an adult male is estimated to cost US$30–60 in Africa, neonatal male circumcision usually costs a small fraction of that amount.[64] Neonatal circumcision could be complemented by 'catch up' programs targeted at adolescent boys and men. These circumcision actions may have a significant impact on HIV/AIDS, particularly in Cunene province where HIV prevalence is high and male circumcision is not common. While constraints associated with the weak healthcare system cannot be ignored, the potential relevance of circumcision actions does make them of special interest.

9.5.4. Promotion and distribution of condoms

Correct and consistent condom use has been shown to be effective in HIV prevention, especially when combined with other interventions. Reported rates of condom use in Angola are low. In a 2005 Population Services International (PSI) survey, only 54% of youth reported using a condom during their last sexual intercourse.[65] Studies have found that consistent condom use is related to the level of education of a person.[66]

In Luanda and some of the provincial capitals, special emphasis has been placed on distributing condoms to at-risk groups such as youth, sex workers, truck drivers, the military, and convicts. Condoms are distributed in urban and border areas at highly subsidized prices, and free condoms are distributed to sex workers.[67] During our country consultations, some organizations expressed concern that condoms were not widely available. They also argued that condoms needed to be distributed free of charge to youth and the unemployed. The problem emphasized by respondents was that distribution occurs largely through public health facilities, whose service coverage is limited to only 40% of the population.[68] Condom distribution through these public health facilities will be deficient when the most vulnerable populations and high-risk groups live in underserved areas.

In 2007, the Ministry of Health distributed close to 21 million male condoms.[48] PEN 2007–2010, outlines plans to distribute a total of 76 million male condoms and 100,000 female condoms.[48] According to PEN 2007–2010, the government is aiming to identify priority populations and strategies for promoting access to female condoms.[48] Although international evidence suggests that male and female condoms have similar effectiveness, acceptance and use of the female condom has been less common.[59] In the Angolan context, the use of female condoms is likely to be less frequent because of gender imbalances in decision-making, and the high cost of female compared to male condoms.

There are a number of different ways that condom distribution and uptake can be improved. One way is to include education on condom use in school curricula, which has been found to have a significant impact on the uptake and use of condoms.[69] Another way is through social marketing of condoms. PSI programs of social marketing of condoms in Cameroon, Madagascar and Rwanda have increased knowledge of proper condom use, awareness of where to buy condoms, and the belief that family and friends support condom use.[70]

9.5.5. Prevention of HIV: Actions of special interest

Certain of the interventions discussed above are currently being implemented to some degree. This is the case with general mass-media information programs and distribution of condoms. Their current scale of operation is inadequate but there are plans to expand them. Assuming that these plans will be implemented, these actions are not of special interest at this stage. Prevention actions targeted at vulnerable groups — such as mobile populations and adolescents and youth — have benefits not only for the groups themselves but for society as a whole. There also appears to be little public action so far to prevent HIV in these groups. Hence interventions designed to prevent HIV among these groups are of special interest. Currently, adult HIV prevalence is much higher in Cunene province than elsewhere in the country. Cunene also has the lowest rates of male circumcision. Hence, free and early male circumcision in Cunene province is an action of special interest.

9.6. Conclusion

Through the review and consultation process four priority areas were identified: (1) income poverty reduction; (2) expansion of healthcare services; (3) strengthening the education system; and (4) prevention of HIV/AIDS. Inaction in any of these areas can have serious implications for children. For each of these areas we have identified a number of actions of special interest, all of which potentially have large costs of inaction. From the list of actions of special interest, we have selected a subset of three actions for further evaluation: a community healthcare system; strengthening the education system; and an adult and infant male circumcision program.

References

1. Corkin L. *Angola's Current Economic Prospects: Oil a Curse or a Blessing?* Madrid, Spain: Real Instituto Elcano, 2009.

2. UNDP. *Human Development Report 2009. Overcoming Barriers: Human Mobility and Development.* New York, NY: Palgrave Macmillan, 2009.

3. Freedom House. *Angola Country Report.* Washington, DC: Freedom House, 2009.

4. World Bank. *World Development Indicators 2011.* Washington, DC: World Bank, 2011.

5. República de Angola. *Estratégia de Combate à Pobreza. Reinserção Social, Reabilitação e Reconstrução e Estabilização Económica. Versao Sumária.* Luanda, Angola: Ministério do Planeamento, 2003.

6. World Bank. Angola: Poverty Reduction Strategy Papers (PRSP). Washington, DC: World Bank, 2010. http://go.worldbank.org/3YA4HPXFY0. Accessed November 11, 2011.

7. Adato M, Basset L. What is the Potential of Cash Transfers to Strengthen Families Affected by HIV and AIDS? A Review of the Evidence on Impacts and Key Policy Debates. Joint Learning Initiative on Children and HIV/AIDS. JLICA Learning Group 1: Strengthening Families. Washington, DC: International Food Policy Research Institute, Food Consumption and Nutrition Division, 2008.

8. Gertler P. Do conditional cash transfers improve child health? Evidence from PROGRESA's control randomized experiment. *American Economic Review* 2004; 94(2):336–341.

9. Sheldon D. Valuing in-kind transfers. *Focus* 1982; 6(1):12–14.

10. Redvers L. Angola: Teenage School Programme Gives Drop Outs Second Chance at Education. Luanda, Angola: IPS, 2009. http://ipsnews.net/africa/nota.asp?idnews=48127. Accessed November 11, 2011.

11. USAID. Community Mapping Gives Villagers Insight on How to Tap Local Asset. 2009. http://www.usaid.gov/stories/angola/ss_ago_honey.html. Accessed June 21, 2010.

12. Dejene Y. *Promoting Women's Economic Empowerment in Africa.* Addis Ababa, Ethiopia: UNECA, 2007.

13. Oikos. *A Oikos e o Micro-Crédito.* http://www.oikos.pt/logos/oikos_microcredito.pdf. Accessed November 27, 2011.

14. World Bank. *10 years of World Bank Support to Microcredit in Bangladesh.* Washington, DC: World Bank, 2007.

15. Consultoria de Serviços e Pesquisas, Consultoria Lda, Consultoria de

Gestão e Administração em Saúde — Consaude Lda, Macro International Inc. *Malaria Indicator Survey 2006–2007*. Calverton, MD: Macro International Inc., 2007.

16. Urassa E, Lindmark G, Nystrom L. Maternal mortality in Dar es Salaam, Tanzania: Socio-economic, obstetric history and accessibility of health care factors. *African Journal of Health Sciences* 1995; 2(1):242–249.

17. OECD. *Promoting Pro Poor Growth Infrastructure*. Paris, France: OECD, 2006.

18. McCord A. *A Typology for Public Works Programming*. Natural Resource Perspectives. Vol. 121. London, UK: Overseas Development Institute, 2008.

19. Kashuupulwa CH. Namibia: Land Reform — Prospects and Challenges. Allafrica.com. 2008. http://allafrica.com/stories/200807180708.html. Accessed November 12, 2011.

20. World Bank. *Angola: Project Information Document (PID) Appraisal Stage*. Report No. AB4517. Washington, DC: World Bank, 2009.

21. WHO. *World Health Statistics 2009*. Geneva, Switzerland: WHO, 2009.

22. Zachariah R, Ford N, Phillips M, Lynch S, Massaguoi M, Janssens V, Harries AD. Task shifting in HIV/AIDS: Opportunities, challenges and proposed actions for sub-Saharan Africa. *Transactions of the Royal Society of Tropical Medicine and Hygiene* 2009; 103(6):549–558.

23. AVERT. Universal access to AIDS treatment: Targets and challenges. West Sussex, UK: AVERT, 2010. http://www.avert.org/universal-access. htm. Accessed November 11, 2011.

24. Rowe AK, de Leon GF, Mihigo J, Santelli AC, Miller NP, Van-Dunem P. Quality of malaria case management at outpatient health facilities in Angola. *Malaria Journal* 2009; 8(275):1–20.

25. Women's Refugee Commission. *Global Survey on Education in Emergencies: Angola Country Report*. New York, NY: Women's Refugee Commission, 2003.

26. Instituto Nacional de Estatistica and UNICEF. *Multiple Indicator Cluster Survey: Assessing the Situation of Angolan Children and Women at the Beginning of the Millennium*. Luanda, Angola: INE and UNICEF, 2003.

27. Republica de Angola and Ministerio da Educação. *Comparação entre o Sistema de Educação em vigor e o Sistema de Educação a Implementar*. Luanda, Angola: Republica de Angola, 2003.

28. International Planned Parenthood Federation (IPPF), UNFPA, Global Coalition on Women and AIDS, Young Positives. *Research Dossier: HIV Prevention for Girls and Young Women — Kenya*. London, UK: IPPF, 2007.

29. Taras H. Nutrition and student performance at school. *Journal of School Health* 2005; 75(6):199—213.

30. WFP. *School Feeding Works for Girls' Education*. Rome, Italy: WFP, 2001.
31. Kayiggwa P. Rwanda: Adolescents Missing School during Menstruation Call for Sanitary Pads. allAfrica.com, 2007. http://allafrica.com/stories/200710120286.html. Accessed November 11, 2011.
32. Chapman DW, Kyeyune R, Lokkesmoe K. *Evaluation of the African Girls Education Initiative — Country Case Study: Uganda*. Kampala, Uganda: UNICEF, 2003.
33. Insingoma J. Makapads: Makere University Makes Affordable Sanitary Pads. Kampala, Uganda: UGPulse.com, 2006. http://www.ugpulse.com/articles/daily/homepage.asp?ID=549. Accessed November 11, 2011.
34. Engle P, Black MM, Behrman JR, Cabral de Mello M, Gertler PJ, Kapiriri L, Martorell R, Young ME, International Child Development Steering Group. Strategies to avoid the loss of developmental potential in more than 200 million children in the developing world. *Lancet* 2007; 369(9557):229–242.
35. Powell C, Baker-Henningham H, Walker S, Gernay J, Grantham-McGregor S. Feasibility of integrating early stimulation into primary care for undernourished Jamaican children: Cluster randomized controlled trial. *British Medical Journal* 2004; 329(7457):1–4.
36. Behrman JR, Cheng Y, Todd P. *The Impact of the Bolivian Integrated "PIDI" Preschool Program*. Philadelphia, PA: University of Pennsylvania, 2000.
37. World Bank. *Early Childhood Development (ECD) Program Evaluations*. Washington, DC: World Bank, 2009.
38. UNICEF. *What's the Difference? An ECD Impact Study from Nepal*. New York, NY: UNICEF, 2003.
39. Boocock S. Early childhood programs in other nations: Goals and outcomes. *The Future of Children* 1995; 5(3):94–114.
40. UNESCO. *National Report on the Development of Adults' Education: Angola*. International Conference on Adults' Education. Bangkok, Thailand: UNESCO, 2003.
41. República de Angola. *Estratégia de Alfabetização e Recuperação do Atraso Escolar, 2006–2015*. Luanda, Angola: República de Angola and Ministério da Educação, 2005.
42. Fundação Evangelização e Cultura. *Educação em Movimento: Promoção da Educação para o Desenvolvimento da Província do Moxico*. Moscavide, Portugal: Relatório de Monitorização, 2008.
43. Brown T, Franklin B, MacNeil J, Mills S. *Effective Prevention Strategy in Low HIV Prevalence Settings*. Durham, NC: Family Health International, USAID, UNAIDS, 2001.
44. UNDP. *Evaluation of UNDP's Role and Contributions in the HIV/AIDS Response in Southern Africa and Ethiopia: Country Studies*. New York, NY: UNDP, 2006.

45. Comunidade dos Paises de Lingua Portuguesa. *The HIV Epidemic in the Portuguese Speaking Countries: Current Situation and Future Perspectives towards Universal Access for Prevention, Treatment and Care.* Lisbon, Portugal: Comunidade dos Paises de Lingua Portuguesa, 2008.
46. USAID. *HIV/AIDS Health Profile: Angola.* Washington, DC: USAID, 2008.
47. República de Angola, Instituto Nacional de Luta Contra a SIDA, UN-AIDS. *Relatório de UNGASS 2007.* Luanda, Angola: República de Angola, 2007.
48. Instituto Nacional de Luta Contra a Sida. *Plano Estratégico Nacional Para o Controlo das Infecções de Transmissão Sexual, VIH e SIDA 2007 a 2010.* Luanda, Angola: Instituto Nacional de Luta Contra a Sida, 2006.
49. Consulado Geral da República de Angola. República de Angola Principais Indicadores Demograficos. http://www.consuladodeangola.org/index.php?option=com_content&task=view&id=14&Itemid=38. Accessed November 27, 2011.
50. Stringer J, Aira T, Bhatta MP, Schwebke J, Sarkar M, Shah SA, Vermund SH. HIV/STD prevention in high risk, low prevalence Asian nations: Bangladesh, Pakistan, and Mongolia. 12th International Conference on AIDS. Geneva, Switzerland: June 28–July 3, 1998.
51. UNAIDS. *Practical Guidelines for Intensifying HIV Prevention towards Universal Access.* Geneva, Switzerland: UNAIDS, 2007.
52. Henry Kaiser Foundation. HIV Prevalence Among Mexican Migrant Workers Three Times as High as General U.S., 2004. http://www.thebody.com/content/art9969.html. Accessed November 27, 2011.
53. IOM. *Baseline Assessment — Preparing for the Implementation of IOM's Health Promotion Projects across Southern Africa.* Pretoria, South Africa: IOM, 2009.
54. Amnesty International. *Angola: Lives in Ruins — Forced Evictions Continue.* London, UK: Amnesty International, 2007.
55. Family Health International. *Corridors of Hope in Southern Africa: HIV Prevention Needs and Opportunities in Four Border Towns.* Durham, NC: Family Health International, 1999.
56. Population Services International, UNICEF, USAID. *Sexual Knowledge, Attitudes, and Behavior among Urban Youth in Angola: A Summary of Results from the 2003 Survey of Knowledge, Attitudes and Practice.* Washington, DC: Population Services International, 2003.
57. Save the Children. *Knowledge, Attitudes and Practice linked to HIV Prevention in Young Children and Adolescents.* Luanda, Angola: Save the Children, 2003.
58. Pozo G, Argandona A. HIV/AIDS prevention among adolescents in low prevalence settings: Lessons from La Paz, Bolivia. 15th International

Conference on AIDS. Bangkok, Thailand: July 11–16, 2004.

59. Coates TJ, Richter L, Caceres C. Behavioural strategies to reduce HIV transmission: How to make them work better. *Lancet* 2008; 372(9639):669–684.

60. Wilson D, Mparadzi A, Lavelle S. An experimental comparison of two AIDS prevention interventions among young Zimbabweans. *Journal of Social Psychology* 1992; 132(3):415–417.

61. Padian NS, Buve A, Balkus J, Serwadda D, Cates W. Biomedical interventions to prevent HIV infections: Evidence, challenges, and way forward. *Lancet* 2008; 372(9638):589–599.

62. WHO, UNAIDS. *Male Circumcision: Global Trends and Determinants of Prevalence, Safety, and Acceptability.* Geneva, Switzerland: WHO, 2007.

63. Marck J. Aspects of male circumcision in sub-equatorial African culture history. *Health Transition Review* 1997; Supplement to Volume 7:337–359.

64. Wamai RG, Weiss HA, Hankins C, et al. Male circumcision is an efficacious, lasting and cost-effective strategy for combating HIV in high-prevalence countries (Letter). *Future HIV Therapy* 2008; 2(5):399–405.

65. Population Services International. *Angola (2005): HIV/AIDS TRaC Study among Youth 12–24 Years of Age. First Round.* Washington, DC: PSI, 2005.

66. Prata N, Vahidnia F, Fraser A. Gender and relationship differences in condom use among 15–24 year-olds in Angola. *International Family Planning Perspectives* 2005; 31(4):192–199.

67. Population Services International. *Angola.* Washington, DC: PSI, 2010. http://www.psi.org/angola. Accessed November 11, 2011.

68. Connor C, Rajkotia Y, Lin Y-S, Figueiredo P. *Angola Health System Assessment.* Bethesda, MD: USAID and Abt Associates Inc., 2005.

69. Kirby D, Obasi A, Laris BA. The effectiveness of sex education and HIV education interventions in schools in developing countries. *World Health Organization Technical Report Series* 2006; 938:103–150.

70. Neukom J, Ashford L. *Changing Youth Behavior through Social Marketing — Program Experiences and Research Findings from Cameroon, Madagascar, and Rwanda.* Washington, DC: PSI, 2003.

CHAPTER 10

A community healthcare system in Angola

10.1. Background

Despite Angola's abundance of resources and relatively high income, the health status of its citizens remains among the worst in the world. The low life expectancy at birth in 2009 of 49 years for males and 52 years for females reflects multiple socio-economic deprivations, including lack of primary healthcare and basic education.[1] The situation is particularly serious for children, who face a very high mortality rate. In 2010 the under-five mortality rate was 161 deaths per 1,000 live births.[1] Maternal mortality is also extremely high, with a rate of 610 per 100,000 live births in 2008.[2] Malaria is the leading cause of mortality and morbidity, with an estimated six million cases of illness per year.[3] Although Angola has one of the lowest levels of HIV prevalence in southern Africa, population mobility has increased after the war and the likelihood of HIV reaching once-isolated communities has risen.[4] Since the end of the war, adult HIV prevalence has increased from 1.7% in 2002 to 2.1% in 2009.[5] The intensity of HIV varies across different parts of the country; lower rates are found in central regions such as the province of Kwanza Norte (1.5%), and higher rates in the border provinces of Cunene and Uíge where adult prevalence is 9.1% and 4.8%, respectively.[6] In the capital city of Luanda, adult prevalence is estimated to be 6.5%.[6]

Health facilities are scarce or dysfunctional throughout the country. At the end of 2002, 12% of hospitals, 11% of health centers, and 85% of health posts were not operational due to serious deterioration (or destruction) of physical infrastructure, lack of staff, and insufficient basic equipment. In 2005, healthcare access was still limited to between 30% and 40% of the population, leaving 60% or more of the population uncovered.[7] The density of doctors in Angola is very low (1 per 10,000 population in 2005) and doctors are highly concentrated in Luanda and other urban centers.[7,8] As a result of the critical shortage of health workers, people are frequently forced to travel long distances to access healthcare, especially in rural areas. The government estimates that 76 % of the rural population in 2009 lived more than 2km (1.2 miles) away from a health center.[9] Limited and costly transportation add to the problems of access.

Primary care for children — including the prevention and treatment of malaria and the vertical transmission of HIV/AIDS — requires the provision of services that are in short supply. Without these services, children will continue to die at a very high rate and many more will continue to suffer from preventable and treatable illnesses. Given that Angola spent 4.6% of its GDP on health in 2009, compared to, for example, Rwanda where 9.0% of GDP was spent on health, Angola clearly has the fiscal space to do more.[1] When it signed the Abuja Declaration in 2001, the Government of Angola committed to allocating 15% of its budget to health,[6] but in 2009 it allocated only 8.4%.[1]

Table 10.1. CHS staff requirements and program costs (2012 US$ million): Selected years

Year	2012	2016	2021
Coverage of CHS			
% of the population covered	6	54	60
Number of people covered (million)	1.0	9.5	10.5
Number of staff			
Community health workers	3,509	35,411	45,392
Community nurses	219	2,213	2,837
Nurse supervisors	5	55	71
Program costs (2012 US$ million)			
Salaries	8.4	84.8	108.7
Training	10.8	9.5	5.8
Consumables	0.6	6.3	8.1
Community clinics	0.3	3.2	4.5
Administration	0.9	9.1	11.7
Total cost (2012 US$ million)	**21.1**	**113.0**	**138.5**

10.2. Description of intervention

A community healthcare system (CHS) is selected as an appropriate intervention to improve access to primary healthcare in the country. It responds to the need for large-scale coverage without placing demands which cannot be met on medical professionals such as doctors. The intervention consists of building and maintaining a community healthcare system, which we evaluate here as a 10-year program from 2012 to 2021. CHS is designed to cover 60% of the country's population that currently has no, or very limited, access to healthcare services.[7]

CHS involves the training and deployment of community health workers (CHWs) and community nurses (CNs) to improve access to primary care. CHWs will provide primary care through home visits. CNs will be based at satellite clinics in the community but will undertake home visits to support and supervise CHWs. CHWs and CNs will be trained, paid and supervised, and will provide services such as dispensing basic medication and referring people for treatment. They will distribute oral rehydration salts and insecticide-treated nets, check whether children have been vaccinated, and provide health information such as guidance on diarrhea prevention and treatment. In addition to providing primary care, they will work to improve malaria and HIV prevention, and assist patients adhere to treatment regimens. They will also provide family planning services. Annex 10A contains further details of the design of CHS.

10.3. Estimation of costs and benefits
10.3.1. Resource requirements and costs

A detailed design for CHS was developed to allow for estimation of its resource requirements and costs of operation. As far as possible, cost data from Angola have been used, and the costing reflects local prices (for details see Annex 10B).

CHS program inputs and costs are calculated on the assumption that the intervention will be scaled-up rapidly — to reach full coverage in five years. The staff requirements and program costs are summarized in table 10.1 for selected years; see Annex 10C for annual estimates between 2012 and 2021. In 2021, CHS will require approximately 45,000 CHWs and 2,800 CNs. Given the limited supply of health workers in Angola, personnel training in large numbers will be an important component of CHS in its early years.

In 2016, five years into the program, coverage will expand to 54% of the population. The total cost of CHS in 2016 will be US$113 million, and the cost per person covered will be US$11. In 2021, 60% of the population will be covered at a cost of US$138.5 million. A high level of investment in training is needed during the first few years of the program, but training costs as a proportion of total costs fall significantly as CHS reaches its full complement of healthcare personnel. Salaries dominate total costs as the program scales up. In 2016, salaries are estimated at US$85 million, which accounts for 75% of total costs.

10.3.2. Constitutive benefits of CHS

The constitutive benefits of CHS are the direct health benefits that arise from implementing the program. The benefits of CHS in Angola were estimated by applying the results of similar programs undertaken in other countries. In Ghana, for example, a community healthcare intervention reduced the risk of infant mortality by 61% — from 85 deaths per 1,000 live births in 1997 to 33 deaths per 1,000 live births in 2003.[10] In Angola, we assume that after three years CHS will reduce the infant mortality rate (IMR) in the population covered by 50%. The reduction of 50% is applied to the population served, whose IMR is taken to be the national IMR in 2010 of 98 deaths per 1,000 live births.[1]

The scale of CHS implies that it will contribute to avoiding a large number of infant deaths. We calculate that in 2021 (year 10) CHS will avoid 23,600 infant deaths. An intervention that covers 60% of the country's population is bound to have a significant effect on indicators at the national level. We estimate that CHS will reduce the national IMR from 98 per 1,000 live births in 2012 to 77 per 1,000 live births in 2021. Apart from infant mortality, CHS will also contribute to reducing the mortality of children aged 1 to 5 years. Thus all under-five mortality will be reduced. CHS will moreover help to decrease morbidity among children under five — here defined as fever, acute respiratory infection, or diarrhea. CHS will also lead to fewer maternal deaths. The effect of CHS on the national maternal mortality rate (MMR) will be to reduce it from 610 per 100,000 live births in 2012 to 457 per 100,000 in 2021. The intervention will have limited impact on adult mortality and morbidity. Its quantified constitutive benefits are summarized in table 10.2 for selected years; see table 10C.6 for annual estimates of benefits during 2012–21.

The decline in infant mortality is expected to arise from the provision of primary care to children and health information to parents and caregivers. The estimated impact on infant mortality is based on the results of similar interventions undertaken in the context of poverty and limited access to healthcare services, notably the Navrongo Community Health and Family Planning Project in the Upper East Region of Ghana.[10] Results of other studies have been used to estimate the impact on child mortality and morbidity.[11-13] A high proportion of the benefits are expected to occur as a result of reduced incidence and severity of malaria. Many studies show that similar interventions deploying CHWs for malaria prevention and treatment are effective.[12]

Evaluations of other programs suggest that CHWs have a significant im-

Table 10.2. Quantified constitutive benefits of CHS: Selected years

Year	2012	2016	2021
Constitutive benefits			
Infant deaths avoided	792	16,889	23,597
Deaths avoided of children age 1–5 years	123	3,111	6,068
Cases of child morbidity avoided	775	19,546	38,125
Number of children immunized	11,256	249,920	264,560
Maternal deaths avoided	30	618	842
Adult malaria deaths avoided	3	60	82
Cases of non-fatal adult malaria avoided	7	151	206
% decline in TFR	6	13	17

pact on children's health as a result of prevention efforts that include vaccination and general health-promotion initiatives. Despite improvements in vaccination coverage, many children in Angola remain inadequately immunized.[14] CHS will significantly increase the number of immunized children, the benefits of which are captured in part by reductions in under-five mortality and morbidity.

Family planning programs using CHWs have been effective in reducing the total fertility rate (TFR) in African countries.[12] We estimate there will be a 17% reduction in TFR among the CHS population in 2021 (on the basis of changes observed in the Ghana project).[10] This will translate into a 10% reduction in the national TFR, which currently stands at 5.6.[15] CHS will also provide a mix of interventions aimed at decreasing morbidity and mortality risks related to pregnancy — including antenatal and postnatal care at home and in community clinics. This will reduce the main risk factors for maternal mortality in Angola, where 54% of deliveries do not currently occur in institutions.[2]

The benefits discussed so far refer to the quantified constitutive benefits of the intervention. However, not all constitutive benefits of CHS were quantified, either because they are qualitative in nature or because of lack of data. For example, CHWs are known to be effective in delivering information on child nutrition,[16] which could not be quantified. Other examples include health benefits to children older than five years, and to adults, from reduction in the incidence or severity of diseases aside from malaria.

10.3.3. Consequential benefits of CHS

The full benefits of CHS consist of both its constitutive and consequential benefits. In contrast to constitutive benefits, which include the health gains shown in table 10.2, the consequential benefits of CHS include non-health gains for individuals, families, broader society, the economy, and future generations. We first consider the consequential benefits arising from the quantified health benefits of CHS — these consequential benefits are summarized in table 10.3. We then consider the quantified and non-quantified consequential benefits arising from employment of CHWs — these benefits are summarized in tables 10.4 and 10.5.

The following sub-sections provide details of the pathways to the consequential benefits identified in table 10.3.

Consequential benefits arising from reduction in under-five morbidity

Child morbidity affects education for a number of reasons. Healthier under-fives are more likely to proceed to primary school, be more efficient learners at school, and have lower dropout rates.[17] Malnutrition and poor health are detrimental to children's cognitive, motor and social-emotional development.[18]

Table 10.3. Consequential benefits arising from quantified health benefits

Quantified benefit leading to consequential benefit	Pathway to consequential benefit	Non-quantified consequential benefit
Reduction in under-five morbidity and increase in number of children immunized	1. Protecting child health leads to improved cognitive, motor and social-emotional skills	• Improved school readiness and attainment (1)
Maternal deaths avoided	1. The presence of mothers is critical for child development, health and education	• Improved child health and education (1)
Reduced fertility	1. Fewer births allow for more investment per child in children's health and education	• Improved child health and education (1)

Consequential benefits arising from reduced maternal mortality

Maternal deaths increase the likelihood that surviving children will die. Studies from Indonesia show that maternal mortality has a large and significant effect on child mortality, with maternally-orphaned children estimated to be four times more likely to die compared to otherwise similar non-bereaved children.[19] For children who survive the loss of their mother, the loss may have a detrimental effect on their nutritional and health status, their physical and cognitive development, and their educational attainment.[19]

In Angola, adult support is needed for children to enroll in and attend school. School transportation is limited and available only in urban centers. Many schools charge fees or require other payments (such as bribes for admission). In this situation, adult mortality can have an adverse effect on a child's education — by delaying school entry or increasing the probability of the child dropping out. Evidence of such consequences is documented in studies of parental loss in many African countries.[19]

The death of an adult who is economically active leads to a reduction in household income and consumption. A reduction in income can push a household into poverty or deepen existing poverty, possibly leading to children dropping out of school.[20]

Consequential benefits arising from reduced fertility

A number of links have been proposed between fertility reduction and investment in children's nutrition, health and education. Families with fewer children tend to spend more on each child, which leads to improved nutrition, health, and school attendance of children.[21]

Benefits consequential to employment of CHWs

Consequential benefits also arise from the employment of CHWs. The implementation of CHS involves the employment of thousands of CHWs which lead to numerous consequential benefits — some quantifiable and others not.

According to the CHS design, CHWs are drawn from communities in which they will end up working. The communities targeted by CHS are those without access (or with only limited access) to healthcare, and are thus likely to have above-average rates of poverty. Employing people from these communities should help to reduce income poverty. It is estimated that in 2021 almost 37,000 households will be above the poverty line (of US$2.5 per person per day) due to CHW employment.

The reduction in household poverty will affect children's well-being in a number of ways. For example, in 2021 an additional 4,000 children from CHW households will be able to attend school as a result of increased income of their families. The spending of income by CHW households will, through

Table 10.4. Quantified consequential benefits from employment of CHWs: Selected years

Year	2012	2016	2021
Consequential benefit Increased income of CHW households (2012 US$ million)	5.5	52.6	62.5
Households moved above the poverty line due to CHW employment	2,843	28,683	36,767
Additional number of children in school from CHW households	295	3,095	4,170

the multiplier, contribute to increasing the incomes of others in the community. Given the large number of CHWs involved, this could mean the injection of significant consumer demand in poor communities. Table 10.4 summarizes the quantified consequential benefits arising from the employment of CHWs.

Other consequential benefits from increased incomes of CHWs cannot be quantified easily, but there is evidence from other countries that they occur. These consequential benefits and the pathways through which they are expected to arise are summarized in table 10.5.

Table 10.5. Non-quantified consequential benefits from employment of CHWs

Quantified benefit from employment of CHWs	Pathway to non-quantified consequential benefit	Non-quantified consequential benefit
Increased income of CHW households	1. More spending on goods and services 2. Spending in the community increases income of other community members	• Improved utilization of health-care and other services (1) • Income poverty reduction (2)

10.4. Summary and conclusion

The community healthcare system is designed to provide primary health-care over a 10-year period to 60% of Angola's population that has no or limited access to health services. The healthcare package consists of elements that have a disproportionately large benefit for children, e.g. immunization, bednets and ORT. Children are particularly susceptible and vulnerable to malaria and diarrhea, but can be protected by simple and inexpensive means. CHS is therefore likely to be an effective intervention for children.

The benefits and costs of CHS have been estimated for the period 2012–21. The cumulative child health benefits over this period are sizeable: 155,000 infant deaths avoided; 34,000 fewer deaths of children between 1 and 5 years of age; 210,000 cases of child morbidity avoided; and 2.1 million children immunized. Moreover, adult-health benefits accrue over this period, e.g. a total of 5,600 maternal deaths avoided. By 2021 there is also expected to be a 17% reduction in TFR among women served by CHS.

The consequential benefits of CHS include an increase in the incomes of people employed as CHWs. Among other things, during the period 2012-21 this results in an additional 3,000 children on average attending school each year. Also the spending of CHW incomes will contribute to an increase in income of poor communities.

Over the period 2012–21 the average annual cost of CHS at 2012 prices is estimated to be US$99.2 million, and the present value of total costs discounted at 3% per annum is US$819.4 million. The intervention, although large in scale, is financially feasible: the average annual cost of CHS is less than 0.5 percent of Angola's annual oil revenues. Per-person served, the annual cost of CHS is *only* US$12.

By selecting an action that is clearly feasible from both a financial and human resources point of view, the identified costs of inaction serve as a powerful instrument to inform policy debate. It is hoped that the analysis presented here will assist policymakers and civil society representatives to address the country's critical shortage of healthcare services for its people. Our results show that large costs of inaction will arise if a community health-care system is not implemented in Angola.

ANNEX
Annex 10A. Description of intervention
Intervention: CHS is a government program which trains and deploys supervised community health workers and nurses to improve access to health services that focus on primary care, malaria prevention and treatment.

Goal: CHS seeks to expand access to primary care to 60% of Angola's population that is presently uncovered. The targeted coverage of 60% is to be achieved in five years. Under primary care for all, the services offered will be particularly beneficial to children from low-income populations, and pregnant women.

Services provided by staff: Community health workers (CHWs) will provide services such as distributing basic medication and referring people for treatment. They will distribute oral rehydration salts and insecticide-treated nets, check if children have been vaccinated, and provide information on diarrhea prevention and treatment. Community health workers will provide households with health information and support patients to adhere to treatment regimens. CHWs trained in HIV prevention will provide psychosocial support to patients, and address issues such as stigma and discrimination. Community nurses (CNs) will be based in satellite clinics in the community and provide clinic-based primary care for half their time. For the rest of their time, CNs will be in the field to supervise CHWs and provide them support and continuing education. CNs, in turn, will be overseen by nurse supervisors (NSs).

Identification and referral: CHWs will work to identify sick people proactively. They will alert CNs if a patient's physical or mental health state is precarious. As required, CHWs will refer patients to the satellite clinics in CHS. Referral to the clinics and hospitals of the existing healthcare system will be done by CNs and NSs.

CHW-to-household ratio: The CHW-to-household ratio required for effective service delivery can vary from site to site depending on population density, logistical demands arising from an area's topography, and the types of patient being served. CHS is designed under the assumptions that each CHW will cover an average of 50 households in rural areas and 80 households in urban areas, that each CN will supervise 16 CHWs, and that each NS will be responsible for 40 CNs.

Selection of CHS staff: CHS staff must be of adult age. Preference will be given to employing CHWs who live in or close to the community in which they will serve. The work arrangements of CHWs are expected to be sufficiently flexible to enable the participation of women. Prior to employment, CHWs must have completed primary-school education, and CNs and NSs must have completed secondary-school education.

Training: CHWs will need to be trained for six months and receive orientation from clinical staff. Basic training will be provided by the National Directorate of Public Health (NDPH). All trainees will be provided with meals and a stipend. Trainers and facilitators will be drawn from staff at existing health centers in the area, and should be competent in participatory-based learning and other training methods. CNs will receive one year of training, and NSs will be required to complete three years of nursing school.

- **Continuing education:** After the initial training program, CHWs will participate in ongoing monthly education sessions. These ongoing sessions will include additional training in areas such as nutrition, malaria, pediatric HIV/AIDS, diarrheal disease, family planning, chronic disease, first aid, the role of traditional healers, and oral hygiene. CHWs with secondary education who have completed at least two years of practice will be eligible for promotion to community nurse, and will be provided training to facilitate this.

Annex 10B. Assumptions and methods

A number of assumptions have been made to estimate the costs and benefits of CHS. Whenever possible, Angolan data were used to inform these estimations. When Angolan data were not available, we used data from similar interventions in other countries in the region.

Population coverage

In order to estimate both costs and benefits it is necessary to make a number of demographic and coverage assumptions for the projection period. Population estimates for Angola during the period 2012–21 are based on recent UN data.[1] The program inputs and costs assume that CHS will be scaled-up in five years to reach full coverage to 60% of the population. This is the proportion of the population that currently has limited or no access to a healthcare facility.[6,7]

Assumptions to estimate costs of CHS

Staff ratios: We assume that CHWs will be responsible for visiting 50 households per month in rural areas and 80 households per month in urban centers.

The level and quality of supervision is widely recognized to play an important role in determining the success of community healthcare programs.[12] CN-to-CHW and NS-to-CN ratios have to be sufficiently large to allow effective supervision. The CN-to-CHW ratio is based on the assumption that CNs will work for half the time in satellite community clinics and supervise CHWs for the remaining half of their time. We assume that each NS will visit 2 CNs per day.

- The CHW-to-household ratio is assumed to be 1-to-50 in rural areas and 1-to-80 in urban areas; the CN-to-CHW ratio is 1-to-16 and the NS-to-CN ratio is 1-to-40.

Urban-rural distribution of households: Healthcare staff needs depend on the distribution of households in urban and rural areas — for which we do not have direct information. We estimate this indirectly by dividing the number of people in each stratum by average household size. Urban areas account for 57% of the total population,[1] and average household size is 5.1 in urban areas and 4.3 in rural areas (2001 data).[22] The larger average household size in urban areas reflects crowded living conditions in cities, particularly Luanda.[23]

- 57% of the population live in urban areas
- On average, urban households contain 5.1 persons and rural households 4.3 persons.

Length of training: High quality training is critical for the success of CHS. The duration of training for CHWs in interventions similar to CHS varies greatly. Some programs have provided just a few days training for CHWs, while others have provided several months of training. Given the range of duties that CHWs are required to perform in CHS, their training needs to be comprehensive.[12]

- CHW training is assumed to be 6 months, CN training 12 months, and NS training 3 years.

Training costs: CHW training costs are based on training that is provided over 6 months for 5 days a week. All participants will be given meals and a stipend to cover transportation costs. Under these assumptions training costs for CHWs are US$200 per month for 6 months. Training costs for CNs and NSs have been estimated on the basis of discussions with and data from private nursing colleges in Angola. Training costs for CNs are taken to be US$250 per month for 12 months, and training costs for NSs US$750 per month for 36 months.

- Monthly training costs are assumed to be US$200 for CHWs, US$250 for CNs, and US$750 for NSs.

Staff attrition: CHW programs often experience high staff attrition because they use volunteers.[24] But CHS in Angola will not be using volunteers. We assume that CHS will have attrition rates for CHWs, CNs and NSs similar to those of other health professionals, viz. an attrition rate of 6% per year. This is comparable to attrition rates for health workers in Kenya of 5% per year.[25]

- The annual attrition rate is assumed to be 6% for CHWs, CNs and NSs.

Salaries: Salary costs for CHS are based on key-informant interviews with people knowledgeable about current salaries of health professionals and similar government staff in Angola.

- CHWs will be paid US$180 per month, CNs will be paid US$300 per month, and NSs will be paid US$500 per month. Salaries are assumed to rise at 2% per annum in real terms.

Consumables: Given the epidemiological context in Angola and the program design of CHS, the main consumables distributed will be oral rehydration therapy (ORT) salts, anti-malarial drugs, insecticide-treated bednets, condoms, and family planning drugs. The assumptions concerning distribution of consumables are as follows.

- Two doses of oral rehydration salts will be distributed per household per year.
- This estimate assumes there are 10 million cases of diarrhea among under-fives each year,[26] and that 30% of the population seeks treatment.
- Anti-malarial medication will be distributed to every household once a year.
- Angola has an estimated 6 million cases of malaria each year,[3] which translates into 1.8 cases per household. We assume that not everyone will seek treatment through CHS.
- Bednets will be distributed once every 5 years.
- Insecticide-treated bednets protect a family of four and are effective for 4 to 5 years.
- 120 condoms will be distributed each year to households that request them, and we assume that 10% of households will request them.
- The number of condoms distributed is estimated on the assumption that they are for one cohabiting couple.
- One implant every 5 years will be offered to women who want an implant, which is assumed to be 5% of all women.
- Uptake is based on reported experience from similar programs such as the Navrongo experiment in Ghana.[10,12]
- Running costs of satellite clinics are assumed to be US$2,500 per year.
- The satellite clinic costs are based on rental costs for a single room.

Assumptions to estimate benefits of CHS
Infant mortality

CHW programs have been shown to lead to declines in infant mortality. The declines are thought to occur because the programs focus on primary care. For example, in the Upper East Region of Ghana, results of the Navrongo Community Health and Family Planning Project show that community healthcare interventions reduced the infant mortality rate from 85 deaths per 1,000 live births in 1997 to 33 deaths per 1,000 live births in 2003.[10] There are similarities between Angola and the Navrongo region in terms of disease profile (high prevalence of malaria and diarrhea), poverty rates, and limited access to services prior to implementation of the intervention. The design of CHS is based on the Navrongo Community Health and Family Planning Project, and it seems reasonable to assume that the impact will be similar. Other community healthcare programs have also reduced infant mortality significantly. For example, in Chhattisgarh, part of the former state of Madhya Pradesh in India, community health workers helped to decrease the infant mortality rate from 85 deaths per 1,000 live births in 2002 to 65 deaths per 1,000 live births in 2005.[27]

In Bangladesh, CHWs have been effective in reducing neonatal mortality. Among infants who survive their first day of life, the 28-day mortality rate among those who were visited by a health worker on the first day was one-third that of those who did not receive such a visit (21 per 1,000 vs 65 per 1,000). Likewise, among infants who survived day 2, the mortality rate was reduced compared to those who never received a visit (13 per 1,000 vs 39 per 1,000). Mortality rates for infants whose first visit occurred after day 2 were not different from rates for unvisited infants.[11]

- **Infant mortality rate:** After 3 years of being covered by CHS, the IMR of children from participating households will be half the rate it would otherwise have been. The IMR in 2012 without CHS is taken to be 98 per 1,000 live births.[1] It is assumed that IMR will fall at 0.5% per year without CHS. The improvement in IMR each year resulting from CHS is calculated by halving the estimated IMR without CHS. The crude birth rate (necessary to estimate the number of births to which the IMR is applied) is taken to be 48 per 1,000 population.[2]

Mortality of children aged 1–5 years

In the implementation area, the Navrongo Project reduced the under-five mortality rate from 188 per 1,000 live births in 1993 to 79 per 1,000 live births in 2003.[10] A Cochrane review cites three CHW interventions that reduced mortality and morbidity among children under five, and finds that compared to control groups the interventions reduced under-five mortality by 25%.[13]

- **Mortality rate of children aged 1–5:** We assume that CHS leads to a reduction in mortality of children aged 1–5 years that is similar to the reductions observed in under-five mortality in randomized control trials. A slightly lower reduction is assumed than the Cochrane review because children aged 1–5 are not likely to benefit as much as infants. We apply a 20% reduction (instead of a 25% reduction) — i.e., we assume the mortality rate of children aged 1–5 years is 0.8 times the rate it would otherwise have been. The mortality rate in 2012 without CHS is taken to be 63 per 1,000 live births, and to decline at 0.5% per year. In each year, the mortality rate of children aged 1–5 covered by CHS will be 0.8 times the rate of children not covered by CHS.

Morbidity among children under five

A Cochrane review of CHW interventions reports that six out of the seven studies which examined morbidity outcomes found CHWs to have a moderate effect in reducing child morbidity (defined as fever, acute respiratory infection, or diarrhea) among children under five years of age).[13] Compared to control groups that were not provided with CHW services, the relative risk of morbidity among children under five covered by a CHW intervention was 0.86 (0.75 to 0.99).[13]

- **Morbidity among children under five**: After five years into CHS, the incidence of morbidity among children aged 0–5 years will be 0.8 times the incidence it would otherwise have been. Morbidity is assumed to decline by 0.5% per year with or without CHS. The incidence of child morbidity in 2012 is assumed to be 10%.

Immunization coverage

A Cochrane review reports that interventions deploying CHWs to promote immunization in children under five increased uptake by 20%.[13]

- **Immunization rate:** After three years of being covered by CHS, immunization uptake among children will be 1.2 times what it would otherwise have been.[13] Immunization uptake is assumed to increase at 0.5% per year with or without CHS. Uptake is assumed to be 88% in 2012.[14]

Impact on fertility

During the Navrongo experiment in Ghana (1997–2003), the total fertility rate (TFR) dropped from 6 to 5 births — a 17% decrease.[10,28]

- **Total fertility rate:** After three years of CHS coverage, TFR will decrease to 0.83 times the rate it would otherwise have been. TFR is assumed to decline at 1% per year with or without CHS. TFR in 2012 is assumed to be 5.6.[15]

Maternal mortality

A review of interventions to train and support traditional birth attendants reports that such interventions decrease maternal mortality by between 50% and 82% (average of 67.6% across all interventions reviewed).[29] The review included an intervention in Angola which trained traditional birth attendants, and led to a 75% reduction in maternal mortality.[29] Save the Children reports that an intervention in Indonesia similar to CHS in Angola resulted in a decrease of 42% in the maternal mortality rate (MMR).[30] In CHS in Angola, CNs and NSs will have midwifery training; CHWs will not, but will encourage pregnant women to visit the satellite clinics where antenatal care is provided.

- **Maternal mortality:** After three years of CHS coverage, MMR among women will be 0.7 times the rate it would otherwise have been. Maternal mortality is assumed to decline at 1% per year with or without CHS. MMR in 2012 is assumed to be 610 per 100,000 live births.[15]

Malaria mortality

The impact of CHS on malaria mortality is based on results from elsewhere which suggest that 65% of households that receive bednets use them correctly, and their use leads to a 50% reduction in malaria incidence.[31] To avoid double counting, only reductions in malaria mortality for adults are considered; the decrease in IMR and U5MR due to CHS capture the impact of bednets for young children.

- **Malaria mortality:** After three years of CHS coverage, the malaria mortality rate among adults will be reduced to 0.85 times the rate it would otherwise have been. The malaria mortality rate among adults is assumed to decline at 1% per year with or without CHS. The malaria mortality rate among adults in 2012 is assumed to be 1,000 per 100,000 adults.[26]

Malaria morbidity

Community healthcare interventions can reduce malaria morbidity and improve the treatment of malaria.[32] In the Katana health zone in the Democratic Republic of Congo, CHWs improved the treatment of malaria.[12] In each of 12 villages in an intervention area, CHWs were trained for two weeks in the use of a simple fever management algorithm and the timing of treatment. CHWs attended monthly meetings and performed their services under the supervision of the nurse in charge of the area's health center. Malaria morbidity and mortality trends were monitored over two years in the project area (area A) and in an ecologically comparable control area (area B) where malaria treatment continued to be available only at the health center. Healthcare behaviors changed dramatically in the intervention area, and by the end of the observation period 65% of malaria episodes were treated by CHWs. Malaria morbidity declined by 50% in area A but remained stable in the control area.[12] From the above assumptions on malaria mortality, we have estimates for the number of malaria fatalities avoided by CHS. We assume that 2.5 cases of malaria will be avoided for every fatality that is avoided. This estimate comes from an analysis of the relationship between malaria incidence and fatality, where the reduction in fatalities occurs due to the distribution of bednets.[31]

- **Malaria morbidity:** We assume that for every adult malaria death avoided as a result of CHS, a further 2.5 cases of malaria morbidity will be avoided.

ANNEX
Annex 10C. Annual estimates of CHS staff, costs and benefits: 2012–21

Table 10C.1 shows the annual number of staff in training each year. Note that we have assumed staff begin training in 2011 (year 0) in order to have trained professionals in 2012 (year 1).

Table 10C.1. Annual number of staff in training; 2012–21

Year	2011	2012	2013	2014	2015	2016	2017	2018	2019	2020	2021
Category of staff in training (number)											
Community health workers	3,409	7,535	8,396	9,301	10,251	7,200	3,603	3,708	3,815	3,926	4,040
Community nurses	577	525	581	641	450	225	232	238	245	252	260
Nurse supervisors – year 1	9	15	17	12	6	6	6	6	6	7	7
Nurse supervisors – year 2	0	9	15	17	12	6	6	6	6	6	7
Nurse supervisors – year 3	0	0	9	15	17	12	6	6	6	6	6
Nurse supervisors (years 1–3)	**9**	**24**	**41**	**44**	**35**	**24**	**18**	**18**	**18**	**19**	**20**

Table 10C.2. Annual costs of training (2012 US$ million) by category of staff: 2011–21

Year	2011	2012	2013	2014	2015	2016	2017	2018	2019	2020	2021
Category of staff											
Community health workers	4.1	9.0	10.1	11.2	12.3	8.6	4.3	4.4	4.6	4.7	4.8
Community nurses	1.7	1.6	1.7	1.9	1.4	0.7	0.7	0.7	0.7	0.8	0.8
Nurse supervisors	0.1	0.2	0.4	0.4	0.3	0.2	0.2	0.2	0.2	0.2	0.2
Total training costs (2012 US$ million)	**5.9**	**10.8**	**12.2**	**13.5**	**14.0**	**9.5**	**5.2**	**5.3**	**5.5**	**5.6**	**5.8**

Table 10C.3. Annual number of staff by category and urban-rural stratum: 2012–21

Year	2012	2013	2014	2015	2016	2017	2018	2019	2020	2021
Category of staff (number)										
Community health workers	**3,509**	**10,834**	**18,580**	**26,766**	**35,411**	**40,487**	**41,661**	**42,869**	**44,112**	**45,392**
Urban	1,454	4,487	7,695	11,086	14,666	16,768	17,255	17,755	18,270	18,800
Rural	2,055	6,347	10,885	15,680	20,745	23,719	24,406	25,114	25,842	26,592
Community nurses	**219**	**677**	**1,161**	**1,673**	**2,213**	**2,530**	**2,604**	**2,679**	**2,757**	**2,837**
Urban	91	280	481	693	917	1,048	1,078	1,110	1,142	1,175
Rural	128	397	680	980	1,296	1,482	1,526	1,569	1,615	1,662
Nurse supervisors	**5**	**17**	**29**	**42**	**55**	**63**	**65**	**67**	**69**	**71**
Urban	2	7	12	17	23	26	27	28	29	29
Rural	3	10	17	25	32	37	38	39	40	42

Table 10C.4. Annual salary costs (US$ million) by category of staff: 2012–21

Year	2012	2013	2014	2015	2016	2017	2018	2019	2020	2021
Salary costs (US$ million)										
Community health workers	7.6	23.4	40.1	57.8	76.5	87.5	90.0	92.6	95.3	98.0
Community nurses	0.8	2.4	4.2	6.0	8.0	9.1	9.4	9.6	9.9	10.2
Nurse supervisors	0.0	0.1	0.2	0.3	0.4	0.4	0.4	0.4	0.4	0.4
Total salary costs (US$ million)	**8.4**	**25.9**	**44.5**	**64.1**	**84.8**	**96.9**	**99.8**	**102.6**	**105.6**	**108.7**

Table 10C.5. Annual cost of consumables (2012 US$ thousand) by type: 2012–21

Year	2012	2013	2014	2015	2016	2017	2018	2019	2020	2021
Type of consumable										
ORT salts	14	42	72	103	137	156	161	166	170	175
Anti-malarial drugs	249	767	1,316	1,895	2,508	2,867	2,950	3,036	3,124	3,214
Bednets	68	209	359	517	684	782	805	828	852	877
Condoms	136	418	718	1,034	1,368	1,564	1,609	1,656	1,704	1,753
Other medicines	113	349	598	862	1,140	1,303	1,341	1,380	1,420	1,461
Total consumables (2012 US$ thousand)	**629**	**1,942**	**3,331**	**4,799**	**6,349**	**7,259**	**7,469**	**7,686**	**7,909**	**8,138**

Table 10C.6. Quantified benefits of CHS: 2012–21

Year	2012	2013	2014	2015	2016	2017	2018	2019	2020	2021
Quantified constitutive benefits										
Infant deaths avoided	792	3,242	7,283	12,110	16,889	20,825	23,140	23,835	23,716	23,597
Deaths avoided of children age 1–5 years	123	505	1,131	2001	3,111	4,210	5,051	5,639	5,976	6,068
Cases of child morbidity avoided	775	3,175	7,108	12,572	19,546	26,450	31,736	35,428	37,550	38,125
Number of children immunized	11,256	46,561	105,640	177,423	249,920	311,264	309,991	294,923	279,779	264,560
Maternal deaths avoided	30	120	269	445	618	758	838	859	851	842
Adult malaria deaths avoided	3	12	26	43	60	74	82	84	83	82
Cases of non-fatal adult malaria avoided	7	29	66	109	151	185	205	210	208	206
% decline in TFR	6	7	10	12	13	15	16	17	17	17
Quantified consequential benefits from employment of CHWs										
Increased income of CHW households (2012 US$ million)	5.5	16.7	28.3	40.3	52.6	59.3	60.1	61.0	61.8	62.5
Households moved above the poverty line due to CHW employment	2,843	8,775	15,050	21,680	28,683	32,794	33,745	34,724	35,731	36,767
Additional number of children in school from CHW households	295	919	1,592	2,316	3,095	3,574	3,715	3,861	4,012	4,170

References

1. World Bank. *World Development Indicators 2011.* Washington, DC: World Bank, 2011.
2. UNICEF. *State of the World's Children 2009: Maternal and Newborn Health.* New York, NY: UNICEF, 2009.
3. World Bank. *Project Information Document (PID) Appraisal Stage.* Report No. AB4517. Washington, DC: World Bank, 2009.
4. Instituto Nacional de Luta Contra a SIDA, UNAIDS. *Relatório de UNGASS 2007.* Luanda, Angola: República de Angola, 2007.
5. UNAIDS and WHO. Adult (15–49) HIV prevalence percent by country, 1990–2007. *2008 Report on the Global AIDS Epidemic.* Geneva, Switzerland: UNAIDS and WHO, 2008. http://data.unaids.org/pub/GlobalReport/2008/20080813_gr08_prev1549_1990_2007_en.xls. Accessed November 25, 2011.
6. WHO. *Health Action in Crises: Angola.* Luanda, Angola: WHO, 2005.
7. Connor C, Rajkotia Y, Lin Y-S, Figueiredo P. *Angola Health System Assessment.* Bethesda, MD: USAID and Abt Associates Inc., 2005.
8. WHO. *World Health Statistics 2009.* Geneva, Switzerland: WHO, 2009.
9. Instituto Nacional de Estatistica. *Inquérito Integrado Sobre o Bem-Estar da População (IBEP) 2008–09 Principais Resultados Grelha de Indicadores.* Luanda, Angola: Ministerio do Planeamento, 2010.
10. Phillips J, Bawah A, Binka F. *Accelerating Reproductive and Child Health Program Development: The Navrongo Initiative in Ghana.* New York, NY: Population Council, 2005.
11. Doskoch P. Early postpartum visits from community health workers reduce neonatal mortality in Bangladesh. *International Perspectives on Sexual and Reproductive Health* 2009; 35(4):208-209.
12. Lehmann U, Sanders D. *Community Health Workers: What do we Know about them? The State of the Evidence on Programmes, Activities, Costs and Impact on Health Outcomes of using Community Health Workers.* Geneva, Switzerland: WHO, 2007.
13. Lewin S, Munabi-Babigumira S, Glenton C, Daniels K, Bosch-Capblanch X, van Wyk BE, Odgaard-Jensen J, Johansen M, Aja GN, Zarenstien M, Scheel IB. Lay health workers in primary and community health care for maternal and child health and the management of infectious diseases (review). *The Cochrane Collaboration* 2010; 3:43.
14. WHO. *Immunization Profile — Angola.* Geneva, Switzerland: WHO, 2009.
15. UNICEF. *Angola — Statistics.* New York, NY: UNICEF, 2011.
16. Mason JB, Sanders D, Musgrove P, Soekirman, Galloway R. Community health and nutrition programs. In: Jameson D, Measham A, Bremer J, Musgrove P, eds. *Disease Control Priorities in Developing Countries.* Washington, DC: OUP/World Bank, 2006.

17. Glewwe P, Miguel E. The impact of child health and nutrition on education in less developed countries. In: Schultz TP, Strauss J, eds. *Handbook
of Development Economics*. Vol. 4. Oxford, UK: Elsevier, 2008.

18. Grantham-McGregor S, Cheung YB, Cueto S, Glewwe P, Richter L,
Strupp B, International Child Development Steering Group. Develop-
mental potential in the first 5 years for children in developing countries.
Lancet 2007; 369(9555):60–70.

19. Gertler P, Martinez S, Levine D, Bertozzi S. *Lost Presence and Presents:
How Parental Death Affects Children*. Berkeley, CA: University of California, Haas School of Business, 2003.

20. Donahue J. Strengthening households and communities: The key to
reducing the economic impacts of HIV/AIDS on children and families. In: Foster G, Levine C, Williamson J, eds. *A Generation at Risk: The
Global Impact of HIV/AIDS on Orphans and Vulnerable Children*. New
York, NY: Cambridge University Press, 2005.

21. Schultz TP. *Population Policies, Fertility, Women's Human Capital, and
Child Quality*. Discussion Paper No. 954. New Haven, CT: Yale University, Economic Growth Center, 2007.

22. Instituto Nacional de Estatistica and UNICEF. *Multiple Indicator Cluster Survey: Assessing the Situation of Angolan Children and Women at
the Beginning of the Millennium*. Luanda, Angola: INE and UNICEF,
2003.

23. Consultoria de Serviços e Pesquisas, Consultoria Lda, Consultoria de
Gestão e Administração em Saúde — Consaude Lda, Macro Interna-
tional Inc. *Malaria Indicator Survey 2006–2007*. Calverton, MD: Macro
International Inc., 2007.

24. Frenk J, Chen L, Bhutta ZA, Cohen J, Crisp N, Evans T, Fineberg H,
Garcia P, Ke Y, Kelley P, Kistnasamy B, Meleis A, Naylor D, Pablos-
Mendez A, Reddy KS, Scrimshaw S, Sepulveda J, Serwadda D, Zurayk
H. Health professionals for a new century: Transforming education to
strengthen health systems in an interdependent world. *Lancet* 2010;
376(9756):1923–1958.

25. Chankova S, Muchiri S, Kombe G. Health workforce attrition in the
public sector in Kenya: A look at the reasons. *Human Resources for
Health* 2009; 7(58):1–8.

26. WHO. *Mortality and Burden of Disease Estimates for WHO Member
States in 2004*. Geneva, Switzerland: WHO, 2009.

27. Haines A, Sanders D, Lehmann U, Rowe AK, Lawn JE, Jan S, Walker
DG, Bhutta ZA. Achieving child survival goals: Potential contribution
of community health workers. *Lancet* 2007; 369(9579):2121–2131.

28. Binka F, Nazzar A, Phillips J. The Navrongo community health and family planning project. *Studies in Family Planning* 1995; 26(3):121–139.

29. Ray A, Salihu H. The impact of maternal mortality interventions using traditional birth attendants and village midwives. *Journal of Obstetrics and Gynaecology* 2004; 24(1):5–11.
30. Save the Children. *Women on the Front Lines of Health Care.* Westport, CT: Save the Children, 2010.
31. Morel C, Lauer J, Evans D. Cost effectiveness analysis of strategies to combat malaria in developing countries. *British Medical Journal* 2005; 331(7528):1–7.
32. Kouyaté B, Some F, Jahn A, Coulibaly B, Eriksen J, Sauerborn R, Gustafsson L, Tomson G, Becher H, Mueller O. Process and effects of a community intervention on malaria in rural Burkina Faso: Randomized controlled trial. *Malaria Journal* 2008; 7(50):1–13.

CHAPTER 11

Strengthening the education system in Angola

11.1. Background

Strengthening the education system is an important intervention for human and economic development in Angola. Education is valuable in and of itself, and because of the many benefits that flow from it. However, availability of, and access to, education in the country is lacking for many children.

As a result of the 27-year civil war, and high rates of income poverty, many children find it difficult to access education, healthcare and other basic services.[1,2] Utilization is restricted because there are not enough schools, and children have to travel a considerable distance to attend one — incurring high transport costs. The government estimated that in 2009, 34.2% of students lived beyond a 1.24-mile radius from a school — 45.4% of students in rural areas and 24.1% in urban areas.[3]

In 2009 early childhood development (ECD) services were virtually non-existent: only 9% of children aged 3 to 5 years were enrolled in an organized preschool program.[3] Since 2004, increased attention has been paid to the education of young children; two national forums on the care and development of children under 5 years of age have been held. Despite such attention, the availability of services remains inadequate — which affects the development and progress of very young children. The first five years of a child's life are critical for brain development, which influences their capacity for future learning.[4]

In 2001 only 56% of children of primary-school age were attending school[4] and only 20% of children of age 12–17 were in secondary school.[2,5] Data on enrollment are limited, but recent figures suggest that the situation has begun to improve since the end of the war in 2002. The government reported that the gross primary-school enrollment rate in 2003 was 91.1%.[6]

UNICEF estimates that gross enrollment in 2011 was more than 140%, but that net enrollment is still well below 100%.[7] A less than 100% enrollment of six-year olds into grade 1 of primary school and high dropout rates mean that many children have no, or inadequate, exposure to the school system.

The standard of education in Angola is also an issue. Standards are compromised by factors such as overcrowded classes, poorly-trained school personnel, lack of materials, inadequate school infrastructure, and limited transportation facilities. These result in irregular attendance at, or dropping out of, school.[8]

Children who are out of school not only miss out on education, but also on primary healthcare services and food-distribution programs that are run through the school system. Schools are the site for several health and nutrition initiatives; for example, primary schools provide de-worming tablets to children. Another example is the school-feeding program, which is jointly administered by the Ministry of Education and the World Food Programme (WFP). The availability of services such as school-feeding can be vital for children living in poverty. Family budgets of the poor are constrained and food consumption levels are low; receiving food at school can contribute to improved nutrition and health. Schools can also offer a safe environment for children — both boys and girls — where they receive information on prevention and treatment of diseases, and links to other services they might need to access.

11.2. Description of intervention

A set of complementary actions was identified to strengthen the education system in Angola over the period 2012–31. Strengthening the education system (SES) consists of building new schools through public works programs; training and deploying teachers to provide ECD services, and primary and secondary education; and developing and teaching school curricula that include information on life-skills and HIV/AIDS prevention. The set of actions is designed to increase grade 1 enrollment by 10 percentage points by the 11th year of the program (2022) and to provide primary- and then secondary-schooling to the children as they progress through the system. In the absence of SES, it is estimated that 90% of six-year olds will enroll in grade 1 in 2012, and 10% will not. SES is designed to increase enrollment in grade 1 to 100% of six-year olds by 2022. It would be unrealistic to run schools with only grade 1 students, so it assumed that a small number of children will be enrolled in *all* grades in 2012. After 2012, all increases in enrollment occur entirely through increased enrollment in grade 1 each year and the progression of these students to higher grades.

Teacher training is expected to be of appropriate quality and new schools are expected to meet international standards — among other things, by in-

cluding sanitary facilities to help keep girls enrolled. A detailed description
of SES is provided in Annex 11A.

The primary goal of SES is to provide children who are currently out-of-
school with an education that includes ECD services. SES will increase access to all levels of basic education, help to reduce HIV transmission through
instruction on health and a protective school environment, and contribute
to increasing the lifetime incomes of students.

11.3. Estimation of costs and benefits
11.3.1. Program coverage and costs

The costs and benefits of SES are estimated for a 20-year period from
2012 to 2031. The estimation of costs is based on the resource requirements
of SES and input prices. Angolan data have been used to estimate costs
wherever possible. To calculate teacher requirements, assumptions relating
to teacher-pupil ratios have been made. Program costs were estimated by
taking account of the length of teachers' training, teacher salaries, school
construction and school-running costs.

Angolan data on repetition and dropout rates were used for the calculation of costs and benefits. For children who do not receive ECD, repetition
rates were assumed to be the same as those currently observed in the country, i.e., 12% for primary school and 13% for secondary school. For children
who do receive ECD services, repetition rates are expected to be lower when
they attend primary and secondary school. We assume that repetition rates
for children who receive ECD will be 20% lower than those currently observed in Angola — i.e., we assume they will be 9.6% for primary school
and 10.4% for secondary school. We also expect repetition rates to fall over
time — we assume they will decrease at the rate of 6% a year for children
who receive ECD services and at 5% a year for those who do not. Dropout
rates for children who do not receive ECD are taken to be 5.8% and 7.4%,
respectively, for primary and secondary school — the Angolan dropout rates
in 2001. As in the case of repetition rates, we assume that dropout rates for
children who receive ECD will be 20% lower — i.e., they will 4.6% and 5.9%,
respectively, for primary and secondary school. A detailed description of the
data and assumptions used in the estimation of costs is contained in Annex
11B.

In 2012, SES will increase enrollment in grade 1 by 0.75 percentage points
from its level in 2011. SES enrollment in grade 1 will be expanded at the rate
of 30% a year until 2022, when the program will enroll 10% of all six-year old
children in the country. One half of these children will have come through
the ECD program. In 2012 (only), SES will also increase enrollment in other
primary-school grades by 0.7 percentage points and in secondary-school
grades by 0.2 percentage points. Subsequent increases in the number of stu-

dents in grades 2–12 occur only as the children who are enrolled in grade 1 of SES progress to these higher grades. In 2021, SES will have increased the primary-school enrollment rate by 4 percentage points. As the intervention focuses first on increasing grade 1 enrollment, by 2021 there will not yet be much of an impact on numbers in secondary school.

The assumption that enrollment in grade 1 can be increased by 10 percentage points in 11 years may be somewhat optimistic. The greatest challenge to meeting this target is likely to be a shortage of teachers in the early years of SES. As in many other African countries, Angola has a shortage of qualified teachers and it may not be possible to expand schooling rapidly until newly-trained teachers become available.[5,9]

SES requires that by 2021 the country trains 10,500 primary-school teachers and at least 1,250 secondary-school teachers. As the children who are enrolled in grade 1 find their way into secondary school, the demand for secondary schooling will increase. By 2031, SES will require close to 15,000 secondary-school teachers (including the 1,250 needed by 2021) to meet the increase in demand. The demand for additional teachers arises mainly because of increased enrollment, but also in part because class sizes are expected to decrease. Our estimates for teacher requirements are based on the average class size in primary school falling from 40 students in 2012 to 35 students in 2017. Secondary-school class size is assumed to be 35 students in 2012, and to decrease to 30 students in 2017. In addition to primary- and secondary-school teachers, the country will need approximately 7,000 ECD teachers in 2021. SES assumes a high staff-to-child ratio for ECD. The ECD teacher requirements are based on a staff-to-child ratio of 1-to-10, with each ECD class of 20 children having one teacher and one teaching assistant.

Teacher salaries are a major cost component of the SES intervention. Teacher compensation is based on market wages in the country, and assistant teacher compensation is set at the Angolan minimum wage. Training costs will rise sharply as the system expands, but become less important as the total size of the teaching workforce stabilizes. Teacher training is assumed to take four years for ECD, primary- and secondary-school teachers. ECD teacher assistants are expected to complete a one-year training program. School-running costs are high; they include not only materials and utilities but also costs of teacher supervision. Annual running costs (in 2012 US$) are based on US$44 per student enrolled in the ECD program, US$63 per student in primary school, and US$250 per student in secondary school. For most of the projection period 2012–31, school construction is a major component of total cost. This is because of the huge shortfall in physical infrastructure and the relatively high costs of construction in Angola.

Table 11.1 summarizes SES enrollment, staffing requirements and pro-

Table 11.1. SES enrollment, teacher requirements, and program costs: Selected years

Year	2012	2016	2021	2026	2031
SES enrollment					
Number of ECD students (1,000s)	6	18	71	77	84
Number of primary-school students (1,000s)	41	74	315	754	883
Number of secondary-school students (1,000s)	14	26	42	178	559
Total number of SES students enrolled (1,000s)	**61**	**118**	**428**	**1,009**	**1,526**
SES enrollment as % of children of primary-school age	0.7	1.1	4.0	8.3	8.9
SES enrollment as % of children of secondary-school age	0.2	0.3	0.4	1.7	4.1
SES enrollment in grade 1 as % of six-year old children	0.8	2.2	8.0	10.0	10.0
Teacher requirements					
ECD teachers	581	1,806	7,138	7,724	8,360
Primary-school teachers	1,236	2,441	10,245	23,623	27,232
Secondary-school teachers	378	721	1,154	5,354	14,309
Program costs (2012 US$ million)					
Teacher salaries	5.6	12.8	49.4	108.3	159.3
Teacher training	2.2	18.4	35.9	30.9	0.0
School-running costs	7.7	14.3	40.9	119.1	262.3
School construction	5.2	20.8	91.8	97.3	46.0
Total cost (2012 US$ million)	**20.7**	**66.3**	**217.9**	**355.5**	**467.5**

gram costs for selected years. The average annual cost of SES (in 2012 prices) over the program period 2012–31 is estimated to be US$243.3 million.

11.3.2. Quantified constitutive and consequential benefits

The constitutive benefit of education is education itself. Education also has instrumental value, as it leads to a whole range of benefits including, but not limited to, increased earning potential, better health, and lower fertility rates. These benefits are important and will be discussed together with other consequential benefits.

In 2021, 428,000 children will be in ECD, primary or secondary school as a result of the intervention and over 19,000 students will complete primary school in that year. In 2031, 1.53 million children will attend ECD, primary or secondary school as a result of SES. In 2031, approximately 133,000 children will complete primary school and 38,000 will complete secondary school. Between 2012 and 2031, 170,000 children will drop out of primary school, 75,000 will complete primary school but not go on to secondary school, and 180,000 will drop out of secondary school before graduating. These children will have received, on average, approximately five years of education before they leave or drop out of school. The educational benefits resulting from the intervention are summarized in table 11.2.

Table 11.2. Constitutive benefits of SES: Selected years

Year	2012	2016	2021	2026	2031
ECD enrollment (1,000s)	6	18	71	77	84
Number of students completing primary school (1,000s)	6	6	19	84	133
Number of secondary-school graduates (1,000s)	2	3	5	11	38

The increases in enrollment will arise not only from more school places being available, but from them being available closer to where people live — and from improvements in infrastructure and teacher training. ECD programs are known to contribute to increased primary-school completion and secondary-school graduation.[10] Reducing distance to schools, and building schools in areas with low enrollment, have been shown to increase educational attainment in terms of number of years of schooling completed.[11] Studies from elsewhere in the world show that years of completed schooling increase when travel time to school is reduced.[12] Equipping schools with private latrine facilities is an important action that can have a significant effect on girls' attendance. An analysis of data from 30 countries in Africa shows that girls are likely to miss classes during menses due to inadequate access to toilet facilities.[13]

SES also has many consequential benefits in addition to its constitutive benefits. A number of these benefits have been quantified, viz. the increase in lifetime incomes of children who receive education, future under-five and maternal deaths avoided, and reduction of fertility. Income returns to education are based on studies that have estimated returns to different levels of education for 25–34 year olds[a] in Africa,[14] and assumptions relating to the earning potential of Angolans without formal education. Estimates of the impact of schooling on U5MR, maternal mortality and TFR are taken from World Bank studies.[15,16] For example, the under-five mortality rate is estimated to fall by 7% per year of education received by a girl. These estimates were applied to the predicted increase in years of education received by children through the SES intervention. Table 11.3 summarizes the consequential benefits which we have been able to quantify.

Table 11.3. Quantified consequential benefits of SES over students' lifetimes

Present value of increased lifetime incomes (2012 US$ million)	4,906
Future under-five deaths avoided (number of children)	240,000
Future maternal deaths avoided (number of women)	11,000
Decline in TFR among SES-educated women (%)	40

Twenty years of the intervention is expected to lead to a cumulative reduction of almost a quarter of a million future under-five deaths, and a reduction of 11,000 future maternal deaths. Increased education received by girls through SES is also expected to lead to a decline in TFR. Improved knowledge and opportunities that come with education lead women to have fewer children.[16] Each year of schooling is assumed to reduce girls' fertility rate by 10%,[16] leading to a total decline of 40% as a result of SES.

The evidence for health impacts has been drawn primarily from World Bank studies.[15,16] Women with formal education tend to have better knowledge about healthcare practices, are less likely to become pregnant at a young age, tend to have fewer and better-spaced pregnancies, and are more likely to seek pre- and postnatal care.[17] These factors all contribute to lower rates of maternal mortality. Women's education also has an impact on their children's health. Women who are more educated are more likely to seek medical care for their children, to ensure their children are immunized, to be better informed about their children's nutritional requirements, and to adopt improved sanitation practices. As a result, their infants and children tend to have higher survival rates and be better nourished and healthier. On average, an additional year of schooling for women is associated with a 5% to 10% reduction in child mortality.[15] Declines in mortality and fertility are also expected to arise from improved access to healthcare services and awareness campaigns at school.

A major benefit of education is that it leads to an increase in future incomes. Apart from influencing the wage rate that is earned, more educated workers are less likely to be unemployed.[18] All levels of education have been linked to improved earnings, even ECD.[19,20] Data on the income returns to education were not available for Angola. Instead, we based our estimates of returns to education from regional figures: 8.9% per year of primary schooling and 14% per year of secondary schooling.[14] The daily wage for secondary-school age individuals with no education is taken to be US$0.50; this wage is assumed to grow by 2% for each additional year in the labor market. On this basis, the present value of increased lifetime incomes, discounted at 3% per annum, of all children enrolled in SES between 2012 and 2031 is estimated to be US$4.9 billion. The present value of the total cost of this in-

Table 11.4. Non-quantified consequential benefits of SES

Quantified benefit leading to consequential benefit	Pathway to non-quantified consequential benefit	Non-quantified consequential benefit
Increased enrollment in ECD, primary and secondary school	1. Education leads to better understanding of healthcare 2. Universalization of basic education 3. More educated labor force	• Improved adult health (1) • Social cohesion (2) • Economic growth (3)
Reduction in maternal mortality	1. The presence of mothers is critical for child development, health and education	• Better educational attainment of children leads to more qualified future labor force (1)
Reduced fertility	1. Lower fertility enables families to spend more per child on nutrition, health and education	• Better child health and nutritional outcomes (1)

tervention discounted at 3% per annum is US$3.0 billion, which yields a net present value of increased future incomes of US$1.9 billion.

The present value of increased future incomes is very sensitive to the discount rate used. The design of SES implies a long delay between the time that children are enrolled in school and the time at which they begin to earn income. The intervention starts by increasing enrollment in ECD and grade 1, and then educating the children through their time in the school system. If the discount rate is increased from 3% to 5%, the present value of increased lifetime incomes of children enrolled in SES decreases from US$4.9 billion to US$2.5 billion, and the net present value from US$1.9 billion to US$0.2 billion.

Expanding ECD coverage from 50% to 100% would increase the cost of the program (in present value terms at a discount rate of 3% per annum) by 22%, and increase other benefits in tables 11.2 and 11.3 by 5%–10%. The reason that ECD improves educational outcomes is that children who receive its services are more likely to stay in the school system. They are also more likely to move through the school system faster (because they do not repeat grades as frequently); this reduces the average cost of their primary and secondary schooling.

The large increase in SES costs from doubling ECD coverage occurs because ECD services are highly resource intensive — they involve a high teacher-to-child ratio, quality facilities and high running costs per child. If the reductions in repetition and dropout rates assumed here to arise from ECD services with a teacher-to-pupil ratio for ECD of 1-to-10 could be achieved with a teacher-to-pupil ratio of 1-to-15, the PV of total costs would not change by providing ECD services to 100% of children.

11.3.3. Non-quantified consequential benefits

Many consequential benefits of SES could not be quantified. Some are inherently non-quantifiable while for others appropriate data were not available for quantification. Table 11.4 provides a summary of non-quantified consequential benefits, and the pathways through which they are likely to arise.

Universal basic education has been linked with a number of social benefits. It promotes a more cohesive, equal and politically stable society. There is a direct relationship between education and social cohesion, and an indirect impact if education results in a more equal income distribution.[21] Education is linked with greater stability of social structures because children learn societal values in school that enable them to act in a more tolerant manner towards others.[18] It helps promote social cohesion by reducing anti-social behaviors such as crime. Educated people with better labor-market opportunities and higher earnings are less likely to engage in crime — in part because the opportunity costs of criminal behavior are higher.[18]

In the US, adults who were provided with ECD services as children have been observed to engage less frequently in criminal activity than adults who grew up in the same community but did not receive ECD services. A study reports that there were 40% fewer arrests among a group of adults who received ECD services as children compared with an otherwise similar group who did not.[10] Other studies have extended the link to reductions in harmful or anti-social behaviors such as smoking,[20] misuse of alcohol, and carrying a weapon or gun.[22]

Quantitative information on private income returns to education was discussed above. The benefits of education, however, are not limited to an increase in the lifetime incomes of individuals who are educated. Education has several important externalities, and is considered to be a key driver of economic growth.[23]

Many consequential benefits of education occur intergenerationally. For example, mothers' education is a significant variable in affecting children's educational opportunities and attainment. Mothers who are educated are more likely to send their children to school.[23] Educated mothers with fewer children will have more resources to invest per child in their children's health and education.

Girls' education ranks among the most powerful tools for reducing their vulnerability to HIV infection. The education of girls has been identified as a means of slowing and reducing the spread of HIV/AIDS — by contributing to female economic independence, delayed marriage, increased uptake of family planning, and increased opportunities to work outside the home.[13,23,24,25] Apart from the protection against HIV infection that results from being in school, there are benefits from the inclusion of an HIV/AIDS curriculum at the secondary level.

In addition to the private income and social returns to education, the construction of schools and the training and employment of teachers will increase the incomes of the persons employed. More people will be employed as teachers and trainers; un- or under-employed laborers from the communities in which schools are built will gain employment; and parents whose children are enrolled in preschool or school will have more time to engage in productive activities. Although employing teachers and temporary laborers is not a constitutive benefit of the intervention, such employment does lead to consequential benefits including poverty reduction. Public works programs, such as school construction through short-term employment, have been observed to reduce poverty.[26]

11.4. Summary and conclusion

Strengthening the education system in Angola involves the implementation of a series of complementary actions. These actions include the construction of schools, and the training, deployment and supervision of teachers. For SES to be effective, teacher-training must be of an appropriate standard. The schools are designed to provide suitable sanitation facilities, which is of particular importance for adolescent girls. ECD services lead to immediate benefits for the children enrolled, and improves their capacity to benefit from primary and secondary education.

Each of these individual actions could be proposed in isolation, but doing so would ignore their complementarities. For example, providing ECD services without increasing access to primary school will forego many of the benefits of ECD. Similarly, increasing primary-school places without expanding secondary education will forfeit some of the benefits of primary schooling. With such complementarities, the benefits of the set of SES actions are greater than the sum of the benefits of each action considered in isolation.

We estimate that implementing SES leads to a present value of increased lifetime incomes of the children educated during 2012–31 of US$4.9 billion (using a discount rate of 3% per annum). The present value of costs over the period 2012–31 is US$3.0 billion, yielding a net present value of US$1.9 billion. Over the period 2012–31, SES will enroll a total of 1.88 million children in grade 1 of primary school. It is estimated that by 2031, 960,000 of these children will complete primary school and 185,000 will complete secondary school. Over the lifetimes of these 1.88 million children, their education is likely to result in 240,000 fewer under-five deaths, 11,000 fewer maternal deaths, and a 40% reduction in the fertility rate of the women educated. Thus in terms of its quantified benefits, the SES intervention appears to be highly desirable. In the context of Angola's fiscal situation, it also seems affordable. Hence the cost of inaction in this case will be very large.

ANNEX
Annex 11A. Description of intervention

Intervention: SES is a government program that expands access to education by building schools; training teachers to provide ECD services, and primary and secondary schooling; and developing academic curricula that include life-skills and sex education with an HIV/AIDS prevention component.

Goal: This set of complementary actions aims to expand access to schooling to the 10% of the country's six-year old children who are not currently enrolled in grade 1. Apart from education, the goals of expanded access include improved student knowledge of healthy sexual practices and HIV prevention. School construction involves public works, and the resultant job creation should help to reduce income poverty.

School construction: School construction will be undertaken as a public works program. To this end, the Ministry of Education and the Ministry of Employment, Administration and Welfare (Ministério da Administarção Pública, Emprego e Segurança Social) will develop and implement a comprehensive plan to recruit laborers from communities where schools are to be built. Laborers must be adults, and the participation of women will be encouraged. The government will provide all the materials necessary for building the schools.

Selection of teachers: In selecting candidates for teacher training, preference will be given to those from the communities where teachers are to be employed. Candidates must have completed secondary school to be considered for teacher training.

Training for teachers: ECD, primary and secondary school teachers will be trained for four years, including one year spent gaining practical experience in classrooms. ECD assistants will be trained for one year. Secondary-school teachers must hold a baccalaureate in teaching (Bachalerato or Licenciatura). Distance-education programs to assist underqualified teachers in meeting the qualification requirements will be offered. The Ministry of Education has already proposed changes in school curricula to include STI and HIV/AIDS awareness and prevention topics. All newly-trained teachers will receive training in these topics.

Teacher supervision: Each school district will be supervised by a designated supervisor. The supervisor will visit the schools in their district to oversee teachers' performance and review students' achievements.

Annex 11B. Assumptions and methods

A number of assumptions were made to estimate the costs and benefits of the SES intervention in Angola. Wherever possible, Angolan data were used for the estimation. Where Angolan data were not available, use was made of evidence from similar interventions that have been implemented in other African countries.

Enrollment assumptions

To estimate enrollment it was necessary to make demographic assumptions in relation to the 20-year projection period of SES. Angola's population for the period 2012–31 was estimated using the Spectrum demographic software package and the UN population data provided for Angola by the package.[27] The program inputs and costs are based on the assumption that SES will enroll 10% of all six-year old children in the country into grade 1, and provide schooling for these children as they progress through the education system. The rate of scale-up of the intervention was set to achieve in 2022 an enrollment rate in grade 1 of 10% of the population of six-year old children. SES starts in 2012 with an enrollment in grade 1 of 0.75% of the six-year old population of children, and increases grade 1 enrollment at 30% a year. It is assumed that in each year 50% of the children begin in an ECD program, and 50% are enrolled directly into grade 1.

Estimation of costs

Repetition rates: Repetition of a grade leads to extra costs of providing a year of completed schooling. The latest data on repetition available to us are from 2001, when repetition rates were 12.2% for primary school and 12.5% for secondary school.[28] Average repetition rates in sub-Saharan Africa are among the highest in the world at 15%; for most African countries the repetition rate is highest in grade 1.[29] There is evidence that ECD services reduce repetition rates.[4] One reason is that ECD programs help the transition from preschool to primary school. Another reason is that educational stimulation in early years can affect children's capacity to learn for many years to come. Studies have shown that the networking of neurons and synapses, as well as learning and reflection capacity, are in place at an early age and these connections made in the brain affect its capacity in the future.[4] A 2003 study examining data from 133 countries shows that ECD interventions reduce repetition rates. This study reported primary-school completion rates of only 50% in the absence of preschool, and 80% when half the children had access to preschool or ECD programs. The study found that preschool experience was associated with a repetition rate of 12%, whereas the absence of preschool was associated with a 25% repetition rate.[30] Longitudinal studies based on randomized control trials have yielded more conservative estimates of the impact of ECD on grade repetition (35%–45% decline in repetition rates in primary school and less than 35% decline in secondary school).[31] We assume that ECD will lead to a 20% decline in repetition rates in 2012, and that repetition rates for ECD students will improve faster over time than for non-ECD students. By the end of the projection period the repetition rates for ECD students will be 35% lower than those of non-ECD students.

- Based on estimates from Angolan data for 2001, and comparison with African averages,[29] repetition rates for children who do not receive ECD services are assumed to be 25% for grade 1, 12% for other years of primary school, and 13% for secondary school. Repetition rates for children who receive ECD services are assumed to be 20% lower than the rates for children who do not receive ECD services — i.e., 20% for grade 1, 9.6% for primary school, and 10.4% for secondary school. Repetition rates for children who receive ECD are assumed to fall at 6% per year, and for children who do not receive ECD they are assumed to fall at 5% per year. Thus by 2031 the repetition rates for children who receive ECD will be 35% lower than for those who do not.

Dropout rates: Dropout rates are based on data from the Angola MICS 2001, where they are reported as 5.8% per year in primary school and 7.4% per year in secondary school.[28] These rates are comparable with average dropout rates in sub-Saharan Africa (SSA).[4] The ECD component of SES is assumed to reduce dropout rates in both primary and secondary school. This assumption is consistent with US longitudinal data on school completion of participants of ECD programs.[10] As the determinants of repetition rates are similar to those of dropout rates, the same reduction factor is used to adjust repetition rates for children who receive ECD compared to children who do not as is used to adjust dropout rates for such children, viz. 20%.

- For children who do not receive ECD services, dropout rates in primary and secondary school are taken to be 5.8% and 7.4% per year, respectively. For children who receive ECD services, the rates assumed are 20% lower, i.e., 4.6% and 5.9% per year in primary and secondary school, respectively.

ECD teacher-to-student ratio: According to UNESCO, the teacher-to-student ratio for ECD programs in Africa is generally 1 teacher to 45 children, whereas the international standard is 1-to-14.[4] A number of studies have documented the results of having a high teacher-to-child ratio and small group sizes. Recommendations range from 1-to-10 to 1-to-20 for children of age 5.[32] Given the benefits attributed to ECD, we considered it appropriate to base costs on the delivery of services with high teacher-to-student ratios. Our evidence of impact of ECD on subsequent outcomes is drawn from studies of ECD programs with high teacher-to-student ratios. Hence we selected a teacher-to-student ratio of 1-to-10 for which we can document the impact.

- For ECD programs the teacher-to-student ratio is assumed to be 1-to-10. A class of 20 will have one teacher with four years' training and one teaching assistant with one year of training.

Primary- and secondary-school class sizes: In 1991, the primary-school class size was estimated to be 32.[33] More recent data are not available to us, but in-country consultation suggested that the primary-school class size was much larger in 2010. There is debate about the educational consequences of class size, but some recent findings suggest that students in smaller classes make better progress in mathematics and language skills.[34] To contribute to better quality of learning, child involvement in class activities, and teacher-child interactions, our class size assumption is based on meeting the UNESCO standard of 40 students per teacher at the primary-school level.[35]

- The primary-school class size is assumed to be 40 students in 2012, falling to 35 students over a 5-year period. The secondary-school class size is assumed to be 35 students in 2012, falling to 30 students over a 5-year period. ECD class size is assumed to be 20 students.

Primary- and secondary-school teacher load: The teacher load is the proportion of the school day that the average teacher spends teaching, as opposed to grading and completing administrative duties. Typically, primary-school teachers are with their class for the entire school day, while in secondary school many teachers, especially mathematics and science teachers, do not teach all the time. In African countries such as Uganda, teachers teach only one-third to one-half of the timetabled periods in school; and in Zambia typical teaching loads are 15-20 periods a week out of 36 timetabled periods.[36]

- For both primary school and ECD programs, teacher load is assumed to be 1. For secondary school the teacher load is assumed to be 0.8, increasing to 0.9 in 5 years (through improvements in school management).

Teacher training: Teacher training is fundamental to the overall quality of any education program, so a high level of training has been assumed. The four-year training assumed for ECD teachers is high relative to the norm. But given the benefits attributed to ECD, we consider it appropriate to base costs on the delivery of high-quality services. In SSA there is a shortage of trained teachers, especially for preschool children. In general, pre-primary education has expanded slowly and teachers receive very little training compared to their primary-school counterparts.[4]

- Training for ECD, primary-school and secondary-school teachers is assumed to be four years. For ECD teacher assistants, training is assumed to be one year.

Compensation of teachers: The salary and compensation assumptions are based on Angolan market wages and in-country consultation. The ECD assistant teacher compensation has been set at the official Angolan minimum wage, which is higher than the wage of many workers in Angola.

- Compensation for ECD assistant teachers has been set at US$120 per month. Primary-school and ECD teachers will be paid US$220 per month and secondary-school teachers will be paid US$250 per month. Salaries are assumed to increase at 1% per annum in real terms from their 2012 levels.

Training costs: Cost estimates for training are based on the 2005 report of the Norwegian non-governmental organization Ajuda de Desenvolvimento de Povo para Povo em Angola (ADPP), which put the annual cost of teacher training at US$2,286 per student-teacher.[37] A slightly lower unit cost is assumed here on the assumption that there will be economies of scale in teacher training.

- Unit costs of training are assumed to be US$2,000 per year for ECD, primary- and secondary-school teachers. One year of training for ECD teaching assistants is assumed to cost US$1,000. All training costs are assumed to increase at 1% per annum in real terms from their 2012 levels.

Attrition: There are no widely available data on attrition in Angola. The assumption of 6% attrition per year has been made after considering teacher attrition rates in eight countries in Anglophone Africa. These rates vary from 2% in Eritrean primary schools to 10% in secondary schools in Lesotho.[38]

- Teacher attrition is assumed to be 6% per year for all staff, falling to 4% per year after 5 years.

School-construction costs: Primary schools are assumed to have 6 classrooms and secondary schools 12 classrooms. In Angola, building costs are reported to range between US$296 and US$319 per square meter of floor space.[39] The lower bound of this range is used for schools because they are relatively simple structures. Assumptions about classroom size are based on the International Institute for Educational Planning (IIEP) and the World Bank's recommendation of 1.2 square meters per student.[39] School construction costs also include construction costs for latrines. The cost of latrines per classroom is assumed to be US$1,294 based on the average construction cost of latrines across 9 African countries.[38]

- Construction costs are taken to be US$97,248 per primary school, US$202,600 per secondary school, and US$16,208 per ECD center.

School-running costs: Running costs include the costs of student materials, teacher supervision and continuing training, management, and maintenance of buildings. Per-student running costs for ECD programs are set at 70% of primary-school running costs, and per-student primary-school costs are set at 25% of secondary-school costs.[40] The per-student secondary-school running cost assumption is based on estimates of secondary-school costs in neighboring Zambia.[36]

- Annual running costs of schools are based on US$44 per student enrolled in an ECD program, US$63 per student enrolled in primary school, and US$250 per student enrolled in secondary school.

Estimation of benefits

Under-five mortality: Mothers' education influences children's health and survival. On average, women with formal education are more likely to seek medical care, to ensure that their children are immunized, to be better informed about their children's nutritional requirements, and to adopt improved sanitation practices. As a result, their infants and children tend to be healthier and have higher survival rates. Researchers suggest that, on average, one additional year of schooling for women is associated with a 5% to 10% reduction in child mortality.[15]

- Child mortality is reduced by 7% for each additional year of education received by a mother.

Maternal mortality: The effect of education on maternal mortality is based on estimates from a World Bank study.[16] Women with formal education have better knowledge about healthcare practices, are less likely to become pregnant at a very young age, tend to have fewer and better-spaced pregnancies, and are more likely to seek pre- and postnatal care.[41]

- It is assumed that one additional year of schooling for each of 1,000 women will lead to two fewer maternal deaths among them.

Reduction in fertility: Women with formal education are more likely to use reliable family planning methods, delay marriage and childbearing, and have fewer babies than women with no education. The effect is particularly pronounced for those with secondary schooling. The assumed rate of reduction in fertility is based on cross-country estimates by the World Bank which suggest that one additional year of female schooling reduces fertility by 8% to 13%.[16]

- It is assumed that one additional year of female schooling will reduce fertility by 10%.

Private income returns: Higher levels of education are associated with higher private incomes. Estimates for income returns to education are not available for Angola. Regional estimates of returns to education vary widely. One review article estimates returns of 25% for primary school and 18% for secondary school in sub-Saharan Africa,[42] while another estimates 5% for primary school and 14% for secondary school for 28 African countries.[43] We use average rates-of-return to primary and secondary education for young men aged 25–34 from a number of African countries. The rates we apply are 8.9% per year of primary schooling (average across four African countries) and 14% per year of secondary schooling (average across seven African countries).[14]

- Returns to an additional year of education are assumed to be 8.9% for primary school and 14% for secondary school. Daily wages for secondary school-age individuals with no education are assumed to be US$0.50. These wages are assumed to grow at 2% per year of employment. Families are assumed to pay US$50 in out-of-pocket schooling expenses each year. These expenses are deducted from the estimate of private income returns. The present value of increased lifetime incomes is calculated using a discount rate of 3% per annum.

Annex 11C. Annual estimates of benefits and costs: 2012–31

Table 11C.1 shows annual enrollment if SES is implemented. The intervention is designed to increase enrollment in grade 1 by 10 percentage points by 2022. To reach this target it is assumed that in 2012, 0.75% of the population of six-year old children is enrolled into grade 1, and this enrollment in grade 1 increases at the rate of 30% per year until the 10 percentage point target is reached in 2022. As the children who become enrolled in grade 1 work their way through the education system, the numbers in primary and secondary school will increase.

Based on the levels of enrollment in table 11C.1, table 11C.2 shows the annual number of teachers required by school type. Teacher requirements are estimated assuming a class size of 20 students for ECD, a class size of 40 students (falling to 35 students by 2017) for primary school, and a class size of 35 students (falling to 30 students by 2017) for secondary school.

Table 11C.3 provides estimates of total salary costs per year by school type, calculated from teacher requirements and salaries. Compensation for ECD assistant teachers is set at US$120 per month; primary-school and ECD teachers are assumed to be paid at the rate of US$220 per month, and secondary-school teachers at US$250 per month. Unit salaries are assumed to rise at 1% per annum in real terms from their 2012 levels.

Table 11C.5 presents annual school-running costs, including the costs of school administration. Running costs per student at secondary level are based on per-student running costs at secondary school in Zambia.[36] ECD running costs have been set at 70% of costs in grade 1, and primary-school running costs are set at 25% of secondary-school running costs.

Table 11C.6 presents annual school-construction costs by school type. Cost estimates are based on construction costs in Angola and school size. The cost of constructing an ECD center is estimated to be US$16,208, a primary school US$97,248, and a secondary school US$202,600.

Table 11C.7 puts together the itemized costs of the SES intervention from tables 11C.3 to 11C.6, and shows the annual cost by expenditure category.

Table 11C.1. SES enrollment in primary and secondary school: 2012–31

Year	2012	2013	2014	2015	2016	2017	2018	2019	2020	2021
SES Enrollment										
Number of ECD students (1,000s)	6	8	10	14	18	24	32	42	56	71
Number of primary-school students (1,000s)	41	43	48	58	74	97	130	175	235	315
Number of secondary-school students (1,000s)	14	17	20	23	26	28	30	32	36	42
Total number of SES students enrolled (1,000s)	**61**	**68**	**78**	**95**	**118**	**149**	**192**	**249**	**327**	**428**
SES enrollment in primary school as % of children of primary-school age	0.7	0.7	0.8	0.9	1.1	1.4	1.8	2.3	3.0	4.0
SES enrollment in secondary school as % of children of secondary-school age	0.2	0.2	0.3	0.3	0.3	0.3	0.3	0.3	0.3	0.4
SES enrollment in grade 1 as % of six-year old children	**0.8**	**1.0**	**1.3**	**1.7**	**2.2**	**2.8**	**3.6**	**4.7**	**6.1**	**8.0**

continued

Table 11C.1. SES enrollment in primary and secondary school: 2012–31 (*continued*)

Year	2022	2023	2024	2025	2026	2027	2028	2029	2030	2031
SES enrollment										
Number of ECD students (1,000s)	73	74	75	76	77	78	80	81	82	84
Number of primary-school students (1,000s)	417	515	606	687	754	803	830	850	867	883
Number of secondary-school students (1,000s)	54	70	96	131	178	242	325	405	486	559
Total number of SES students enrolled (1,000s)	**543**	**659**	**777**	**894**	**1,009**	**1,123**	**1,235**	**1,336**	**1,435**	**1,526**
SES enrollment in primary school as % of children of primary-school age	5.1	6.1	7.0	7.7	8.3	8.7	8.8	8.8	8.8	8.9
SES enrollment in secondary school as % of children of secondary-school age	0.6	0.7	1.0	1.3	1.7	2.2	2.9	3.5	3.9	4.1
SES enrollment in grade 1 as % of six-year old children	**10.0**	**10.0**	**10.0**	**10.0**	**10.0**	**10.0**	**10.0**	**10.0**	**10.0**	**10.0**

Table 11C.2. SES annual teacher requirements by school type: 2012–31

Year	2012	2013	2014	2015	2016	2017	2018	2019	2020	2021
Teacher requirements (number)										
ECD teachers and assistants	581	783	1,029	1,357	1,806	2,401	3,187	4,224	5,588	7,138
Primary-school teachers	1,236	1,337	1,547	1,896	2,441	3,261	4,344	5,796	7,712	10,245
Secondary-school teachers	378	480	585	690	721	723	688	718	860	1,154

Year	2022	2023	2024	2025	2026	2027	2028	2029	2030	2031
Teacher requirements (number)										
ECD teachers and assistants	7,251	7,368	7,484	7,604	7,724	7,848	7,972	8,100	8,228	8,360
Primary-school teachers	13,455	16,460	19,209	21,630	23,623	25,051	25,806	26,317	26,775	27,232
Secondary-school teachers	1,581	2,154	2,925	3,962	5,354	7,212	9,588	11,802	13,446	14,309

Table 11C.3. SES teacher salaries (2012 US$ million) by school type: 2012–31

Year	2012	2013	2014	2015	2016	2017	2018	2019	2020	2021
Teacher salaries (2012 US$ million)										
ECD teachers and teaching assistants	1.2	1.6	2.2	2.9	3.9	5.2	6.9	9.3	12.4	16.0
Primary-school teachers	3.3	3.6	4.2	5.2	6.7	9.1	12.2	16.4	22.1	29.6
Secondary-school teachers	1.2	1.5	1.8	2.2	2.3	2.3	2.2	2.3	2.8	3.8
Total	**5.6**	**6.7**	**8.1**	**10.2**	**12.8**	**16.5**	**21.3**	**28.0**	**37.2**	**49.4**

Year	2022	2023	2024	2025	2026	2027	2028	2029	2030	2031
Teacher salaries (2012 US$ million)										
ECD teachers and teaching assistants	16.4	16.8	17.2	17.7	18.1	18.6	19.1	19.6	20.1	20.6
Primary-school teachers	39.3	48.5	57.2	65.0	71.7	76.8	79.9	82.3	84.6	86.9
Secondary-school teachers	5.3	7.2	9.9	13.6	18.5	25.1	33.8	42.0	48.3	51.9
Total	**60.9**	**72.5**	**84.3**	**96.2**	**108.3**	**120.5**	**132.7**	**143.8**	**152.9**	**159.3**

Table 11C.4. SES teacher-training costs (2012 US$ million) by school type: 2012–31

Year	2012	2013	2014	2015	2016	2017	2018	2019	2020	2021
Teacher-training costs (2012 US$ million)										
ECD teachers and assistants	0.8	1.9	3.3	4.3	5.7	7.5	9.3	7.5	4.9	1.7
Primary-school teachers	1.3	3.2	5.7	9.1	12.3	16.3	21.2	25.1	27.4	27.7
Secondary-school teachers	0.1	0.2	0.2	0.3	0.5	1.2	2.1	3.4	4.8	6.6
Total	**2.2**	**5.2**	**9.2**	**13.7**	**18.4**	**24.9**	**32.6**	**35.9**	**37.1**	**35.9**

Year	2022	2023	2024	2025	2026	2027	2028	2029	2030	2031
Teacher-training costs (2012 US$ million)										
ECD teachers and assistants	1.6	1.6	1.6	1.5	1.5	1.5	1.5	1.0	0.5	0.0
Primary-school teachers	25.3	22.1	17.7	13.4	9.8	7.4	5.1	3.3	1.6	0.0
Secondary-school teachers	8.9	11.9	15.8	18.8	19.6	17.6	11.9	6.5	2.4	0.0
Total	**35.8**	**35.5**	**35.0**	**33.6**	**30.9**	**26.4**	**18.4**	**10.7**	**4.5**	**0.0**

Table 11C.5. SES school-running costs (2012 US$ million) by school type: 2012–31

Year	2012	2013	2014	2015	2016	2017	2018	2019	2020	2021
School-running costs (2012 US$ million)										
ECD	0.3	0.4	0.5	0.6	0.8	1.1	1.5	2.0	2.7	3.4
Primary school	3.1	3.3	3.8	4.5	5.7	7.5	10.1	13.6	18.3	24.5
Secondary school	4.3	5.2	6.1	7.1	7.8	8.5	9.0	9.6	10.8	13.0
Total	**7.7**	**8.9**	**10.3**	**12.2**	**14.3**	**17.1**	**20.6**	**25.2**	**31.7**	**40.9**

Year	2022	2023	2024	2025	2026	2027	2028	2029	2030	2031
School-running costs (2012 US$ million)										
ECD	3.5	3.6	3.7	3.8	3.9	4.0	4.1	4.2	4.3	4.4
Primary school	32.5	40.2	47.4	53.9	59.4	63.6	66.2	68.2	70.1	72.0
Secondary school	16.4	21.7	29.6	40.7	55.8	76.2	103.1	131.7	159.7	185.9
Total	**52.4**	**65.5**	**80.7**	**98.3**	**119.1**	**143.8**	**173.4**	**204.1**	**234.1**	**262.3**

Table 11C.6. SES school-construction costs (2012 US$ million) by school type: 2012–31

Year	2012	2013	2014	2015	2016	2017	2018	2019	2020	2021
School-construction costs (2012 US$ million)										
ECD centers	2.7	3.6	4.8	6.4	8.6	11.5	15.4	20.6	27.6	35.6
Primary schools	1.1	2.8	4.8	7.5	11.3	16.5	22.3	29.7	39.6	50.7
Secondary schools	1.5	1.5	1.5	1.1	1.0	0.7	0.9	1.9	3.4	5.6
Total	**5.2**	**7.8**	**11.0**	**15.0**	**20.8**	**28.7**	**38.6**	**52.1**	**70.6**	**91.8**

Year	2022	2023	2024	2025	2026	2027	2028	2029	2030	2031
School-construction costs (2012 US$ million)										
ECD centers	36.5	37.4	38.4	39.4	40.4	41.5	42.6	43.7	44.8	46.0
Primary schools	47.9	44.3	39.4	32.8	23.7	12.7	8.7	7.9	7.9	0.0
Secondary schools	8.6	12.8	18.0	24.6	33.2	43.6	46.1	44.6	41.1	0.0
Total	**93.0**	**94.5**	**95.8**	**96.7**	**97.3**	**97.7**	**97.3**	**96.1**	**93.8**	**46.0**

Table 11C.7. SES costs (2012 US$ million) by expenditure category: 2012–31

Year	2012	2013	2014	2015	2016	2017	2018	2019	2020	2021
Expenditure category										
Teacher salaries	5.6	6.7	8.1	10.2	12.8	16.5	21.3	28.0	37.2	49.4
Teacher training	2.2	5.2	9.2	13.7	18.4	24.9	32.6	35.9	37.1	35.9
School-running costs	7.7	8.9	10.3	12.2	14.3	17.1	20.6	25.2	31.7	40.9
School construction	5.2	7.8	11.0	15.0	20.8	28.7	38.6	52.1	70.6	91.8
Total cost (2012 US$ million)	**20.7**	**28.5**	**38.6**	**51.0**	**66.3**	**87.1**	**113.0**	**141.1**	**176.5**	**217.9**

Year	2022	2023	2024	2025	2026	2027	2028	2029	2030	2031
Expenditure category										
Teacher salaries	60.9	72.5	84.3	96.2	108.3	120.5	132.7	143.8	152.9	159.3
Teacher training	35.8	35.5	35.0	33.6	30.9	26.4	18.4	10.7	4.5	0.0
School-running costs	52.4	65.5	80.7	98.3	119.1	143.8	173.4	204.1	234.1	262.3
School construction	93.0	94.5	95.8	96.7	97.3	97.7	97.3	96.1	93.8	46.0
Total cost (2012 US$ million)	**242.0**	**267.9**	**295.7**	**324.8**	**355.5**	**388.4**	**421.8**	**454.7**	**485.2**	**467.5**

Table 11C.8. Quantified constitutive benefits of SES: 2012–31

Year	2012	2013	2014	2015	2016	2017	2018	2019	2020	2021
Quantified constitutive benefits of SES										
ECD enrollment (number)	5,811	7,832	10,283	13,568	18,057	24,003	31,869	42,241	55,876	71,382
Number of students who complete primary school	6,314	6,391	6,400	6,246	6,074	5,440	7,072	10,015	13,787	18,706
Number of secondary-school graduates	2,015	1,922	1,836	2,380	2,504	2,484	3,795	4,672	5,036	5,110

Year	2022	2023	2024	2025	2026	2027	2028	2029	2030	2031
Quantified constitutive benefits of SES										
ECD enrollment	72,510	73,673	74,836	76,037	77,238	78,477	79,717	80,996	82,275	83,595
Number of students who complete primary school	25,403	34,453	46,583	62,790	84,349	110,296	121,797	126,903	130,193	133,167
Number of secondary-school graduates	5,071	4,755	5,529	7,574	10,593	14,643	20,164	20,164	27,691	37,880

Endnote

a. We have estimates of rates-of-return to years of primary and secondary education for young men from a number of African countries. The rates we applied were 8.9% per year of primary schooling (average across four African countries) and 14% per year of secondary schooling (average across seven African countries). These rates-of-return were applied to schooling received by both men and women.

References

1. WHO. *World Health Statistics 2009*. Geneva, Switzerland: WHO, 2009.
2. World Bank. *World Development Indicators 2011*. Washington, DC: World Bank, 2011.
3. Instituto Nacional de Estatistica. Inquérito Integrado Sobre o Bem-Estar da População (IBEP) 2008–09: Principais Resultados Grelha de Indicadores. Luanda, Angola: Ministerio do Planeamento, 2010.
4. UNESCO. Early Childhood Care and Education: Regional Report — Africa. World Conference on Early Childhood and Education. Moscow, Russian Federation, September 27–29, 2010.
5. UNICEF. *State of the World's Children 2009: Maternal and Newborn Health*. New York, NY: UNICEF, 2009.
6. Republic of Angola, UNDP. Objetivos de Desenvolvimento do Milénio: Relatório de Progresso 2005. Luanda, Angola: UNDP, 2005.
7. UNICEF. *Angola — Statistics*. New York, NY: UNICEF, 2011.
8. Women's Refugee Commission. *Global Survey on Education in Emergencies: Angola Country Report*. New York, NY: Women's Refugee Commission, 2003.
9. Republic of Angola and UNDP. Angola: Millennium Goals Report Summary 2005. Luanda, Angola: Republic of Angola and UNDP, 2005.
10. Temple J, Reynolds A. Benefits and costs of investment in preschool education: Evidence from the Child-Parent Centers and related programs. *Economics of Education Review* 2007; 26:126–144.
11. Duflo E. Schooling and labor market consequences of school construction in Indonesia: Evidence from an unusual policy experiment. *American Economic Review* 2001; 91(4):795–813.
12. Glewwe P, Kremer M. Schools, teachers, and education outcomes in developing countries. In: Hanushek E, Welch F, eds. *Handbook of the Economics of Education*. Vol. 1. Amsterdam, Holland: North Holland, 2005.
13. Herz B, Sperling G. *What Works in Girls' Education: Evidence and Policies from the Developing World*. New York, NY: Council on Foreign Relations Press, 2004.
14. Colclough C, Kingdon G, Patrinos H. The Pattern of Returns to Educa-

tion and its Implications. Policy Brief No. 4. Cambridge, UK: Research Consortium on Education Outcomes and Poverty, 2009.
15. Herz B, Subbarao K, Habib M, Raney L. *Letting Girls Learn: Promising Approaches in Primary and Secondary Education*. Washington, DC: World Bank, 1991.
16. Abu-Ghaida D, Klasen S. *The Economic and Human Development Costs of Missing the Millennium Development Goal on Gender Equity*. Washington, DC: World Bank, 2004.
17. Schultz TP. Population policies, fertility, women's human capital, and child quality. In: Schultz TP, Strauss J, eds. *Handbook of Development Economics*. Vol. 4. Oxford, UK: Elsevier, 2008.
18. Vila L. The outcomes of investment in education and people's well-being. *European Journal of Education* 2005; 40(1):3–11.
19. Belfield C, Nores M, Barnett S, Schweinhart L. The High/Scope Perry Preschool Program: Cost-benefit analysis using data from the age 40 followup. *Journal of Human Resources* 2005; 41(1):162–190.
20. Barnett W, Masse L. Comparative benefit-cost analysis of the Abecedarian Program and its policy implications. *Economics of Education Review* 2007; 26:113–125.
21. Green A, Preston J, Sabates R. *Education Equity and Social Cohesion: A Distributional Model*. Research Report No. 7. London, UK: Centre for Research on the Wide Benefits of Learning, Institute of Education, 2003.
22. Davis T, Byrd R, Arnold C, Auinger P, Bochhini JA. Low literacy and violence among adolescents in a summer sport program. *Journal of Adolescent Health* 1999; 24(6):403–411.
23. World Bank. *Education Quality and Economic Growth*. Washington, DC: World Bank, 2007.
24. Kohler H, Thornton R. Conditional Cash Transfers and HIV/AIDS Prevention: Unconditionally Promising? BREAD Working Paper No. 283. Durham, NC: Bureau for Research and Economic Analysis of Development, 2010.
25. Baird S, Chirwa E, McIntosh C, Ozler B. The short-term impacts of a schooling conditional cash transfer program on the sexual behavior of young women. *Health Economics* 2010; 19 Suppl(Sep):55–68.
26. McCord A. *Public Works in the Context of HIV/AIDS: Innovations in Public Works for Reaching the Most Vulnerable Children and Households in East and Southern Africa*. Cape Town, South Africa: University of Cape Town, SALDRU Public Works Research Project, 2005.
27. UNAIDS. Spectrum/EPP 2011. Demographic and Epidemiologic Data from Spectrum Files Using Country-Specific Data from UNAIDS and UN Population Division. UNAIDS, 2011. http://www.unaids.org/en/dataanalysis/tools/spectrumepp2011/. Accessed December 2, 2011.

28. Instituto Nacional de Estatistica and UNICEF. *Multiple Indicator Cluster Survey: Assessing the Situation of Angolan Children and Women at the Beginning of the Millennium.* Luanda, Angola: INE and UNICEF, 2003.

29. UNESCO. *Education for All by 2015: Will We Make It?* EFA Global Monitoring Report. Paris, France: EFA Global Monitoring Report Team, 2008.

30. Arnold C, Bartlett K, Gowani S, Merali R. Is Everybody Ready? Readiness, Transition and Continuity: Lessons, Reflections and Moving Forward. Paper commissioned for the EFA Global Monitoring Report 2007, Strong Foundations: Early Childhood Care and Education. Paris, France: UNESCO, 2007.

31. Molofeeva E, Daniel-Echols M, Xiang Z. *Findings From the Michigan School Readiness Program 6 to 8 Follow Up Study.* Ypsilanti, MI: High/Scope Educational Research Foundation, 2007.

32. Barnett WS, Schulman K, Shore R. Class Size: What's the Best Fit? *Preschool Policy Matters,* Issue 9. New Brunswick, NJ: National Institute for Early Education Research, 2004.

33. UNESCO Institute of Statistics. Data Centre. Montreal, Canada: UNESCO Institute for Statistics, 2008. http://stats.uis.unesco.org/unesco/ReportFolders/ReportFolders.aspx. Accessed November 28, 2011.

34. Blatchford P, Russell A, Bassett P, Brown P, Martin C. The effect of class size on teaching of pupils aged 7–11 years. *School Effectiveness and School Improvement* 2007; 18(2):147-172.

35. UNESCO. *Projecting the Global Demand for Teachers: Meeting the Goal of Universal Primary Education by 2015.* Technical Paper No. 3. Montreal, Canada: UNESCO Institute for Statistics, 2009.

36. World Bank. Strategies for Sustainable Financing of Secondary Education in Sub-Saharan Africa. Africa Human Development Series. Working Paper No. 136. Washington, DC: World Bank, 2008.

37. Lexow J, Klove E. *Review/Appraisal of Possible Norwegian Support.* Ajuda de Desenvolvimento de Povo para Povo em Angola. Luanda, Angola: Norwegian Embassy in Luanda, 2005.

38. Mulkeen A. *Teachers in Anglophone Africa: Issues in Teacher Supply, Training and Management.* Development Practice in Education. Washington, DC: World Bank, 2010.

39. Theunynck S. *School Construction Strategies for Universal Education in Africa: Should Communities be Empowered to Build their own Schools?* Washington, DC: World Bank, 2009.

40. Myers R. Costing Early Childhood Care and Development Programmes. Online Outreach Paper 5. The Hague, Netherlands: Bernard van Leer Foundation, 2008.

41. UNICEF. *Progress for Children: A Report Card on Maternal Mortality.* Report No. 7. New York, NY: UNICEF, 2008.

42. Psacharopoulos G, Patrinos H. Returns to investment in education: A further update. *Education Economics* 2004; 12(2):111–134.
43. Appleton S. Education and Health at the Household Level in Sub-Saharan Africa. CID Working Paper No. 33. Cambridge, MA: Harvard University, Center for International Development, 2000.

CHAPTER 12

HIV prevention through male circumcision in the province of Cunene

12.1. Background

HIV prevalence in Angola is much lower than in its neighboring countries. The low national average of 2.1% adult HIV prevalence, however, masks large regional variations. The highest prevalence in the country is reported for the province of Cunene, where it is estimated that 9.1% of the adult population is infected.[1] The two most important factors contributing to high prevalence in this province are generally thought to be its proximity to and connections with Namibia — where adult HIV prevalence is 13.1% — and the province's relatively low rate of male circumcision. [2] Male circumcision in Angola nationally is estimated to be as high as 80%, but in Cunene it is much lower because it is not practiced by the Kuayamas who make up the majority of the population in the province.[3,4]

Cunene is the southernmost province of Angola bordering with Namibia. In geographic area the province is the size of Belgium and the Netherlands combined, and its population is approximately 750,000 people.[5] During the civil war, Cunene did not play a major role in the conflict, but one of its main ethnic groups was associated with support for UNITA against the government forces of MPLA.[6] The effects of the 27-year conflict are evident in high rates of poverty, and lack of infrastructure to support the delivery of basic services such as health and education. In 2007, it was reported that Cunene had 4 hospitals, 6 health centers and 68 health posts serviced by 48 doctors (7 Angolans and 41 expatriates).[5] The province's international border to the south is a major point of entry for imports, which leads to the local population having frequent contact with HIV-risk groups such as truck drivers and sex workers.

HIV prevention in Cunene can be improved in a number of ways. HIV-prevention education can be integrated into the school system, media campaigns can be run, and voluntary counseling and testing can be promoted. Male circumcision is known to be an effective intervention and can be implemented in Cunene. In this chapter we examine male circumcision of both adults and infants as an HIV-prevention strategy.

Male circumcision (MC) reduces the probability of HIV transmission from HIV-positive women to HIV-negative men by more than half.[7] It may also be protective in preventing male-to-female HIV transmission.[7,8] Although the protective effect during sexual contact is far greater for men, MC is also likely to reduce HIV prevalence among women because fewer of their male partners are infected.

There are a number of concerns about relying exclusively on male circumcision to prevent HIV. First, there is a concern that men will overestimate the protective effect of MC leading to decreased condom use, and a net increase in risk of HIV infection.[8] Secondly, there is a concern that other HIV-prevention services will be scaled back because they are mistakenly seen as no longer needed. Thirdly, MC does not address the underlying social determinants of risk such as gender relations and poverty. To mitigate some of these concerns it is essential to maintain existing HIV-prevention efforts and provide counseling services that emphasize the importance of safe sexual behavior.[9] Counseling also provides an opportunity for education on sexual and reproductive health, and for family-planning initiatives.

Male circumcision programs are an opportunity for men to be tested and to discover their HIV status. Unlike women who have more contact with the health system through visits to clinics for antenatal and postnatal care, where they might be tested for their HIV status, men visit health centers infrequently. Hence HIV-positive men tend to be identified at a later stage of their illness, and consequently face lower rates of treatment success.[10]

12.2. Description of intervention

The intervention consists of two programs, both aimed to increase the level of MC in Cunene province. One program covers adults and adolescents, and the other covers infants up to the age of 60 days. Both actions will provide free male circumcision at public hospitals and through mobile units. The adult male circumcision program (AMCP) is a three-year program in Cunene province designed to increase the proportion of adult men who are circumcised from 10% to 80% in the three-year period. The infant male circumcision program (IMCP) is a 10-year program which aims to increase the proportion of male infants circumcised to 80% in five years, and to maintain this rate thereafter.

AMCP will affect HIV incidence in the short term and IMCP will affect it in the long term. We include IMCP because circumcision done before adolescence, particularly in early infancy, has the advantage of being cheaper and technically easier.[9] It is cost effective to provide circumcision to infants rather than run an adult campaign when the infants come of age.

AMCP will offer free MC through health facilities and mobile health units for a period of three years from 2012 to 2014. After the three-year intensive program, MC will continue to be offered, but only on a request basis in health centers and hospitals. To generate demand for AMCP, a large-scale awareness campaign will be undertaken involving mass media and meetings with community members. Men who present for MC will be provided with counseling and life-skills training on HIV prevention, sexual risk behavior, and condom use. Adult MC will be preceded by HIV counseling and testing. An HIV-positive test result will not preclude a client from being circumcised, but will prompt additional counseling on the risks and benefits given his status. Counseling and testing will be conducted by lay counselors. Routine adult MC will be performed by trained nurses, who will be supervised by a medical doctor. The doctor will also attend to complex cases.

IMCP will use mobile units. Mobile units will rotate between nine sites in each of the six municipalities of Cunene: Curoca, Cahama, Ombadja, Cuvelai, Cuanhama, and Namacunde. A unit will stay at a site for one week to conduct MC for infants born in that week or in the previous eight weeks. Infant MC will be performed by specialized nurses. At least one doctor at a local hospital in the province will be trained to deal with difficult cases and complications. Infants requiring the doctor's services will be referred to the nearest hospital and transportation will be provided. See Annex 12A for a detailed description of the design of AMCP and IMCP.

12.3. Estimation of costs and benefits

Costs and benefits have been estimated on the basis of the design of the intervention, and recent studies on the effect of MC in reducing the probability of HIV infection. The annual cost of AMCP is calculated by multiplying the unit cost per circumcision by the number of MCs performed each year. The unit cost per circumcision consists largely of the cost of the procedure which includes surgical materials and staff time. The material costs and time required are based on the use of the Prepex device. This is a new device which decreases the risk of complications and reduces the time needed for surgery. To the cost of the procedure we add media and administrative costs, which are calculated by assuming the same ratio between these costs and the cost of the procedure in similar programs.[11] The costs of IMCP are based on the number of sites and cost of materials used to conduct infant male circumcisions. The cost per site is based on the composition of the team specified in the design. Material costs are based on the use of Accu-circ for infant MC.

The constitutive benefits of AMCP are reductions in the incidence of adult HIV and deaths from AIDS. These benefits have been quantified for a 15-year period from 2012 to 2026. Longer-term projections have not been made due to the degree of uncertainty about the future path of HIV in Cunene. It is not clear for how long HIV prevalence will continue to rise, or what will happen when it peaks; it may remain at its peak or it may start to decline. For similar reasons, the software that is commonly used (see below) to quantify the reduction in HIV incidence and AIDS deaths due to adult male circumcision limits itself to a 15-year projection period.

The constitutive benefits of AMCP were estimated by using the UNAIDS Decision Maker's Program Planning Tool (DMPPT)[12] and the UNAIDS Epidemic Projection Package (EPP).[13] EPP was used to predict the time path of HIV prevalence in the absence of AMCP. This prediction is made by identifying the epidemic curve which best fits the provincial data on HIV prevalence in Cunene. EPP thus provides the time path of HIV-prevalence *without* the AMCP intervention.

To calculate the benefits of AMCP, we need to forecast the time path of HIV-prevalence *with* this intervention. This is based on the time path of HIV-prevalence *without* AMCP and the proportion of circumcised adult males in each period (as a result of AMCP). Given these inputs, DMPPT generates a time path of HIV-prevalence *with* AMCP. The difference between the time paths *with* and *without* AMCP provides the reduction in HIV-prevalence that is attributable to AMCP.

From the time paths of HIV-prevalence *with* and *without* AMCP, we obtain the time path of the reduction in adult HIV-prevalence due to AMCP. DMPPT then calculates the number of adult infections and deaths avoided as a result of AMCP. To do this, the time path of reduction in adult HIV-prevalence is used together with data on the size and age structure of the population in each year.

The quantified consequential benefits of AMCP include child infections and deaths avoided, and reduction in the number of orphans. These consequential benefits were quantified by using the Spectrum demographic projection software.[13] The Spectrum software makes projections of infections and deaths by age group according to the time path of adult HIV-prevalence. Two projections were made of child infections and deaths (and of orphans) — one *without* and one *with* AMCP. The difference between the two projections provides the quantified consequential benefits in terms of child infections and deaths avoided.

We do not quantify the benefits of IMCP. The benefits of IMCP in terms of reduction in HIV incidence will start to occur only after the infants grow up and become sexually active. It is difficult to quantify the impact of IMCP on HIV incidence so far into the future, and in any case DMPPT limits projections to a 15-year period because of increasing uncertainty with time regarding the progression of HIV prevalence. However, WHO and UNAIDs recommend infant male circumcision — as well as adult male circumcision — as an HIV-prevention strategy in high-prevalence settings such as Cunene.[14] If the goal is to maintain high rates of adult male circumcision over time, a current infant male circumcision program would appear to be cost-effective in comparison to circumcising the infants when they become adults. The cost per circumcision is much lower for infants than for adults. We examine the costs of IMCP over a 10-year period from 2012 to 2021. Details of the assumptions used to estimate the costs and benefits of AMCP and IMCP are provided in Annex 12B.

12.3.1. AMCP resource requirements and costs

AMCP is a three-year program designed to reach a target proportion of 80% males circumcised by the end of the third year. Given this target, DMPPT is used to estimate the uptake of adult male circumcision in each year based on an S-shaped scale-up. This generates the number of MCs to be performed each year during the three-year program. The absolute number of adult men who are circumcised, and the prevalence of adult male circumcision, are shown in table 12.1.

To provide circumcisions at this scale, we use an intervention design which does not rely on doctors performing MC, because they are in very short supply in the country. Routine MC surgery will be conducted by nurses, with doctors attending only to complicated cases. This will require policy changes to ensure that such a practice is legal. To reduce pressure on nurses, HIV counseling and testing will be conducted by non-medical staff. We base the AMCP design on MOVE (models for optimizing volume and efficiency) which curbs the demand for highly-trained staff.[15] In line with MOVE, assistant nurses will prepare clients for surgery, and surgical specialists will be responsible only for the surgery (and not for preparation of clients). Based on this design it is assumed that a trained surgical nurse can, with the support of two trained assistant nurses, perform 40 adult MCs per day using the disposable Prepex device, which requires no anesthetics and involves swift procedure and recovery times. The device is more expensive than reusable instruments, but removes the need for staff to spend time sterilizing equipment. Doctors only play a supervisory role and may be called to address complicated cases. Given this design, a single doctor is sufficient for the implementation of AMCP in year 1, and less than one doctor in years 2 and 3. The design also implies other staff requirements to implement AMCP over its three-year period, which are shown in table 12.1.

Table 12.1. AMCP coverage and staff requirements

Year	2012	2013	2014
Coverage of AMCP			
Number of adult males circumcised	78,534	38,593	28,229
Prevalence of adult male circumcision (%)	51	68	80
Number of staff			
Surgical nurses	10	5	4
Assistant nurses	20	10	7
Doctors (urologists)	1	0.48*	0.35*
Counselors/attendants	26	13	10
Total staff	57	28*	21*

Note: *Doctor's work counted for fraction of time.

The total cost of AMCP comprises training costs, procedure costs, costs of treatment following complications, media costs, and administrative costs. Training costs are based on one week of training for each staff member. Procedure costs consist largely of the cost of HIV testing kits and surgical kits, and the cost of staff time spent in counseling, testing and surgery. The cost of responding to complications is taken from similar programs conducted elsewhere in the region.[11] We include the costs of a media campaign to promote uptake in order to reach the target coverage of 80% in three years; and we include administrative costs associated with the program. Media costs are assumed to be 30% of the procedure costs and administrative costs are assumed to be 10% of the procedure costs.[11] Table 12.2 presents a disaggregation of the total costs of AMCP by item.

Table 12.2. Costs of AMCP (2012 US$ thousand)

Year	2012	2013	2014
Item			
Training costs	6	0	0
Procedure costs	2,403	1,181	864
Costs of treatment following complications	83	41	30
Media costs	721	354	259
Administrative costs	321	158	115
Total cost (2012 US$ thousand)	**3,534**	**1,734**	**1,268**
Unit cost per circumcision (2012 US$)	**45**	**45**	**45**

Total cost is highest in year 1 (2012) because the number of MCs performed is largest in that year. Thereafter costs fall with the number of MCs performed. The present value (PV) of the costs of implementing AMCP over three years is US$6.4 million using a discount rate of 3% per annum.

To maintain 80% male circumcision coverage after the three-year program ends, approximately 7,000 MCs per year will need to be undertaken to keep pace with population growth. The cost of performing these procedures will be US$215,000 a year after year 3 (2014).

12.3.2. IMCP resource requirements and costs

IMCP is an intervention proposed for an initial 10-year period. Its resource requirements are based on a rapid roll-out of the service: all 36 sites of IMCP (six sites in each of the six municipalities) are visited by staff from year 1 onwards. Although all sites are visited from the start of IMCP, it will take time to generate demand for the service. For year 1, we assume that only 16% of mothers will elect to have their infant boys circumcised; in year 5 this rate will reach 80%. The absolute number and percentage of infant males who are circumcised are shown for selected years in table 12.3. For annual estimates during the period 2012–21, see table 12C.1 in Annex 12C.

In order to provide MC to infants in the first 60 days after birth, a mobile unit will visit each site for one week every nine weeks. This design implies that one mobile unit will rotate between 9 sites and hence IMCP will require 4 mobile units to cover the 36 sites. Each mobile unit comprises 3 staff (2 nurses and 1 assistant). Together the 4 mobile units are intended to provide MC coverage to 80% of infant males each year.

The total cost of IMCP comprises training costs, procedure costs, costs of treatment following complications, media costs, and administrative costs. Training costs are based on one week of training for each staff member. Procedure costs consist of surgical kits, staff time and a small transport subsidy to mothers. As with AMCP, media and administrative costs have to be added to provide the total cost of IMCP. Because mothers can be contacted through the antenatal care system, they are easier to reach than adult males. Media costs for IMCP are therefore assumed to be only 15% of procedure costs, as opposed to 30% for AMCP. We assume administrative costs to be 10% of procedure costs. For selected years, table 12.3 presents estimates of the total cost of IMCP. The annual cost of IMCP during 2012–21 is shown in table 12C.1.

We have assumed that annual staff numbers remain constant throughout the period 2012–21 despite the fact that in the first four years fewer than 80% of infant males will be circumcised (see table 12C.1). The mobile unit team of 2 nurses and 1 assistant was considered to be of minimum viable size for the infant MC procedure (in case of problems with the surgery). As

Table 12.3. IMCP coverage and costs (2012 US$ thousand): Selected years

Year	2012	2016	2021
Coverage of IMCP			
Number of infant males circumcised	6,104	33,469	34,729
% of infant males who are circumcised	16	80	80
Costs of IMCP (2012 US$ thousand)			
Training costs	1	0	0
Procedure costs	127	390	403
Costs of treatment following complications	3	18	18
Media costs	19	56	58
Administrative costs	13	41	42
Total cost (2012 US$ thousand)	**163**	**505**	**521**
Unit cost per infant MC (2012 US$)	**27**	**15**	**15**

uptake increases over time the total cost of IMCP will rise. However, the unit cost per infant MC will fall because the same number of staff will perform more circumcisions each year until the target coverage of 80% is reached. The unit cost per infant MC will stabilize at US$15 (see table 12C.1). As expected, the unit cost per infant MC of US$15 is much smaller than the unit cost per adult MC of US$45.

12.3.3. Constitutive and consequential benefits of AMCP

Adult male circumcision in Cunene will have the constitutive benefit of reducing the rate of HIV infection and AIDS deaths among adults in the province. These constitutive benefits have been quantified and are reported below. AMCP will also have a number of consequential benefits, viz. reduced costs of adult treatment, fewer orphans, reduced rates of mother-to-child transmission which lead to fewer infant infections and child deaths, and reduced costs of infant treatment. Some other benefits could not be quantified because of lack of data or because of the nature of the benefit.

Quantified constitutive benefits of AMCP

Estimates of male circumcision on the probability of HIV infection are based on results from randomized control trials in a number of African countries. A randomized study in Uganda found that the risk of female-to-male transmission of HIV was reduced by 60%.[16] These findings are similar to data from other studies which found that risk was reduced by 76% in a semi-urban population of 18–24 year-olds in South Africa,[17] and by 60% in an urban population of 18–24 year-olds in Kenya.[18] It is also claimed that male circumcision combined with low viral loads (of less than 50,000 copies/mL) reduces the risk of male-to-female transmission.[8] Table 12.4 presents the quantified constitutive benefits of AMCP for selected years. See table 12C.2 for annual estimates of the quantified constitutive benefits during 2012–26.

Table 12.4. Quantified constitutive benefits of AMCP: Selected years

Year	2016	2021	2026
Constitutive benefit			
Number of adult infections averted	1,435	1,593	1,233
Cumulative number of adult infections averted	3,821	11,723	18,661
Number of adult deaths avoided	3	172	850
Cumulative number of adult deaths avoided	4	369	3,085

The results suggest that 1,435 adult infections will be averted in 2016, and 1,233 in 2026. Cumulatively, by the end of the 15-year projection period chosen, i.e., 2026, 18,661 adult infections will be averted. There will be a delay before reduced mortality benefits are seen, but in 2026, 850 deaths will be avoided. By 2026, a cumulative total of 3,085 deaths will have been avoided.

The number of adult infections averted each year is likely to decline over time. This is because HIV incidence in Cunene is probably close to its peak (based on a review of surveillance data in the province). As incidence falls, so will the number of infections averted.

Figure 12.1 shows the time path of adult HIV incidence in Cunene *without* and *with* AMCP.

Reduced HIV incidence *with* AMCP will lead to lower HIV prevalence. Annual HIV incidence and prevalence estimates for the period 2012–26 *without* and *with* AMCP are shown in table 12C.3. *Without* AMCP, HIV prevalence is expected to peak at 15.3% of adults; *with* AMCP, it is expected to peak at 13.2%. In 2026, *without* AMCP, HIV prevalence is estimated to be 14.3%; *with* AMCP, it is estimated to be 9.7%.

Quantified consequential benefits

As a consequence of avoiding adult HIV infections, fewer children will be infected by their mothers, and hence fewer children will die. Based on observed vertical transmission rates, the Spectrum model assumes that the probability of transmission from mother-to-child is 0.32.[19] In the absence of antiretroviral treatment (ART), 60% of children who are infected with HIV at birth will die before they reach the age of 5, and 90% will die before they are old enough to attend school.[19,20]

Figure 12.1. Adult HIV incidence in Cunene *without* and *with* AMCP

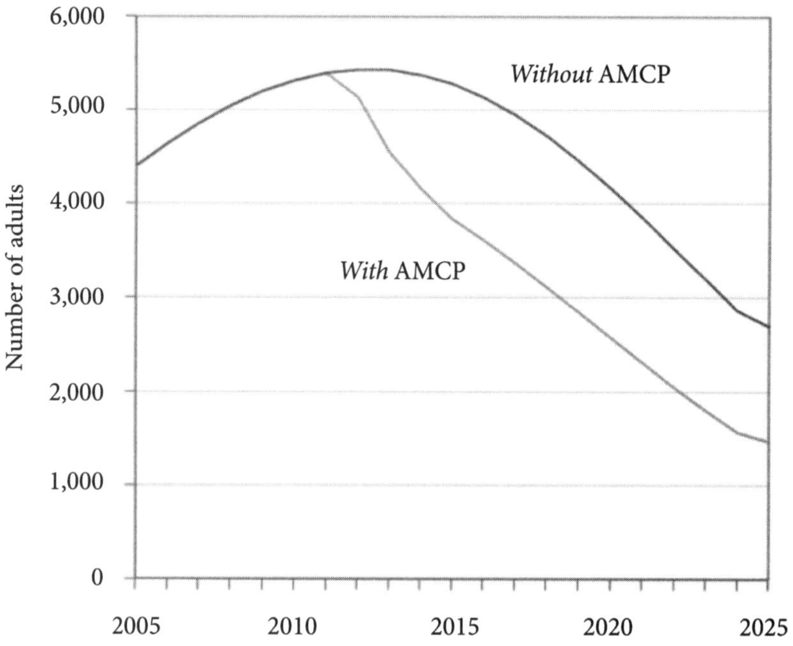

Table 12.5 summarizes the quantified consequential benefits of AMCP for selected years. Table 12C.4 contains annual estimates of these benefits for the period 2012–26. In 2016, 88 infant infections, 26 infant deaths, and 60 deaths of children 1–14 years old will be avoided as a result of AMCP. As the difference in HIV prevalence *with* and *without* AMCP becomes larger over time, the number of infections and deaths avoided will increase. In 2026, 668 infections will be averted, and 198 infant deaths and 493 deaths among children 1–14 years old will be avoided.

Table 12.5. Quantified consequential benefits of AMCP: Selected years

Year	2016	2021	2026
Consequential benefit			
Number of infant HIV infections averted	88	399	668
Number of infant AIDS deaths avoided	26	118	198
Number of AIDS deaths avoided of children 1–14 years old	60	266	493

AMCP reduces the number of adult AIDS deaths, as a consequence of which there will be fewer orphans — maternal and paternal. Fewer children will suffer the loss of one or both parent. These consequential benefits have been estimated by use of the Spectrum software package.[13] By the end of our projection period, i.e., 2026, the model estimates that there will be 3,000 fewer maternal orphans and 2,200 fewer paternal orphans due to the AMCP intervention.

Preventing HIV infections saves the cost of treating those who would otherwise be infected. To estimate these cost savings over our 15-year projection period, we need to know the costs of treatment and the proportion of HIV-infected adults who would have been treated. Data on the costs of treatment in Angola were not available to us. We used an estimate from South Africa of US$8,000 per person of the present value of the lifetime cost of treating HIV/AIDS.[21] Also, we assume that the proportion of HIV-infected adults in Cunene who would have been treated will increase from its current level of 39% to 50% in 2026. Based on these assumptions, the present value of treatment costs saved as a result of infections avoided over the 15-year period is US$52 million using a discount rate of 3% per annum. Even if we assume that the proportion of HIV-infected adults who would have been treated stays *constant* at its current level of 39%, the present value of treatment cost savings is US$45 million.

The consequential benefit of averting mother-to-child transmission of HIV as a result of AMCP also yields savings in the cost of treating AIDS in children. We assume that the present value of lifetime treatment costs per child is US$5,000 (see Annex 12B) and the proportion of HIV-infected children who would have received treatment increases from 10% to 30% over the 15-year period. Based on these assumptions, the present value of pediatric treatment costs saved is US$7 million. The combined present value of treatment costs saved for adults and children is US$59 million.

Non-quantified consequential benefits

Not all consequential benefits could be quantified. Below we discuss the non-quantified consequential benefits that arise from the quantified constitutive and consequential benefits, and the evidence that supports their consideration. These consequential benefits and pathways through which they arise are summarized in table 12.6.

Consequential benefits for children of reduced adult morbidity and mortality

Adult morbidity and mortality can have a detrimental effect on children's education and health.[22,23] Losing both parents is likely to have a larger impact on education and health than losing one parent.[23] Living with a parent ill with HIV/AIDS, or being orphaned, increases the probability of a child not attending school because education costs cannot be met or because the child needs to care for the sick parent.[24] Older children are more likely to

Table 12.6. Non-quantified consequential benefits of AMCP

Quantified benefit leading to non-quantified benefit	Pathway to non-quantified consequential benefit	Non-quantified consequential benefit
Reduced adult morbidity and mortality	1. Reduced illness leads to higher levels of labor-force participation 2. Reduced adult morbidity and mortality has positive impact on child outcomes	• Reduced income poverty (1) • Improved child education and health (2)
Reduced incidence of HIV in children	1. Reduced morbidity	• Improved child development (1)

be involved in caring for sick parents.[25] The situation for children may be worse when a parent dies. A number of studies have reported that orphans are more likely to drop out of school and go to bed hungry.[26,27] Moreover, orphans are more likely to suffer psychological problems related to mood, anxiety and depression — which undermine their long-term mental health.[26,28]

Consequential benefits of reduced HIV-incidence in children
We have quantified the health impact of HIV-infection averted in infants through child deaths avoided. But there are a number of other ways in which children suffer as a result of HIV-infection. HIV can lead to learning disabilities (due to central nervous system dysfunction) that affect attention, memory and language.[29] Distress associated with HIV can lead to behavior problems such as aggression and social withdrawal. A study in India found that 81% of HIV-positive children were reported to have behavior problems (assessed using the Child Behavior Check List) compared with 18.3% of HIV-negative children in the control group.[30] HIV-infection can have a detrimental effect on children's growth patterns, in terms of both height and weight.[31,32]

Reduced incidence of STIs as a result of AMCP
Studies have found that male circumcision reduces the incidence of STIs such as Herpes Simplex Virus 2 (HSV-2) and Human Papilloma Virus

(HPV). A 25-year longitudinal study of a cohort of more than 500 New Zealand males showed that uncircumcised males were three times more likely to have STIs than circumcised males.[8] In rural Uganda, another study found that circumcision of men reduced the incidence of HSV-2 by 25% and of HPV-infection by 35% among them.[33] Reduction in male incidence of HPV has been shown to lead to a subsequent reduction in female incidence.[34]

12.4. Summary and conclusion

The present value (PV) of the costs of implementing AMCP over three years is US$6.4 million at a discount rate of 3% per annum. If this investment is made, we estimate that between 2012 and 2026, a cumulative total of approximately 18,700 adult HIV infections, 3,100 adult AIDS deaths, 4,400 infant HIV infections and 4,300 child AIDS deaths will be averted. Moreover, US$59 million in adult and child treatment costs will be saved. In addition to the quantified benefits, there will be numerous non-quantified benefits of AMCP relating to child health, education and development.

IMCP will cost approximately US$0.5 million per annum. If IMCP is implemented it will avoid the need for adult MC campaigns in the future, because 80% of males will have been circumcised as infants. Circumcising infant males rather than adult males will save costs because the unit cost of infant circumcision is only one-third that of adult circumcision.

Male circumcision in Cunene will have a significant impact on HIV-infection in the province, which also has many consequential benefits. The gross benefits result from a relatively small cost of undertaking AMCP and IMCP.

ANNEX
Annex 12A. Description of intervention

Background: In 2009 the adult HIV prevalence rate in Angola was 2.1%.[1] Although this prevalence is low relative to other countries in the region, it masks wide variation between provinces of Angola. The adult HIV prevalence rate is 9.1% in Cunene province, which has an international border with Namibia where adult prevalence is 13.1%.[1,2] Male circumcision (MC) is common in Angola, but not in Cunene.[3,4]

Goal: The goal of AMCP and IMCP is to reduce the incidence of HIV and deaths from AIDS in Cunene province in Angola.

Intervention: AMCP and IMCP will be implemented in Cunene province only. AMCP is a three-year intervention and IMCP is a 10-year intervention. Both AMCP and IMCP will provide free MC in public hospitals and mobile units. Both AMCP and IMCP will conduct media campaigns to generate demand. Prior to the surgical procedure, AMCP and IMCP will provide counseling for clients and parents, respectively. AMCP will also provide HIV testing. An HIV-positive test result for an AMCP client will not preclude him from being circumcised, but will prompt additional counseling on condom use to protect his sexual partners. AMCP clients will also be examined for STIs and, if necessary, referred for treatment prior to surgery.

Target age-groups: AMCP will target men in the age-group of 15 to 49 year-olds. Sexually active men older than 49 years who present for MC will not be turned away. IMCP will target infant males less than 60 days old. This combination of age-groups will provide both immediate and long-term reductions in HIV incidence.

Service-delivery model: Mobile units will be used for both AMCP and IMCP. For AMCP, the mobile unit will visit each of the six municipalities in Cunene: Curoca, Cahama, Ombadja, Cuvelai, Cuanhama, and Namacunde. The unit will remain at a municipality for the period necessary to meet demand in that region. For IMCP, 4 mobile units will rotate between 36 sites (6 sites per municipality), remaining one week in each site. IMCP will provide a transportation subsidy of US$1 to mothers to bring their child to the mobile unit.

Staff and training: For AMCP, counseling and testing will be conducted by lay counselors. Routine MC will be performed by trained nurses. The nurses will be supervised by a doctor (urologist), who will also attend to complicated cases. For IMCP, nursing assistants will provide counseling to mothers and prepare infants for surgery. Trained nurses will perform the surgery. One doctor, able to deal with difficult cases and complications, will be available in the province. Lay counselors will be provided with four weeks of training. Nurses and doctors will receive one week of training in the use of the device and in dealing with possible complications.

Materials: Materials and equipment used for a standard adult MC include a rapid test kit, a surgical kit containing sterile and disposable materials, and a disposable adult male circumcision clamp (Prepex). Circumcision of infants will be conducted using Accu-circ or Plastibell disposable infant circumcision clamps. Necessary surgical materials will be provided in a kit which includes disposable gloves for examination, sterile disposable gloves for the provider doing the circumcision, and a surgical mask.

Media campaign: To generate demand for adult and infant MC, media campaigns will be conducted. For AMCP, the campaign will run for three years and involve mass media and meetings with community members. The media campaign for IMCP will involve training community members and local health professionals to encourage pregnant women to have their newborn male infants circumcised.

Annex 12B. Assumptions to estimate costs and benefits
Coverage assumptions for AMCP and IMCP

Adult male population covered by AMCP: The size of the total population of Cunene province is assumed to be 750,000.[5] The age structure of the province is taken to be similar to that of the country as a whole; hence 23% of Cunene's population are assumed to be males in the age group 15 to 49 years.

- The number of males in the age group 15–49 years is assumed to be 170,000 (approximately 23% of 750,000).

Male circumcision target of AMCP: We assume that prior to the intervention 10% of the adult male population in Cunene is circumcised. Although MC is not common among the ethnic group which makes up the majority of the population in Cunene, people from other ethnic groups who practice MC also live in Cunene. Hence some males in Cunene province will be circumcised — we assume this number is 10% of the adult male population. AMCP aims to increase the adult MC rate to 80% in three years. This target is not unrealistic. A study on the acceptability of male circumcision for prevention of HIV/AIDS in sub-Saharan Africa found that the proportion of uncircumcised men willing to become circumcised ranged from 29% to 87%. Moreover, 71% of women were found to favor circumcision for their partners.[35]

- We assume that 10% of adult men in Cunene are already circumcised, and that AMCP will increase this proportion to 80% in year 3.

Number of infant male births during IMCP intervention period: We assume that the total population of Cunene is 750,000 and that the province has the same fertility rate as the rest of the country. We then use the Spectrum demographic projection software to forecast the number of male infants born each year during 2012–21.

Infant male circumcision target for IMCP: We assume that without IMCP a negligible proportion of male infants will be circumcised at birth, as this is not common practice in Cunene or elsewhere in the country. With IMCP we assume that the rate of uptake will increase to 80% in 2016 and will be maintained at this level. This assumption is consistent with a survey on the acceptability of male circumcision in sub-Saharan Africa, which found that 81% of mothers were willing to have their infant sons circumcised.[35]

- We assume that without IMCP, 0% of mothers will have their male infants circumcised. With IMCP, we assume that uptake will increase to 80% in 2016, and will be maintained at this level.

Staff and material requirements

Staff and materials required for AMCP: The AMCP design is based on models for optimizing the volume and efficiency (MOVE) of male circumcision services.[15] MOVE is designed to limit the need for highly-trained staff. A lay counselor conducts HIV counseling and testing, a nurse assistant then prepares the client for surgery, and a senior nurse trained in surgery conducts the procedure. The procedure uses the Prepex disposable circumcision kit, which is a disposable device that limits the need for sterilization. Circumcision of an adult male using Prepex takes approximately 3 to 5 minutes. Based on this design, we make the following assumptions in relation to staff and materials.

- A surgical nurse will perform an average of 40 adult MCs per day with the support of 2 trained assistant nurses.
- A doctor (urologist) will supervise 10 surgical nurses and respond to complications.
- The equipment used for a standard adult MC will be as follows: a rapid HIV test kit; standard surgical materials; a disposable adult male circumcision clamp; and materials for post-circumcision wound dressing.

Staff and materials required for IMCP: Male infants are expected to be circumcised within 60 days after birth. Circumcision of an infant takes approximately 5 minutes. Staff numbers are determined by the number of sites to be visited by a mobile unit. For 36 sites, IMCP will require 4 mobile units. One mobile unit comprises 3 staff (2 nurses and 1 assistant). The following equipment will be used for infant male circumcision: standard surgical materials; disposable infant male circumcision clamp; and materials for wound dressing.

Assumptions to estimate costs

Salaries: Staff costs are based on current salaries of health professionals in Angola. A transportation subsidy is added for staff to reach remote sites. For the doctor, an additional accommodation and travel subsidy is included on the assumption that he/she will come from Luanda.

- Monthly salaries (including subsidies) are assumed to be US$580 for a surgical nurse; US$280 for an assistant nurse; US$3,080 for a doctor (urologist); and US$230 for an attendant/lay counselor.

Training costs: Prior to deployment, staff will be provided with one week of training on MC.

- Training costs are set at US$100 per trainee.

Media costs: The cost of conducting a media campaign is based on US-AID estimates for a media campaign undertaken for a male circumcision program in Swaziland.[11]

- Media costs are set at 30% of total procedure costs for AMCP and at 15% of total procedure costs for IMCP.

Administrative costs: Administrative costs are based on USAID estimates for administrative costs of a male circumcision program in Swaziland.[11]

- For AMCP and IMCP, we set administrative costs at 10% of total procedure costs.

Transportation subsidy: For IMCP, we assume it is necessary to cover transportation costs to and from the site for mother and child.

- Mothers of MC infants get a transportation subsidy of US$1 per child.

Assumptions to estimate benefits

Reduced risk of HIV transmission: Male circumcision has been shown to reduce the risk of female-to-male transmission of HIV in randomized controlled trials in Africa. These studies confirm that male circumcision reduces the risk of HIV acquisition by men from women by more than half.[7] MC is not as protective for men who have sex with men.[9] A randomized control trial in Uganda found that the reduction in risk of female-to-male transmission was 60%.[16] In South Africa a 76% reduction was observed, and in Kenya a 60% reduction was reported.[17,18] MC combined with lower viral loads of less than 50,000 copies/mL reduces the risk of male-to-female transmission.[8]

- MC reduces the risk of HIV transmission from HIV-positive women to HIV-negative men by 60%.

ART coverage: ART coverage assumptions affect our estimates of cost savings from infections averted as a result of AMCP. The higher the rate of ART coverage the greater will be the opportunity for cost savings. It is estimated that in 2010, 39% of adults who were in need of ART were receiving it, and 10% of children who were in need of ART were receiving treatment.[36] ART coverage in Angola has been increasing over time, and we assume it will continue to do so.

- ART coverage for adults is assumed to be 39% in 2012, increasing linearly to 50% in 2026. ART coverage for children is assumed to be 10% in 2012, increasing linearly to 25% in 2026.

Lifetime costs of HIV treatment: The present value of lifetime costs of HIV treatment for adults is based on an estimate from South Africa of US$8,000 per person (US$4,000 to US$12,000).[21] The present value of lifetime costs of HIV treatment for a child is assumed to be $5,000. The latter figure is derived from a 2006 estimate of lifetime treatment costs of pediatric HIV in African countries of US$3,500.[37] The estimate of US$3,500 for 2006 has been adjusted upwards for inflation and higher labor costs in Angola.

- The present value of lifetime treatment cost of HIV is set at US$8,000 for an adult and at US$5,000 for a child.

Annex 12C. Costs of IMCP and benefits of AMCP

Table 12C.1. IMCP coverage and costs (2012 US$ thousand): 2012–21

Year	2012	2013	2014	2015	2016	2017	2018	2019	2020	2021
Coverage of IMCP										
Number of infant males circumcised	6,104	12,574	19,358	26,348	33,469	33,862	34,144	34,359	34,554	34,729
% of infant males who are circumcised	16	32	48	64	80	80	80	80	80	80
Costs of IMCP (2012 US$ thousand)										
Training costs	1	0	0	0	0	0	0	0	0	0
Procedure costs	127	190	254	322	390	394	397	398	401	403
Costs of treatment following complications	3	7	10	14	18	18	18	18	18	18
Media costs	19	28	37	46	56	57	57	57	58	58
Administrative costs	13	20	27	34	41	41	41	42	42	42
Total cost (2012 US$ thousand)	163	245	328	416	505	510	513	515	519	521
Unit cost per infant MC (2012 US$)	27	19	17	16	15	15	15	15	15	15

Table 12C.2. Quantified constitutive benefits of AMCP: 2012–26

Year	2012	2013	2014	2015	2016	2017	2018	2019	2020
Constitutive benefit									
Number of adult infections averted	0	297	868	1,221	1,435	1,517	1,574	1,606	1,612
Cumulative number of adult infections averted	0	297	1,165	2,386	3,821	5,338	6,912	8,518	10,130
Number of adult deaths avoided	0	0	0	1	3	10	26	55	102
Cumulative number of adult deaths avoided	0	0	0	1	4	14	40	95	197

Table 12C.2. Quantified constitutive benefits of AMCP: 2012–26 (continued)

Year	2021	2022	2023	2024	2025	2026
Constitutive benefit						
Number of adult infections averted	1,593	1,547	1,479	1,391	1,288	1,233
Cumulative number of adult infections averted	11,723	13,270	14,749	16,140	17,428	18,661
Number of adult deaths avoided	172	266	386	528	686	850
Cumulative number of adult deaths avoided	369	635	1,021	1,549	2,235	3,085

Table 12C.3. Adult HIV incidence and prevalence *without* and *with* AMCP: 2012–26

Year	2012	2013	2014	2015	2016	2017	2018	2019	2020
Adult HIV incidence *without* AMCP (%)	1.7	1.7	1.7	1.7	1.7	1.7	1.7	1.7	1.6
Adult HIV incidence *with* AMCP (%)	1.7	1.7	1.5	1.4	1.3	1.2	1.2	1.1	1.0
Adult HIV prevalence *without* AMCP (%)	11.9	12.6	13.2	13.7	14.2	14.5	14.9	15.1	15.3
Adult HIV prevalence *with* AMCP (%)	11.9	12.6	13.0	13.2	13.2	13.2	13.1	12.9	12.6

Table 12C.3. Adult HIV incidence and prevalence *without* and *with* AMCP: 2012–26 (*continued*)

Year	2021	2022	2023	2024	2025	2026
Adult HIV incidence *without* AMCP (%)	1.5	1.5	1.4	1.3	1.2	1.1
Adult HIV incidence *with* AMCP (%)	0.9	0.9	0.8	0.7	0.6	0.5
Adult HIV prevalence *without* AMCP (%)	15.3	15.3	15.1	14.9	14.5	14.3
Adult HIV prevalence *with* AMCP (%)	12.2	11.7	11.2	10.6	10.0	9.7

Table 12C.4. Quantified consequential benefits of AMCP: 2012-26

Year	2012	2013	2014	2015	2016	2017	2018	2019	2020
Consequential benefit									
Number of infant HIV infections averted	0	12	25	48	88	141	200	265	331
Number of infant AIDS deaths avoided	0	3	7	13	26	41	59	77	98
Number of AIDS deaths avoided of children 1–14 years old	0	10	21	35	60	91	130	173	218

Table 12C.4. Quantified consequential benefits of AMCP: 2012-26 (*continued*)

Year	2021	2022	2023	2024	2025	2026
Consequential benefit						
Number of infant HIV infections averted	399	465	527	583	631	668
Number of infant AIDS deaths avoided	118	137	156	173	187	198
Number of AIDS deaths avoided of children 1–14 years old	266	314	362	410	453	493

References

1. Republic of Angola. *Relatório sobe o Progresso do País para dar Seguimento aos Compromissos da Sessão Especial sobre VIH e SIDA da Assembleia Geral das Nações Unidas.* Luanda, Angola: UNAIDS and Instituto Nacional de Luta Contra a SIDA, 2010.

2. UNAIDS. *Report on the Global AIDS Epidemic.* Geneva, Switzerland: UNAIDS, 2010.

3. Drain P, Halperin D, Hughes J, Klausner J, Bailey R. Male circumcision, religion, and infectious diseases: An ecologic analysis of 118 developing countries. *BMC Infectious Diseases* 2006; 6(1):172.

4. Integrated Regional Information Networks. The pros and cons of snipping. IRIN, 2007. http://www.aegis.com/news/irin/2007/IR070231.html. Accessed November 24, 2011.

5. Rebelo P, Jorgensen S. *Mid-Term Review of Inter-sectoral Response to HIV/AIDS in Angola.* NORAD Collected Reviews. Vol. 28. Oslo, Norway: Norwegian Agency for Development Cooperation, 2008.

6. Vakulukuta A. O kuayama mais influente da historia da UNITA. ClubK, 2012. http://www.club-k.net/index.php?option=com_content&view=article&id=6656:antonio-vakulukuta-ex-comandante-da-unita-no-cunene&catid=41004:quem-e-quem&Itemid=633. Accessed February 16, 2012.

7. UNAIDS. *Practical Guidelines for Intensifying HIV Prevention: Towards Universal Access.* Geneva, Switzerland: UNAIDS, 2007.

8. Sawires S, Dworkin S, Coates T. *Male Circumcision and HIV/AIDS: Opportunities and Challenges.* Los Angeles, CA: UCLA Program in Global Health, 2007.

9. Padian N, Buve A, Balkus J, Serwadda D, Cates W. Biomedical interventions to prevent HIV infections: Evidence, challenges, and way forward. *Lancet* 2008; 372(9638):589–599.

10. United Nations, Department of Economic and Social Affairs, Division for Social Policy and Development. *Men in Families and Family Policy in a Changing World.* New York, NY: United Nations, 2011.

11. USAID. *Costing Male Circumcision in Swaziland and Implications for the Cost-Effectiveness of Circumcision as an HIV Intervention.* Washington, DC: USAID, 2007.

12. Bollinger L, Plosky W, Stover J. Male Circumcision: Decision Maker's Program Planning Tool. Washington, DC: USAID, Health Policy Initiative, 2009. http://www.malecircumcision.org/about/documents/DMPPT_manual_110909.pdf. Accessed February 16, 2012.

13. UNAIDS. Spectrum/EPP 2011. Demographic and Epidemiologic Data from Spectrum Files Using Country-Specific Data from UNAIDS and UN Population Division. UNAIDS, 2011. http://www.unaids.org/en/

dataanalysis/tools/spectrumepp2011/. Accessed December 2, 2011.

14. UNAIDS, WHO. *Joint Strategic Action Framework to Accelerate the Scale-Up of Voluntary Medical Male Circumcision for HIV Prevention in Eastern and Southern Africa, 2012–2016.* Geneva, Switzerland: UNAIDS, 2011.

15. WHO. *Considerations for Implementing Models for Optimizing the Volume and Efficiency of Male Circumcision Services.* Geneva, Switzerland: WHO, 2010.

16. Gray R, Kigozi G, Serwadda D. Male circumcision for HIV prevention in men in Rakai, Uganda: A randomised trial. *Lancet* 2007; 369(9562):657–666.

17. Auvert B, Taljaard D, Lagarde E, Sobngwi-Tambekou J, Sitta R, Puren A. Randomized, controlled intervention trial of male circumcision for reduction of HIV infection risk: the ANRS 1265 Trial. *PLoS Medicine* 2005; 2(11):e298.

18. Bailey R, Moses S, Parker C, Agot K, Maclean I, Krieger J, Williams C, Campbell R, Ndinya-Achola J. Male circumcision for HIV prevention in young men in Kisumu, Kenya: A randomised controlled trial. *Lancet* 2007; 369(9562):643–656.

19. Mahy M. *Measuring Child Mortality in AIDS-Affected Countries.* Workshop on HIV/AIDS and Adult Mortality in Developing Countries. New York: UN Department of Economic and Social Affairs, 2003.

20. Bennell P. The impact of the AIDS epidemic on the schooling of orphans and other directly affected children in sub-Saharan Africa. *Journal of Development Studies* 2005; 41(3):467–488.

21. Kahn J, Marseille E, Auvert B. Cost-effectiveness of male circumcision for HIV prevention in a South African setting. *PLoS Medicine* 2006; 3(12):e517.

22. Gertler P, Martinez S, Levine D, Bertozzi S. *Lost Presence and Presents: How Parental Death affects Children.* Berkeley, CA: University of California, Haas School of Business, 2003.

23. Case A, Paxson C, Ableidinger J. Orphans in Africa: Parental death, poverty, and school enrollment. *Demography* 2004; 41(3):483–508.

24. Commission on HIV/AIDS and Governance in Africa. *The Impacts of HIV/AIDS on Families and Communities in Africa.* Addis Ababa, Ethiopia: Economic Commission for Africa, 2003.

25. Sharma M. Orphanhood and schooling outcomes in Malawi. *American Journal of Agricultural Economics* 2006; 88(5):1273–1278.

26. Makame V, Ani C, Grantham-McGregor S. Psychological well-being of orphans in Dar es Salaam, Tanzania. *Acta Paediatrica* 2002; 91:459–465.

27. Case A, Ardington, C. The impact of parental death on school outcomes: Longitudinal evidence from South Africa. *Demography* 2006; 43(3):401–420.

28. Atwine B, Cantor-Graae E, Bajunirwe F. Psychological distress among AIDS orphans in rural Uganda. *Social Science and Medicine* 2005; 61(3):555–564.
29. Bisiacchi P, Suppiej A, Laverda A. Neuropsychological evaluation of neurologically asymptomatic HIV-infected children. *Brain Cognition* 2000; 43(1-3):49–52.
30. Grover G, Pensi T, Banerjee T. Behavioural disorders in 6-11-year-old HIV-infected Indian children. *Annals of Tropical Paediatrics* 2007; 27(3):215–224.
31. McKinney R, Wesley J, Robertson R, Unit DPACT. Effect of human immunodeficiency virus infection on the growth of young children. *Journal of Pediatrics* 1993; 123(4).
32. Mishra V, Arnold F, Otieno F, Cross A, Hong R. Education and Nutritional Status of Orphans and Children of HIV-Infected Parents in Kenya. DHS Working Paper No. 24. Washington, DC: USAID, 2005.
33. Tobian A, Serwadda D, Quinn T, et al. Male circumcision for the prevention of HSV-2 and HPV infections and syphilis. *New England Journal of Medicine* 2009; 360(13):1298–1309.
34. Wawer A, Tobian A, Kigozi G, et al. Effect of circumcision of HIV-negative men on transmission of human papillomavirus to HIV-negative women: A randomised trial in Rakai, Uganda. *Lancet* 2011; 377(9761):209–218.
35. Westercamp N, Bailey R. Acceptability of male circumcision for prevention of HIV/AIDS in sub-Saharan Africa: Review. *AIDS and Behavior* 2007; 11(3):341–355.
36. WHO, UNAIDS, UNICEF. *Global HIV/AIDS Response. Epidemic Update and Health Sector Progress towards Universal Access. Progress Report 2011.* Geneva, Switzerland: WHO, 2011.
37. Stover J, Bertozzi S, Gutierrez J, Walker N, Stanecki K, Greener R, Gouws E, Hankins C, Garnett G, Salomon J, Boerma J, De Lay P, Ghys P. The global impact of scaling up HIV/AIDS prevention programs in low- and middle-income countries. *Science* 2006; 311(5766):1474–1476.

CHAPTER 13

The cost of inaction: Summary and discussion

The cost of *not* undertaking an action can be much greater than the cost of undertaking it. Inaction can lead to serious negative consequences — for individuals, society, and the economy. The consequences of a failure to address extreme poverty, for example, include child malnutrition, lack of basic education, preventable morbidity, premature mortality, and other costs borne by the poor and by society. As another example, failure to provide schooling to children can lead to lower future incomes, higher HIV/AIDS risk behaviors, increased fertility, and numerous other costs. In this book we have attempted to clarify the meaning of 'cost of inaction' and provide an approach to its evaluation. The conceptual framework emphasizes the need to select appropriate actions against which inaction is evaluated.

To illustrate the application of the COI approach, we have conducted six case studies — three in Rwanda and three in Angola. The case studies demonstrate the steps involved in the approach, viz. the identification of areas of inaction (priority areas); feasible interventions which respond to each priority area (actions of special interest); estimation of the constitutive and consequential benefits of the selected actions and the costs of implementing them; and interpretation of the results in terms of cost of inaction. The case studies highlight the importance of identifying appropriate interventions as *sets* of complementary actions, not simply as isolated single actions.

The case studies illustrate the COI approach and provide empirical evidence on the net benefits of six specific interventions in Rwanda and Angola. These interventions are found to have large constitutive and consequential benefits relative to their cost of implementation. Given these findings, the interventions should be of significant interest to policymakers in the countries. The chapter includes a brief summary and discussion of the case study results.

The case studies focus on children affected by poverty and HIV/AIDS, but the COI approach is quite general and can be applied to other areas. Later in this chapter we briefly mention another area where the approach might usefully be applied, viz. climate change. This has three important features in common with inaction in relation to children: (i) seriousness of the harm resulting from inaction; (ii) length of time over which the consequences of inaction are experienced; and (iii) irreversibility of the harm caused by inaction.

The chapter concludes with a discussion of the distinctive features of the COI approach and how it contrasts with traditional benefit-cost analysis (BCA). BCA involves reducing all benefits and costs to monetary values, and ignores those that are not — or cannot be — monetized. Applying BCA on the basis of monetary returns only can lead to conclusions that differ from those reached through COI analysis. Later we discuss the nature and implications of the differences between the two approaches.

13.1. The case studies

To illustrate the COI approach we have selected two countries in which to conduct case studies — Rwanda and Angola. These two countries were selected because they are similar in some respects but quite different in others. Both have relatively low HIV prevalence, high poverty rates, and have recently undergone major civil conflicts. On the other hand, Angola is an order of magnitude richer than Rwanda (national income per capita in 2010 of US$4,423 compared to US$530), but is doing far less to deal with its social and economic problems. We therefore expect the costs of inaction to be greater in Angola than in Rwanda.

The COI exercise involves identifying priority areas and actions of special interest in each country. It is more difficult to do this in Rwanda than in Angola, because many worthwhile actions are already being undertaken in Rwanda — despite its resource limitations. In Angola the task of identifying areas of inaction is much easier.

In choosing appropriate actions, we take account of the country's economic and social situation, its existing policies and programs, and actions under consideration by its policymakers. To gain first-hand knowledge of areas of inaction, we conducted consultations in each country with government departments, international organizations, NGOs, community groups, and others. Of special interest were the views of people knowledgeable about children affected by HIV/AIDS and poverty. The in-country consultations were a critical part of the process of identifying priority areas and actions. The process of identification generated many more interventions than we are able to analyze in this book, especially in the case of Angola. In the end we selected three actions for study in each country.

In Rwanda, all three actions are extensions of ongoing programs: a scaled-up FXB (SFXB) intervention; expanded secondary schooling (ESS); and an expanded school-feeding program (ESFP). In Angola, by contrast, two of the three interventions selected are not part of existing programs. These two interventions are a community healthcare system (CHS), and an adult and infant male circumcision program (AMCP and IMCP). The third intervention selected in Angola — strengthening the education system (SES) — is incremental to the existing school system.

A principal criterion for selecting an action is that it should potentially have a large net benefit. In one case, however, a different criterion was applied. In Angola, the male circumcision intervention in Cunene province was selected because we wanted to include an HIV-prevention action, despite its expected net benefit being small relative to that of other possible interventions. Angola has a national HIV prevalence that is low compared to neighboring countries, but there is concern that HIV incidence will increase because of expanded trade with its neighbors and improved domestic transport infrastructure. Compared to a national HIV prevalence of 2.1%, HIV prevalence in Cunene province is 9.4%. With increased population mobility, such a steep gradient between Cunene and the rest of the country places other provinces at heightened risk. For this reason we have included an HIV-prevention intervention in Cunene province in Angola.

Estimation of the cost of implementing an action, and its constitutive and consequential benefits, requires the preparation of a detailed design. For example, the design of a community healthcare system requires specification of the population to be covered, the scope and nature of the services to be provided, the categories of staff who will deliver the services, the consumables that are needed (e.g. bednets, ORT salts, condoms), and so on. The detailed design must also take into account the physical and human resource constraints that need to be overcome in implementing the action.

The following sub-sections briefly review the results of the six case studies. The actions have not been ranked in terms of their net benefit summarized as a scalar number. COI analysis is not intended to supply a mechanical decision rule, but rather it provides information to policymakers about the benefits of an action in different dimensions (which can be thought of as a vector) and the costs of implementing the action. Many value judgements in, and trade-offs across, different spaces are involved in assessing the constitutive and consequential benefits of an action. The COI approach provides both quantitative and qualitative information to support such discussion on the evaluation of outcomes.

13.2. Case studies in Rwanda

13.2.1. Scaled-up FXB (SFXB) intervention

SFXB is simply a scaled-up version of the existing FXB-Village Program in Rwanda. It is an integrated poverty reduction intervention that seeks to lift people out of extreme poverty by enhancing their basic capabilities. An important instrument of SFXB is assistance to households for the development of their IGAs or microenterprises. SFXB starts by addressing ultra-poor households' immediate basic needs — including nutrition, sanitation, healthcare and education. When such needs are met, households have the opportunity to launch and grow their IGAs. The assistance to households for microenterprise development includes training, an initial asset transfer, and their integration into existing microfinance institutions. IGAs help households to lift themselves out of poverty and sustain incomes at higher levels. Higher incomes in turn lead to numerous consequential benefits, including improvements in children's health and education.

The costs of implementing SFXB are incurred during three years of intervention support. The present value of the total costs of the intervention for 2,000 households over the 3-year period 2012–14 in 2012 US$, discounted at 3% per year, is US$4.5 million.

A 30-year projection period is considered for the benefits of this intervention. Two types of constitutive benefit are attributable to SFXB: immediate gains during years 1–3 in the health and education of children in participating households; and increases in income during years 1–30 (in-kind transfers in years 1–3 and income increases from IGAs/microenterprises in years 4–30). In years 1–3, the intensive support is expected to lead to a 7% increase in years of primary education for children of primary-school age, and an 84% increase in years of primary education for over-age children. Also, during years 1–3, there is expected to be a 212% increase in years of secondary education received, and a 14% decline in under-five mortality. On the income side, the intervention results in a present value of increased household incomes in 2012 US$ over the 30–year period of US$21.2 million, using a discount rate of 3% per annum. With the present value of costs estimated at US$4.5 million, the *net present value* of increased incomes resulting from SFXB is US$16.7 million.

A number of consequential benefits arise from increased incomes. The consequential benefits that we have quantified include increases in the number of years of primary and secondary schooling during years 4–15 — e.g. a 241% increase in years of secondary education. Other consequential benefits during years 4–15 include a 6% reduction in under-five mortality. Non-quantified benefits consist of improvements in child development, family health, and employment and income of community members.

It is important to evaluate the SFXB intervention over an appropriately long time period. If the intervention were evaluated simply over the three-year period of its implementation, only the immediate benefits of SFXB would be taken into account and its long-term benefits would be ignored.

A 30-year period for income, and a 15-year period for health and education benefits, was considered suitable for measuring the returns on the SFXB investment made during years 1–3.

13.2.2. Expanded secondary schooling (ESS)

As a result of the government's drive to increase primary-school enrollment, larger numbers of children are graduating from primary school. This in turn is leading to greater demand for secondary-school places. But if the supply of secondary-school places is not increased, the proportion of primary-school graduates who can attend secondary school will decline. The expanded secondary schooling (ESS) intervention increases the supply of secondary-school places by an amount which allows the transition rate from primary to secondary school to be maintained at its current level. To meet the extra demand for secondary education between 2012 and 2031 requires the construction of 1,000 additional secondary schools and the training of 130,000 additional secondary-school teachers. The present value of the total costs of ESS during 2012–31 discounted at 3% per annum is US$2.1 billion.

The constitutive benefit of ESS is increased education of children. Over the period 2012–31, ESS leads to an annual average of 450,000 additional children being enrolled in secondary school, i.e., an average increase in the enrollment rate over the period of 28 percentage points. The increased enrollment will lead to 1.7 million additional children completing secondary school between 2012 and 2031, assuming that 2012 Education Sector Strategic Plan (ESSP) targets relating to dropout and repevtition rates are achieved and continue to be met during 2012–31. Quantified consequential benefits of ESS include a present value of increased future incomes discounted at 3% per annum of US$6.0 billion, 154,000 fewer under-five and 9,000 fewer maternal deaths in the future, and a 33% decrease in TFR. In addition to the quantified benefits there are several non-quantified consequential benefits such as reduction in HIV/AIDS risk behavior and incidence, and improved health outcomes.

This case study emphasizes the importance of not only increasing secondary-school enrollment but also reducing dropout and repetition rates. If the dropout and repetition rate targets of ESSP are not met, then the benefits of ESS will be much reduced. For example, if dropout and repetition rates continue at 2007 levels (latest available data), the present value of increased future incomes will be reduced from US$6.0 billion to US$3.6 billion.

The Government of Rwanda formulates impressive plans on various social fronts. However, it cannot be assumed that such plans are being implemented because they are included in a published government document. There is need for regular monitoring and evaluation of proposed government actions, including those relating to dropout and repetition rates in ESSP.

13.2.3. Expanded school-feeding program (ESFP)

The school-feeding program in Rwanda currently covers 14% of children enrolled in primary and lower-secondary schools. The expanded school-feeding program (ESFP) is intended to increase coverage from 14% in 2012 to 50% in 2021. This 10-year program will provide one meal a day to children with the goal of improving their nutritional status and school participation. ESFP will work in partnership with the government's School Garden Project and assist communities to assume responsibility for school-feeding in local schools.

The constitutive benefits of ESFP are improvements in children's nutritional and educational outcomes. There is international evidence that nutritional outcomes improve significantly as a result of school-feeding. Unfortunately, we were unable to quantify the nutritional benefits of ESFP because baseline data are not available on the nutritional status of the children served in Rwanda. However, we are able to quantify improvements in educational outcomes attributable to ESFP, viz. additional school enrollment and completion. We estimate that during 2012–21 ESFP will lead to an annual average of 174,000 additional children being enrolled in primary and lower-secondary school, owing to both increased intake and retention. We also estimate that between 2012 and 2021 increased enrollment will lead to 220,000 more children graduating from primary school and 80,000 more children graduating from lower-secondary school.

ESFP results in a range of consequential benefits, some of which we have quantified. Because more children graduate from lower-secondary school, more children are likely to attend upper-secondary school, which is not served by ESFP. Between 2012 and 2021, 9,600 of the children who complete lower-secondary school as a result of ESFP will go on to complete upper-secondary school. There are also likely to be consequential benefits for the preschool siblings of children who receive meals at school. We estimate that during 2012–21 an annual average of 25,000 cases of stunting among preschool children will be avoided.

The costs of implementing ESFP are significant. During 2012–21 the average annual cost of ESFP is US$28.2 million, and the present value of total costs discounted at 3% per annum is US$236.2 million.

The government already operates a school-feeding program, but there is scope for the scale of the program to be increased. Much support was expressed in Rwanda for expanding the program, and it is hoped that the examination of benefits and costs provided here will inform the debate on the appropriate scale of expansion.

13.3. Case studies in Angola

13.3.1. Community healthcare system (CHS)

An estimated 60% of the population of Angola have no or limited access to healthcare. Thus the provision of healthcare in this resource-rich country would seem to be an obvious intervention. Given the scarcity of high-level medical professionals in the country and the time taken to train such personnel, a community healthcare system (CHS) was identified as an appropriate action that could be implemented rapidly. CHS involves the training and deployment of community health workers (CHWs) and of community nurses (CNs) — drawn from local communities where possible. Compared with the training of medical doctors which can take several years, the training time for CHWs is six months and for CNs one year.

Three critical elements are necessary to ensure a competent and stable CHS workforce: training, supervision, and payment. The services provided by CHWs and CNs will greatly expand access to primary healthcare through home visits and a network of community-based satellite clinics. In addition to providing primary care, the health workers will offer services to improve prevention of malaria and HIV, and assist patients adhere to antiretroviral drug regimens. CHWs will distribute basic medication and supplies (including oral rehydration salts and insecticide-treated bednets), check whether children are vaccinated, and provide guidance on diarrhea prevention and treatment. As appropriate, CHWs will identify patients for referral to satellite clinics, and CNs will refer them on to health centers and hospitals.

The benefits and costs of CHS have been estimated for a 10-year period from 2012 to 2021. The constitutive benefits during this period are large: 189,000 fewer deaths of children under five; 210,000 fewer cases of child morbidity; 2.1 million more children immunized; 5,600 fewer maternal deaths; and a 17% reduction in TFR among the population of women served. There are also consequential benefits of CHS, e.g. over the period 2012–21 an annual average of 3,000 more children will be in school as a result of their parents being employed as CHWs. In addition to these quantified benefits, the program should lead to improved educational outcomes as healthier children tend to do better at school. Furthermore, spending by CHWs of their increased wages can lead to a rise of employment and income in poor communities. During 2012–21 the average annual cost of CHS is estimated as US$99.2 million, and the average annual cost per person served is a mere US$12. The present value of total costs during 2012–21, discounted at 3% per annum, is US$819.4 million.

The CHS case study shows that primary healthcare in Angola is an intervention which has large costs of inaction. Although CHS does not replace the need for higher-level medical care, it does respond to the need for primary healthcare rapidly and at low cost. Moreover, by employing community members as CHWs and CNs, the intervention should help contribute to the reduction of income poverty in the country.

13.3.2. Strengthening the education system (SES)

Strengthening the education system (SES) is identified as a priority area because 10% of children in Angola do not even enroll in grade 1 of primary school, and a large percentage of those who do enroll drop out. The intervention we identify as a response to this serious shortcoming is a set of complementary actions to increase enrollment in both primary and secondary schools over a 20-year period from 2012 to 2031. Included in the intervention is the provision of one year of ECD services, which will help to improve children's performance in both primary and secondary school.

The set of SES actions involves building new schools as part of a public works program; training and deploying teachers to provide ECD, primary and secondary education; and developing and teaching school curricula that include life-skills education and HIV/AIDS prevention.

SES begins by increasing enrollment in both ECD and grade 1 of primary school. Of the population of children served, 50% are assumed to enroll in ECD and go on to grade 1, and 50% to wait one year and enroll directly into grade 1. Both groups of children are provided primary and secondary schooling through SES.

As SES expands in scale (more schools are built and teachers are trained) the enrollment of children will increase. By 2031 SES will have increased national primary-school enrollment by 9 percentage points, and national secondary-school enrollment by 4 percentage points.

Between 2012 and 2031, SES is expected to result in a total of 1.88 million more children being enrolled in grade 1. By 2031, 960,000 of these children will have completed primary school. Of the remainder, 750,000 will still be in primary school and 170,000 will have dropped out of primary school. Of the 960,000 who complete primary school by 2031, 75,000 will not go on to secondary school, 520,000 will still be in secondary school, 180,000 will have dropped out of secondary school, and 185,000 will have graduated from secondary school.

In addition to these constitutive benefits, there are a number of consequential benefits of SES. The education received by children through SES will — over their lifetimes, extending beyond 2031 — lead to 11,000 fewer maternal deaths among them, 240,000 fewer under-five deaths of their children, and a 40% reduction in TFR among the women served. There will also be a significant increase in incomes of those who receive education through SES. Over a 30-year period after completion of their education, the present value of increased incomes of SES participants, at a discount rate of 3% per annum, is US$4.9 billion. The present value of the costs of implementing SES during 2012–31 is US$3.0 billion. Hence the net present value of increased future incomes of participants is US$1.9 billion.

The substantial benefits of SES taken together — in terms of education, under-five and maternal mortality, fertility, and increased incomes — suggest that the intervention, although requiring considerable financial resources, is worthwhile. From our review of Angola's economy and fiscal position, the country appears to have the necessary resources to implement this important intervention.

13.3.3. Adult and infant male circumcision programs (AMCP and IMCP) in Cunene province

Cunene province has the highest prevalence of HIV in Angola and one of the lowest rates of male circumcision. Male circumcision is well known to reduce the risk of female-to-male HIV transmission and hence second-round partner risks of HIV infection. We consider two actions designed to increase medical male circumcision in Cunene province — one targeting adult and adolescent males, and the other targeting infant males (between birth and 60 days old). The adult and adolescent male program affects HIV/AIDS in the short term, and the infant program affects it in the long term.

The adult male circumcision program (AMCP) involves a three-year campaign to increase the proportion of men who are circumcised in Cunene from 10% in 2012 to 80% in 2014. To maintain the proportion of circumcised men at 80% from 2015 onwards, male circumcision will continue to be offered on a request basis in health centers and hospitals. For the three-year campaign to reach its goal of 80% adult male circumcision, a large-scale awareness program will be conducted. Men will be offered HIV testing and counseling, and trained nurses will perform routine adult male circumcision.

The infant male circumcision program (IMCP) is designed to increase the proportion of infants who are circumcised to 80%. The benefit of IMCP is that it circumvents the need for more expensive adult male circumcision in the future. The unit cost of an adult male circumcision is three times that of an infant male circumcision.

The present value of the costs of AMCP during years 1–3 of implementation, at a discount rate of 3% per annum, is US$6.4 million. The constitutive benefits of this action are evaluated for a period of 15 years because the main model (DMPPT) for estimating the epidemiological impact of male circumcision is limited to a 15-year future projection. The constitutive benefits of IMCP occur more than 15 years after an infant is circumcised, and therefore cannot be quantified. The benefits of AMCP intervention are estimated for the 15-year period 2012–26. The constitutive benefits of AMCP during this period consist of preventing 18,700 adult HIV infections and 3,100 adult AIDS deaths. Its consequential benefits include avoiding 4,400 infant HIV infections and 4,300 child AIDS deaths, and saving approximately US$59 million in treatment costs for adults and children. Numerous non-quantified benefits also accrue — for example, avoidance of family pain and suffering that accompanies HIV/AIDS illness and death, and the associated financial costs.

13.4. Comparison of country case studies

The case studies from both Rwanda and Angola consist of interventions that have large costs of inaction. In Rwanda the selected actions are based on existing programs, viz. FXB-Villages, secondary education, and school-feeding. In Angola the focus is on new interventions, viz. a community health-care system and male circumcision.

All three actions in Rwanda augment the scale of existing programs. Our results imply that the existing programs are effective but that large net benefits will ensue by expanding them. Expanding the scale of current interventions does require overcoming financial and human resource constraints. Given Rwanda's tight fiscal position, the expansions are likely to require a measure of external support.

The case studies from Angola include two interventions which are large in scale and scope, and one intervention that is a focused action. The community healthcare system is an ambitious large-scale intervention which seeks to provide primary healthcare to 60% of the population. The intervention requires a substantial investment of financial and human resources, but its expected benefits are enormous. The government has the financial resources to implement CHS, and can if necessary hire skilled personnel from outside the country to provide training and assistance in establishing administrative systems. CHS is clearly desirable and there will be huge costs of inaction if it is not undertaken. The education intervention (SES) is large in both scale and scope, and has obvious net benefits. Again, the resources required for its implementation do not pose a financial problem for an oil-rich country like Angola. The male circumcision intervention (AMCP and IMCP) is much smaller, but generates important net benefits. The program relies mainly on nurses for its implementation, for which the number needed is small relative to their availability in the country.

Much infrastructure was damaged in Angola during the prolonged civil war, including infrastructure for social services. The government has started to repair and rebuild infrastructure, including healthcare and education facilities, but has prioritized the transportation network. Rebuilding roads is indeed critical to the country's recovery, but so too is the building and expansion of social services. The construction of health and education systems afresh provides an opportunity for the country to incorporate the latest findings on effective delivery mechanisms.

The Government of Angola currently appears to be emphasizing economic growth rather than human and social development. GDP has been growing rapidly in the country, but its human and social development indicators remain very poor. In this context, the large-scale health and education interventions proposed here would seem to be necessary and desirable.

13.5. Application of COI to other areas

The country-case studies from Rwanda and Angola include children affected by poverty and HIV/AIDS. The COI approach is clearly not limited to actions in this area or in these countries, but is applicable more generally. Other issues affecting children, and actions in other areas, can be readily examined through use of the template developed in this book.

One application is to use COI in a purely descriptive way to evaluate the cost of inaction relative to an action that has been (exogenously) suggested as a candidate to prevent the cost of inaction. Unlike our (endogenous) selection of counterfactual actions, this candidate action may not have been proposed with the object of generating a large net benefit, but suggested merely as a means of avoiding the negative consequences of inaction — with few constitutive benefits. The COI template can still be used here for the *descriptive* purpose of measuring the cost of inaction relative to the suggested action, without having to regard the latter as a desirable or optimal action. By contrast, our selection of actions in this book against which the cost of inaction is assessed is *normative* — we attempt ex ante to select those actions that we believe will have a large net benefit.

Interventions directed at children lend themselves particularly to cost-of-inaction analysis because the negative consequences of inaction in relation to children are experienced over a long period of time — their entire lifespan. Obversely, the benefits of investment in children occur over a long time horizon, viz. their age-specific life expectancy in years. Indeed such benefits can be stretched through parallel investments, e.g. in child health, that contribute to an extension of life expectancy. Given this long (and extendible) time horizon, investments in children's early development, nutrition, health, and education will generate large aggregate benefits.

There is another reason why the costs of inaction in relation to children can be particularly large. The damage caused by not undertaking certain actions on behalf of children can be *irreversible*. Thus if a child suffers from severe malnutrition, he or she can become stunted — a condition that is difficult to reverse. If damage to neural networks occurs, it is almost impossible to undo. Irreversibility of arrested development in the case of children is a condition whose consequences are experienced over a long period of time.

By contrast, similar actions on behalf of adults tend to have smaller aggregate benefits, partly because life expectancy for adults is smaller than for children. For example, the gains from clearing landmines in Angola are likely to be larger for children than for adults. If a child loses a limb he will

suffer for a longer period of time than an adult. If an adult suffers from malnutrition he will not become stunted, unlike a child who may. Moreover, in
similar circumstances, children are more susceptible to malnutrition than
adults. Thus actions in relation to children, compared to similar actions on
behalf of adults, are likely to generate larger benefits.

Another area where the costs of inaction are expected to be particularly
large is climate change. As mentioned earlier, failure to act on the environment shares three important features with inaction in relation to children:
(i) significance of the harm due to inaction; (ii) length of time over which its
consequences are felt; and (iii) irreversibility of the damage caused by inaction. Mutatis mutandis, the COI approach can be usefully applied to environmental protection. Failure to act will lead to enormous costs because the
harm is significant, the period of time (in this case, generations) over which
the consequences are experienced is very long or permanent, and many of
the consequences are *irreversible* — or reversible only at great cost.

13.6. Distinctive features of the COI approach

Inaction can certainly lead to negative consequences. However, not all
negative events can be reckoned as costs of inaction; some negative outcomes are unavoidable. Only those negative events that are avoidable by
some action can be considered to be costs of inaction. Then the question
arises as to *what* action should be undertaken to avoid these negative consequences. This leads us to wanting to do the action that has the largest net
benefit — measured as the costs avoided by doing it *plus* its constitutive
benefits, minus the cost of implementing the action.

In COI analysis a plural approach is taken to identify and value benefits.
Like the human development approach and its associated index, benefits
in COI are quantified in three main dimensions: health, education, and income. Health and education benefits are measured through use of multiple
indicators — e.g. child and maternal mortality avoided, HIV/AIDS deaths
prevented, educational enrollment and graduation rates, years of schooling
completed, and so on.

The COI approach makes a distinction between constitutive and consequential benefits. The distinction is important because in addition to the
direct constitutive benefits, the consequential benefits of an action — e.g.
avoiding the negative consequences of inaction, and positive externalities
— should obviously form part of the information set to evaluate an action.
Without an explicit recognition of consequential benefits, they may tend
to get overlooked. For example, reducing maternal mortality benefits both
mothers and their children. The constitutive benefit of an intervention to
reduce maternal mortality is fewer maternal deaths. But the consequential
benefits to children should also be counted. The distinction draws attention

to the inclusion of both types of benefit. Saving mothers has obvious intrinsic value, but also instrumental value in protecting children.

The inclusion of consequential benefits highlights the fact that actions in one area can lead to benefits in other areas, e.g. health interventions can have poverty reduction benefits and vice versa. Thus, if the goal is to improve health, income poverty reduction may be an effective action. In other words, the COI approach forces the evaluator to consider the value of an action across different sectors. For instance, the evaluation of an education intervention should take account of its consequential health benefits — as we did in evaluating ESS and SES in Rwanda and Angola, respectively.

Another distinctive feature of the COI approach is that ex ante there may be no pre-existing actions to evaluate. We start with a *tabula rasa* and first seek to identify possible actions which avoid the negative outcomes that are observed. Then through a dynamic process we construct an intervention with a significant net benefit. The environment is not seen as static in COI analysis: if there are additional actions which increase net benefit, they are included in the intervention. For example, in the process of proposing an action, constraints that hinder its implementation may come to light. Further actions are then identified to ease these constraints. The process may also lead to the recognition that an isolated action is inadequate to respond to an area of inaction. Further actions — in type or scale — will then be sought to improve net benefit. Such processes lead to an iterative identification of a set of actions. When these actions are complementary, the set as whole will have a larger net benefit than the sum of each action considered separately.

In our case studies there are several examples of sets of complementary actions. An excellent example is the integrated SFXB intervention in Rwanda which consists of a set of tightly-knit complementary actions. The IGA component of the intervention involves the transfer of an asset to help ultra-poor households develop a microenterprise. But without the basic support package of SFXB, which eases pressure on poor households' budgets and time, an isolated IGA action may fail — as has been observed in other contexts. Ultra-poor people have very high discount rates and may choose to sell the transferred asset in order to meet their immediate consumption and healthcare needs. Similarly, extremely poor people may not be willing to invest time in the training offered for IGA development if other activities yield immediate income to meet short-term needs.

As discussed in chapter 2, the COI approach can be viewed as similar to conducting a full and comprehensive benefit-cost analysis. Yet the distinctive features of COI lead to significant differences between it and traditional benefit-cost analysis (BCA) — in terms of both process and analysis. The process difference relates to the starting point of the approaches. BCA starts with a specific intervention to evaluate, whereas COI does not. COI seeks to identify alternative interventions that can avoid the negative outcomes observed. The analytical difference is that BCA is conducted as an economic exercise in purely monetary terms, whereas COI is not. The COI exercise requires the inclusion of monetary and non-monetary benefits in various dimensions — economic, social and human.

The benefits of an intervention typically arise in different dimensions. BCA attempts to aggregate all benefits — monetary and non-monetary — into a single money figure. However, it is not always appropriate to put a money value on non-monetary benefits — e.g. on lives saved or illness averted. Moreover, use of a single money aggregate — accomplished through monetary valuation in diverse dimensions using different methods — can lead to the loss of useful information. Policymakers need appropriate disaggregated information to consider the many value judgements and trade-offs involved in reaching a decision on an action.

In the COI exercise the different types of benefit arising in different spaces are listed separately. We can think of such a list as a *vector* of benefits. The vector includes both constitutive and consequential benefits, and quantified and non-quantified benefits, with the quantified benefits specified in monetary or non-monetary terms. No attempt is made at reducing values in different dimensions to a common money metric. By listing benefits in different spaces as a vector, the COI approach provides quantitative and qualitative information that encourages discussion about the relative value of different outcomes.

The COI approach provides a framework to support the evaluation of actions that respond to the negative consequences of inaction. It does not lead to an automatic ranking of such actions. Difficult decisions have to be made by policymakers, and there is no mechanical formula that can generate a decision on what should be done. Many value judgements must be taken into consideration in the areas of human and social development. People's values often differ, and there should be room for debate. The COI approach seeks to promote such discussion, not to avoid it.

Index